Early Church Records of Somerset County, New Jersey

Volume 1

F. Edward Wright

HERITAGE BOOKS
2020

HERITAGE BOOKS
AN IMPRINT OF HERITAGE BOOKS, INC.

Books, CDs, and more—Worldwide

For our listing of thousands of titles see our website
at
www.HeritageBooks.com

Published 2020 by
HERITAGE BOOKS, INC.
Publishing Division
5810 Ruatan Street
Berwyn Heights, Md. 20740

Originally printed in 2002

International Standard Book Number
Paperbound: 978-1-68034-969-6

CONTENTS

CHURCH RECORDS OF SOMERSET COUNTY[1]

GERMAN REFORMED

Pluckemin (On the Mountain) was established ca. 1714, as one of four German Reformed congregations in the Raritan Valley.. All four congregations build churches between ca. 1725 and 1731. In the later 1740s Pluckemin refused to join in building one central church for the four congregations as recommended by Henry Melchior Muhlenberg. The other three churches were Whitehouse (Leslysland), Potterstown (Rockaway) and Fox Hill The other three congregations joined as Zion church at Smithfield, later New Germantown, which was dedicated on December 2, 1750. Pluckemin's second church, constructed of stone by a congregation now known as Bedminster, was dedicated as St. Paul's in 1758. The Bedminster congregation remained part of the New Germantown parish until it became extinct ca. 1800.[2] Surviving records: Baptisms, 1841 to date. Marriages, 1841 to date. Membership, 1802 to date. Consistorial records, 1840 to date. Deaths, 1840 to date. (The names of "Members of Consistory" (1758-1886) were published in Thompson's *Historical Sketch of the Bedminster Church* in 1887).

LUTHERAN

Church on the Millstone (German Lutheran) existed in 1724. Certain baptisms of the church were published in the 1903 "Year Book" of the Holland Society of New York City.

DUTCH REFORMED

Neshanic Reformed church. Organized 1752. Surviving records: Baptisms, 1762 to date. Marriages, 1821 to date, with some meager previous records. Membership, 1752 to 1785, incomplete; 1821 to date. Consistorial records, 1752 to 1775, and 1785 to date. Deaths, 1875 to date. Baptisms, 1762-1800, are contained in this volume.

Somerville. First Reformed Church (Raritan). Organized 1699. Surviving records: Baptisms, 1699 to date. Marriages, 1800 to date. Membership, 1699 to date. Consistorial records, minutes of organization, 1699; then from 1721 to

1. This introduction is largely based on comments made in Vol. 6, No. 3 of the *Somerset County Historical Quarterly*.

2. Charles H. Glatfelter, Vol. 1, *Pastors and People: German Lutheran and Reformed Churches in the Pennsylvania Field, 1717-1793*. Breinigsville, PA: The Pennsylvania German Society (1980).

date, with various omissions. Baptisms from 1699 to 1800 are contained in this volume.

Readington Reformed church. Organized 1719. Surviving records: Baptisms from 1720 to date. Marriages from 1833 to 1853 and from 1869 to date. Membership from 1721 to date. Consistorial records from 1720 to date, with a few breaks. Deaths from 1869 to date. (Church Officers (1719-1881) and Members (1721-1880) published in Thompson's *Readington Church History*, (1882). Baptisms, 1720-1800 are contained in this volume.

Millstone Reformed church. Organized 1766. Surviving records: Baptisms, 1767 to date. Marriages, 1782 to date. Membership, 1766 to date. Consistorial records, 1766 to date, except from 1810-1814. (Church Officers (1776-1866), and Members (same period), with early Subscription Lists, etc., published in the *Centennial Memorial* (1866) Baptisms, 1767-1800 are contained in this volume.

Six-Mile Run. Reformed church. Organized 1710. Surviving records: Baptisms, 1743 to date. Marriages, 1798 to date. Membership, 1796 to date. Consistorial records, 1796 to date. Deaths, from 1796 with numerous omissions. Baptisms, 1743 to 1800, are contained in this volume.

Harlingen Reformed church. Organized 1727. Surviving records: Baptisms, marriages, membership lists and Consistorial records complete from 1727 to date. Deaths, 1727 to 1900. Some of the early baptisms have been published in the *New York Genealogical and Biographical Record*. Baptisms, 1727-1800, are contained in Volume 2 of this series.

PRESBYTERIAN

Bound Brook. Presbyterian church. Organized between 1710 and 1725. Surviving records: Baptisms, 1816 to date. Marriages, 1830 to date. Membership, 1815 to date. Session records, 1804 to date. Deaths, 1830 to date.

Basking Riodge Presbyterian church. Organized about 1725. Surviving records: Baptisms, marriages, deaths and Session records from 1795 to date. Membership, very incomplete from 1765 to date. Brief and irregular Trustees' records from 1764 to date. Baptisms, 1795-1800 are contained in this volume.

Lamington Presbyterian church. Organized about 1739. Early records of this church (except of the Trustees), as of most Presbyterian churches, were considered the personal property of the early pastors and have disappeared.

Surviving records: Baptisms, 1810 to date. Membership, 1795 to date. Session records, 1810 to date. Trustees' reports, 1748 to date. Deaths, recent years only. Contributors' records, 1740-1809. A few other records. The Contributors (1740-1809) and Members (1800-1890) were published in the "Manual" of the church in 1890.

Kingston Presbyterian church was founded ca. 1723 near the junction of Middlesex, Somerset, and Mercer counties in Franklin Township. Surviving records: All surviving records (the earliest ones were burned) from 1791 through about 1900 were microfilmed by the Rutgers University Library. It is from these films that the present abstracts have been made. Volume 2 of this series contains the baptisms, 1791-1800.

BAPTIST

Mount Bethel Baptist church. King George's Road, Mt. Bethel,

Organized 1767. First constituent members received letters of dismissal form the Scotch Plains Baptist Church. First services were held in a meeting house near Plainfield built in 1761. This building was moved in 1768 to a site donated by Messrs. George Cooper, William Alward and Benjamin Enyart. The same building was later moved to the present site (date unknown). First resident clergyman, Rev. Henry Crossley, 1767-91.

Early records were lost, except a few minutes of organization, etc. in private hands. Surviving church minutes (including baptisms, marriages, members, deaths and financial records) begin in 1913.

SOURCE OF RECORDS

These volumes cover the earliest surviving records through 1800. Most of these records (baptismal) were taken from the *Somerset County Historical Quarterly*. The first issue of the *Quarterly* was published in January, 1912 in Somerville, New Jersey under the auspices of the Somerset County Historical Society. Its editor was A. Van Doren Honeyman of Plainfield, New Jersey. The Somerset County Historical Society was organized 21 November 1882, at Somerville. The *Quarterly* was last published (Volume 8) in October 1919.

F. Edward Wright
Lewes, Delaware
2002

NESHANIC REFORMED CHURCH BAPTISMAL RECORDS

These records begin in Volume 1 (1912) of the Quarterly, page 133.

The first volume of baptismal entries in what was formerly known as the Neshanic Reformed Dutch Protestant Church (the name now being simplified in this denomination to the Reformed Church) dates from 1762 and ends with 1796. The entries were made in Dutch until shortly after the Revolutionary War, after which date they appear in very poor English. Another, and the volume now in use by the church, begins with 1796 and continues to the present, and is well written, especially when the pastor was the Rev. Gabriel Ludlow, who served the Church from 1821 to 1878. In the first volume the names of those baptized are entered in usual order according to date, but in the second volume the order is the unusual one of alphabetical. In copying these records, therefore, it has been deemed best to make the list alphabetical throughout, which has been done by the Editor of the *Quarterly.*

The minutes of the earliest Consistories are fully preserved in a volume begun August 25, 1752, and continued until July 10, 1785, which is still in its original pigskin binding, and well preserved. The account books of John DeMott and Dirk Low, showing in detail the amounts expended in erecting the church building, 1759-1772, while those two men who were the building committee of the church were erecting the first structure, are still in existence, being deposited in the Sage Library at New Brunswick, while a copy of them is in possession of the church.

In presenting the baptismal entries which follow it is to be noted that the spelling of names of parents and children are in all cases just as the record gives them, or are so intended to be, except that, as the Dutch language had no "y," but letters were used similar to "ij," which has now become in English, in most cases, "y," we have used the latter letter. We have also used the English spelling for the months. Where spellings of a certain family vary, even to the extent of disturbing a strict alphabetical arrangement, we have classified the baptisms in such family together, for the sake of convenience of reference.

1762-1796

Aeten, Tomas and Aentie-Johannis, bap. June 17, 1781.
Alli-Jannite, bap. June 17, 1787.
Amerman, Albert and Jannite-Hendrick, bap. May 29, 1785.
Amerman, Albert and Maria-Poulus, bap. Oct. 31, 1779.

Amerman, Albert and Maria-Lamete, bap. April 29, 1787.
Amerman, Albert and Maria-Eyda, bap. Oct. 18, 1789.
Amerman, Albert and Maria-Jan, bap. Aug. 5, 1792.
Amerman, Ouken and Seytie-Aeltie, bap. Jan. 30, 1780.
Amerman, Ouken and Seytic-Neltie, bap. Apr. 1, 1781.
Amerman, Ouken and Seytie-Gertie, bap. May 20, 1784.
Amerman, Ouken and Seytie-Janite, bap. Mar. 26, 1786.
Amerman, Ouken and Seytie-Poulus, bap. July 29, 1787.
Amerman, Ouken and Seytie-Wilimte, bap. Nov. 27, 1791.
Aten, Gerrit and Deyna-Antie, bap. Feb. 7, 1774.
Aten, Tomas and Antie-Tomas, bap. July 21, 1776.
Bennet, Johannis and Maria-Abraham, bap. April 22, 1764.
Bennit, Johannis and Maria-Aeltie, bap. June 29, 1766.
Bennit, Peiter and Eleisabeth-Maregreitie, bap. March 20, 1768.
Bergen, Joris and Maria-Sara, bap. Sept. 5, 1762.
Bergen, Peiter and Jannitie-Greitie, bap. June 26, 1768.
Bergen, Peiter and Janite-Petrus, bap. Aug. 24, 1783.
Berger, Johannis and Aeltie-Evert, bap. July 14, 1771.
Berger, Johannis and Aeltie-Cornelius, bap. May 21, 1775.
Berger, Peiter and Jannite-Jannite, bap. Mar. 26, 1775.
Bertu, Peiter and Casie-Peiter, bap. Sept. 7, 1783.
Beyaert, More-Hendrick, bap. Sept. 25, 1762.
Bleekene, Jorge and Nelle-Anna, bap. April 8, 1770.
Borrel, Johnle and Annatie-Willim, bap. Nov. 17, 1782.
Brets, John and Gertie-Adam, bap. May 6, 1792.
Briton, Jannite (wife of Samuel)-Johannis, bap. Dec. 12, 1773.
Broca, Abraham and Eleisabet-Maria, bap. Sept. 17, 1780.
Broco, Abraham and Eleisabet-Eleisabet, bap. Feb. 10, 1782.
Broco, Abraham and Eleisabet-Abraham, bap. May 29, 1785.
Broco, Abraham and Eleisabet-Annati, bap. Jan. 17, 1790.
Broka, Joris and Greite-Maria, bap. Nov. 27, 1763.
Broka, Joris and Greitie-Jan, bap. Dec. 22, 1765.
Broka, Joris and Greitie-Greitie, bap. Sept. 16, 1768.
Broca, Joris and Greitie-Magdalena, bap. June 23, 1771.
Broca, Joris and Greitie-Isaack, bap. Oct. 30, 1774.
Brocka, Peiter and Rebecka-Abraham, bap. Dec. 5, 1784.
Broca, Peiter and Rebecka-Isack, bap. July 8, 1787.
Broca, Seimon and Maria-Bergon, bap. Jan. 23, 1780.
Broca, Seimon and Maria-Leuse, bap. Oct. 7, 1781.
Broch, Adam and Annatie-Jan, bap. Nov. 9, 1766; witness, Lena vaen Derypen.

Bullerd, Nette and Maregrita-John, bap. July 25, 1784.
Bullerd, Nete and Maregreita-Janite, bap. Nov. 12, 1786.
Bullerd, Nete and Magret-Mary, bap. Apr. 5, 1790.
Buys, Deneys and Antie-Leideia, bap. May 25, 1766.
Buys, Deneys and Antie-Aeltie, bap. Aug. 7, 1768.
Buys, Deneys and Antie-Cornelus, bap. Apr. 21, 1771.
Buys, Deneys and Antie-Marial bap. Aug. 1, 1773.
Buys, Deneys and Antie-Johannis, bap. April, 1778.
Buys, Deneys and Antie-Catelyna, bap. Nov. 12, 1780.
Cerel, Josif and Maria-Dirick Lou, bap. June 8, 1777.
Chaberlain, Bill-Annia, bap. Oct. 18, 1793.
Chroson, Joseph and Eleisabeth-Catreina, bap. Aug. 26, 1770.
Cock, Edwerd and Mary-Jacob, bap. Aug. 20, 1786.
Cock, Edword and Mary-Edword, bap. May 17, 1789.
Cock, Derick and Judick-Mary, bap. Nov. 2, 1777.
Cock, Gysum and Maria-Cateleynte, bap. July 25, 1776.
Cock, Girsum and Maria-Cornelia, bap. Sept. 5, 1790.
Cock, Goerges and Eleisabeth-Thomas, bap. June 6, 1767.
Cock, Henry and Alaria-Gorge, bap. July 29, 1764.
Cock, Hendrick and Alaria-Jacob, bap. Mar. 20, 1768.
Cock, Henry and Mary-Unic, bap. Nov. 28, 1770.
Cock, Maria-Aeltie, bap. April 21, 1771; witness, Daniel Hont.
Cock, Henri and Maria-Maria, bap. Feb. 23, 1777.
Cock, Jacob and Blandina-Eleisabet, bap. July 27, 1783.
Coeck, Jacob and Blandeina-Mary, bap. April 29, 1787.
Cock, Jacob and Blandeina-John, bap. April 12, 1789.
Cock, Jacob and Cate-John, bap. April 22, 1764.
Cock, Jacob and Catrina-Maria, bap. Sept. 21, 1766.
Cock, John and Enne-Jacob Dinnis, bap. Oct. 19, 1788.
Cock, John and Enne-Gerrit, bap. Nov. 28, 1790.
Cock, John and Ennei-John, bap. Sept. 23, 1792.
Cocke, John-Caety, bap. July 26, 1795.
Cock, John and Jannite-Jannite, bap. May 19, 1765.
Cock, John and Janetie-Cornelus, bap. Jan. 29, 1769.
Cock, Jan and Jannite-Eleisabeth, bap. May 24, 1772.
Cock, Jan and Sara-Neeltie, bap. Oct. 24, 1762.
Cock, John and Sara-Wyllim, bap. June 9, 1765.
Cock, Nete and Mary-Catrin, bap. Feb. 27, 1791.
Cock, Reinert and Jtidick-Jurin, bap. April 21, 1771.
Cock, Rinert and Judick-Lena, bap. Mar. 25, 1781.

Cock, Renerd and Judick-Jorgs, bap. Aug. 15, 1784.
Cock, Tomas and Eyda-Eyda, bap. Aug. 9, 1767.
Cock, Tomas and Eyda-Jacob, bap. Mar. 8, 1772.
Cock, Tomas and Eyda-Maria, bap. May 29, 1774.
Cock, Tomas and Eyda-John, bap. June 8, 1777.
Cock, Tomas and Eyda-Maregreite, bap. Aug. 6, 1780.
Cock, Willim and Maria-Willim, bap. Aug. 31, 1777.
Cock, Willem and Maria-Gerit Van Wagenen, bap. Nov. 1, 1778.
Cock, Willim and Maria-Catleyntie, bap. April 1, 1781.
Cock, Willim and Poli-Cornelia, bap. May 25, 1788.
Cock, Willim and Polli-Coenraet, bap. July 25, 1790.
Coevert, Abraham and Areyaentie-Lucas, bap. May 26, 1776.
Coevert, Abraham and Areyaentie-Petrus, bap. June 25, 1780.
Coevert, Abraham and Areyaente-Janite, bap. May 29, 1785.
Coevert, Bergon and Femite-Ariaentie, bap. April 16, 1775.
Coevert, Bergen and Femete-Johannis, bap. April 20, 1777.
Coevert, Bergen and Femmite-Femmite, bap. Sept. 26, 1784.
Coevert, Judewee (?) and Susanna-Jassense Coson, bap. Jan. 1, 1787.
Coevert, Jasewe (?) and Susanna-Femmite, bap. May 6, 1792.
Cool, Wyllim and Sara-John, bap. Mar. 27, 1774.
Coll, Willim and Sara-Antie, bap. Aug. 13, 1775.
Cornel, Petrus and Rachel-Annatie, bap. Nov. 21, 1779.
Cornel, Teunis and Maria-Sara, bap. Aug. 14, 1763.
Cornel, Teunis and Maria-Peterus, bap. June 30, 1765.
Cornel, Willim and Sara-Cornelus, bap. Dec. 25, 1781.
Corsum, Joseph and Eleisabet-Johannis, bap. Jan. 29, 1764.
Corsum, Joseph and Eleisabeth-Gertie, bap. Mar. 30, 1766.
Corsum, Joseph and Eleisabeth-Catreina, bap. Oct. 9, 1768.
Corson, Joseph and Eleisabet-Jostia, bap. Nov. 8, 1772.
Corson, Josiph and Eleisabet-Josua, bap. Oct. 30, 1774.
Coson, Josip and Eleisabet-Reiter, bap. Nov. 17, 1776.
Coson, Josua and Maria-Maregreita, bap. July 16, 1780.
Corson, Jostia and Maria-Annatie, bap. Feb. 10, 1782.
Coson, Johannis and Annatie-Eleisabet, bap. May 6, 1792.
Counoven, Jan and Catrina-Maria, bap. June 6, 1773.
Counoven, Jan and Catreina-Annatie, bap. Oct. 9, 1774.
Counoven, Jan and Catreina-Janite, bap. April 8, 1776.
Counoven, Jan and Catreina-Antie, bap. Feb. 1, 1778.
Croesen, Jan and Blandeina-Wylhelmus, bap. Oct. 9, 1774.
Cyhim, Drick and Maregreita-Steven Voorhees, bap. May 18, 1783; witnesses,

Steven and Marigret Voorhees.
Dearys, John and Mgret-Sara, bap. July 16, 1780.
Debeld, Josif and Catreina-Maria, bap. Nov. 12, 1780.
De Hart, Cornelus and Eyda-Jannite, bap. May 23, 1773.
Demot, Abraham and Christina-Eleisabet, bap. April 5, 1778.
Demot, Abraham and Hanna-James Van Horn, bap. July 30, 1786.
De Mot, Abraham and Hanna-Peiter Clover, bap. May 25, 1788.
Demot, Dirick and Sara-Eleisabet, bap. Dec. 9, 1779.
De Mot, Dirick and Sara-Gerit Gerisen, bap. Oct. 28, 1781.
De Mot, Dirick and Sara-Johannis, bap. July 13, 1783.
De Mot, Derick and Sara-Sara, bap. April 16, 1786.
Demot, Dirick and Lena-Andris, bap. April 9, 1787.
De Mot, Drick and Lena-Lotiwerens, bap. Dec. 11, 1783.
Demott, Johannis and Catreina-Johannis, bap. Jan. 16, 1774.
Demot, Johannis and Catreina-Gerritt, bap. Mar. 24, 1776.
Demot, Johannis and Catreina-Eleisabet, bap. April 18, 1779.
De Mot, Louwerens and Dortie-Debora, bap. Nov. 6, 1763.
Demott, Louwerens and Dortie-Abraham, bap. April 19, 1766.
Demott Louwerens and Dortie-Johannis, bap. July J6, 1769.
Demot, Marta-Rachel, bap. April 12, 1789.
Dumont, Peiter and Maria-Maria, bap. Nov. 17, 1771.
Demont, Peiter and Maria-Leidea, bap. Dec. 12, 1773.
Deumon, Peiter and Maria-Catreina, bap. Jan. 1, 1776.
Demon, Peiter and Maria-Hendrick, bap. April 20, 1778.
DeMont, Peiter and Maria-Petrua, bap. Aug. 6, 1780.
De Mont, Peiter and Maria-Bregye, bap. Sept. 15, 1782.
Demun, Peiter and Maria-Gerrit, bap. Aug. 20, 1786.
Deumon, Peitermon and Susanna-Jan Betist, bap. Aug. 15, 1784.
Demon, Peter Devroome-Abraham Low, bap. Aug. 17, 1794.
Dets, Jacobus and Catreyntie-Isack, bap. Nov. 10, 1782.
Devis, Steyntie (wife of Joseph)-Sara, bap. July 10, 1774.
Ditmas, Peiter and Aeltie-Nicolaes, bap. April 10, 1774.
Ellon, Naton and Mary-Maria, bap. Dec. 25, 1785.
Flag, Jacob and Eleisabeth-Jacob, bap. Augustus 11, 1765.
Flag, William and wife-Eleisabeth, bap. May 27, 1794.
Flag, William-Abraham, bap. July 5, 1795.
Flamerfelt, Zacharias and Maria-Susanna, bap. April 26, 1767; witness, Johannis Speder.
Genoo, Abraham and Jannite-Eleisabet, bap. July 11, 1773.
Genoo, Abraham and Jannite-Steven, bap. April 9, 1775.

Geno, Jorgs and Eleisabet-Steven, bap. July 30, 1786.
Geno, Jorgs and Eleisabet-Mary, bap. July 24, 1791.
Gerritsen, Gerrit and Sara-Gatreina, bap. Mar. 27, 1774.
Gerritsen, Gerrit and Sara-Antle, bap. Sept. 15, 1776.
Geulick, Jacobus and Maregreita-Gertie, bap. Aug. 25, 1776.
Geulick, Petrus and Gerrite-Johannis, bap. Sept. 20, 1778.
Geulick, Teunis and Maria-Samuel, bap. Nov. 26, 1775.
Geulick, Teunis and Maria-Maria, bap. July 20, 1777.
Geulick, Teunis and Maria-Annatie, bap. April 4, 1779.
Geulick, Teunis and Maria-Abraham, bap. April 29, 1781.
Geulick, Teunis and Maria-Teyne, bap. May 30, 1784.
Greis, Wyllim and Annatie-Abraham, bap. Dec. 2, 1787.
Greigs, Wyllim and Annatie-Annatie, bap. Mar. 1, 1789.
Greis, Willim and Janite-John, bap. July 3, 1791.
Hall, Abraham and Sara-John, bap. Nov. 18, 1770.
Hall, Abraham and Sara-Magdalena, bap. Sept. 20, 1772.
Hall, Abraham and Sara-Abraliam, bap. July 20, 1777.
Hall, Henry and Maria-Frederick, bap. Aug. 1, 1773.
Hall, Henry and Eleisabet-Mary, bap. June 8, 1777.
Hall, Henry and Eleisabet-Catryn, bap. July 16, 1780.
Hall, Henery and Eleisabet-Anni, bap. Aug. 20, 1786.
Hall, Hennery and Eleisabet-Edword, bap. Oct. 18, 1789.
Hall, Isack and Judi-Petti, bap. July 17, 1787.
Hall, Jack and Judick-Greite, bap. May 5, 1782.
Hall, John and Marta-Isaak, bap. Sept. 5, 1762.
Hall, Jan and Marta-Joris, bap. Aug. 9, 1767.
Hall, Johannis and Marta-Johannis and Tomas, bap. Sept. 19, 1769.
Hall, John and Marta-Eleisabeth, bap. July 2, 1775.
Hall, John and Marta-Richerd, bap. April 20, 1778.
Hall, John and Hanna-Marv, bap. Nov. 27, 1791.
Hall, Jorge and Maregreita-Edwerd, bap. Jan. 19, 1772.
Hall, Jeorge and Maregritta-John, bap. Mar. 27, 1774.
Hall, Joris (?) and Peage-Abraham, bap. Feb. 21, 1779.
Hall, Jorgs and Pegey-Bylly, bap. May 19, 1782.
Hall, Jorgs and Marygret-Abram, bap. April 16, 1786.
Hall, Jorge and Sara-Jorge, bap. April 5, 1778.
Hall, Jorgs and Sara-Louwerens, bap. Mar. 27, 1780.
Hall, Jorgs and Sara-Sara, bap. Dec. 23, 1781.
Hall, Jorgs and Sara-Derite, bap. May 25, 1788.
Hall, Tomas and Mary-Mary, bap. Dec. 26, 1779.

Hall, Tomas and Mary-Caty, bap. April 26, 1786.
Hall, Thomas and Outie-Johannis, bap. Mar. 27, 1763.
Hall, Thomas and Outie-Maria, bap. July 8, 1764.
Hall, Tomas and Otie-Jacob, bap. June 26, 1768.
Hall, Tomas and Atey-Tomas Hall, bap. Dec. 24, 1780.
Hammer (see Hommer).
Hardenbroeck, Abraham and Rachel-Johannis, bap. Oct. 31, 1779.
Hardenbroeck, Hendrick and Maria-Henneri, bap. May 21, 1775.
Hardenbroeck, Hendrick and Maria-Cetie, bap. Nov. 22, 1778.
Hardenbroeck, Hendrick and Maria-Neltie, bap. April 1, 1781.
Hardenbroeck, Hendrick and Maria-Femmite, bap. Sept. 14, 1783.
Hardenbroeck, Hendrick and Maria-Jorgs, bap. July 30, 1786.
Hegeman, Andris and Rachel-Andris, bap. Aug. 4, 1782.
Hegeman, Adriyain and Greite-John, hap, June 4, 1786.
Hegeman, Arieaen and Jannite-Arieaen, bap. April 19, 1772.
Hegeman, Areyaen and Janite-Symon, bap. Aug. 27, 1780.
Hegeman, Areyaen and Jannite-Christeyaen, bap. Oct. 5, 1783.
Hegeman, Christeyaen and Geertie-Ariaen, bap. May 29, 1774.
Hegeman, Christeyaen and Gertie-Christeyaen, bap. May 26, 1776.
Hegeman, Deneys and Treyntie-Aentie, bap. Aug. 4, 1782.
Hegeman, Deneys and Breyntie-Johannis, bap. Dec. 2, 1787.
Hegeman, Deneys and Breyntie-Sofie, bap. Jan. 29, 1792.
Hegeman, Frans and Eleisabet-Nisye, bap. May 26, 1776.
Hegeman, Frans and Eleisabet-John Smit, bap. June 8, 1778.
Hegeman, Frans and Eleisabet-Sara, bap. Jan. 30, 1780.
Hegeman, Frans and Elcisabet-Catreina, bap. Oct. 23, 1781.
Hegeman, Frans and Eleisabet-Josip, bap. Aug. 24, 1783.
Hegeman, Frans and Eleisabet-Leidia, hap, Aug. 17, 1788.
Hegeman, Jacobus and Eleisabet-Petrus, hap, May 23, 1762.
Hegeman, Jacobus and Eleisabeth-Jacobus, bap. Feb. 16, 1766.
Hageman, Joseph-Natie, bap. Oct. 18, 1793.
Hegeman, Seymon and Maria-Seymon Weykof, bap. April 28, 1776.
Herder, Christeyaen and Antie-Seymen, bap. July 7, 1782.
Herder, Filipus and Nelti-Nicholas Du Boeys, bap. Oct. 19, 1788.
Hertogt, Engelbert and Enni-Cornelia, bap. July 30, 1786.
Herstoght, Engelbert and Enne-Maria, bap. June 15, 1788.
Hertstogt, Engelbert and Enne-Enne, bap. July 4, 1790.
High, Heugh and Marigreita-Robbert, bap. June 5, 1763.
High, Hugh and Marigreita-Maregreita, bap. Aug. 11, 1765.
Hoff, Abraham and Neltie-Teunis, bap. July 31, 1774.

Hoff, Abraham and Neltie-Sara, hap, Feb. 23, 1777.
Hof, Dirick and Eleisabet-Bergon, bap. Feb. 21, 1779.
Hoff, Derick and Eleisabet-Nicolaes, bap. Mar. 30, 1783.
Hoff, Dirick and Eleisabet-Dirick, bap. Feb. 19, 1792.
Hof, Isaac and Catrina-Abraham, bap, June 5, 1763.
Hoff, Jan and Antie-Peiter, bap. Aug. 8, 1762.
Hoff, John and Roeti-Mary, bap. Aug. 17, 1788.
Hoff, John and Routy-John, bap. Oct. 16, 1791.
Hoff, Nicolaes and Janita-Bergon, bap. Oct. 19, 1788.
Hoff, Nicolaes and Janite-Neltie, bap. April 5, 1790.
Hoff, Nicolaes and Janite-Fransseynte, bap. April 1, 1792.
Hoff, Peiter and Aeltie-Bergon, bap. May 29, 1774.
Hoff, Peiter and Aeltie-Deneys, bap. Feb 25, 1776.
Hoff, Peiter and Aeltie-Peiter, bap. July 18, 1779.
Hoff, Peiter and Aeltie-Sara, bap. May 25, 1783.
Hoff, Peiter and Sara-John, bap. July 30, 1786.
Hoff, Peiter and Sara-Sara, bap. May 25, 1788.
Hoff, Peiter and Sara-Peiter, bap. July 13, 1791.
Hoof, Peter-George, bap. Oct. 20, 1793.
Hoff, Teunis and Maria-Elsye, bap. Sept. 9, 1787.
Hoff, Teunis and Maria-Lenti, bap. Jan. 17, 1790.
Hoff, Tom and Deyaen-Steven, bap. June 13, 1791.
Hogelant, Abraham and Susanna-Tobeias, bap. Dec. 2, 1787.
Hogelant, Albert and Maria-Martynes, bap. Nov. 23, 1788.
Hogelant, Christoffel and Maria - Jannitie, bap. Nov. 12, 1769.
Hogelant, Christoffel and Maria-Christoffel, bap. July 12, 1772.
Hogelant, Christofel and Maria-Maria, bap. Mar. 16, 1777.
Hogelant, Christoffel and Maria-Joris, bap. June 13, 1788.
Hogelant, Dirick and Judick-Maregreie, bap. Aug. 25, 1782.
Hogelant, Elbert and Maria-Elbert, bap. Nov. 14, 1762.
Hogelant, Elbert and Maria-Martynus, bap. Nov. 6, 1768.
Hogelant, Harmanus and Eleisabeth-Maria, bap. Mar. 26, 1775.
Hogelant, Harmanus and Eleisabet-Cornelus, bap. Feb. 18, 1781.
Hogelant, Harmanus and Eleisabet-Elbert, bap. May 25, 1788.
Hogelant, Harmanes-Elsie, bap. May 27, 1794.
Hogelant, Harmanus and Jannite-Martynus, bap. Mar. 3, 1776.
Hogelant, [?no name], Harmanus and Janite-Jannite, bap. May 17, 1789.
Hogelant, Hendrick and Jannite-Cornelus, bap. Aug. 21, 1774.
Hogelant, John and Femite-Mary, bap. April 1, 1781.
Hogelant, Lucas and Maria-Harmanus, bap. Mar. 27, 1774.

Hogelant, Lucas and Maria-Edwerd, bap. Jan. 31, 1779.
Hogelant, Lucas and Maria-Hendrick, bap. Aug. 19, 1781.
Hogelant, Lucas and Maria-John, bap. Oct. 5, 1783.
Hogelant, Lucas and Maria-Stynte, bap. Jan. 15, 1786.
Hogelant, Lucas and Maria-Eyni, bap. Nov. 23, 1788.
Hogelant, Lucas and Maria-Leucas, bap. May 10, 1792
Hogelant, Peiter and Maria-Maria, bap. April 27, 1783.
Hogelant, Peiter and Maria-Elbert, bap. Nov. 7, 1790.
Hommer, Baltus and Eleisabet-Johannis, bap. Jan. 16, 1763.
Hammer, Baltus and Eleisabeth-Eleisabeth, bap. April 21, 1765.
Hammer, Balthus and Eleisabeth-Balthus, bap. April 26, 1767.
Hommer, Baltus and Eleisabet-Teunis, bap. Sept. 20, 1772.
Hammer, Meykel and Maregreita-Cornelus, bap. Aug. 9, 1767.
Hammer, Mychel and Maregreita-Eleisabeth, bap. Aug. 6, 1769.
Hunt, Daniel and Catleynte-Catlyntie, bap. May 23, 1762.
Jansen, Hendrick and Susanna-Hendrick, bap. June 5, 1763.
Jong, Jacob and Maria-Jacob, bap. Aug. 6, 1769.
Jong, Jacob and Maria-Alaria, bap. April 1, 1771.
Jorolman, John and Leideya-James, bap. July 24, 1785.
Koevert, Bergon and Femmite-Jannite, bap. June 6, 1773.
Laen, Willim and Maria-Abraham, bap. Nov. 17, 1782.
Lefelaer, Jacob and Lena-Peiter, bap. Sept. 1776.
Lebelaer, Jacob and Lena-Tohannis, bap. Oct. 9, 1778.
Lefelaer, Jacob and Lena-Peiter, bap. Dec. 24, 1780.
Lebelaer, Jacob and Lena-Jacob, bap. May 18, 1783.
Letli, Herman and Gertie-John Lou, bap. July 8, 1787.
Leydel, Andrias and Sara-Safya, bap. Dec. 6, 1767.
Lou, Abraham and Eyda-Catreina, bap. June 29, 1766.
Lou, Abraham and Maria-Abraham, ba Feb. 20, 1780.
Lou, Abraham and Maria-Gerit, bap. July 31, 1785.
Lou, Abraham and Maria-Peiter, bap. July 6, 1788.
Lou, Abraham and Maria-Cornelus, bap. July 24, 1791.
Lou, Maria-Hendrick, bap. Mar. 20, 1768; witness, Dirick Lou.
Lou, Beniaman and Neltie-Gisbert, bap. Sept. 25, 1762.
Lou, Benjamen and Neeltie-Isack, bap. June 29, 1766.
Lou, Cornelus and Catelyna-Cornelus, bap. Mar. 27, 1774.
Lou, Cornelus and Catleyna-Deneys Stryker, bap. Oct. 19, 1777.
Lou, Dirck and Rebeca-Jeudick, bap. Oct. 16, 1763.
Lou, Dirck and Rebecka-Abraham, bap. Oct. 20, 1765.
Lou, Dirck and Rebeca-Jacob, bap. June 6, 1767.

Lou, Dirick and Rebeca-Sara, bap. July 16, 1769.
Lou, Dirick and Rebecka-Isaack, bap. April 19, 1772.
Lou, Dirick and Dorite-Rebecka, bap. June 18, 1775.
Lou, Dirick and Dorite-Debora, bap. Oct. 30, 1778.
Lou, Diricck and Dorite-Dirick, bap. Nov. 12, 1780.
Lou, Dirick and Dorite-Maria, bap. Oct. 27, 1782.
Lou, Gerrit and Rachel-Sara, bap. April 1, 1764.
Lou, Gerrit and Rachel-Gysbert, bap. Feb. 16, 1766.
Lou, Gerrit and Rachel-Abraham, bap. Aug. 7, 1768.
Lou, Geysbert and Persila-Maria, bap. Dec. 12, 1773.
Lou, Hendrick and Johanna-Maria, bap. Nov. 8, 1772.
Lou, Hendrick and Anna-Eleisabeth, bap. Sept. 11, 1774.
Lou, Jan and Maria-Isaac, bap. May 2, 1773.
Lou, Jan and Maria-Willim, bap. May 16, 1776.
Lou, Peiter and Sara-Daniel, bap. Mar. 1, 1767.
Low, Willam and ___ -Neiltie, bap. Jan. 24, 1796.
Lupardua, Rem and Annatie-Antie, bap. April 19, 1766.
Leupardus, Christeyaen and Annatie-Jacob Weykof, bap. Mar. 25, 1787.
Luyster, Peiter and Antie-Neltie, bap. Jan. 29, 1769.
Luyster, Peiter and Antie-Jacob, bap. June 24, 1770.
Luyster, Peiter and Antie-Abraham and Isaack, bap. April 19, 1772.
Luyster, Peter and Antie-Jacob, bap. Mar. 27, 1774.
Luyster, Peiter and Antie Jacob Peiter, bap. Aug. 25, 1776.
Leuyster, Piter and Antie-Eva, bap. April 29, 1781.
Meseco, Ruben and Efye-Isack, bap. Aug. 28, 1768.
Middagh, Derrick and Maria-Teunis, bap. July 20, 1766.
Middagh, Dirick and Maria-Efraim, bap. Aug. 28, 1768.
Middagh, Dirick and Maria-Eleisabeth, bap. Aug. 5, 1770.
Middagh, Gerrit and Nelltie-Neeltie, bap. Dec. 2, 1765; witnesses, ---- Peiter and Maritte Middagh.
Miller (?) Andris and Pete-Peiter, bap. Dec. 21, 1783.
Mocinne, Cornelus and Cetie-Eleisabet, bap. July 2, 1775.
Mocinne, Cornelus and Cetie-Jacob, bap. Feb. 22, 1778.
Mocime, Cornelus and Catreina-Henderick, bap. June 4, 1780.
Molet, Dirick and Nellie-Abraham, bap. Nov. 28, 1773.
Moncalm, Heue and Maria-Aertsobel, bap. April 10, 1768.
Moncalm, Heue and Maregreita-Luwerens, bap. Nov. 8, 1772.
Moncalm, Heue and Maria-Maria, bap. Feb. 23, 1777.
Moncalm, Heue and Maria-Hendrick, bap. Aug. 8, 1779.
Monfoor, Peiter and Johanna-Catreina, bap. October 26, 1763.

Monfoort, Peiter and Johanna-Arrei, bap. Mar. 31, 1765.
Monfoort, Peiter and Johanna-Jan, bap. Aug. 30, 1767.
Monfoor, Hendrick and Aenti-Enne, bap. April 15, 1792.
More, Hendrick and Eyda-Hendrick, bap. June 9, 1764.
More, Hendrick and Eyda-Ouken, bap. Mar 12, 1769.
Moor, John and Eleisibet-Cateleyntie, bap. July 20, 1777.
Moor, John and Eleisabet-Henderick, bap. Jan. 31, 1779.
Moor, John and Eleisabet-Gertie, bap. Mar. 11, 1781.
Nevius, Cornelus and Janite-Nelli, bap. Dec. 25, 1786.
Nevius, Jacobus and Peiternelle-Eleisabeth, bap. Sept. 1, 1765.
Nevius, Jacobus and Peiternellite-Greitie, bap. April 10, 1768.
Nevius, Jacobus and Peiternelete-Jannite, bap. April 19, 1772.
Nevius, Johannis and Sara-Cornelus, bap. Feb. 11, 1784.
Nevius, Johannis and Sara-Willim, bap. Nov. 11, 1787.
Nevius, Johannis and Sara-Cresye, bap. Apr. 10, 1761.
Nevius, Roelof and Maria-Meinnen, bap. Sept. 15, 1782.
Nevius, Roelof and Maria-Maria, bap. April 12, 1784.
Nevius, Roelof and Maria-Petrus, bap. July 30, 1786.
Nevius, Roelof and Maria-Gerrit Voorhees, bap. Mar. 21, 1788.
Nevius, Roelof and Maria-Johnnis Marteinas, bap. Nov. 28, 1790.
Nevis, Rulef and Maria-Catielana, bap. Jan. 19, 1794.
Nevius, Tobias and Rebecka-Jannite, bap. May 19, 1765.
Nevius, Tobias and Rebecka-Annatie, bapt. Oct. 12, 1766.
Neveus, John and Sara-John, bap. Aug. 13, 1775.
Nivin, John and Sara-Joris Schamp, bap. April 20, 1778.
Onderdonck, Henry and Lidea-James Draek, bap. April 4, 1790.
Persel, Iserel and Greite-Jinne and John, bap. April 4, 1790.
Peyher, Henderick and Maria-Eleisabet, bap. July 2, 1775.
Peitersen, Cornelus and Annatie-Cornelia, bap. June 9, 1764.
Peitersen, Cornelus and Annatie-Cornelus, bap. Sept. 1, 1765.
Peitersen, Cornelus and Annatie-Rihsert, bap. April 5, 1767.
Peitersen, Cornelus and Annatie-Joris, bap. May 15, 1768.
Peitersen, Cornelus and Annatie-Roelof, bap. May 16, 1773.
Peitersen, Cornelus and Annatie-Gerrit, bap. April 28, 1776.
Peitersen, Cornelus and Annatie-Jeronems, bap. Nov. 22, 1778.
Peitersen, Cornelus and Annatie-Annatie, bap. May 6, 1781.
Peitersen, Cornelus and Annatie-Aeltic, bap. Oct. 24, 1783.
Peterson, Cornelus-Annatie, bap. July 5, 1795.
Peitersen, Gerit and Catleyna-Lena, bap. Dec. 25, 1767.
Peitersen, Gerrit and Catreyntie-Sara, bap. Jan. 22, 1775.

Peitersen, Gerit and Catrina-Mattie, bap. Nov. 2, 1777.

Peitersen, Peiter and Catrina-Roelof, bap. Mar. 6, 1763; witnesses Roelof and Sara Peitersen.

Peitersen, Peiter and Maria-Roelof, bap. Mar. 8, 1772.

Peitersen, Peiter and Maria-Johannis, bap. June 19, 1774.

Peitersen, Petrus and Annatie-Petrtis, bap. May 17, 1767.

Peitersen, Petrus and Annatie-Cornelus, bap. Nov. 8, 1772.

Peitersen, Peiter and Betsey-Annatie, bap. May 17, 1789.

Peitersen, Petrus and Eleisabet-Neltie, bap. Apr. 10, 1791.

Peitersen, Roelof and Sara-Christinte, bap. Jan. 29, 1764.

Peitersen, Roelof and Sara-Harpert, bap. Dec. 22, 1765.

Peterson, Ruleph-Sarah, bap.

Peitersen, Roelof and Sara-Maria, bap. Jan. 19, 1772.

Peitersen, Roelof and Sara-Mettie, bap. Feb. 6, 1774.

Peitersen, Roelof and Sara-Femete, bap. Feb. 23, 1777.

Piepenser, Abraham and Maregreitie-Hendeick, bap. May 27, 1767; witnesses Hendrick and Maria Piepenser.

Pittenser, Abraham and Maregreita-Josua, bap. July 15, 1770.

Pittenser, Abraham and Maregreita-Rehsert, bap. Dec. 26, 1774.

Pipenser, Abraham and Maregreita-Maregreita, bap. Feb. 23, 1777.

Pipenser, Abraham and Maregreita-Abraham, bap. Feb. 21, 1779.

Pipenser, Abraham and Maregreita-John, bap. Aug. 19, 1781.

Pipenser, Abraham and Maregreita-Susanna, bap. Aug. 24, 1783.

Pipenser, Jan and Annatie-Hendrick and Nicolaes, bap. Nov. 27, 1763; witnesses, Hendrick Maria Pipenser and Niecolaes Maria Weykof.

Piepenser, Johannis and Cnertie-Joris, bap. Mar. 20, 1768.

Pittenser, Johannis and Cnertie-Sara, bap. Apr. 21, 1771.

Pipenser, Johannis and Cnertie-Peiter, bap. Feb. 21, 1779.

Pipenser, John and Cneirtie-Maria, bap. April 16, 1786.

Pittenser, Josif and Magdalena-John, bap. Nov. 20, 1774.

Pipenser, Josif and Lena-Josif, bap. Sept. 1, 1776.

Pittenser, Richert and Rebeca-Abraham, bap. Jan. 16, 1763.

Pittensen, Richart and Rebecka-Richart, bap. Aug. 11, 1765.

Post, Christoffel and Greitie-Jacob, bap. Oct. 31, 1773.

Post, Christofel and Greitie-Maria, bap. Aug. 25, 1776.

Post, Christofl and Greite-Eyda, bap. Sept. 15, 1782.

Post, Hendrick and Maregreita-Aeltie, bap. June 6, 1773.

Post, Hendrick and Maregreita-Willim, bap. June 18, 1775.

Post, Hendrick and Maregreita-Hendrick, bap. May 10, 1778.

Post, Hendrick and Alaregreita-Maregreita, bap. May 15, 1780.

Post, Willim and Marigreita-Willim, bap. May 19, 1765.
Post, Wylhelmus and Susanna-Johannis, bap. Mar. 12, 1769.
Post, Wyllim and Susanna-Cliristoffel, bap. Sept. 8, 1771.
Post, Willim and Susanna-Abraham, bap. Mar. 27, 1774.
Post, Hendrick and Maregreita-Gertruy, bap. Feb. 11, 1787.
Post, Willim and Susanna-Aeltie, bap. Nov. 26, 1775.
Probasco, Jacob and Antie-Gorge, bap. June 29, 1766.
Probasco, Jacob and Antie-Jacob, bap. June 26, 1768.
Post, John and Catie-Lentie, bap. Nov. 27, 1791.
Post, Teunis and Scytie-Willim, bap. Mar. 31, 1777.
Post, Teunis and Seytie-Maria, bap. Feb. 21, 1779.
Post, Teunis and Seytie-Jorisbergen, bap. Aug. 27, 1780.
Post, Wyllim and Maragreita-Eyda, bap. May 12, 1763.
Probasco, Jacob and Antie-Joseph, bap. April 21, 1771.
Probasco, Jacob and Antie-Eleisabet, bap. Nov. 8, 1772.
Prsel, Olevert and Leneresye-Gerit Willimse, bap. Oct. 18, 1789.
Pruse, Christofor and Maria-Eleisabeth, bap. Sept. 12, 1773.
Queck, Jacobus and Maregreita-Maregreita, bap. Oct. 30, 1774.
Quyck, Peiter and Aeltie-Annatie, bap. Nov. 12, 1780; witnesses Jogom and Catreina Quick.
Reynersen, Barent and Eleisabet-Berent, bap. Feb. 19, 1764.
Rynersen, Berent and Eleisabeth-Eleisabeth, bap. April 19, 1766.
Reynersen, Barent and Eleisabeth-Nicholaes, bap. Dec. 3, 1769.
Post, Henderick and Maregreita-Henderick, bap. Jan. 5, 1783.
Reyneirsen, Barent and Sara-Cetie, bap. June 17, 1781.
Ryneirsen, John and Antie-Maria, bap. April 29, 1787.
Reyneirsen, Reynein and Judick-Barint, bap. Oct. 23, 1781.
Reneirsen, Reyneir and Jeudick-Rebecka, bap. Mar. 30, 1783.
Schamp, Adriaen and Rebecka-Styntie, bap. May 24, 1772.
Schamp, Adriyaen and Catleyna-Samuel, bap. Oct. 22, 1775.
Schamp, Areyaen and Catleytie-Nicolaes, bap. Aug. 31, 1777.
Scamp, Maria-Hendrick, bap. Mar. 26, 1786.
Scylman, John and Maria-Maria, bap. Jan. 30, 1780.
Sebring, Roelof and Femite-Aeltie, bap. Sept. 17, 1780.
Sebring, Roelof and Femmite-Cornelus, bap. Mar. 24, 1782.
Sebring, Roelof and Femmite-Roelof, bap. April 11, 1784.
Sebrant, Rulef and Phebe-Harp Peterson, bap. Oct. 20, 1793.
Senders, John and Aentie-Aentie, bap. Sept. 17, 1780.
Sydel, Andrias and Sara-Annatie, bap. Dec. 1, 1765.
Seydel, Andrias and Sara-Catreina, bap. June 2, 1771.

Sickels, Sekerias and Maragretta-Neltie, bap. July 18, 1779.
Sickels, Sekerias and Nensei-Cetie, bap. July 18, 1779.
Sickels, Seckerius and Marygret-Willim, bap. June 17, 1781.
Sitvin, Geysbert and Gertie-Aeltie, bap. Oct. 7, 1770.
Sitvin, Jan and Janetie-Maria, bap. January 13, 1765.
Sitvin, Jan and Jannitie-Aeltie, bap. Jan. 26, 1766.
Sitvin, Jan and Janniteie-Lea, bap. June 8, 1767.
Sitvin, Jan and Jannitei-Jacob, bap. April 29, 1770.
Sitvin, Jan and Jannite-Jan and Jannite, bap. Mar. 26, 1775.
Sitvin, Stout and Funtie-Lou, bap. Mar. 17, 1776.
Slegt, Abraham and Gertie-Henderick, bap. Jan. 31, 1779.
Smali, Isack and Seytie-Hendrick, bap. May 17, 1767; witnesses Hendrick and Maria Piepenser.
Smali, Isaak and Seytie-Isaak, bap. Oct. 6, 1771.
Smali, Isaac and Seytie-Abraham, bap. May 29, 1774; witnesses Abraham and Maregreita Pipenser.
Smock, Matyas and Hanna-John, bap. April 9, 1787.
Speder, Bergen and Eleisabet-Willim, bap. Aug. 20, 1786.
Speder, Bergen and Eleisabet-Eleisabet, bap. Oct. 19, 1788.
Speder, Wyllim and Maria-Daniel, bap. Dec. 27, 1767.
Speder, Wyllim and Maria-Abraham, bap. Sept. 16, 1770.
Speder, Willim and Maria-Jonathan, bap. Aug. 23, 1772; witness, Jonatan Speder.
Speder, Willim and Maria-Peiter, bap. Aug. 20, 1775.
Speder, William and Sara-Maria, bap. Aug. 6, 1780.
Speder, Willim and Sara-Eleisabet, bap. Feb. 6, 1783.
Stevens, Josf and Aeltiei-Maregreite, bap. July 23, 1782.
Stothof, Elbert and Else-Annatie, bap. Jan. 1, 1773.
Stothof, Elbert and Else-Eyda, bap. Feb. 21, 1779.
Staets, Reyneier and Sara-Annatie, bap. Nov. 22, 1778.
Staets, Reyneir and Sara-Hendreick, bap. May 31, 1784.
Stryker, Abraham and Ontie- ---, bap. July 5, 1795.
Streyker, Christoffel and Judick-Rachel, bap. Nov. 12, 1786.
Stryker, (?) ---- -Peiter, bap. Jan. 26, 1766.
Stryker, Domenicus and Maria-Peiter, bap. June 26, 1763.
Streyker, Dominicus and Maria-Dominicus, bap. Jan. 17, 1768.
Streyker, Dominicus and Maria-Samuel, bap. Dec. 3, 1769.
Stryker, Dominicus and Maria-Maria, bap. Mar. 8, 1772.
Streyker, Isack and Janite-Johannis, bap. July 20, 1777.
Streyker, Isack and Janite-Cornelia, bap. April 16, 1781.

Streyker, Isack and Janite-Isack, bap. Aug. 25, 1782.
Streyker, Isack and Jannite-Peiter, bap. July 31, 1785.
Streyker, Isack and Janite-Hendrick, bap. Dec. 5, 1787.
Streyker, Johannis and Maria-Johannis, bap. Mar. 26, 1775.
Suams, John and Maria-Samuel, bap. May 12, 1776.
Saums, John and Maria-Minnen Voorhees, bap. Sept. 21, 1779.
Sauems, John and Maria-Hendrick, bap. Mar. 31, 1782.
Saums, John and Maria-Catreina, bap. May 20, 1784.
Saums, John and Maria-Leucresye, bap. July 29, 1787.
Saeums, John and Maria-Maria, bap. Oct. 18, 1789.
Sudam, Isack and Sara-Maria, bap. April 5, 1767.
Sudam, Isaac and Sara-Anna, bap. Feb. 9, 1772.
Sudam, Sara-Isaack, bap. Oct. 27, 1776.
Sudam, Peiter and Janite-Isack, bap. Mar. 26, 1786.
Sudam, Peiter and Jannite-Davit, bap. Dec. 2, 1787.
Sudam, Peiter and Janite-Johannis, bap. April 4, 1790.
Sudam, Peiter and Jannite-Helena, bap. April 1, 1792.
Ten Eyck, Peiter and Debora-Neeltie, bap. Dec. 30, 1764.
Terheunen, Steven and Margreita-Greite, bap. Mar. 11, 1764.
Teter, Willit and Jannite-Maria, bap. July 30, 1786.
Teysen, Abraham and Maria-Abraham, bap. Jan. 1, 1781.
Teysen, Abraham and Maria-Sara, bap. Aug. 15, 1784.
Titort, Abraham and Antie-Catie, bap. Mar. 20, 1768.
Titort, Abraham and Antie-Jacob, bap. Dec. 24, 1769.
Titort, Abraham and Aentie-Blandina, bap. May 2, 1773.
Titort, Abraham and Antie-Henrei, bap. July 9, 1775.
Titort, Abraham and Maregreita-Abraham, bap. June 9, 1764.
Tietort, Abraham and Margreite-Catleyntie, bap. April 26, 1767.
Titort, Abraham and Maregreita-Efye, bap. Oct. 6, 1771.
Titort, Abraham and Maregretta-Maregreita, bap. July 9, 1775.
Titort, Abraham and Maregreita-Willim, bap. April 16, 1780.
Titort, Peiter and Annatie-Efye, bap. Aug. 28, 1768.
Titort, Peiter and Annatie-Harpert, bap. Nov. 18, 1770.
Titort, Peiter and Annatie-Femmite, bap. Jan. 16, 1774.
Titort, Peiter and Annatie- ----, bap. May 26, 1776.
Titort, Peiter and Annatie-Annatie, bap. Aug. 8, 1779.
Titort, Peiter and Catlyna-Isaac, bap. June 20, 1772.
Titort, Peiter and Catleynte-Peiter, bap. Oct. 22, 1780.
Titort, Willem and Elsye-Sara, bap. Aug. 17, 1788.
Titswort, Jacob-George, bap. Aug. 17, 1794.

Van Aersdalen, Abraham and Else-Abraham, bap. Jan. 1, 1772.
Van Aersdalen, Fillipus and Annatie-Annatie, bap. Feb. 1787.
Van Aersdalen, Fillipus and Aenatie-Sara, bap. Mar. 23, 1788.
Van Aersdalen, Filipus and Annatie-Polli, bap. Oct. 18, 1789.
Vanarsdalen, Phillip-Fammitie, bap. July 26, 1795.
Van Aersdalen, Jan and Annatie-Judick, bap. Jan. 29, 1769.
Van Aersdalen, Jan and Annatie-Joris, bap. April 21, 1771.
Van Aersdalen, Jan and Annatie-Jannite, bap. Aug. 4, 1774.
Van Aersdalen, Jan and Anatie-Isaak, bap. Mar. 31, 1777.
Van Aersdaten, Jan and Anatie-John, bap. Aug. 9, 1778.
Van Aersdalen, Ouke and Maria-Cornelus, bap. Nov. 14, 1762.
Van Arsdalen, Oilken and Maria-Eyda, bap. Dec. 24, 1769.
Van Ailen, Dirick and Gertruy-Caatreina Johanna, bap. Mar. 27, 1780.
Van Alen, Dirick and Gertruy-Tomas, bap. Aug. 4, 1782.
Van Campen, Tomas and Catleyna-Cornelus, bap. May 29, 1774.
Van Camp, Tomas and Catryn-Teunis and John, bap. Sept. 26, 1784.
Van Kampen, Jan and Lea-Cornelus, bap. Sept. 20, 1772.
Van Derypen, Harmen and Cornelia-Cornelus, bap. Aug. 1, 1773.
Van De Reypen, Haermen and Catleyntie-Aeltic, bap. Aug. 31, 1777.
Van De Reypen, Harmen and Cornelia-Maria, bap. June 4, 1780.
Van Derypen, Johannis and Ariaentie-Jurian, bap. Oct. 27, 1771.
Van De Reypen, Johannis and Areyaentie-Lena, bap. June 8, 1777.
Van Dereypen, Johannis and Areyaentie-Peiter Deneyck, bap. Aug. 8, 1779.
Van De Reypen, Johannis and Areyacntie-John, bap. April 11, 1784.
Van De Reypen, Johannis and Areyaentie-Andreis, bap. Feb. 11, 1787.
Van De Reypen, Johannis and Arreyaentie-Maria, bap. Feb. 19, 1792.
Van Der Veer, Lauwerens and Maria-Joseph, bap. April 8, 1770.
Van Derveer, Louwerens and Maria-Femetie, bap. May 3, 1772.
Van Der Veer, Louwerens and Maria-Hendrick, bap. Nov. 27, 1774.
Van Der Veer, Louerens and Alaria-Johannis, bap. Oct. 31, 1779.
Van Der Veer, Louwerens and Maria-Jacob, bap. June 4, 1786.
Van Der Veer, Lotiwerens and Maria-Rachel, bap. April 26, 1789.
Van Der Veer, Peiter and Antie-Seytie, bap. Jan. 23, 1785.
Van Deusen, Cetie-Johannis, bap. Aug. 7, 1782.
Van Dooren, Christeyaen and Aeltie-Jannite, bap. April 21, 1765.
Van Doren, Christeyaen and Aeltie-Christeyaen, bap. May 17, 1767.
Van Doorn, Christeyaen and Aeltie-Aeltie, bap. Aug. 6, 1769.
Van Doorn, Christeyaen and Aeltie-Barnardus, bap. Mar. 7, 1773.
Vandorn, Crityane and Annate-Neeltie, bap. Aug. 11, 1793.
Van Doren, Josip and Sara-Neltie, bap. June 6, 1779.

Van Doren, Josip and Sara-Sara, bap. May 3, 1781.
Van Doren, Josip and Sara-Maria, bap. May 25, 1783.
Van Doren, Josip and Sara-Aentie, bap. Mar. 6, 1785.
Van Doren, Josip and Sara-Catreina, bap. July 8, 1787.
Van Doren, Josip and Sara-Josip, bap. April 12, 1789.
Van Doren, Josip and Sara-Jeromus Van Derbilt, bap. Apr. 10, 1791.
Van Doren, Josip and Sara-Jeromus Van Derbilt, bap. April 1, 1792.
Van Dorn, Joseph and Sarah-Abraham, bap. April 6, 1794.
Van Dooren, Peiter and Franseynte-Catelyna, bap. Oct. 6, 1771.
Van Duyn, Wyllim and Sara-Susanna, bap. Aug. 21, 1774.
Van Duyn, Wyllim and Sara-Cornelia, bap. Aug. 19, 1787.
Van Dycke, Domienicus and Marigrita-Hendrick, bap. Aug. 25, 1763.
Van Dyck, Domenicus and Marigreita-John, bap. Aug. 11, 1765.
Van Deyck, Dominicus and Hanna-John Cock, bap. Dec. 2, 1787.
Van Dyck, Hendericus and Styntie-Hendericus, bap. April 26, 1767.
Van Deyck, Hendericus and Christeyntie-Roelof, bap. July 23, 1775.
Van Dyck, Johannis and Annatie-Johannis, bap. June 23, 1771.
Van Dyck, Johannis and Annatie-Gerrit, bap. Sept. 28, 1773.
Van Deyck, Johannis and Annatie-Maregreita and Annatie, bap. April 16, 1775.
Van Dyck, Petrus and Rachel-Rebecca, bap. Nov. 6, 1768.
Van Deyck, Verdenanttis and Aeltie-Catreina, bap. Nov. 28, 1784.
Van Deyck, Verdenantus and Aeltie-Hendericus, bap. Feb. 11, 1787.
Van Deyck, Verdenantus and Aeltie-Antie, bap, Aug. 18, 1789.
Van Deyck, Wyllim and Maria-Dominacus, bap. June 21, 1782.
Van Engelen, Cornelus and Sara-Cornelus, bap. July 15, 1770.
Van Houten, Gertruy-Jorge Hall, bap. April 19, 1772; witness Edward Hall.
Van Hotiten, Johannis and Gertruy-John, bap. Aug. 21, 1774.
Van Houten, Johannis and Gertruy-Cornelus, bap. Nov. 3, 1776.
Van Houten, Johannis and Gertruy-Cetie, bap. Feb. 21, 1779.
Van Houten, Johannis and Gertruy-Maria, bap. July 8, 1781.
Van Nist, Jan and Sara-Johannis, bap. June 26, 1763.
Van Nist, Jan and Sara-Maria, bap. Oct. 12, 1766.
Van Nist, Jan and Sara-Isack, bap. May 26, 1776.
Van Nist, Magdalena-Sara, bap. April 30, 1775; witness Jan Van Nist.
Van Nist, Magdalena-Sara Stevins, bap. July 18, 1779.
Van Nuys, Corneltis and Neeltie-Magdalena, bap. Nov. 15, 1771.
Van Nuys, Cornelus and Neltie-Sara, bap. Sept. 16, 1768.
Van Sant, Bernardus and Neeltie-Magdalena, bap. Jan. 16, 1763.
Van Vleit, Frederick and Lea-Rebecka, bap. Dec. 25, 1785.
Van Vleit, Fredrick and Lea-Maregreita, bap. May 17, 1789.

Van Vleit, Frederick and Lea-Mary, bap. Apr. 15, 1792.
Van Vleit, Gerrit and Catleyna-Josiph, bap. Oct. 10, 1773; witnesses Josiph and Nesseie Hegeman.
Van Vleit, Jan and Eleisabet-Greite, bap. Oct. 23, 1785.
Van Vliet, Maria-Leideya, bap. Nov. 16, 1783; witness Willim Van Vleit.
Van Vleit, Wyllim and Ariaentie-Abraham, bap. May 29, 1774.
Ver Bryck, Barnardus and Catleyntie-Jannite, bap. July 31, 1774.
Ver Breyck, Barnardus and Catleyntie-Eleisabet, bap. Sept. 15, 1776.
Ver Breyck, Barnardus and Catleynte-Barnadus, bap. Mar. 10, 1782.
Ver Breyck, Barnardus and Catleynte-Catleyna, bap. Dec. 5, 1784.
Ver Breyck, Bernardus and Catleyntie-Maria, bap. June 17, 1787.
Ver Bryck, Wyllbelmus and Dortie-Jannitie, bap. May 15, 1768.
Ver Breyck, Wylhelmus and Doritte-Louwerens, bap. April 8, 1770.
Ver Breyck, Wylhelmus and Rebecka-Dorite, bap. Feb. 22, 1778.
Ver Breyck, Wylhelmtis and Rebecka-Rebecka, bap. Aug. 29, 1779.
Ver Breyck, Wilhelmus and Rebecka-Barnardus, bap. June 3, 1781.
Ver Breyck, Wylhelmus and Rebecka-Dirick, bap. Mar. 30, 1783.
Ver Breyck, Wyhelmus and Rebecka-Sara, bap. Mar. 20, 1785.
Ver Breyck, Wilhelmus and Rebecka-Wylhelmus, bap. April 16, 1786.
Ver Breyck, Wylhelmus and Rebecka-Jan, bap. May 25, 1788.
Ver Breyck, Wilhelmus and Rebecka-Jeudick, bap. June 13, 1790.
Ver Breyck, Wylhelmus and Rebecka-Nelle, bap. June 24, 1792.
Vlaeck, Jacob and Cristina-Rebecka, bap. April 30, 1786.
Vlaeck, Jacob and Catreina-Annatie, bap. April 4, 1790.
Vlaeck, Jacob and Enne-Jacob, bap. Nov. 7, 1790.
Vlaeck, Susanna-Jacob Gno, bap. April 30, 1786; witness Jacob Vlaeck.
Voorhees, Abraham and Maria-Gerrit, bap. June 26, 1763.
Voorhees, Abraham and Maria-Treyntie, bap. Sept. 16, 1768.
Voorhees, Abraham and Maria-Nelle, bap. April 21, 1771.
Voorhees, Abraham and Maria-Jacob, bap. Nov. 2, 1777.
Voorhees, Abraham and Maria-Johannis, bap. May 15, 1780.
Voorhees, Abraham and Willimte-Abraham, bap. Sept. 16, 1781.
Voorhees, Coert and Eleisabet-Aeltie, bap. April 6, 1788.
Voorhees, Coert and Eleisabet-Maria, bap. Nov. 7, 1790.
Voorhees, Dirick and Simyme-Abraham, bap. Feb. 23, 1777.
Voorhees, Derick and Simije-Lena, bap. Feb. 1, 1778.
Voorhees, Dirick and Simye-Isack, bap. Mar. 21, 1779.
Voorhees, Gerardus and Maria-Gerrit, bap. May 13, 1790.
Voorhees, Jacob and Symmeye-Sara, bap. Sept. 10, 1775.
Voorhees, Jacob and Sara-Eleisabet, bap. Nov. 22, 1778.

Voorhees, Jacob and Sara-Johannis, bap. Nov. 21, 1779.
Voorhees, Minnen and Maria-Gerrit, bap. Aug. 23, 1772.
Voorhees, Mynnen and Maria-Arnoldus, bap. June 4, 1775.
Voorhees, Minnen and Tyni-Abraham, bap. Feb. 5, 1775.
Voorhees, Minen and Tyni-Cornelus Lou, bap. Mar. 16, 1777.
Voorhees, Minnen and Catleyna-Maria, bap. Dec. 9, 1779.
Voorhees, Minnie and Catleyna-Minne, bap. June 23, 1782.
Voorhees, Stefanus and Maregreita-Hendericus, bap. Sept. 19, 1769.
Voorhees, Steven and Maregreita-Johannis, bap. Mar. 8, 1772.
Voorhees, Steven and Maregreita-Catleyntie, bap. Oct. 9, 1774.
Voorhees, Steven and Maregreita-Aeltie, bap. Oct. 6, 1776.
Voorhees, Steven and Maregreita-Annatie, bap. Dec. 21, 1783.
Vroom, Hendrick and Jacameyntie-Petrus, bap. July 7, 1782.
Vroom, Hendrick and Saertie-Peiter, bap. Sept. 15, 1782.
Vroom, John and Nensi-John, bap. Oct. 22, 1786.
Vroom, Peiter and Maria-Eyda, bap. April 29, 1781.
Vroom, Peiter and Maria-Petrus, bap. July 13, 1783.
Vroom, Peiter and Maria-Janete Demon, bap. Nov. 8, 1789.
Waldrom, Catrena-Elesabeth, bap. July 26, 1795.
Waldrom, Jeronemus and Leideya-Jannike, bap. May 23, 1773.
Waldrom, Jeromus and Eleisabet-Catreina, bap. Oct. 23, 1785.
Waldrom, Jeronemus and Eleisabet-Gretie, bap. Oct. 18, 1789.
Waldrom, Johannis and Janite-Johannis, bap. Oct. 9, 1778.
Waldrom, Samuel and Neltie-Catreina, bap. Feb. 13, 1785.
Weimer, Jacob and Genye-Neltie, bap. Sept. 9, 1787.
Weykof, Abraham and Areyaentie-Petrus, bap. May 19, 1765.
Weykof, Abraham and Areyaentie-Josua, bap. June 28, 1767.
Weykof, Abraham and Ariaentie-Catreina, bap. Aug. 5, 1770.
Weykof, Abraham and Areyaentie-Annatie, bap. Nov. 8, 1772.
Weykof, Cornelus and Antie-Annatie, bap. July 10, 1774.
Weykof, Cornelus and Antie-Mary, bap. June 8, 1777.
Weykof, Cornelus and Enne-Febe, bap. June 27, 1779.
Wicoff, Jan and Sarah-Neeltje, bap. May 23, 1762; witnesses Nicholas and Neeltje Ammorman.
Weykof, Jan and Sara-Petrus, bap. Nov. 4, 1764.
Weykof, Jan and Sara-Nicolaes, bap. April 5, 1767.
Weykof, Nicolaes and Susanna-John and Pieter, bap. April 5, 1790.
Weycof, Nicolaes and Susanna-Willim, bap. May 20, 1792.
Winter, Peiter and Lena-Hendrick, bap. Mar. 6, 1763; witnesses Hendrick Dils and Eleisabet Vlack.

Winter Peiter and Magdalena-Samuel, bap. June 6, 1773.
Winter, Peiter and Malli-Johannis, bap. Feb. 16, 1766; witnesses Johannis and Antie Kese.
Willimsen, Cornelus and Catreina-Gertie, bap. April 4, 1790.
Willemsen, Gerrit and Gertie-Antie, bap. April 26, 1767.
Willimsen, Gerrit and Geertie-Lucreesie, bap. Jan. 29, 1769.
Wyllimsen, Johannis and Geeysye-Aert, bap. Mar. 26, 1775.
Willimsen, Johannis and Gesy-Henderick, bap. April 21, 1776.
Willimsen, Johannis and Gesye-Antie, bap. Jan. 31, 1779.
Willemsen, Johannis and Geysie-Sara, bap. April 1, 1781.
Wyllemsen, Johannis and Gesye-Davit, bap. June 4, 1786.
Wyllimsen, Johannis and Gesye-Gerrit, bap. Mar. 1, 1789.
Weytknegt, Cornelus and Catlyna-Abraham, bap. April 21, 1765.
Weytknegt, Joseph and Catreina-Aeltie, bap. Feb. 4, 1770.
Wytknegt, Joseph and Catreina-Johannis, bap. Aug. 23, 1772.

Records, 1796-1800

The second book of Baptismal Records of the Neshanic Reformed Church began in the pastorate of Rev. William R. Smith (1794-1817), of whom Rev. Henry Polhemus was a colleague (1798-1808), and continues through the pastorates of Rev. Peter Labagh (1809-'21) and Rev. Gabriel Ludlow (1821-'78). The names were entered in plain English spelling, and vary but little in orthography. Accordingly, instead of repeating the names of the parents the list is presented in a manner easy of reference, being alphabetical as to the parents and in consecutive order as to the children. The arrangement was made from the records by the Editor of the *Quarterly*. The parents are first stated and then the children; and where there are variations in a parent's name, they are stated in parentheses.

The second book covers the period, 1796-1878; only the records up to 1801 are included here.

Baranhart (Barnheart), Peter and Tine Cock:
Mary, b. Jan. 3, 1798; bap. Apr. 8.
William Cock, b. Jan. 13, 1800; bap. Feb. 16.
Bennet, Abraham and Mary Arrowsmith:
Letty Lane, b. Sept. 13, 1798; bap. Nov. 11.
Boorum, Cornelius and Deborah Vanderipe:
Nelly, b. Jan. 9, 1798; bap. Feb. 25.

John Van Deripe, b. Dec. 3, 1799; bap. Jan. 19, 1800.
Brokaw, Bergun and Letty Post:
Henry, b. Feb. 17, 1798; bap. June 10.
Cock, Edward and Mary Post:
Ann Reading, b. Aug. 27, 1798; bap. Sept. 30.
Cock, Jeremiah and Anne Hall:
Crishee, b. Aug. 28, 1796; bap. Dec. 30.
George, b. Apr. 28, 1799; bap. July 30.
Cock, John and Anne Williamson:
Caty Dennis, b. June 30, 1798; bap. Sept. 30.
Cock, Margret:
Hannah Cock, b. Sept. 8, 1799; bap. Feb. 16, 1800.
Corsant, James and Deborah Whitehead:
Elizabeth Lambert, b. Sept. 19, 1796; bap. Dec. 4.
Coshun, Joshua and Tiney Voorhees:
Margaret, b. June 25, 1797; bap. Aug. 20.
Stephen, b. Nov. 3, 1798; bap. Feb. 3, 1799.
Coshun, Peter and Sarah Whiteneght (Whitenack):
Elizabeth, b. Sept. 28, 1799; bap. Jan. 19, 1800.
Ditmars, George and Charity Voorhees:
Mary, b. Jan. 8, 1800; bap. Feb. 8, 1801.
Flagg, Jacob J. and Anne Stoteoff:
Elisabeth, b. July 6, 1797; bap. July 30.
Albert Stotehuff, b. ----; bap. Apr. 20, 1800.
Flagg, John and Nancy Arrowsmith:
Christian, b. Sept. 10, 1798; bap. Sept. 25.
Gano, George and Elizabeth Cock:
Rebekah, b. Dec. 11, 1797; bap. Feb. 25, 1798.
Hageman, Francis and Elizabeth Hobbard:
Thomas, b. Nov. 30, 1796; bap. May 28, 1797.
Hageman, Francis Van Dike and Martha Beekman:
Dennis, b. June 11, 1797; bap. July 9.
Mary, b. Apr. 28, 1799; bap. May 26.
Hageman, Joseph and Altie ----:
Margret, b. Aug. 12, 1796; bap. Sept. 11.
Jinne, b. Aug. 28, 1799; bap. Oct. 19.
Hall, Thomas E. and Eunis Cock:
Charity, b. Jan. 2, 1798; bap. Feb. 11.
Mary Ann, b. Jan. 20, 1800; bap. Apr. 20.
Hartough, Angleburt and Ann Gulick:

Sarah, b. Sept. 19, 1797; bap. Oct. 14.
Hat, John, alias Chapalow, and Mary Stout:
Orraminar Cumting, b. Feb. 23, 1799; bap. May 26.
Herder, Abraham and Catharine Hoagland:
Elenor, b. June 22, 1797; bap. Aug. 20.
Mary, b. Feb. 11, 1799; bap. Apr. 28.
Lucas Hoagland, b. Aug. 31, 1800; bap. Oct. 5.
Herder, Henry and Ann Staats:
Peter Staats, b. Mar. 14, 1800; bap. July 13.
Hoagland, Albert H. and Mary Kingsland:
Catharine Hoagland, b. Oct. 29, 1796; bap. Dec. 4.
Elizabeth, b. Jan. 30, 1799; bap. Apr. 7.
Hoagland, Herman and Jane Vroom:
Peter, b. Oct. 22, 1797; bap. Nov. 26.
Hoagland, John and and Sarah Bergen:
John Bergen, b. Oct. 21, 1797; bap. Dec. 6.
Hoagland, Lucas and Mary Bunn:
Abraham, b. ----; bap. May 28, 1797.
Hoagland, Peter and Mary Van Cleaf:
Ann Striker, b. Feb. 15, 1799; bap. Apr. 28.
Huff, Bergun and Mary Van Fleet [or Vanvliet]:
Frederick Huff, b. June 15, 1796; bap. July 31.
Huff, Peter and Sarah Van Nest:
Peter, b. Apr. 28, 1798; bap. June 10.
Huff, Tunis and Mary [Maria] Voorhees:
Jonneche, b. Feb. 3, 1799; bap. May 19.
Jessup, Daniel and Catharine Jessup:
Joseph, b. Oct. 13, 1796; bap. Apr. 30, 1797.
Jeroloman, Nicholas and Elisabeth Jessup:
Elisabeth, b. Feb. 18, 1797; bap. May 28.
Nicholas, b. May 14, 1800; bap. Sept. 27.
Labertude, John and Phebe:
Peter, b. Nov. 28, 1792; bap. Dec. 9, 1796.
Joseph, b. Dec. 5, 1794; bap. Dec. 9, 1796.
Labertude, William and Eve Van Cleve:
Catharine, b. Nov. --, 1794; bap. Dec. 9, 1796.
Lisk, Abraham and Jane Thomson:
Rachel, b. Dec. 5, 1785; bap. Feb. 19, 1797
Alexander, b. Feb. 11, 1788; bap. Feb. 19, 1797.
John Teneike, b. July 3, 1790; bap. Feb. 19, 1797.

Abraham, b. Feb. 22, 1794; bap. Feb. 19, 1797.
Henry H. Schenk, b. Dec. 26, 1796; bap. Feb. 19, 1797.
Caty, b. July 25, 1799; bap. Oct. 13.

Low, Garrit, Jr.:
Judah, b. Dec. 8, 1798; bap. Oct. 1799.

Low, John and Mary Striker:
Frederick Van Fliet, b. Oct. 27, 1795; bap. June 19, 1796.
Garret, b. June 26, 1797; bap. Sept. 7, 1798.

Low, William H. and Frances Huff:
Sarah, b. May 11, 1799; bap. Oct. 13.

Miner, Henry and Mary Monfort:
William, b. May 29, 1798; bap. July 8.

Miner, John and Mary Allen:
Margery, b. Aug. 29, 1797; bap. Oct. 15.

Miner, William and Altie [Letitia] Voorheese:
Peggy Voorhees, b. Feb. 10, 1798; bap. May 19.

Mitler, Samuel and Rebekah:
Levi, b. last of March; bap. Apr. 30, 1797.

Monfort, Peter H. and Sarah Miller:
Anna, b. Nov. 26, 1793.
Mary, b. Oct. 31, 1795; bap. Jan. 1796.
Elisabeth, b. Aug. 3, 1797; bap. Sept. 10.
Johannah, b. aug. 15, 1799; bap. Feb. 16, 1800.

Moore, John and Elisabeth Hagaman:
Elisabeth, b. Dec. 24, 1799; bap. Aug. 30, 1801.

Parsell, Oliver and Lucretia Williamson:
Nicholas Williamson and Altie Peterson, b. Nov. 23, 1797; bap. Dec. 27.

Peterson, Cornelius and Elenor Voorhees:
Minna Voorhees, b. Jan. 30, 1798; bap. Mar. 14.
Garrit, b. Nov. 20, 1800.

Peterson, Peter P. and Elisabeth Boerum:
Elisabeth Hoagland, b. May 17, 1799; bap. July 23.

Peterson, Reulif and Magdelene:
John, b. Nov. 6, 1796; bap. Feb. 12, 1797.

Philips, William and Mary Voorhees:
Simeon, b. Dec. 12, 1799; bap. Mar. 30, 1800.

Quick, James, Jr., and Maria Hagaman:
James, b. Jan. 31, 1798, bap. Mar. 14.
Camelia, b. Sept. 17, 1799; bap. Oct. 19.

Quick, John and Lenah Van Nest:
John Van Nest, b. Jan. 17, 1798; bap. Apr. 8.
Jacobus, bap. Oct. 5, 1800.
Renton, James and Margaret [Nevius]:
John Nevius, b. April 29, 1797; bap. May 28.
Runyou, George and Sarah Brocaw:
Rebekah, b. Oct. 12, 1798; bap. Dec. 23.
Schenck, Henry H. and Nelly Hardenbergh:
John Frelinghuysen, b. July 6, 1799; bap. July 30.
Skillman, Isaac and Cornelia Quick:
Thomas, b. Sept. 22, [1796]; bap. Dec. 9.
Smith, William R. and Rachel Stidham:
Anne Dubois Smith, b. Sept. 14, 1795; bap. Jan. 18, 1796.
Elizabeth Smith, b. Oct. 19, 1796; bap. Oct. 29.
Mary Colesberry, b. Jan. 3, 1797; bap. July 8.
Robert Stidham, b. Feb. 19, 1800; bap. Apr. 26.
Stryker, Abraham and Anne Lapordus:
Hannah, b. Mar. 13, 1798; bap. Apr. 29
Stryker, John D. and Catharine Bogart:
Sarah Van Middlesworth, b. Nov. 20, 1797; bap. Feb. 4, 1798.
Stryker, Stephen and Mary Bogart:
Maria, b. Oct. 22, 1797; bap. Nov. 26.
Sutphen, John D. and Aletta Van Doren:
Derick Sutphen, b. July 20, 1796; bap. Aug. 28.
Mary Ann, b. Aug. 11, 1800; bap. Sept. 14.
Sutphin, Theodotia (wife of Christopher), b. Aug. 10, 1789; bap. Aug. 4, 1811.
Sydam, Peter and Jennette Voorhees:
Isaac, b. Feb. 19, 1786.
David, b. Nov. 11, 1789.
Johannes, b. Mar. 2, 1790.
Hellenah, b. Feb. 16, 1792.
Sarah, b. May 27, 1794.
Peter, b. Aug. 8, 1796; bap. Sept. 11.
Daniel, b. Aug. 22, 1798; bap. Sept. 30.
Van Arsdalen, Philip and Anne Peeterson:
John, b. June 2, 1798; bap. Sept. 9.
Ver Bryck, William and Rabeca Low:
Peter Clover, b. Jan. 8, 1796; bap. Apr. 29, 1799.
Jean, b. May 26, 1798; bap. Apr. 29, 1799.
Van Deripe, Jerry and Anna Voorhees:

Jerry Ann, b. Oct. 5, 1798; bap. Dec. 16.
Van Deripe, John and Arian Ten Eist:
Nelly, b. Nov. 3, 1798; bap. Dec. 16.
Van Deripe and Anne Vorhees:
John, b. Oct. 11, 1796; bap. Nov. 13 or 20.
Van Derveer, Hendrick and Charity Cline:
John, b. May 5, 1800; bap. June 15.
Van Derveer, John and Rachel Ackerman (Ockerman):
Peter Stryker, b. June 16, 1796; bap. July 10.
David, b. Aug. 2, 1798; bap. Sept. 15.
Maria Stryker, b. Dec. 1, 1800; bap. Mar. 2, 1801.
Van Derveer, Peter S. and Nancy (Anna) Phillips:
John, bap. Aug. 2, 1799.
Elias Philips, b. Dec. 29, 1800; bap. Feb. 22, 1801.
Van Doren, Abbey:
Peter, b. Feb. 19, 1797; bap. July 30.
Van Dyck (Van Dyke), William and Mary Labryteaux:
John, b. July 7, 1797; bap. Oct. 15.
Henry, b. Nov. 8, 1799; bap. Apr. 20, 1800.
Van Horn, John and Phebe Ten Eick:
John Ten Eick, b. July 29, 1796; bap. Sept. 11.
Van Liew, Denice and Mary Suydam:
Johannes, b. Sept. 30, 1798; bap. Nov. 4.
Ann, b. July 11, 1800; bap. Aug. 10.
Van Middlesworth, John and Lydia Kenedy:
Peter Dumont, b. June 21, 1800; bap. July 13.
Vanordstrand, Jacob and Anne Sydam:
Aaron, b. Oct. 19, 1797; bap. Nov. 26.
Van Zant, John and Eunace Tenbrook:
Nicholas, b. July 13, 1797; bap. ----.
Voorhees, Court and Lucretia Hagaman:
John, b. Oct. 18, 1799; bap. ----.
Voorhees, John and Jinny Nevius:
James Nevius Voorhees, b. June 24, 1796; bap. Aug. 7.
Stephen, b. June 2, 1800; bap. Sept. 7.
Vroom, Peter and Mary ----:
Hendrick, b. June 22, 1797; bap. July 30.
Waldrun, William and Mary:
Anne, b. Nov. 14, 1797; bap. Apr. 13, 1798.
Witeknaght, Abraham and Anne Coshun:

Joseph, b. Apr. 5, 1797; bap. May 28.
Sarah, b. Dec. 7, 1800; bap. Feb. 1, 1801.

Willet, Thomas and Anna Case:
Elisa Ann, b. Sept. 4, 1797; bap. Sept. 24.
Anna, b. July 4, 1799; bap. Sept. 1.

Williamson, Cornelius and Catharine Simonson:
Garrit, b. Oct. 11, 1797; bap. Nov. 26.
Magdalane Ten Eyck, b. Jan. 21, 1800; bap. Mar. 2.

Wilson, Abraham and Susannah Low:
Peter Vroom, b. June 23, 1800; bap. July 27.

Wilson, John D., Sr., and Mary Sims:
John Van Harler, b. Feb. 10, 1798; bap. July 29.

FIRST REFORMED CHURCH, RARITAN (SOMERVILLE) BAPTISMS

The introduction to these records begins in Volume II (1913) of the Quarterly, page 38.

The earliest known ecclesiastical organization in Somerset County was that of the First Reformed Church of Raritan (now Somerville), originally known as the Reformed Dutch Church of Raritan. It was organized March 9, 1699. If a church building was then, or soon after, erected, the fact and the location are at present unknown, but as to this we shall refer again presently. In 1721, however, a building was erected on the north side of the Raritan river, near Finderne, where the ground was donated by Michael Van Veghten, (usually spelled in the church records Van Vechten), and remained standing there until burned down by British raiders under Lieut.-Colonel Simcoe on Oct. 27, 1779. In 1784 a new (brick) church was built in present Somerville, which, with several enlargements, stood until 1896, when the present handsome stone edifice took its place. The church baptismal records are preserved from the beginning, the first three baptisms recorded being March 8, 1699, made, no doubt, by Rev. Guiliam Bertholf, of Hackensack, in whose presence, next day, the first elder and first deacon of the Raritan church were installed. Bertholf probably supplied the organization with preaching until 1717. The next known minister to officiate was the Rev. Theodorus Jacobus Frelinghuysen, who was called from Holland and arrived in 1720, becoming pastor of the four churches of Raritan, Three-Mile Run, Six-Mile Run and North Branch (Readington).

The history of this mother church of Somerset County is fully given in Dr.

Messler's *Memorial Sermons and Historical Notes* (1873), and in various other works.

The baptisms were written out in the Dutch language until 1720, when English, with some Dutch intermixed, was substituted. Some of the early entries, while admirably kept and well preserved, are exceedingly hard to decipher, owing to the unusual spellings (often greatly varied) of the proper names.

The fact that the baptisms are not always entered upon the record in chronological order would seem to indicate that the local scribe, or Clerk of Consistory, after recording the baptisms celebrated in the home congregation, would then copy Domine Bertholf's notes of baptisms made by him in other parts of the congregation, as, e.g., in Readington (then known as North Branch), which he occasionally visited. This supposition is the more plausible in view of the fact that in 1893 William Riker, the then living well-known librarian and antiquarian, wrote to the Rev. Dr. Searle, the minister of the First Church, Somerville, saying that he had discovered certain manuscripts which he believed to be fragments of Domine Bertholf's diary. Bertholf (if it were he) declares that on such and such a date he baptized certain children "in the new church on the Raritan." A comparison with the record shows the same names recorded, the year being 1709. Incidentally, this would not only go to prove that the old Dutch Domine kept notes of his doings as he rode about his circuit, but admits also of the inference that the Raritan church had a house of worship as early as 1709, or twelve years prior to the earliest date assigned by Rev. Dr. Messler. Moreover, this is in harmony with the documentary history according to which the Readington part of the congregation had a church edifice in 1718-19. Would the older and more considerable part of the congregation at Raritan be likely to have no building until two or three years later?

It is with much regret, however, that we have to relate the end of the Riker matter. Before the Rev. Dr. Searle could communicate with Mr. Riker the latter died. A rigid search, instituted some time later by Rev. Dr. Cranmer, who succeeded to Dr. Searle in the pastorate of the "Old First," failed to bring to light again this strangely discovered and, doubtless, most valuable document.

The instalments given below and to be continued for some time are believed to be printed as nearly as the proper names were spelled as possible; where there is great uncertainty an interrogation mark after a name will indicate it. Some years ago Mr. William F. Wyckoff, of Brooklyn, had the whole record carefully translated into English and copied by a student from Rutgers College, and has kindly placed the same at the disposition of the Editor of the *Quarterly*. Another copy is in the possession of the Holland Society of New York City. The Wyckoff record the Editor expects to copy with care and then compare with the original record, to make sure there are no omissions, and to try to verify the peculiar spellings (not always certain), and in this will have the cheerful and valued co-operation of the present pastor of the church, Rev. Wm. Stockton Cranmer, D.D. An exact chronological order will be followed. In the original the child's name appears first and then the parents, but, for purposes of reference, the parents are now printed first, and then the name of the child.

Until about 1727 the sponsors, or witnesses, to baptisms were generally noted in the baptismal book, and, as these are important, often showing family relationships and giving names not appearing elsewhere, they will be included in the published record. After 1727 the names of witnesses appear only at infrequent intervals.

It should be noted by those who refer to the records as now printed that surnames ending in *se or sen* were so written, indifferently, and sometimes s only with or without a flourish after it; as an example in the latter case, Cornelis Powels for Cornelis Powelsen. Also that the relationship of the sponsors is often uncertain, even when the word "vrou" (wife) appears followed by another surname. For example, "Johannes Sebrige and vrou Merledt." This may mean Sebrige's wife was a Merledt, or it may mean the wife of a Merledt was the second witness. We do not undertake in such cases to go beyond the record, but shall give them as written, so far as possible.

BAPTISMAL RECORDS FROM 1699

1699.

Mar. 8. Van Neste, Hironimus and Neeltie Van Neste-Judith.
Witnesses: Cars. Vroom and wife.
Thuenissen, Cornelis and Neeltien-Abraham.
Witness: Michiel Hansson and______
Van Neste, Piter and wife-Jaquemina.
Witnesses: Derek Middage and wife.

May 6. Aallyn, Andrias and Meery-Amarias, Milleson, Obillom, Marsie.

Sept. 19. Van Vechten, Michiell and wife-Dirck.
Witnesses: Jan and Kataleyne Thuenissen.
Gerritse, Fredrick and wife-Jan.
Thuenissen, Jan and wife-Abraham.

Witnesses: Cornelis Thuenisse and wife.
Woertman, Jan and wife-Lisebet.
Witnesses: Michiel Van Vechten and wife.

1700.
Apr. 30. Vroom, Cors and wife-Hendrick.
Witnesses: Jacob Sebrege and wife.
Sept. 26. Middage, Derck and wife-Piter.
Witnesses: Isack Bodyn and wife.
Thuenissen, Cornelis and wife-Abraham.
Witness: Jan Thuenissen.
Alleyn, Ameries and wife-Thammes.

1701.
Mar 11. Van Neste, Piter and wife-Jan.
Witnesses: Isack Bodyn and wife.
June 11. Van Neste, Hironimus and wife-Catleyntie.
Witnesses: Joris and Rutryntis(?) Van Neste.
Van Vechten, Michiel and wife-Jantien.
Witnesses: Piter De Mondt and wife.
Drinckwater, Eedvbert and wife-Sara and Lisebedt.
Witnesses: Jan Thuenissen and wife; Jan Otman and wife.
Nov. 18. Monwersen, Monwers and wife-Fredrick.
Witnesses: Piter Van Neste, Enyeltie ----.

1702.
Apr. 21. Vroom, Cors and Catryn-Jan.
Witnesses: Jeronimas Van Neste and wife.
Jansen, Auken and wife-Barber.
Witnesses: Jan Sebrege and wife.
Oct. 27. Van Neste, Joris and wife-Jantien.
Witnesses: Hendrick Reyniersen and wife.

1703.
Mar. 23. Daniels, Johannes and wife-Pouvbell(?).
Witnesses: Michiel Van Vechten and wife.
Lebersten, Gabriell-Piter.
Sebrege, Johannes and wife-Jaentien.
Witnesses: Jan Roelfsen and wife.
Middage, Derck and wife-Derck.
Witnesses: Jacob Sebrige and wife.
Possell, Thomas and wife-Elisabedt.
Witnesses: Piter and Judit Van Neste.

June 30.	Van Neste, Piter and wife-Joris.
	  Witnesses: Joris Van Neste and wife; Edvbert Garrell and wife.
	Drinckwater, Eedwert and wife-Hester.
	  Witnesses: Joost Jansen, Maria Sebrege.
	Pouwelsen, Cornelis and wife-Elisabet.
	  Witnesses: Cornelis Thuenissen and wife.
	Woertman, Jan and wife-Jan.
	  Witnesses: Hanse Hoverden and wife.

Oct. 19.	Bodyn, Isack and wife-Jan.
	  Witnesses: Piter Van Neste and wife.
	Koelie, Aerte and Susan-Jacob.
	  Witnesses: Josias Merlet, Susanna Morises.
	Hendricksn, Folkert and wife-Elisabet.
	  Witnesses: Jan Thuenissen and wife.
	Neyssen, Ellen-Elisabet.
	  Witnesses: Cornelis Thuenissen and wife.
	Andriessen, Andries and wife-Madalena.
	  Witnesses: Jan Woertman and wife.
	[Parents' names not inserted]-Marytie, Lisabet, Maria, Cornelis, Benjamin, Jesaias, Willem, Jan.
	  Witnesses: Cornelis Pouwels and wife.

1704.	

Apr. 20.	Op Dyck, Lourens and wife-Wilhelmus.
	  Witnesses: Jan Koeverden and wife.
	Oldin, Willem and wife-Lisebett.
	[Parents' names not inserted]-Jan, Willem, Anneken, Saertien, Mertien, Hanna.
	  Witnesses: Cornelis Pouwels, Willem Claessen.
	Thuenissen, Cornelis and wife-Jan.
	  Witnesses: Piter De Mondt and wife.
	Van Neste, Hironimus and wife-Maryrieton.
	  Witnesses: Jacob Sebrege, Judit Van Neste.
	Jansen, Ouke and wife-Jaentien.
	  Witnesses: Jacob and Maria Sebrige.

Aug. 1.	Beten, Gabriel de and Constans-Jantien, b. June 17.
	  Witness: Jantien Cure.
	Bordt, Andries and wife-Mary.
	Laenssen, Willem and wife-S. Jeems.
	  Witness: Derk Volckers.

Brulle, Willem and Albertina-Maria.
Witnesses: Gerrit Bolmers and wife.
Korssen, Kors and wife-Kristiaen.
Witnesses: Joris Van Neste and wife.
Antony, ---- and Maria-Britjert.
Witness: Wife of Broekaerts.
[Parents blank]-Meery.
Witness: Wife of Jan Hauss Hoeverden.
de Mont, Piter and wife-Jan.
Witnesses: Tan Thuenissen and wife.
Oct. 25. Van Neste, Joris and wife-Joris.
Witnesses: Jacob Sebrige and wife.
Oeldien, Willem and wife-Margriet.
Witnesses: Cornelis Pouwels, Abraham Merlet.
Koenraets(?), Octaviaen and Maria Langevelt-Marytie.
Witnesses: Cornelis Langevelt and wife.
Bordt, Andries and wife-Katryn.
Witnesses: Piter and Katryn Broeckaer.
Lavors, Jan and wife-Abrabam.
Witnesses: Johannes Sebrige and wife, Merledt.
Pouwels, Cornelis and wife-Maria.
Witnesses: Abraham Merledt and wife.
Claessen, Willian and wife-Gerbrandt.
Witnesses: Michiel Van Vechten and wife.
Woertman, Jan and wife-Hermtien.
Witnesses: Piter de Mondt and wife.
Bordt, Joris and wife-Joris.
Witnesses: Thammes and Marya Bordt.
Wickhoff, Simon and wife-Geertien.
Witnesses: Cornelis and Geer(?) Wickhoff.
Porssell, Thomas and wife-Piter.
Witnesses: Michiell Van Vechten and wife.

1705.
Aug. 28. Middage, Derck and Kataleyn-Theunis.
Witnesses: Reydt Koorse, Jantien Van Neste.
Hooff, Pieter and wife-Peter.
Witnesses: Piter Lafever and wife, Broeckarts.
Sebrige, Johannes and wife-Lefkers.
Witnesses: Hendrick Reyniersse and wife.
Nov. 14. Van Neste, Piter and wife-Annatien.

Witnesses: Abraham Merledt and wife.
Volkers, Derck and wife-Annetien.
Witnesses: Hendrick Reyniersse and wife.
Broeckaer, Jan and wife-Kalleyntie.
Witnesses: Jan Theunissen and wife.
Lafeber, Piter and wife-Jantien.
Witnesses: Hans Koverden, Katryna Broeckaw.

1706.

Apr. 3. Van Duynen, Abraham and Geertien-Isack.
Witnesses: Jan and Kaetleyn Teunissen.
Teunissen, Cornelis and Neeltien-Sara.
Witnesses: Michiel and Jantien Van Vechten.
Rappelje, Jacob and Saertien-Joris (b. Jan. 24).
Witnesses: Jan and Kaetleyn Tetinissen.
Janse, Auke and wife-Jan.
Witnesses: Daniel and Lisebet Sebrige.
Vroom, Kors and wife-Michiell.
Witnesses: Derck Middage and Kaetien Kurs.

Apr. 14. Malet, Abraham and Elisabet-Joris, b. Apr. 14.
Witnesses: David Willemsen and wife.
Drinckwater, Net and Antien-Eduert.
Witnesses: Willem and Maria Halee.
de Mon, Piter and Femmichien-Abraham.
Witnesses: Michiel and Jannetien Van Vechten.
Van Neste, Jeronimus and Neeltien-Jeronimus.
Witnesses: Derck and Katleyn Middage.
Andriessen, Andries and wife-Mary.
Witnesses: Piter Hoff and wife.
[Parents not named]-Maria.
Witnesses: Abraham van Duynen and wife.

Aug. 6. Marschan, Hendrick and wife-Andries.
Witnesses: Andries Bort and wife.
Koevers, Hans and wife-Maria.
Witnesses: Cornelis and Neeltien Teunissen.
Bort, Joris and Helena-Maria.
Witnesses: Andries Bort and Andries Marshan.

Oct. 30. Broka, Piter and wife-Katleyn.
Witnesses: Piter Van Neste and wife, Broka.
Joosten, Jan and wife-Sara.
Witnesses: Joost Jansen, Katleyn Bodyn.

Van Neste, Joris and wife-Reynier.
Witnesses: Derck Middage and wife.
Dorlandt, Gerrit (the younger) and wife-Maria.
Witnesses: Jacob Wickhoff and wife.

1707.
Apr. 30. Lafeber, Piter and wife-Katryn.
Witnesses: Jan and Catryn Broka, Michiell Van Vechten.
Oldien, Willem and wife-Thomas.
Witnesses: Michiell Van Vechten and wife.
Bort, Andries and wife-Borgon.
Witnesses: Tam Bort and wife.
[Parents not named; says "Mother"]-Margriet.
Witnesses: Abraham Merlet and wife.
Bodyn, Isack and wife-Jantien.
Witnesses: Joris Haall and wife.
Claessen, Willem and wife-Hanna.
Witnesses: Cornelis and Neeltien Thuennissen.
Muelenaer, Hendrick and Katleyn-Joost Adriaensen.
Witnesses: Adriaen Muelenaer and wife.
Hendricksen, Folkert and wife-Grietjen.
Witnesses: Michiell Van Vechten and wife.
Fonteyn, Jannes and wife-Abraham.
Witnesses: Jacob Sebrege and wife.
Pouwels, Cornelis and wife-Elsjen.
Witnesses: Andris Jurjensen and wife.
Wuertman, Jan and wife-Anna.
Witnesses: Jan Broecka and wife.
Nias, Anna-Tammes.
Witnesses: Tammes --- and wife.

Aug. 3. Rappelje, Jacob and wife-Abraham.
Witnesses: Abraham Jorisse and wife, de Mon.
Broeckaer, Jan and wife-Femmichjen.
Witnesses: Jan Thunnissen and wife, Broekaer.
Hoff, Piter and wife-Borgon.
Witnesses: John Broekaers and wife, Koevers.
Willemsen, Davidt and wife-Judit.
Witnesses: Peter and Seyne Van Neste.

Oct. 29. Post, Willem and wife-Johannes.
Witnesses: Louwert Opdwck, Barber Willemsen.
Bort, Tham and wife-Thomas.

Witnesses, Andries Bort and wife, Koevers.
Thissen, Cornelis and wife-Mathias.
Witnesses: Jan Brockaer and wife.

1708.
Apr. 28. Backer, Jacob and wife-Susanna.
Witnesses: Jan Laross and wife.
Kuesa, Antony and wife-Jannetje.
Witnesses: Jan Thuenissen and wife.
Thuenissen, Cornelis and wife-Dneyes(?).
Witnesses: Tuenis and Saertien Middelswart.
Siebridge, Johannes and wife-Annetje.
Witnesses: Jacob and Maria Siebrige.
Van Neste, Piter and wife-Bernerdus.
Witnesses: Michiell Van Vechten and wife.
Wickhoff, Simon and wife-Jan.
Witnesses: Jacob Wickhoff and wife.
Bossell, Cammes and wife-Dinnes.
Witnesses: Hans Koevers and wife.
Joosten, Jan and wife-Johannes.
Witnesses: Isack Bodyn, Van Kocke.
Brocka, Piter and wife-Maryrietien.
Witnesses: Piere and Aryntien Van Neste.
Vroom, Kors and wife-Abraham.
Aug. 4. Janse, Auke and wife-Willem.
Witnesses: Rolef Sibrige; Seyne Van Neste.
Andriessen, Andries and wife-Jannetien.
Witnesses: Jacob Probasco and wife.
Oct. 27. Lafeber, Piter and wife-Judick.
Witnesses: Isaac Broeckaer, Judick Marell.
Merlet, Abraham and wife-Derck.
Witnesses: Derck Middage and wife.
Lafos, Jan and wife-Niclaes.
Witnesses: Willem Ooldien and wife.
Hael, Tam and wife-Ritfelt.
Witnesses: Michiell Van Vechten and wife.
Koch, Jan and wife-Neeltien.
Witnesses: Jan Palen and wife.
Ten Eyck, Albert and wife-Jennehen.
Witnesses: Michiel Van Vechten and wife.

1709.

Apr. 26. Probasco, Jacob and wife-Stoffell.
Witnesses: Jacob Wyckhoff and wife.
Van Neste, Jeronimus and wife-Willem.
Witnesses: Jacob Sibrige and wife.
Van Neste, Joris and wife-Abraham.
Witnesses: Adrean Meulenaer; Katien Vroom.
Middage, Derck and wife-Joris.
Witnesses: Davit Wilemsen; Maryken Van Neste.
Meulenaer, Hendrick and wife-Maryken.
Witnesses: Jacob Bodyn and Kataleyn.
Bodyn, Isack and wife-Fredrick.
Witnesses: Abraham Merlet, Arientien Van Neste.

Apr. 27. Rappelje, Jacob and wife-Antien.
Sebrige, Rolof and wife-Derck.
Witnesses: Derck Volkers and wife.
Beten, Gabriel and wife-Benjamin.
Witness: Lisebet Beten.
Joosten, Jan. and wife-Maria.
Witnesses: Albert Louw and wife.
Dumont, Piter and wife-Katleyntien.
Witnesses: Cornelis and Nieltien Teunissen.
Woertman, Jan and wife-Abraham.
Witnesses: Derck Volckers and wife.

Aug. 4. Halderinck, Willem and wife-Elsjen.
Witnesses: Jan Broecka and wife, Van Vechten.

Oct. 26. Briss, Folkert and wife-Jurjan(?).
Witnesses: Hendrick Reyniersen, Angenietien Barentsen.
Dorlant, Gerrit and Merritien-Lisebet.
Witnesses: Jan Laeten and wife.
Broka, Jan and wife-Jan.
Witnesses: Thunis Middleswart, Cataleyn Theunissen.
Koevers, Hans and wife-Barbara.
Witnesses: Michiel Van Vechten and wife.
Hoff, Piter and wife-Derck.
Witnesses: Piter and Maria Broka.
Van Dyck, Lambert and wife-Achias.
Witnesses: Jacob and Annatien Van Dyck.
Thisson, Cornelis and wife-Annetien.

Witnesses: Piter Van Neste and wife.
Broka, Piter and wife-Piter.
Witnesses: Jan and Catleyntie Broka.

1710.

Apr. 27. Lambers, William and wife-Joseph.
Witnesses: Davit Willemsen and wife.
Backer, Jacob and wife-Lauwerens.
Witnesses: Jan Sebrege and wife.
Vroom, Kors and wife-Isaack.
Witnesses: Hendrick Meulenaers and wife.
De Bardt, Giesbert and wife-Antien.
Witnesses: Davit Willemsen and wife.
Kinnen, Piter and wife-Davit.
Witnesses: Davit Willemsen and wife.
Neyes, Anna (?) and, wife-[child not entered].

Aug. 2. Buys, Jacob and wife-Merritien.
Witnesses: Willem Claessen and wife.
Brees, Cornelis and wife-Thomas.
Witnesses: Jan Brocka; Merritien Buys.
Pouwels, Cornelis and wife-Neettien.
Witnesses: Hendrick Reyniersen; Helena Fonteyn.
Bort, Andries and wife-Abraham.
Witnesses: Abraham Brooka; Kaetleyn Bort.
Bort, Tham and wife-Merrietien.
Witnesses: Hans Koevers; Marietien

Oct. 25. Rappelie, Jacob and wife-Aeltien (b. Sept. 16, 1710).
Witnesses: Cornelis Theuiiisse and wife.
Louw, Albert and wife-Louwerens.
Witnesses: Michiel Van Vechten and wife.
Lafeber, Piter and wife-Jan.
Witnesses: Andries Bort and wife.
Wüertman, Jan and wife-Jan.
Witnesses: Hans Koevers and wife.
----, Ouke and wife-Ouke.
Witnesses: Derck Middagh and wife.
Andriessen, Andries and wife-[child's name omitted].

1711.

Apr. 25. Kock, Jan and wife-Madalena.
Witnesses: Jan Kock; Madalena Kock.
Schermerhoorn, Luyckas and wife-Luykas.

Witnesses: Derck Middagh and wife.
Meriet, Abraham and wife-Jan (b. Mar. 15, 1711).
Witnesses: Jan Theunissen and wife.
Post, Willem-Marya.
Witnesses: Derck Volckers and wife.
Bodien, Jacob and wife-Maryken.
Witnesses: Daniel and Marya Sebregh.
Boegert, Cornelis and wife-Johannes.
Witnesses: Jan Theunissen and wife.
Broka, Piter and wife-Judith.
Witnesses: Jan Broka; Catryna Van Neste.
Borckloo, Kuen and wife-Marya.
Claessen, Willem and wife-Thomas.
Witnesses: Jacob Buys and wife.
Muelenaer, Hendrick and wife-Jan.
Witnesses: Isaack Bodien and wife.
Ten Eyck, Marya Van Vechten (wife of Albert Ten Eyck, deceased)-Albert.
Witnesses: Conraedt Ten Eyck; Margrietie Van Vechten.

Aug. 1. Artsen, Thomas and wife-Thomas.
Witnesses: Hendrick Brees; Sara, wife of Jan Brokaw.
Van Neste, Joris and wife-Judith.
Witnesses: Piter Van Neste; Jacob Jan Middagh.

Nov. 2. Probasko, Jacob and wife-Ida.
Witnesses: Abraham Blou and wife.
Sebrege, Roeloff and wife-Annetien.
Witnesses: Johannes Sebrege and wife.
Bodien, Isack and wife-Kateleyn.
Witnesses: Jacop Bodien and wife.
Vroom, Kors and wife-Jacob.
Witnesses: Anna Beeckmans; Jacob Stoll.

1712.

Apr. 30. Lafeber, Piter-Annetje.
Witnesses: Jurgen Oortman and wife.
Herris, Willem and wife-Elisabet.
Witnesses: Willem Odyn and wife.
Hoff, Piter and wife-Kataleyn.
Witnesses: Isack Brooka; Hilletje Broocka.
Bodyn, Piter and wife-Jan.
Witnesses: Isack and Cataleyn Bodyn.

Middagh, Derck and wife-Gerrit.
Witnesses: Jan Theunissen and wife.
Pouwelsen, Cornelis and wife-Kornelis.
Witnesses: Hendrick and Elisabet Bries.
Rappelje, Jacob and wife-Sara.
Witnesses: Jan Theunissen and wife.
Doti, Eduert and wife-Jan.
Witnesses: Reyst Vroom; Katryna Van Neste.
Haell, Joris and wife-Elisabet.
Witnesses: Isack Bodyn and wife.
Aug. 6. Haall, Tham and wife-Katarina.
Witnesses: Jan Theunissen and wife.
Casaert, Anthony and wife-Anthony.
Witnesses: Willem Hendricksen; Neeltien Theunissen.
Stevens, Joseph and wife-Sara.
Witnesses: Jacob Sebrenge and wife.
Dorlant, Gerrit and wife-Geertjen.
Witnesses: Abraham Merlet and wife.
Broka, Jan and wife-Bergon.
Witnesses: Hans Koevers; Merritjen Theunissen.
de Lameter, Abraham and wife-Sara.
Witnesses: Cornelis Bogert and wife.
Meulenaer, Hendiick and wife-Lisebet.
Witnesses: Katrina Van Neste; Pier Van Neste.
Broeka, Abraham and wife-Cataleyntie.
Witnesses: Wife Bergon; Jan Broeka.
Vroom, Hans and wife-Jesyntien.
Witnesses: Isack Bodien and wife.
Vroom, Hans and wife-Meritien.
Witnesses: Jesyntien ----; Daniel Sebrege.
Bogert, Cornelis and wife-[child's name omitted].
Lameter, Abraham and wife-[child's name omitted].
Sebrege, Johannes and wife-[child's name omitted].
Stoll, Jacob and wife-[child's name omitted].
Lafasi, Jan and wife-[child's name omitted].
Buys, Jacob and wife-[child's name omitted].

1713.
Aug. 9. Bort, Thammes and wife-Hannes.
Witnesses: Theunis Kors; der Jaentien.
Schermerhoorn, Luyckas and wife-Elisabet.

Witnesses: Hendrick Beeckman and wife.
Traphagen, Hendrick-Blandina.
Witness: Andries Ten Eyck.
Oct. 27. Bris, Hendrick [his wife baptized on confession].
Ban, Benjemin and wife-Willem.
Van Vechten, Abraham and wife-Jantien.
Witnesses: Michiel Van Vechten and wife.
Manus, Borger and wife-Engeltien.
Witnesses: Hans Koevers and wife.
Remer, Jurjen and wife-Elisabet.
Witnesses: Piter Hoff; wife of Tam Bort.
Van Neste, Joris and wife-Abraham.
Witnesses: Adriaen and Helena Meulenaer.
Oct. 28. Roos, Andries and wife-Johannes; also Elisabet.
Witnesses: Jacob Wickhoff and wife.
Van Middelswaert, Theunis and wife-Femmichjen.
Witnesses: Jan Theunissen and wife.

1714.
June 3. Schol, Piter and wife Elsjen (?).
Witnesses: Piter Hoff and wife.
Cock, Jan and wife-Jan.
Witnesses: Jacob and Mechtelt Stol.
Van Oudegem, Cornelis-Stientien.
Witnesses: Hendrick Jansen and wife.
Doti, Eduvert and wife-Jeremias.
Witnesses: Jan Broka and wife.
Herrissen, Willem and wife-Matitien.
Witnesses: Neeltie Theunissen; Meme Stavasy.
Passen, Niclaes and wife-Maria Lies.
Witnesses: Jacob Moer; Elisabet Laurense.
Fiell, Jeremias and wife-Jeremias.
Witnesses: Hendrick Bris and wife.
Konyn, Derck and wife-Andries.
Witnesses: Abraham Van Vechten and wife.
Vroom, Kors and wife-Petrus.
Witnesses: Isack Bodyn and wife.
Michiny, Mordechaey and wife-Jan.
Witnesses: Roeloff Sebrege and wife.
Mesenaer, Rutser and wife-Rutser.
Witnesses: Gerrit and Robert Bolmer.

Oct. 9. Louw, Jan and wife-Gysbert.
Witnesses: Albert Louw; Mertien Beeckmas.
Buys, Johannes and wife-Mertien.
Witnesses: Jacob Buys and wife.
Probasko, Jacob and wife-Frederick.
Witnesses: Hendrick Van Leeuwe and wife.
Buerum, Hendrick and wife-Niclaes.
Witnesses: Abraham Blauw and wife.
Bodyn, Jacob and wife-Jan.
Witnesses: Isack Bodyn and wife.
Hael, Joris and wife-Eduaert.
Witnesses: Jan Koch and wife.

1715.
May 18. Van Etten, Manuel and wife-[no child's name].
Witnesses: Willem Roos; Antien Van Etten.
Betue, ---- and wife-Maria.
Witness: --- Merkiese (?)
Boegert, Cornelis and wife-Raechell.
Witnesses: Daniel Sebreges; Seytie Van Neste.
Haell, Tam and wife-Tammes.
Witnesses: Albert Louw and wife.
Jansen, Jilles and wife-Johannes.
Witnesses: Wilhelmes and Beletie Pos.
Broka, Jan and wife-Isaack.
Witnesses: Piter Broka; Jantien Koevers.
Hoff, Piter and wife-Egjen (?).
Witnesses: Hans Koevers; Aeltie Spieten.
Schermerhoorn, Luykas and wife-Marya.
Witnesses: Peter Bodyn; Jacob Jen Middagh.
Bodyn, Isaack and wife-Isaack.
Witnesses: Abraham Bodyn; Kataryna Van Neste.
Manus, Borgert and wife-Johannes.
Witnesses: Jacob Korssen and wife.
Fiel, Jeremey and wife-Jan.
Witnesses: Abraham Van Vechten and wife.
Aerten, Thomas and wife-Mertien.
Witness: Jeremey Fiell.
Van Midderswaert, Theunis and wife-Hendrickus.
Witnesses: Hendrick Beeckman and wife.
Laforsi, Jan and wife-Davit.

Witnesses: Abraham Bodyn; Janitjen Middagh.
Bouman, Thomas and wife-Neeltien.
Witnesses: Merten Vandevort; Jantien Slecht.
Davits, Thammes "von Be Jaerde" [after confession, baptized].

Aug. 25. Ban, Benjemin and wife-Mery.
Artsen, Benjemin and wife-Millessen.
Witnesses: Willem and Seeri Annisse.
Hendricksen, Jan and Weyntie Ten Eyck-Matheus.
Witnesses: Mathys Ten Eyck and wife.
Jansen, Ouke and wife-Ida.
Witnesses: Jan and Janneetie Butin.
Machkini, Morcdihay and wife-Willem.
Witnesses: Jacob Bodyn and wife.

Oct. 26. Bibou, Petrus and Christina Mollissen-Mertien.
Witnesses: Jan Mollisse; Mettien Bibou.
Bolmer, Roobert and Maria Spoonheymer-Antien.
Witnesses: Gerhit Bolmer; Antien Spoonheymer.

1716.

Apr. 12. Van Neste, Joris and wife - Hendrick.
Witness: Abraham Bodien.
Heyt, Niclaes and wife-Hendrick.
Witnesses: Hendrick Vechte and wife.
Dey, Willem and wife-Willem.
Witnesses: Willem Piterse; Sara Van Genee.
Bort, Tammes and wife-Endri.
Witnesses: Kataleyn and Piter Broka.
Vondgem, Cornelis and wife-Cornelis.
Witnesses: Adriaen and Susanna Hendricksen.
Stoll, Jacob and wife-Jan.
Witnesses: Marten Beeckman; Mechtelt Stoll.
Sickeler, Johannes and wife-Reynier.
Witnesses: Arjaen [Adrian] Laen and wife.

Aug. 22. Kock, Jan and wife-Dammes.
Witnesses: Joris Hael and wife.
Vroom, Kors and wife-Reyst.
Witnesses: Hendrick Vroom and wife.
Van Middleswaert, Thonis and wife-Mertien.
Witnesses: Jan and Sara V. Middelswaert.
Van Vechten, Abraham and wife-Elisabet.

Witnesses: Leenhert Witbrok; Jatien V. Vechten.
Bodien, Jacob and wife-Jaentien.
Witnesses: Ouke Jansen and wiie.
Devoor, Daniel and wife-Matheus.
Witnesses: Hendrick Reyniersen and wife.
Passen, Niclaes and wife-Madalena.
Witnesses: Kasper Haltbeg and wife.
Wüertman, Jan and wife-Femmichyen.
Witnesses: Cornelis and Femmichyen V. Middelswaert.
Oct. 17. Crom, Willen and wife-Hendrick.
Witnesses: Adriaen Muclenaer and wife.
Harissen, Willen and wife-Jan.
Witnesses: Siemon Haeven and wife.
Buys, Jan and wife-Mertien.
Witnesses: Joris and Femmechyen Buys.
Pouwels, Cornelis and wife-Poulus.
Witnesses: Hendrick Bries and wife.
Lou, Jan and wife-Bengemin.
Witnesses: Adriaen Muelenaer and wife.
Andrissen, Andries and wife-Mertien; also Prissilla.
Witnesses: Piter Dumon and wife [as to Mertien];
Jurgen Andrissen and Helena Bort [as to Prissilia].
Fiell, Jeremias and wife-Michiell.
Witnesses: Derck and Jannetje Van Vechten.

1717.
Apr. 3. Douty, Ellert and wife-Sara.
Witnesses: Derck Konyn and wife.
Maenissen, Borghert and wife-Grietien.
Witnesses: Jan Louw; Judit Van Neste.
Roos, Willem and wife-Geertien.
Witnesses: Conraet Ten Eyck and wife.
Boegert, Cornelis and wife-Abraham.
Witnesses: Albert Louw and wife.
Hendricksen, Jan and wife-Hendrick.
Witnesses: Adriaen Hendricksen and wife.
Wessels, Luyckas and wife-Wessel.
Witnesses: Jan Broeka and wife.
Schol, Pieter and wife-Mergriet.
Witnesses: Piter Broeka and wife.
Korssen, Jacob and wife-Johannes.

Witnesses: Hans Koevers and wife.
Ellick, Willem and wife Ellinck-Annanias.
Witnesses: Annanias --- and wife.
Bries, Hendrick and wife-Hendrick.
Witnesses: --- Aertsen; wife Bries.
Maghiny, Mardighaey and wife-Daniel.
Witnesses: Daniel Sebregh and wife.
Dumont, Piter and wife-Hendrick.
Witnesses: Walraen Dumon; Gerrite Vechte.
Bodien, Piter and wife-Davit.
Witnesses: Kataleyn Middagh; Abraham Bodien.
Bolmer, Roobert and wife-Johannes.
Witnesses: Gerrit Bolmer; Antien Spoonheymer.

July 31. Elemeteren, Abraham and wife-Catrina.
Witnesses: Albert Louw and wife.
Dey, Willem and wife-Maria.
Witnesses: Nicklaes Heyt and wife.
[Parents' names omitted)-Jan Lafleur.
Witnesses: Johannes Sebrege and wife.
Hoff, Piter and wife-Maria.
Witnesses: Abraham Brocka and wife.
Bouman, Thomas and wife-Thomas.
Witnesses: Jan Van Sickelen; Mertien v. d. Hueven.
Kerter, Beniemin and wife-Nias.
Witnesses: Jacob Corssen and wife.
Bodien, Isaack and wife-Abraham.
Witnesses: Piere v. Neste; Engeltien Daent.
Van Etten, Manual and wife-Thammes.
Witnesses: Tham Hael and wife.
----, Joris and Femmechien Van Middelswaert-Neeltien.
Witnesses: Cornelis Theunissen and wife.

Oct. 15. Heyt, Niclaes and wife-Cataleyn.
Witnesses: Hendrick Wever and wife Wevers.
Ten Eyck, Andries and wife-Neeltien.
Witnesses: Jan Hendricksen; Weyntien Ten Eyck.
Konyn, Derck and wife-Jannetien.
Witnesses: Derck and Jannetien Van Vechten.
Vroom, Hendrick and wife-Josyntien.
Witnesses: Jacob Sebregh and wife.
Tarl, Kellep and wife-Kellep.

Broka, Jan and wife-Catalentien.
Witnesses: Kataleyn Hoff; Jan Van Middelswaert.
Pieert, Jacob and wife-Rachel.
Fiel, Jeremy and wife-Mergrietien.
Witnesses: Derck and Jannetien Van Vechten.
Franss, Caper and wife-Dorotea.
Witnesses: Jan Van Roem; Mergriet Karmen.
Hael, Joris and wife-Tammes.
Witnesses: Joris Hael; Geertruyt Stevens.

1718.
Mar. 22. Hayman, Nicolaas and Willemyntje-Sara.
Witnesses: Pieter and Cattelyntje Hoff.
Van Ouwdgem, Corn. and Styntje-Henderick.
Witnesses: Jan and Wyntje Henderickze.
Dirckze, Folkert and Dyna-Dirck.
Witnesses: Dirck Volkertze; Grietje Zynielse.
Mar. 23. Ban, Benjamin and [En Can]-Betje.
Stol, Jacob and Annaje-Antje.
Witnesses: Hendrick and Maria Beeckman.
Van Middelswart, Corn. and Rebecka-Neeltje.
Witnesses: Theunis and Neeltje Van Middelswart.
Jans, Oucke and Catryntje-Abraham.
Witnesses: Johannis and Aaltje Sebringh.
July 29. Van Sicklen, Kornelis and Maria-Neeltie.
Witnesses: Jan and Lena v. Sicklen.
Van Sicklen, Jan and Leena-Andries.
Witnesses: Kornelis and Marya Van Sicklen.
Casan, Niclaes and Madeleen-Marieya.
Witness: Frans Lokas.
—, Lauriens and ---- -Frans.
Witness: Madeleen ---
Hael, Tammes and Geertie ---- -Elysabet.
Witnesses: Kornelis and Neeltic Tuenis.
Emans, Jan and Ragel-Jan.
Witness: Raegel ---
Oct. 22. Laen, Mattus and Korane Heyene (?) ---- Aderjanes.
Witnesses: Hendrick and Maertie Jansen.
Jansen, Jielles and Baerra-Willem.
Witnesses: Tuenis and Lysbet Hoff.
Kock, Jan and Geertrui-Willem.

Witnesses: Jan and Machter Stol.
Du Bouis, Abraham and Maerieytue-Franssynte.
Witnesses: Pieter Biljoo; Katryn Mairgen.
Vroom, Kors and Katryn-Katryntie.
Witnesses: Andries and Arejaentie Teniech.
Boogaert, Kornelis and Kornelea-Isack.
Witnesses: Theunis Middelswaer; Rebecka Boegaert.

1719.

Jan. 21. Van Middelswaert, Tunnis and wife, Susanna-Piete.
Apr. 4. Krom, Willem and wife, Wintie-Johannis.
Witnesses: Willem Roos and wife, Enlysabet.
Lou, Jan and wife, Jannitie-Marytie.
Witnesses: Cornelis Lou and wife, Juedie.
Herres, Willem and wife, Enlysabet-Willem.
Witnesses: Willem and Marytie Olden.
They, Willen and wife, Eva-Lysabet.
Witnesses: Casspari Fransen and wife Lysbet.
Ferley, Joris and wife, Femmitye-Kelp.
Apr. 5. Bries, Hendreck and wife, Antie-Jannitye.
Witnesses: Cornelis and Antjie Pouwelsen.
Ellen, Wiliam and Sarah Ellen-Wiliam.
Witnesses: Niclaas and Susanna Hydt.
Brocaarde, Abraham and Marytie-Isack.
Witnesses: Pieter Brocaarde and Engeltie Davids.
Minkinge, Mardachai and Maritie-Jacob.
Witnesses: Jacob and Josyntie Sebring.
Bodyn, Jacob and Lysbet-Jacob.
Witnesses: Jacob and Judie Poijon.
July 26. Van Koort, Lyas and wife, Enni-Elyas.
Witnesses: Daniel Korpur; Abiegel Sebring.
Band, Benjamen and wife-Henne.
July 27. Rapale, Jacop and wife, Saara-Jacop.
Witnesses: Maghiel Van Vegten and wife, Jannetie.
Demon, Pieter and wife, Jannitie-Jan Patist (Baptist].
Witnesses: Dirck and Janniten Van Vegten.
Tenyck, Jacob and wife, Jacomyntien-Kattrintie.
Witnesses: Koenrat Tenik and wife, Kaaten.
Oct. 13. Van Vechten, Abraham and wife, Angenietie-Dirck.
Witnesses: Dirrick Van Vegt and wife, Berber.
Lou, Albert and wife-Abram; also Cornelis.

Witnesses: Abram Lameter and wife; Cornelis Lou and wife.

Lou, Cornelis and wife-Dirck.
Witnesses: Pieter and Cattalyna Middag.

Fransen, Casparis and wife-Susanna Kattrina.
Witnesses: Willim Dey; Kattrina Bruyn.

Colman, Robbert and wife-Rissina.
Witnesses: Albert Roskam; Maddalena Spankener.

Oct. 14. Dirricsen, Folkert and wife-Vrdrik(?)
Witnesses: Jacop Parrabaska and wife.

Jansen, Koert and wife-Marytie.
Witnesses: Arie Laan and wife.

Fiel, Jerimyas and wife-Marytie.
Witnesses: Pieter Demon and wife.

Van Nitte, Manuel and wife-Petris.
Witnesses: Joris Haal and wife.

Bodyn, Isak and wife-Elisabet.
Witnesses: Pieter Bodyn and wife.

Van Sikaal, Ritsaart and wife-Marya.
Witnesses: Tuenis Middelswa; Niltie Teunis.

Van Neste, Pieter and wife-Marigritie.
Witnesses: Pieter Broeka and wife.

Ater, Adriaan and wife-Antie.
Witnesses: Pieter and Katalyna Middag.

Van Neste, Joris and wife-Jacop.
Witnesses: Pouwel Ater and wife.

1720.

Jan. 31. Schol, Pieter and wife-Jannike.
Witnesses: Benjamen and Jannitie Van Vegten.

Feb. 28. Middelswart, Tuenes and wife, Susanna-Jan.
Witnesses: Jan Broecka; Mary Beekman.

Vroom, Hindrick and wife, Jannitie-Sara.
Witnesses: Daniel Sebring and wife Kaatie.

Hoff, Pieter and wife, Kattryntie-Isack.
Witnesses: Wilhelmus Post; Sara Broekaa.

Mar. 27. Korse, Jacop and wife, Ariyantie-Jannike.
Witnesses: Bragon and Jannitie Koevert.

Apr. 23. Basing, Nicklaas and wife, Marya-Rosina.
Witnesses: Robbert Bolmer and wife, Rosina.

June 19. Woertman, Bout and wife, Belitie-Jan.

Witnesses: Tuenes Koevers and wife, Marrytie.
Ferlie, Joris and wife, Femmitie-Sara.
Witnesses: Cornelis Middelswart and wife, Rebecka.
[Here begin entries in handwriting of Rev. Theodorus J. Frelinghuysen].

Aug. 12. Van Middelswaart, Cornelis and wife, Rebecka-Fliep.
Witnesses: Flip Folkers; Christiena Sebering.
Bogaert, Cornelis and wife, Cornelia-Jacob.
Witnesses: Henderick Reiniersen; Gridje ---

Dec. 10. Fiel, Jeremias and wife, Marietje-Maria.
Witnesses: Dirck Konyn and wife, Ragel.

1721.

Jan. 8. Van Koert, Leier and wife, Annatje-Moses.
Witnesses: Paulus and Susanna [Bettue?]
Makingi, Mordechai and wife, Marietje-Annetje.
Witnesses: Hanse Sebring and wife, Aeltje.

Mar. 5. Heit, Nicholaes and wife, Susanna-Susanna.
Witnesses: Baerent Veter and wife, Elisabeth.
Brouwer, Henderick and Elisabeth-Adam.
Witnesses: Thomas and Neltje Bouman.
Monde, Joseph and wife, Elsye-Joseph.
Witnesses: Jacob Bois; Lyben Gidion.

Apr. 2. Konyn, Dirck and wife, Rachel-Seitje.
Witnesses: Jeremias Fiel and wife, Marietje.
Madalet, Thomas and wife, Neeltje-Margarietje.
Witnesses: Willem and Susanna Titzor.

May 7. Bris, Henderick and wife, Hanna-Neeltje.
Witnesses: Leonaerd Smack; Elizabeth Bris.
Broeckae, Abraham and wife, Maria-Brugon.
Bodyn, Jacob and wife, Elisabeth-Catharina.
Witnesses: Pieter and Marietje Bodyn.

May 28. Ten Eyck, Jacob and wife, Jacomyntje-Mattheus.
Witness: Mattheus Ten Eyck.
Herris, William and wife, Lysabeth-Thomas.

Sept 17. de Groote, Jacob and wife, Seitje-Margarieta.
Witness: Gerrit de Groot.
Aerten, Adrian and wife, Intje-Dirck.
Witnesses: Thomas Aerten and wife, Elsche.
Feerly, Callep and Margarietje-Meindert.
Witness: Maria Bort.

Nov. 17.	Woertman, Janevers and Belletje-Withemus.
	Bolmer, Robbert and Marietje-Gerrit.
Dec. 17.	Oolen, Willem and Abigail-Aeltje.
	Witnesses: Hans Sebering and wife, Aeltje.
	Elaesien, Jesaias and Eggie-Aeltje.
	Witnesses: Jellis Jansen and wife, Barbara.
	Moor, Jacob and Anna Poloni-Elisabeth.
	Witnesses: Jan Meier and wife, Elisabeth.
1722.	
Mar. 11.	Corsse, Jacob and Ariaentje-Metje.
	Claessen, Cornelis and Marretje-Cornelis.
	Witnesses: Esaios Claessen and wife, Eggje.
May 6.	Bogaert, Cornelis and Cornelia-Maerten.
June 3.	Basinck, Nicolaes and wife, Maria-Anna.
	Hegeman, Jacobus and Jannetje-Micheel.
	Witnesses: Dirck and Jannetje Van Vegten.
	Ellen, Willem and Cery-Jan.
	Brouwer, Henderick and Elisabeth-Henderick.
	Witnesses: Thomas Mellot and wife, Neeltje.
	La Meter, Abraham and Catharina-Isaac.
	Witness: Aynietje van Vegten.
July 8.	van Coort, Elias and wife, Anna-Jannetje.
	Witness: Hans Sebering,
Sept. 2.	Schol, Pieter-Pieternelletje.
	Witnesses: Jan van Middelswaert and wife, Pieternelletje.
Dec. 25.	Grauw, Johannes and Antje-Gerritje.
	Witnesses: Robbert Bolmer and wife, Rosina.
1723.	
Jan. 13.	Coevers, Teunis and Marretje-Anna Maria.
Feb. 20.	Ronseval, Pieter and Rebecca-Henne.
	Lucas, Frans and Jannetje-Maria.
Mar. 17.	Fiel, Jeremias and Marietje-Michael.
	Mollet, Thomas and Neeltje-Abraham.
	Middag, Cornelis and Eycke-Dirck.
	Witness: Pieter Middag.
Apr. 12.	Jansen, Jellis and Barbara-Elisabeth.
14.	Moor, Jacob and Anna Polonia-Jacob.
15.	Coesaert, Anthoni and Judith-Elisabeth.
May 12.	Herrison, William and Elisabeth-Jacobus.
June 2.	Titzor, Wilm and Marietje-Margarietje.

Witness: Neeltje Mollet.
Ellen, William and Cery-James.
12. Lafas, Jan and Francentje-Isaac.
Aug. 4. Konyn, Dirck and Rachel-Dirck.
Ten Eyck, Jacob and Jacomyntje-Pieter.
Witness: Pieter van Est.
Sept. 1. Moor, Johannes and Magdalena-Lisabeth.
29. van Neste, Pieter and Leentje-Pieter.
Aaerten, Adriaen and Jantje-Henderick.
Bodyn, Jacob and Lesbetje-Cornelis.
Dec. 25. Hageman, Jacobus and Jannetje-Deneys.
Witnesses: Du Mee Hageman and wife, Gertrui.
Oolen, Wilm and Abigail-Lisabeth.
Scheffer, Bemhardus and Antie-Johannes.
Bodyin, Isaac and Jannetje-Hester.

1724.
Feb. 9. de Groot, Jacob and Seitje-Johannes.
Woertman, Jan Everts and Nelletje-Maria.
Witness: Andreas Woertman.
Bries, Hendrick and Antje-Jurisee.
Mar. 15. Bolmer, Robbert and Marietje-Albertus.
Apr. 12. Bason, Nicolaes and Maria-Margarietje.
May 19. van Coert, Elias and Annatje-Daniel.
20. Older, Hannes and Maria-Magdalena.
June 17. Ackervelder, Johan Pieter and Elisabeth-Anna.
Wilm, Johan and Antje Mary-Johan Wilm.
Aug. 30. Volkersen, Dirck and Geertie-Maria.
Sept. 27. Bogaart, Cornelis and Cornelia-Samuel.
Oct. 25. van Middelswaart, Jan and Picternelle-Jan.
Witnesses: Teunis van Middelswaart and wife, Susanna.
Haegemond, Jan and Leibetje-Catharina.
Witnesses: Joost van Pelt; Aeltje Hoogeland.
Nov. 22. Aersen, Jan and Barbara-Oucke.
Witnesses: Abraham Bodyn and wife, Arriaentje.
Coevert, Teunis and Marretje-Hermtje.
Dec. 20. La Faers, Jan and Cery-Jan.
Corss, Jacob and Ariaentje-Margaritje.
Graeuer, Jan and Antje-Catharina.

1725.
Jan. 10. Dinksen, Voickert and Ditia-Volckert.

Caof, Jacob and Magdalena-Johannes.
Witnesses: Hans Jurgen and - Speeneman.
Marrelet, Thomas and Neeltje-Jan.
Feb. 7. Konyn, Dirck and Rachel-Dirck.
Woertman, Andrees and Jannetje-Jan.
Kotter, Bernardus and Lisabeth-Susanna.
Witnesses: Hans Louwrens and wife, Anna Mary.
Apr 4. Jong, Hannes and Mecheld-Margarietha.
Ellen, Neys and Henne-Henna.
Bodyn, Abraham and Arriaentje-Catrina.
Coesaert, Jacob and Henna-Lisabeth.
May 2. Fiel, Jeremi and Marietje-Benjamin.
Jansen, Jellis and Barbara-Jannetje.
Oucke, Abraham and Antje-Abraham.
Schoebeer, David and Leibetje-Jannetje.
Voorn, [Hoorn?] Hieronymus J. and Anna Elisabeth-Catharina.
30. Herris, William and Lysebeth-Saertje.
Pescheerer, Jacob and Barbara-Lisabeth.
Witnesses: Hans Lourence and wife, Margarietha.
Aug. 1. Doorland, Gerrit and Marietje-William.
Coesaer, Antoni and Judith-David.
29. Lucas, Frans and Jannetje-Elsche.
Sept. 26. Bois, Jan and Seitje-Seitje.
Ten Eyck, Jacob and Jacomyntje-Conraed.

1726.
Jan. 1. van Twickel, Simon and Dina-Evert.
Witnesses: Philip Volkert and wife, Metje.
Vanist, Jan and Marietje-Catharyntje.
Feb. 6. Pouwlsen, Andres and Jannetje-Alaria.
Hoogeland, Willem and Lena-Jan.
Mar. 6. Aerten, Adrean and Jabje-Catholyntje.
Older, Hannes and Maria Catharina-Lisabeth.
Witnesses: Hieronymus Hoorn and wife, Lisabeth.
Apr. 3. La Foercy, Jan and Cery-Francentje.
Witnesses: Jan La Foerscy and wife, Francentje.
29. van Koovd, Eelyas and Metie-Anggenite.
May 8. van den Berg, Goosen and Annaetje-Cornelia.
29. Claessen, Jesaias and Lysabeth-Jesaias.
Titzoor, Willem and Marietjc-Willem.

van Sickelen, Johannes and Jannetje-Johannes.
June 26. van Middelswaert, Jan and Pieternelletje Bogaert-Pieternelletje.
Witnesses: Philipp Volkert and wife, Metje.
Bolmer, Robbert and wife, Marietje-Marietje.
Aug. 21. Schol, Pieter and Debora-Elisabeth.
Bodyn, Jacob and Lisabetb-Antje.
Dec. 1. Fiel, Jeremias and Maerietje-Dirck.
Vissher, Henderick and Elisabeth-Volckert.
Bodyn, Abraham and Arriaentje-Pieter.

1727.
Feb. 5. Bries, Henderick and Hanna-Volckert.
Woertman, Jan Evert and Belletje-Sara.
Haegewoud, Jan and Elisabeth-Pieter.
Witnesses: Daniel and Annatje Hoogeland.
Woertman, Andrees and Jannetje-Agnietje.
Sebering, Johannes and Aeltje-Johannes.
Witnesses: Hans Sebering and wife, Aeltje.
de Groot, Jacob and Seitje-Margaritha.
Apr. 2. Dircksen, Volckert and Dina-Dina.
30. Hegeman, Jacobus and Jannetje-Deneys; also Johanna.
Witnesses: Jeremias Fiet, Kros Haritie and Judit ----(?).
Kotter, Bernherdus and Lisabeth-Pieter.
Middag, Cornelis and Eycke-Dina.
Witness: Catholina Middag.
Bescheerer, Jacob and Barbara-Lena.
May 28. Montangne, Ide and Lisabeth-Abraham.
June 25. Brouwer, Henderick and Marietje-Willem.
Groeuer, Johannes and Antje-Marietje.
Witnesses: Hans Jurgen and ---- Spoeneman.
Oucke, Abraham and Antie-Maria.
July 23. Corsse, Jacob and Arriaentje-Teunis.
Jansen, Jelles and Barbara-Maria; also Agnietje.
Sept. 17. Lucas, Frans and Jannetje-Frans.
van Coert, Elias and Annatie-Jannetje.
Nov. 19. Volckersen, Dirck and Geertje-Dirck.

1728.
Jan. 14. Mollet, Thomas and Neeltje-Catholyntje.
Plees, Joseph and Vincentje-Joseph.
Hoogeland, Christoffel and Catholyntje-Christoffel.

19. Harrison, William and Lysabeth-Pieter.
Ooff, Jacob and Magdalena-Jacob.
Feb. 11. van der Berg, Goosen and Annatje-Goosen.
Witnesses: Jan van Nist; Catje Ten Eyk.
May 5. Blauw, Henderick and Aeltje-Aeltje.
June 2. Balljuw, Isaac and Jannetje-Marietje.
Koriell, David and Elsche-Agnietje.
Sept. 1. Schoeler, Philip Jacob and Maria Christina-Christina; also Sarah.
Dec 1. Fiel, Jeremias and Maria-Sara.
25. Bolmer, Robbert and Marietja-Lena.
1729.
Jan. 12. Pescheerer, Jacob and Barbara-Johannes.
Witness: Johannes Pescheerer.
van Sickelen, Abraham and Elysabeth-Abraham.
Apr. 4. Scheffer, Bernhardus and Catharina-Lisabeth.
6. Volckersen, Volckert and Dina-Debora.
Van Coort, Elias and Henna-Thomas.
Titzoor, Willem and Marietje-Lisabeth.
May 14. Visser, Henderick and Leibetje-Maria.
25. Muller, Wilhelm and Margaritha-Gerrit.
Apr. 16. Blau, Henderick and Aeltie-Elsie.
1730.
May 10. Post, Tunis and Annatje-Annatje.
Merten, Hertie-Davit.
June 27. Loisi, Jan and Jannitie-Marya.
Brouwer, Jan and Aegye-Dirck.
Teuhunen, Gerrit and Aeltie-Marya.
Aug. 16. Sweet, Aeouont and Eva-Pieter.
Botyu, Eysack and Jannetje-Eysack; also Jantietie.
Herris, Willem and Wesse-Benijamin.
van Laa, Gabriel and Pryntye-Gerrit.
Oct. 25. Louw, Cornelis and Judick-Judick.
Witnesses: Dirck Middag; Maertie de Mot.
Oof, Jacob and Maerdelena-Abram.
Ellen, Annanyes and Semie-Jynne.
Clasen, Tammes and Antie-Junien.
Dec. 6. Layn, Abraham and Ariaentie-Jan.
van Neste, Pieter and Marigrita-Maria.
Luckes, Soans and Jannetie-Tomis.

Davids, Fiel and Judick-Jannety.
Janaten ---- and Lysbetie-Kosi (?).
27. Fiel, Jeremias and Maria-Antje.
1731.
Mar. 14. Broeca, Abraham and Marya-Engeltie.
Smack, Jan and Leya-Lena.
Mickel, John and Engeltye-Neltye.
Betu, Pieter-Josup.
Witness: Henne Bries.
May 16. Belyer, Lukes-Mareya.
Marlet, Tomas-Tomas.
Koryel, Davet-Jannete.
Laforse, Nicolaes-Sacrias.
Bolman, Roobert-Lisabet.
July 4. Dirckese, Volker and Dyna-Pettrus.
Aug. 1. Brouer, Jakop and Marike-Annatie.
Bosserie, Jakop-Jakop.
Sept. 26. Van Neste, Jeronimus and Susanna-Joris.
Van Neste, Jan and Marytye-Peterus.
Witnesses: Barnardus Van Neste and Catelytie.
Oct. 24. Fisser, Henderick and Syetie-Neeltie.
Nov. 20. Woertman, Piter and wife, Maragrete-Peterus.
Vannist, Pieter and wife, Grite-Jan.
Sebrin, Volkert and wife, Malle-Jan.
Dec. 19. Montanye, Teunes and Lisebet-Jacobus.
Witness: Wife of Ide Mont.
1732.
Feb. 13. Vannist, Bernardus and wife, Catleynte-Bernardis.
Mar. 12. Sweed, Arnout and wife, Eva-Elisabet.
Apr. 9. Lamantanye, Eide and wife, Elisabet-Eide.
Janse, Jillis and wife, Barbera-Jannete.
Folckerse, Flip and wife, Maregrite-Elisabet.
Oof, Jakop and wife Madelena-Jannete.
May 28. Swik, Johannes and wife-Egie.
Witnesses: Tam Bort and wife.
Sebren, Johannes and wife-Elisebet.
Sefer, Bernandus and wife-Bernerdus.
Aug. 6. Brouer, Piter and wife, Susanna-Peterus.
Laforse, Niclas and wife-Jannete.
Witness: Neelte Laforse.

Van Koort, Leyyes and Ante-Abram.
Witnesses: Abram Bodeyn and wife, Annatt.
Toevenbagh, Johannes and wife-Susanna.
Witness: Susanna Hove.
Sept. 6. Aten, Tomes and wife, Seyte-Pouel.
Koeuert, Lukas and wife, Femmete-Lukas.
Oct. 1. Post, Teunes and Annate-Willim.
22. Van Sikelen, Abraham and wife, Elisabet-Jakop.
Van Laar, Gaberel and wife, Preynte-Johannes.
Brouer, Sammel and wife, Maragrite-Annate.
Deves, Jores and wife, Judit-Judit.
Witness: Maragrita Woertman.
Dec. 25. Van Nist, Jeronemus and wife, Susanna-Ferdenandus.
Bolman, Robbert and wife, Mariya-Abram.
1732/3.
Jan. 22. Housen, Johannes and wife, Nelte-Mariya.
Mar. 28. Folkenburger, Crysstoffel and wife, Maragrita-Maragrita.
Witnesses: Jacobus Hegeman and wife, Jannete.
Bries, Henderik and wife, Ante-Eyda.
Bolyve, Isak and wife, Jannete-Catryna.
Brouer, Jakop and wife-Sara.
1733.
Apr. 15. Bodeyn, Abram and wife, Areyaente-Abram.
Brokaer, Abram and wife, Mareyte-Jan.
Puetue, Piter and wife, Jemyme-Poules.
Witness: Mariya Puetue.
May --. Hagewout, Jan and wife, Leybite-Sara.
June 24. Gerrese, Jakobus and wife, Sara-Samuel.
Resenar, Nikolas and wife, Cornelia-Maregrite.
Aug. 25. Van Deventer, Isak and wife, Sara-Abram.
Lukas, Frans and wife, Jannete-Elisabet.
----, Jurre and wife, Else-Elisabet.
Ammerman, Nicolaes and wife-Jan.
Keryel, Danyel and wife-Moses.
Kilse, Mateys and wife, Tina-Catrina.
Sept. 20. Koneyn, Dirk and wife, Susanna-Davet.
Witness: Steynte Kosart.
Folkerse, Joseph and wife, Alte-Fliph.
Witnesses: Dirk Volkerse and wife.
Oct. 29. Kosaert, Jores and wife, Lisabet-Jannete.

Witness: Steynte Kosart.
Nov. 20. Vannist, Bernardus and wife, Katleyn-Mareyte.
Dec. 23. Kosart, Jakop and wife-Lideya.
Witness: Susanna Koneyn.

1733/4.
Jan. 5. Swik, Jahnes and wife, Barbara-Martgie.
Witness: Luykes Koevert.
Hegeman, Jacobus and wife, Jannete-Maragrita; also Jakobus.
Witnesses: Kornelis Van Horne and wife; Angenite Van Veghten.
Feb. 4. Hertoog, Piter and Anna Maragrita-Piter.
Mar. 10. Sebrin, Folkert and wife, Nelli-Folkert.
Streyker, Piter and wife-Maregrite.
Streyker, Hannes and wife-Dominekes.

1734.
May 1. Lafors, Jan-Ragel.
Witness.: Areyaente Bodeyn.
Probasko, Stoffel and wife, Elisabet-Maregrite, born Sept. 9, 1734 [evidently 1733].
Bilyue, Danyel and wife, Sara-Isak.
5. Moor, Johannes and wife-Elisebet.
Teger, Rusyan-Anna Mari.
Witnesses: Fillip Jong; Anna Mariya Winaker.
23. Blau, Henderik and wife-Maryya.
July 21. Aten, Jan and wife-Jakop.
Miller, Hannes and wife, Matte-Jakop.
Montanye, Tuenes and wife, Rebekke-Sara.
Oct. 25. Bulyue, Lukas and wife, Barbera-Kateleyna,
Marlet, Tomes and wife, Nellie-Markes.
Koopman, Johannes and wife, Eva-Johannes.
Van Laer, Gaberel and wife, Preynte-Jannete.
20. Sebrandt, Hannes and wife, Nelle-Cerstina.
Jong, Fillip and wife-Mareya.
Witnesses: Jakop and Mareyta Weynaker.
Van Kleef, Lou and wife, Mareya-Mareyte.
Nov. 17. Koevert, Lukes and wife, Harmte-Isak.
1734/5.
Jan. 19. Bulyue, Piter and wife, Maragrita-Eyda.
Witness: Henna Moor.
Ellen, Neyes and wife, Henna-Gissem.

Brouer, Samel and wife, Maregrita-Anate.
Brouer, Jakop and wife, Mareyte-Mareyte.
Folkerse, Joseph and wife, Alte-Sara.
Witnesses: Abram Rapelye and wife, Jenneke.

1735.
Mar. 2. Van Nist, Jeronemus and wife, Susanna-Jakobus.
Witness: Catrina Teneyk.
Van Veghten, Benjamin and wife, Sara-Bennamen.
Fase, Johannes and wife, Rosina-Jan.
23. Aten, Jan and wife-Jan.
Aten, Tomes and wife-Helena.
Apr. 20. Bodeyn, Abram and wife, Areyante-Judick.
Bolmer, Robbert and wife, Rosina-Jannete.
Dirkse, Folkert and Dina-Debora.
Hertogh, Piter and Anna Maragrita-Nikolaes.
Bulyue, Daniel and wife, Sara-Sara.
16. Bullue, Isak and wife, Jannete-En.
May 3. Willumse, Piter and wife, Willimte Petrus.
June 15. Post, Willim and wife, Eyda-Willim.
Woertrnan, Leybete-Anate.
29. Rimer, Piter and wife, Wynte-Wynte.
July 13. Vannuys, Isak and wife, Catryna-Cornelus.
Kosaert, Davit and wife, Katleynte-Steynt.
Aug. 17. Buys, Jakop and wife, Neelte-Lisebet.
Van Deventer, Isak and wife, Sara-Sara.

1735.
Aug. 7. Petue, Piter and wife, Jemyma-Marya.
Witness: Marya Petue.
Nov. 9. Simonis, Hermanes and wife-Willum.
Witnesses: Johan Willum Engel and wife, Judit.
Maraselis, Eide and wife, Areyante-Anna.
Witness: Preynte Van Laer.

1735/6.
Jan. 18. Denes, Jores and wife, Judet-Katleynte.
Feb. 16. Lukes, Frans and wife, Jannete-Abram.
Sebring, Folkert and wife, Nelli-Elisabet.

1736.
Apr. 11. Aten, Jan and wife-Jan.
Van Laer, Gabriel and wife, Preynte-Sara.
Wilson, Henderick and wife, Annate-Piterus

Bodeyn, Jan and wife, Kate-Peterus.
Van Koert, Leyyes and wife, Ante-Elisabet.
Woertman, Isak and wife, Ragel-Femmete.
May 9. Van Nist, Bardenardus and wife, Katleynte-Freynte.
Witness: Immes Wittenton.
Post, Johannes and wife, Alte-Tohannes.
June 17. Laforse, Nicolaes and wife-Niklaes.
Witness: Nelle Merlet.
July 25. Koneyn, Dirk and wife, Susanna-Johannes.
Witness: Jores Kosart and wife Elizabet.
Klasen, Willem and wife, Sara-Maryya.
Witnesses: Jores Buys and wife Seyte.
Middagh, Piter and wife, Marete-Marete.
Witness: Jores Middagh.
Teneyk, Jakop and wife, Jakemeynte-Jakemeynte.
Koopman, Tunnes and wife-Maregrite.
Aug. 22. Van Kleef, Lou and wife, Maritie-Johannes.
Sept. 19. Vanist, Peterus and wife, Margrietye-Joris.
Oct. 15. Konyn, Philip and wife, Janetye-Rachel.
17. V'Dyck, Hendrik and wife, Margrietye-Jacob.
Smak, Hendrik and wife, Antye-Lidia.
Witnesses: Cornelus Buys, Lidia Van Duyn.
18. Loder, John and Johanah-Beyemen.
Nov. 14. Cosaert, Jacob-Jacob.
Witnesses: David Cosaert, Katlyntye ----.
Haris, Wm. ---- Rachel.
Witness: Abigeltye ----.
Graw, Johanes and wife, Antye-Sufya.
Dec. 19. Tunesen, Nyes and Saertie-Neeltie.
1736/7.
Jan. 30. Van Neste, Jeronimus and wife, Susanna-Petrus.
Witnesses: Pieter Broca, Judick
Feb. 13. Fiel, Jeremyes and Femmetie-Marya.
Witnesses: Jeremyes Fiel, Marytie.
Stiven, Henry and Catlyn-Joseph.
Bellu, Luckes and Barbara-Luckes.
Hertsoggt, Pieter and Anna Maria-Lisabet.
Van Sickelen, Rynier and Martie-Jannetie.
Mar. 13. Coesaert, Johannis and Catelyntie-Antoni.
1737.

July 10. Bodyn, Abraham and Ariaentie-Isack.
Post, Willem and Eyda-Jacop.
Lockert, Samuel and Caterintie-Ouke.
May 8. Brise, Henderick and wife, Antye-Antye.
Millers, Johannis and wife, Mareytye-Thomas.
Stilwel, Nickolaes and wife, Matye-Johannis.
Folkerse, Joseph and wife, Aeltye-Antye.
Pouwelse, Anderies and wife, Jannetye-Elisabet; also Jannetje.
Aug. 7. Van Aersdale, Abraham and wife, Catreyntye-Wilhelmus.
Bollemer, Robbert and wife, Mareytye-Robbert.
Oct. 9. Blau, Henderick and wife, Aeltye-Deyna.
Ellen, Ananeys and wife, Hanna-Isaack.
Nov. 6. Post, Tuenis and wife, Annaetye-Catreyntye.
Belyue, Daniel and wife-Daniel.
Dec. 4. Brokas, Frans and wife, Jannetye-Elsye.
1737/8.
Jan. 1. Tuenisse, Thuenis and wife, Adriyaentye-Johannis.
Smack, Jan and wife, Lea-Abraham.
Jan. 29. Dewit, Piter and wife, Elisabet-Sara.
Witness: Bernardus Vannist.
Koriel, Abraham and wife, Catareyntye-Abraham.
Mar. 26. Voskamp, Albert and wife, Geesye-Jannetye.
Coevert, Bergon and wife, Annaetye-Jacob.
Hertsog, Piter and wife, Margriet-han Jurg.
Van Laer, Gabriel and wife, Preyntye-Catrina.
Willemse, Piter and wife, Mareytye-Willem.
Ate, Jan and wife, Leyhetye-Elsye.
Janse, Willem and wife, Sefya-Willem.
Sloon, Ida-Catryna.
1738.
July 23. Van Mater, Isaeck and wife, Elsye-Piter.
May 7. Weykof, Cornelus and wife, Catreyntye-Neeltye.
Smack, Lucas and wife, Jannetye-Henderick.
Witnesses: Henderick Brise and wife, Antye.
Middagh, Joris and wife, Elisabet-Dirck.
Koevert, Lukas and wife, Harmpye-Abram.
Kille, Elisebet-Jan,
28. Fasz, Johannis and wife, Antye-Willem.
June 25. Van Aersdale, Philippus and wife, Jannetye-Philipus.
Carbel, Mateys and wife, Dina-Mareya.

Witnesses: Stoffel Filburg and wife.
July 23. Middagh, Dirck and wife, Eengettye-Dirck.
Wels, Philip and wife, Cataleyntye-Mareya.
Aug. 20. Buys, Cornelus and wife, Lidea-Lidea.
Sebering, Volkert and wife, Mareytye-Cornelus.
Sept. 17 . Coesaerd, Daved and wife, Cataleyntye-Daved.
Oct. 15. Davedse, Jores and wife, Yudick-Peterus.
Marselus, Jan and wife, Arreyaentye-Catreyntye.
Witness: Aeltye Sebering.
Van Derbilt, Aris and wife, Catreyna-Cornelia.
Belyu, Piter and wife, Margrita-Mareytye.
Witness: Elisabet Croek.
Nov. 12.Belyu, Lucas and wife, Barbaraetye-Lucas.
Arosman, Adman and wife, Alarya-Antye. [Name said to represent Arrowsmith].
Ate, Thomas and wife, Hilletye-Pouwel.
Ferli, Kilp and wife, Febi-Margrita.
Koopman, Johannis and wife, Eva-Eva.

1738/9.
Jan. 1. Derimer, Isack and wife, Geertye-Marya.
Feb. 4. Coesaert, Antoni and wife, Wilpye-Antoni.
Mar. 4. Coneyn, Anderies and wife, Jannetye-Dirck.
Witnesses: Adriyaen Hogelant, Feytye Coneyn.
Coriel, David and wife, Elsye-Abraham.
Van oven, Cornelus and wife, Mareitye-Cornelus.
Witnesses: Barint Hegeman and wife, Steyntye.
Coneyn, Philip and wife, Jannetye-Dirck.
Van Court, Elyas and wife, Antye-Maghiel.

1739.
Apr. 1. Clase, Willem and wife, Sara-Willem.
Lafosse, Nickolaes and wife, Raghel-Franceyntye
May 13. Vanderveer, Jacobis and wife, Femmetye-Jan.
Witness: Femetye Van der veer.
Grau, Johannes and wife, Antye-Willem.
Miller, Johanis and wife, Mareitye-Jan.
Winterstien, Jacobus and wife, Antye-Jacobus.
Witness: Cornelia Engel.
Dumont, Jan and wife, Annaetye-Abraham.
Hoff, Bergon and wife, Frantceyntye-Catolintye.
Post, Johannis and wife, Aeltye-Mareytye.

June 3. Smack, Mateys and wife Mareytye-Jan.
Merlet, Jores and wife Veshefy-Fenson.
Amerman, Isack and wife, Jannetye-Wilhelmus.
Post, Wilhelmus and wife, Eyda-Mareya.
July 1. Van Mapele, Jogom and wife, Mareytye-Ari.
29. Ditmars, Douwe and wife, Aeltye-Johannis.
Teneyck, Jacob and wife, Yackemeyntye-Peterus.
Volkerse, Joseph and wife, Aeltye-Jacob.
Pouwelse, Anderies and wife, Jannetye-Angenietye.
Nov. 18. Bedeyn, Abreham and wife, Arreyaentye-Ouken.
Dewit, Titus and wife, Elisabet-Margrita.
Sept. 16. Volkerse, Philipus and wife, Margrita-Volkert.
Coevert, Bergon and wife, Annaetye-Mareytye.

1739/40.
Jan. 1. Coneyn, Dirck-Jacob.
Witnesses: Willem Krock and wife, Elisabet.
Coesaert, Johannis and wife, Cataleyntye-Johannis.
Jan. 27. Brise, Henderick and wife, Antye-Antye.
Janse, Willem and wife, Sufya-Ouke.
Feb. 24. Middagh, Joris and wife, Elisabet-Joris.
Willemse, Piter and wife, Marytye-Jacob.
Rapelle, Jores and wife, Marejtye-Jacob.
Bollemor, Robbert and wife, Marytye-Sufya.
Leforse, Abraham and wife, Raghel-Jan.
Smit, Jan and wife, Maria-Piter.
Mar. 23. Wyckof, Comelus and wife, Catreyntye-Cornelus.
Aten, Jan and wife, Leybetye-Thomas.
Van laer, Gabriel and wife, Preyntye-Elisabet.

1740.
Apr. 20. Belyue, Lucas and wife, Barbera-Isack.
Smack, Lucas and wife, Jannetye-Lucas.
Vandeventer, Jacob and wife, Marigrita-Jeremias.
Fiel, Jeremias and wife, Femmetye-Thuenis.
June 1. Mareytye ---- Dirck.
Witness: Philippus Coneyn.
Coryell, Emanuel and wife, Sara-Neeltye.
Herres, John and wife, Mareytye-Johannis.
June 29. Post, Teunis and wife, Annaetye-Tuenis.
Coesaert, David and wife, Cataleyntye-Geertye.
Van Tuyle, Abram and wife, Margreeta-Mareya.

July 27.	Arosmit, Adman and wife, Mary-Joseph.
Sept. 21.	Visser, Henderick and wife, Lybetye-Abram.
	Walderom, Daniel and wife, Hepye-Antye.
	Freest, Isack and wife, Mareytye-Mareytye.
Dec. 7.	Sebering, Volkert and wife, Mareytye-Mareytye.
1740/1.	
Jan. 1.	Beeckman, Peter and wife, Neeltye-Neeltye.
	Folkerse, Joseph and wife, Aeltye-Antye.
	Coesaert, Frans and wife, Margrita-Mardelena.
	Kelli, Robbert and wife, Leybetye-Harmpye.
Feb. 22.	Van nist, Peter and wife, Grietye-Reynier.
	Davetse, Jores and wife, Judick-Grietje.
	Witnesses: Cornelis Van Nist, Maritie
	Jurval, Rishard and wife, Elsye-Sara.
	Caste, Mateys and wife, Dina-Mateys.
	Vankleef, Louwerens and wife, Marya-Wilhelmus.
	Winterstien, Jacobus and wife, Antye-Jacobus.
	Witness: Cornelia ----.
Mar. 22.	Van nist, Abraham and wife, Sara-Johannis.
	Middagh, Cornelus and wife, Aeltye-Margrita.
28.	Davetse, Jores and wife, Judick-Adriaen.
	Witnesses: Cornelis [Dumond?] and Maritie.
1741.	
Jan. -.	De mon, Abraham and wife, Metye-Johannis.
	Witnesses: Jan Van midelswart and wife, Mareytye.
	Berca, Bergon and wife, Metye-Evert.
	Witnesses: Abran Van nist and wife, Sara.
May 24.	Van derveer, Jacob and wife, Femmetye-Louwerens.
	Raugh, Noach and wife, Elisabet-Catrina.
	Koopman, Johannes and wife, Eva-Jacob.
	Hertsog, Piter and wife, Margriet-Henderick.
	Off, Jacob and wife, Mardelena-Robbert.
	Hegeman, Barent and wife, Steyntye-Steyntye.
	Tyler, Samuel and wife, Lea-Samual.
	Post, Willem and wife, Eyda-Stoffel.
	Witness: Stoffel Perbasco.
June 28.	[Parents omitted]-Tunis.
	Tuenrse, Cornelus and wife, Rebecka-Tuenis.
	Smit, Adam and wife, Hanna-Raghel.
	Brouwer, Jan and wife, Mardelena-Catrina.

	Amerman, Isaeck and wife, Janntye-Isaeck.
Aug. 22.	Bantyn, Jacob and wife, Elisabet-Lea.
23.	Boesem, Johannes and wife, Engeltye-Jan.
	Bilyeu, Luykus and wife, Barbera-Cornelus.
Oct. 18.	Koevert, Burgon and wife, Annatye-Lucas.
	Weykof, Cornelus and wife, Catryentye-Abraham.
	Laforsee, Jan and wife, Saertye-Sartye.
Nov. 1.	Bedyen, Abram and wife, Ariaentye-Araentye.
	Jonglof, Jesais and wife, Mrya-Josip.
	Post, Johannes and wife, Aeltye-Abram.
	Ditmaers, Douwe and wife, Aeltye-Willemtye.
Dec.13.	Dewitt, Tietus and wife, Elisabet-Thomas.
	Vanlaer, Gabriel and wife, Prvntye-Mareytye.
	Middaegh, Jorus and wife, Elisabet-Saertye.
	Witness: James Mckrelis.
1742.	
Jan. 31.	Hof, Burgon and Franseyntye-Mareyya.
Feb. 26.	Vanoven, Cornelus and Mareya-Elisabet.
	Broeckaar, Jan and Mareytye-Sara.
28.	Maselusen, Yden and Ariaentye-Lena.
	Fast, Johannes and Antye-Rosina.
	Cryel, David and Arye-Leyyis.
June 6.	Vantuyl, Abraham and Margritie-Walter.
	Arosmit, Edmen and Marya-Marya.
	Graue, Johannis and Antie-Antie.
	Coesaert, Davit and Catlyntie-Susanna.
	Van Ogen, Henderick and Ragel-Hendericks.
	Brouwer, Jacob and Maria-Sara.
	Day, Willem and Elisabet-Abraham.
	Hegeman, Denis and Marya-Joseph.
	Witnesses: Coenraet Teunis and Jannetie Br----.
	Aten, Tomes and Hilletie-Dirck.
	Bellis, Abraham and Marya-Abraham.
Nov. 14.	Conyn, Dirck and Catelyntie-Pieter.
Dec. 22.	Rappele, Joris and Marytie-Jeremyes.
	Conyn, Anderis and Jannetie-Styntie.
	---- and Attie-Jacop.
	Stienert, Ebeneser and Saertie-Marya.
1743.	
Jan. 9.	Saylh, Joneten and Maryte-Adem.

Witness: Ragel Smit.
Tunesen, Tunes and Areaentie-Sara.
Coevert, Luykes and Harpie-Maria.
Bellu, Pieter-John.
Rolont, Elseie-Antie.
Feb. 9. Ferle, Celp and Febe-Willem.
----, Noagh and Elisabet-Elisabet.
Roscam, Albert and Geetie-Meitie.
Mar. 6. Bras, Johannis and Sefia-Saertie.
Tenise, Jan and Maria-Anderis.
Middagh, Dirck and Engyelie-Dirck.
Apr. 3. Wissien, Jacobus and Antie-Flippus.
Van derbilt, Rick and Geertie-Pieterus.
May 1. Post, Tunis and Annatie-Peterus.
Middagh, Cornelis and Aeltie-Catelintie.
Corse, Douwe and Jannetie-Jacob.
Broecka, Eysack and Malle-Abraham.
June 5. Coryel, Abraham and Catrietie-Joost.
Witness: Antie Van Coort.
Jacobs, Tomes and Marytie-Tomes.
Coesaert, Frans and Margritie-Davit.
Fisser, Henderick and Elisabet-Margrite.
Clasen, Willem and Rosina-Jesaes.
Bellu, Daenyel and Saertie-Eva, also Marya.
July 3. Davets, Joris and Judick-Isack.
Caelsits, Matys and Albertina-Marytie.
Sebrengh, Volkert and Marya-Cristina.
Mantanie, Joseph and Marya-Isack.
Bort, Enderi and Margritie-Lisabet.
July 31. Bellu, Luykes and Barbera-Daenyel.
Aug. 18. Tunesen, Denis and Saertie-Neeltie.
Hertsogh, Pieter and Margrita-Catrina.
Derveest, Isack and Malle-Johannis.
Pieterse, Haupert and Annatie-Annatie.
Hogelant, Areaen and Elisabet-Elisabet.
Witnesses: Jan Hage and Lybetie.
Swick, Hannis and Barberatie-Peterus.
Miller, Johannis and Marretie-Joris.
Sept. 25. Coopman, Hannis and Eva-Abraham.
Nov. 23. Dichmas, Douwe and Aeltie-Pieter.

Dec. 18. Oof, Jacob and Leetie-Cornelis.
Van Nist, Abraham and Saertie-Marya.
Witnesses: Pouwel ----; Maria Aten.
Wyckof, Cornelis and Cateryntie-Peterus.
Vanagen, Cornelis and Marya-Henderick.
Vantuyl, Abram and Marregrite-Saertie.
Bedys, Jacop and E---- -Johannis.

1744.
Jan. 14. Coevert, Bergon and Annatie-Annatie.
Conin, Fliph and Elisabet-Dirck.
Broecka, Jan and Maritie-Beniamin.
Feb. 11. Ten nicke, Terces and Aeltie-Anderis.
Mar. 11. Folkerse, Joseph and Aeltie-Rebecka.
Seberen, Leffert and Jannetie-Jacop.
Vange, Noagh and Lisabet-Johannis.
Morlet, Gideon and Pieternelle-Jeremias.
Middagh, Joris and Elisabet-Catelintie.
Witnesses: Jacob Eli and Engeltie Middagh.
Coens, Edden and Eva-Nicklaes.
Stuckert, Ebneser and Saertie-Johannis.
May 27. Tunesen, Cornelis and Rebecka-Johanna.
Harppending, Henderick and Maritie-Lea.
Douti, Jan and Marytie-Jeremyes.
Smack, Luykes and Jannetie-Luyckes.
Van Neste, Jeronimus and Catelyntie-Mareya.
Aten, Jan and Lyetie-Lisabet.
June 24. Bellu, Abraham-Catrina.
Walderom, Daenyel and Heppe-Tomes.
July 22. Coens, Johan Miggel and Maria Elisabeth-Anderis.
Witness: Anderis Mindaug.
Hall, Richard and Elisabet-Tobyaes.
Witnesses: Tobyais and Rebecka Tennyck.
Aug. 18. Coesart, Davit and Catelyntie-Catelyntie.
Herris, John and Marya-Elisabet.
Ackerman, Galyn and Ragel-Grietie.
Witnesses: Johannis Seberig and Aeltie.
Nov. 11. Buys, Ari and Lisabet-Lisabet.
Witness: Anntie Van ----.
Hof, Bergon and Sintic-Peterus.
Pouwlse, Cornelis and Marytie-Cornelis.

G--el, Ritser and Elsie-Aeltie.
Dec. 9. Pris, George and Angenitie-Tenis.
Fisser, Henderick and Effe-Henderick.
Hegeman, Magiel and Jannetie-Jacobus.

1745.
Jan. 25. Willemse, Piter and Maritie-Teodoris.
Feb. 17. Daly, Cornelis and Marytie-Marytie.
Vantyn, Jacob and Elisabet-Catrina.
Winterstien, Jacobus and Antie-Jacop.
Apr. 12. Folkerse, Phlip and Annatie-Saertie.
Witness: Saertic Van Fegte.
Van middelseart, Abraham and Matte-Jan.
Witness: Barber Jansen.
Post, Johannis and Aeltie-Willem.
Clasen, Willem and Rosina-Marya.
Deforest, Isack and Marya-Catrina.
14. Arresmet, Edmond and Marya-Barent.
May 19. Fose, Johannis and Antie-Robbert.
Boerem, Johannis and Enggeltie-Henderick.
Coevert, Luyckes and Harpie-Tunis.
Hof, Dirck and Cornelia-Cornelia; also Annatic.
Witness: Jannetie ----.
Coryet, Davit and Elsie-Jannetie.
June 9. Ferle, Celph and Femmetie-Sare.
Bort, Enderi and Grietie-Tomes.
Schek, Abraham and Elsie-Neeltie.
Van Cleef, Louwerens and Malle-Marta.
July 7. Coryel, Abraham and Tuyntie-Moses.
Aug. 11. Van ogen, Henderick and Ragel-Stintie.
Coopman, Johannis and Eva-Isack.
Sept. 7. Morlet, Jan and Malle-Dirck.
Sudum, Carels and Ariaentie-Eyda.
Fiel, John and Lisabet-Marya.
Jacops, Tammes and Malle-Danyel.
Oct. 6. Raugh, Johannis-[adult baptism?].
Coesaert, Davit and Catelyntie-Jacobus.
Van Norden, Tobyes and Syntie-Ragel.
Nov. 3. Davits, Isack and Angenitie-Isack.
Raugh, Noagh and Lisabet-Marya.
Hertsogh, Pieter and Margrita-Marya.

1746.

Jan. 12. Sebering, Folkert and Marya-Tomes.
Smack, Matis and Marytie-Jacob.
Spaenders, Jan and Jannetie-Jan.
Bras, Johannis and Sofia-Luykes.

Feb. 9. Woertman, Pieter and Grietie-Margritie.
Buys, Jacob and Malle-Joris.
Aten, Tomes and Hilletie-Tomes.
Lucas, Arie and Saertie-Isaes.
Bellu, Luycas and Barberatie-Marya.

Mar. 9. Harpending, Henderick and Marytie-Caterintie.
Broecka, Jan and Marytie-Isack.

Apr. 13. Coevert, Bergon and Annatie-Tunis.
Wyckof, Cornelis and Catrintie-Maria.
Smack, Jan and Lea-Maria.
Van Noert Wick, Wilhelmus and Blandina-Sara.
Witnesses: Cornelis Middagh and Aeltie.
Heath, Samuel and Marya-Jan.
Sebering, Leffirt and Jannetie-Fitie.

May 11. Douti, Jan and Maritie-Peterus.

July 6. Folkerse, Joseph and Aeltie-Abraham.
Montanye, Joseph and Maritie-Bergon.
Van derbilt, Nyes and Sara-Jacop.
Wycof, Nickolaes and Maritie-Jannetie.

Nov. 30. van derveer, Jacob and Femetye-Elias.

Sept 1. Fisser, Henderick and Lybetie-Jeremiaes.

1747.

Feb. 8. Van Deventer, Isack and Saertie-Isack.
Deforeest, Isack and Marya-Lisabet.
Vanys, Noagh and Lisabet-Lea.

May 5. Smack, Luykes-Jannetie.
Broecka, Bergon and Jannetie-Marya.
Witness: Lisabet Hof.
Titsvort, Marck and Eagie-Abraham.
Hogelant, Jan and Marya-Henderick.
Winterstien, Jacobus and Antie-Nickalaes.
Witness: Nickalaes
Coesaert, Davit and Catelinti-Jannetie.
Hegeman, Magiel and Jannetie-Jannetie.
Aersle, Matews and Marretie-Hester.

	Middagh, Joris and Lisabet-Joris.
July 31.	Stryker, Pieter and Antie-Lidia.
	Buys, Jacop-Jacop.
	Witness: Sytie Buys.
	Field, John and Lisabet-Lisabet.
	Wycof, Jan and Neeltie-Elisabet.
	Lafeber, Johannis and Ruth-Samuel.
	Douwe, Johannis and Annatie-Henderick.
	Witness: Maregrit Barense.
	Hof, Dirck and Cornelia-Daeniel.
	Bort, Endru and Gritie-Catelintie.
	Tem Broeck, Wessel and Neeltie-Johannis.
	Tem Broeck, Cornelis and Margrita-Catrina.
	Witnesses: Jacob Tem Broeck and Jence Lou.
	Roelant, Elsie-Elsie.
	Brouwer, Pieter and Susanna-Marya.
	Jansen, Anderis and Jannetie-Neeltie.
	Degroot, Johannis and Aeltic-Elisabet.
	Dy, Willem. and Lisabet-Marya,
Oct. 2.	Meselis, Harmanis and Annatie-Peterus.
	Van Nest, Jacobus and Trintie-Peterus.
	V. Midde[lswaer]t, Henderick and Neeltie-Anderiaes.
	Hof, Bergon and Fransyntie-Fransintie.
	Coevert, Luycas and Harpeie-Jannetie.
Nov. 13.	Hardenbroeck, Lodewyck and Catryntie-Marytie.
Dec. 11.	Aerse, Lewes, and Mareya-Baerbera.
	Witness: Baerberra Bellu.
	Smack, Yaen and Lea-Lea.
1748.	
Apr. 1.	Van Nest, Jeronimus and Catelyntie-Tryntie.
	Wycof, Cornelis and Catrintie-Gerrit.
	Middagh, Dirck and Engeltie-George.
	Van Cleef, Louwerens and Marytie-Tunis Post.
Sept. 28.	Broecka, Jan and Marytie-Sara.
	Winterstien, Jacobus and Antie-Henderick.
	Swick, Johannis and Barber-Jannetie.
1749.	
Mar. 5.	Berck, Isack and Aente-[child's name omitted].
	Witness: Jacob Vaenoertstein.
Apr. 2.	Van Norden, Tobyes and Jannetie-Ertsebil.

Dewit, Tytus-Pieter.
Broecka, Isack and Maritie-Marigrity.

May 7. Errosmith, Edmon and Marytie-Johannis.
Hegeman, Magiel and Jannetie-Dirck.
Witness: Maregrite Vaen der Spigel.
Titsoort, Markes and Egie-Egie.
Bolmer, Robbert and Risina Clasen-Willemtie.
Waelderom, Daneel and Heppe-Marigrite.
Poest, Johannes and Aelte-Henderick.
De frest, Isack and Maelle-Abraem.
Strang, Noag and Lisebet-Peteris.
"The above date, May 7, 1749, marks the time after which T. J. F. did not baptise any more children at Raritan, and to nearly his death." *(Note inserted by Rev. Dr. Messler).*

June 9. Mataemie, Josep and Mareya-Jaennei.
Coens, Adaen and Eva-Mendoen.
Concyn, Derck and Gerte-Ragel.
Wellemse, Coert and Aente-Enne.

Aug. 6. Lafeber, Johannes and Ret-Wiellen.
Hutsien, Johannes and Elisebet-Abigel.
Witness: Abigel Oelden.
Cosaert, Tone and Willemte-Peteries.

Sept. 24. douwen, Jan, and Anate-Derck.
Coasert, Johaennes and Catleyn-Jaenneke.
Maerresen, Jaen and Betse-Jaennete.
Boerd, Anderi and Griete-Griete.

1750.

Aug. 5. Wyenter Stien, Jacobus and Aente-Anate.
Coesaert, David and Calyna-Fraens.
Buys, Jacobes and Egye-Marya; also Sara.
Witnesses: Marya Buys; Sara Messelaer.
Bergen, Evert and Jannete-Jaennete.
Witnesses: Josep and Jaennete Hegeman.

Sept. 2. La Veber, Johannes and Rot-Mette.
Hoef, Bergoen and Fraenseynte-Isack.
Vaenoert Weyck, Wellem and Blaendina-Blaendina.

1751.

Mar. 3. Vaen Malen(?) Corneles and Marya-Vrederick.
Demoen, Henderick and Catriente-Johannes.
Coerrt, Adaem and Eva-Sara.

Aresmit, Ned and Mereye-Edmon.
Bes, Yacobeh and Marya-Sara.
Berca, Bergoen and Mette-Vemmete.
Witnesses: Jan Vaen Metaelswart and Sara Berca.
Mar. 31. Berca, Isack and Marya-Marya.
Apr. 21. Raeug, Noag and Elisebet-Margrite.
Bries, Jure and Catrina-Anatie.
Berca, Jaen and Mareya-Derck.
May 12. Cosaert, Vraens and Mari Grite-Jacob.
June 22. Kock, Wiellem and Cornelia-Johannes.
Aug. 4. Folkerse, Jacob and Marya-Folkert.
Witness: Marritie Folkerse.
Amerman, Kobes-Jacobes.
Van Norde, Tobyes and Jannetie-Tobyes.
Witness: van Cagge (Housewife).
Aug. 25. Aten, Tomas and Hillete-Feyte.
Hutsen, Johannis and Bette-Elisebet.
Witness: Beegelte Oelden.
Sept. 22. Vaen niest, Piter and Elisbet-Aberaem.
Cosaert, Aentone and Wielliemte-Eliaes.
Teunese, Deneys and Sara-Teunes.
Witnesses: Tunes Tunesse and Areyaente ----.
Oct. 13. Lagrange, Jelles and Anate-Catlyna.
Witness: ----(?).
Nov. 3. Vaen Neste, Peteres and Jaennete-Aente.
Nov. 24. Frelinhuysen, Johannes and Deyna-Eva.
Witnesses: Bergen and Loura de Vroem.
Preyn, Piter and Eva-Necklaes.
Reckmeyyer, Jacobes and Saefeya-Vemmete.
Witnesses: Jacobes Reckmeyyer, Jr. and Mareya Reckmeyyer.
Graen, Gerret and Leddeya-Robbert.
[One baptism cut out here.]
Dec. 25. Dumont, Hendrick and Catrena Oethout-Hendrick.
Witnesses: Johanes T. Tenbroock and wife, Elesebedt.
Vroom, Peter and Janetie Dumont-Peter.
Witnesses: Peter Dumont and wife, Brege.
1752.
Jan. 20. De Wet, Poules and Marya-Catrina.
Witnesses: Comeles and Mareya Vaenoven.

Cosaert, Daved and Aeleyea-Efye.
Bries, Henderick and Rael-Aentie.
Mar. 22. Laen, Wellem and Jaennetie-Anatie.
Apr. 19. Tencyck, Matewes and Aelte-Jaennetie.
[One baptism cut out here.]
Copman, Johannes and Eva-Mareya.
Bodyen, Piter and Mareya-Mareya.
Witness: Elisebet Bodeyn.
Coeweyn, Anderies and Jaennetie-Ragel.
Oct. 28. Doute, Jeremyes and Haemite-Marite.
Nov. 18. Sebering, Johannis and Gerte-Ariyaente.
Dec. 9. Bergen, Jores and Mareya-Nettie.
Dec. 30. Teler, Benyemen and Matye-Maerretie.
Berca, Isack and Aente-Catlyna.
Witnesses: Aberaem Bercka and Aente Vaenoertstaent.

1751 [so dated].
Jan. -. Coneyn, Derck and Calya-Peteris.
Dec. 20. Br--ces, Johannes and Savoya-Daved.
Smack, Mateys and Marya-Mateys.
Brieys, Are and Elisebet-Anate.
Sebering, Leffert and Jaennete-Feyte.
Stoel, Jaen and Jaennete-Jaennete.

1751 [so dated].
Feb. 10. Aersse, Matewes and Marya-Johannes.
May 7. Douwe, Jaen and Anate-Liedeya.
Sedaem, Henderick and Nelte-Maria.
Houf, Borgoen and Seyt-Elisebet.
Hoef, Derck and Cornelia-Neelaes.
Het, Semel and Maerya-Elisebet.
Doute, Jeremyas and Haernete-Sara.
May 24. Vaen Nest, Jeromes and Callyna-Aberaem.
Neefyes, Luykes and Mette-Grite.
July 6. Vaelckerse, Josep and Aelte-Josep; also Aelte.
Hegemaen, Maghiel and Jaennete-Ragel.
Witness: Jaennete Hegemaen.
July 26. Borea, Aberaem and Judeck-Johannes.
Witnesses: Jaen and Sara Boercka.
Weycoef, Cornelies and Catrynte-Gerte.
de groet, Jaen and Aelte-Wiellem.
Loue(?), Coerneles and Catrina-Sara.

Witnesses: Deneyes and Sara Vaen Dueyn.
Boert, Henderi and Grite-Marya.
Aug. 15. Davedse, Jores and Judeck-Peteris.
Witnesses: Piter and Judeck Berca.
Laveber, Johannes and Roet-Aberaem.
Nov. 24. Veghte, Hendereck and Neelte-Jaen.
Vaen noertweyk, Wellem and Blaendina-Corneleya.
Sebering, Derck and Marya-Marya.
V. meddelswaet, Tunes and Jaennete-Catlyna.
Oct. 15. Wiellen, Meynert and Aente-Willem.
Nov. 5. Berca, Isack and Aente-Caespares.
Vaen mideelswaert, Henderikes and Neelte-Aenderis.
Best, Jacobes and Marya-Elisebet.
Dec. 12. Wilsen, Henderick and Neelte-Henderick.
Dec. 31. Schenck, Henderick and Lena-Gerte.
1753.
Jan. 1. Sebering, Johaennes and Gerte-Jores.
[One baptism cut out here.]
Jan. 20. Wiellemse, Wiellem and Catrina-Catrina.
Feb 11. Borca, Jores and Grite-Piter.
Mar. 4. Tunesse, Pelep and Debera-Engette.
Teneyck, Coenrat and Elsse-Treynte.
Witness: Cate Dencyck.
25. Wienterstien, Jacobes and Aente-Jaennete.
Coevert, Piter and Mareya-Johaennes.
Seberieng, Leffert and Jaennete-Aelte.
Macenne, Daneet and Rebeca-Neckelaes.
Apr. 15. Lagraense, Jielles and Aente-Criesteyaen.
Witnesses: Criesteyaen and Catlyna Lagraense.
May 6. Vrelinhuysen, Johannes and Deyna-Frederick.
Witnesses: Todores and Marigrite Vrelenhuysen.
Teler, Bengemen and Maereti-Vemmete.
Witnesses: Jaen Staegt and Vemmete Stats.
26. Berca, Isack and Maryte-Saerte.
June 24. Aerresmet, Ned and Mareya-Bennejemen.
Streyker, Jacobes and Gerte-Aente.
Demoen, Henderick and Catriente-Aberaem.
Witnesses: Abraham and Metie Dumond.
July 15. Berca, Jaen and Maria-Mareya.
Loet, Aberaem and Gertruy-Aenderies.

	Witnesses: Samuel Staets Coeyemaen and Gertruyd Couyemaens.
	Hoef, Daennes and Nette-Daneel.
Sept. 9.	Middag, Jores and Elisebet-Elisebet.
	Poosden, Temmes and Jaemeynte-Johannes.
Oct 3.	Daveds, Isack and Aengenite-Elisebet.
	Witness: Henderick Bries.
	Richmeyer, Jacobes and Soveya-Lodeweyck.
	Witnesses: Haennes Speder and Lisebet Rickmeyer.
	Wiessen, Jaen and Elisebet-Maria.
	Witness: Robbert Bottemer.
Oct. 20.	Kock, Willem and Cernelea-Tunes.
21.	Aerse, Matewes and Marya-Matewes.
	Smack, Mateys and Mareya-Maria.
Nov. 11.	Douwe, Jaen and Conate-Maktelye.
Dec. 2.	Stelwel, Josep and Pesyeus-Daneel.
	Bries, Jaerry and Caterina-Jacobes.
	Coens, Adaem and Eva-Lisebet.
1754.	
Jan. 12.	Grau, Gerret and Elidea-Wiellem.
	Preyn, Piter and Eva-Piter.
Feb. 3.	Tunessen, Corneles and Jaennete-Areyaente.
Apr. -.	Teneyt, Matewes and Neite-Corneles.
	Vechte, Henderick and Piternelte-Reyner.
	Cosaert, Daved and Catryna-Mareya.
	Vaen Noerden, Tobeyes and Gienne-Maria; also Samaules.
Apr. 28.	Faerle, Cilp and Vebe-Vebe.
May 19.	Coevert, Piter and Mareya-Tomaes.
	Berca, Bergoen and Jaennete-Piter.
May 23.	Broeka, Bergon; Broka, Jan and Mettye-Jan.
	[Perhaps Bergon, above, was witness; entry not clear.]
	Harpending, Henderick and Maryte-Piter.
	Voorhes, Kneelis and Neeltye-Knelis.
	Wilson, Meyndert-Henderick.
	Wilson, Henderic-Iassya.
June 9.	Tunesse, Deneys and Saerte-Derck.
	Vaen niest, Johaennaes and Aelte-Teunes.
	Witnesses: Teunes and Arreyaente Teunesse.
June 30.	Vermeulen, William and Blandina-Nelte.
	Witness: Cornelius Middagh.

	Smit, Henderick and Ragel-Adam.
Sept. -.	Teneyt, [Ma]tewes and Aeltie-Treynte.
	Kock, Taemmes and Maria-Elisebet.
	Bries, Henderick and Rut-Henderick.
	Reynerse, Oucke and Elsse-Gerret.
	Sebering, Gores and Myreya-Johannes.
Sept. 22.	Detmaes, Douwe and Aelte-Aelte.
	Aemmertnaen, Poules and Alidae-Poules.
	Albrecht, Jacop and Lena-Lena.
Nov. 3.	Teneyck, Coenrades and Elsse-Vrereck.
	Hegemaen, Magiel and Jaente-Maergrite.
	Witness: Mgrite Hegemaen.
	Teneyck, Peteries and Debera-Peteries.
	Reyke, Hendereck and Nelle-Elisebet.
1755.	
Jan. 5.	Vaen mulene, Coerneles and Maryte-Coersting.
Feb. 2.	Hutsen, Jaen and Bette-Tomaes.
	Degroet, Jaen and Aelte-Veyte.
	Van Neste, Jeronimus and Catelytie-Diena.
Apr. 20.	Douwe, Jaen and Anate-Johaennes.
	Tunese, Flip and Debera-Rabeca.
	Witnesses: Cornelis Tunesse and Rabeca.
	Voelckerse, Flip and Maergrite-Josep.
	Witness: Aelte Voescke.
	Baenta, Henderick and Aente-Peter.
	Vaen Voerhes, Jaen and Marya-Marya.
June 7.	Visser, Henderick and Effe-Maria.
8.	Boelmer, Aberaem and Elisebet-Robbert.
	Bort, Enderi and Marigrite-Derck.
	Raeug, Noag and Elisebet-Jacobes.
	Sebering, Johannes and Gerte-Aelte.
	Waelderoem, Daneel and Heppe-Leffert.
Sept. 7.	Cosaert, Fraens and Marigrite-Stynte.
	Grau, Gerrit and Elidea-Isack.
	Stpper, Ebbeneser and Catryna-[No child's name].
	Witnesses: Stryker Belyu and Caerber.
1756.	
Feb 4.	Berca, Bergoen and Mette-Sara.
	Berca, Aberaem and Maelle-Catlyna.
	Vaen Nest [?] Peteris and Jaennete-Maergrite.

Swet, Piter and Jaennete-Eva.
Messelaer, Cornelius and Eva-Lena.
Esbert, Jannes and Mayen-Jacob.
Berca, Jaen and Mareyte-Bergoen.
July 1. Teneyt, Conract and Elsse-Gerrete.
Teneyck, Piter and Debera-Dorete.
Coevert, Piter and Mareya-Mareya.
Vaen Nist, Piter and Catrite-Coernelies.
Engel, Niclaes and Mareyte-Flip.
Biem, Henderick and Cornelia-Anate.
Aresmit, Ned and Maelle-Niclaes.
Vaen niest, Haennes and Aelte-Jeromes.
Aug. 22. Wititerstien, Jacobes and Aente-Marigrite.
Cock, Taemmes and Meri-Jacob.
Hoef, Derck and Cernelia-Bergoen.
Vaen Voerhes, Jaen and Marya-Aberaem.
Cosaert, Daved and Caleyte-Nelte.
Oct. 30. Bedeyn, Jaen and Vemmete-Areyaente.
1757.
---- Matiewes and Aelte-Wilbelmus.
Vectie, Henderick and Nelte-Sara.
Tunesse, Deneys and Saerte-Aente.
Ate, Tomes and Hellete-Jaen.
Nov. -. Reyk, Henderick and Nelle-Corneles.
Witnesses: Corneles Socaen and Maryte.
Bodeyn, Aberaem and Mareyte-Corneles.
Vaenderbilt, Jaen and Aengenite-Piter.
Matanye, Eide and Elisebet-Elisebet.
Vaen niest, Jeromes and Catlytie-Isack.
1756 (8?).
Apr. 13. Coevert, Piter and Marya-Lisebet.
Hutsen, Jaen and Elisebet-Johaennes.
Aerst, Matewes and Marya-Hester.
Renser, Enoag and Elisebet-Anate.
Vaen noertwick, Cristeuennes and Caettrierte-Henderick.
Sebering, Jores and Marya-Jores.
Vaenniest, Piter and Elisebet-Aberaen.
Coevert, Luykes and Anate-Luykes.
Aug. 13. Bodeyn, Jaen and Femmete-Aberaem.
Sweed, Piter and Jaennete-Catlyna.

	Boellemer, Aberaem and Elisebet-Garret.
Dec. 10.	Willemse, Piter and Deyna-Piter.
	Vaen nist, Jchannes and Aelte-Sosaena.
Aug. 29.	Cosaert, Fraens and Maregrite-Elisebet.
1759.	
	Voerhes, Aberaem and Saevya-Johannes.
	Vaen niest, Peteris and Catleyte-Maryte.
	Vaenmittelswart, Tueses and Jaennake-Tueses.
Mar. 25.	Tencyck, Piter and Debera-Aenderis.
	Hoef, Bergoen and Neelte-Nelte.
	Messelaer, Coernelis and Laemrnete-Corneles.
Apr. 22.	Berck, Bergoen and Jaennete-Bergoen.
	Sebering, Jaen and Nelle-Foelkert.
	Ubert, Jonaes and Marya-Truyte.
	Vaendoren, Wellem and Catlyte-Bergoen.
May 20.	Haerdenberg, Jacob Rutsen and Deyna-Johannes.
	Teneyt, Jacob and Magrita-Jacob.
July 8.	Berca, Eysack and Maryte-Eysack.
	Coevert, Piter and Marya-Aente.
	Degroet, Jaen and Aelte-Johannes.
Aug. 5.	Streyker, Jacobes and Gerte-Gerte.
	Demoen, Piter and Aderyana-Aderyana.
Oct. 7.	Vaen oerden, Tobeyes and Ginne-Piter.
	Witness: Catrina Naerret.
Nov. 4.	Vaen mulene, Corneles and Maryte-Deyna.
Dec. 2.	Te neyke Koenrot and Elsse-[child's name omitted].
Dec. 25.	Mataenye, Eide and Elisebet [child's name omitted].
	Witnesses: Jacobes Wienters [tien] and Aente.
1760.	
Feb. 24.	Tuneste, Fillip and Debera-Nelte.
Apr. 20.	Bennit, Johannis and Marya-Johannis.
	Smack, Teys and Gerte-Teys.
May 15.	Berca, Isack and Treynte-Aberaem.
	Witnesses: Aberaem and Jetide Berca.
June 1.	Sebering, Jores and Marya-Daved.
	Coevert, Luykes and Anate-Eide.
	Aersse, Teues and Reya-Johannes.
July 27.	Reyke, Henderick and Nelte-Henderick.
	Hegeman, Magiel and Jaennete-Magiel Vaen Vegte.
	Witness: Jaennete Hegeman.

Aug. 23. Middelswaert, Hendericks and Nelte-Femrnete.
Aug. 24. Welsen, Peteris and Ecye-Henderick.
Witness: Henderick Welsen.
Nov. 30. Vaendoren, Wellem and Catleyte-Aberaem.
Demon, Derck and Ragel-Jaen.
Dec 25. Sweed, Piter and Jaennete-Peteres.
Devyse Saerra and En-En.
Jan. 11. Haemberg, Jacobes Ruts and Dyna-Nela.
Biem, Henderick and Cerneliya-Neleya.
Feb. 8. Hoef, Bergoen and Nelte-Tunes.
Vaenniest, Peteris and Catleyte-Peteries.
Apr. 5. Teneyt, Jacob and Jaennete-Jaennete.
Coevert, Piter and Marya-Luycas.
Wielsen, Meyndert and Aente-Clesia[?].
Teneyt, Mattewes and Nelle-Sara.
June 14. Ate, Tomas and Hellete-Aron.
Vaennist, Johaennes and Aelte-Areyaente.
Messelaer, Coerneles and Marya-Laemmeta.
Herpendeyn, Henderick and Marya-Aenderis Menton.
Nov. 8. Vaen middelswart, Tunes and Jaennete-Susanna.
Dec. 25. Berca, Isack and Treynte-Bergon.
1762.
Jan. -. Vaen aersdale, Wilhelms and Catryna-Catryna.
Feb. 20. Ate, Pouwel and Marya-Tomas.
Mataenye, Eide and Elisebet-Eide.
Mar. 14. Ate, Arey and Elisebet-Johannes.
Teneyt, Koenraet and Mrya-Jacob.
[Name blank-Bennet?] Johannes and Marya-Henderick.
Mar. 28. Tennick, Coenraet and Elsie-Jacop.
May 9. Koevert, Luykes and Anate-Johaennes.
Coemten, Jaen and Catryn-Jaen.
Coseyn, Corneles and Aente-Johaennes.
May 20. Vaen Vegte, Derck and Sara-Derck.
Tuenesse, Flip and Debera-Johaennes.
Witness: Jaen Vaen der Spigel.
July 12. Sebereng, Jores and Marya-Jacop.
Aug. 1. Coevert, Daenyel and Annaetye-Marya.
Demon, Pieter and Ariaentye-Peteris.
Oct. 26. Smack, Teys and Gerte-Aelte.
Schenck, Henderick and Lena-Aberam.

Nov. 28. Merel, Niclaes and Lidea-Villep.
Aersse, Matewes and Mareya-Catria.
Teneyck, Aeersen and Saerte-Aenderies.

1763.
Jan. 23. Douwe, Jaen and Anate-Wilhelmes.
Gertse, Gert and Saerte-Marya.
Feb. 6. Reyke, Henderick and Nellie-Sarel.
Ate, Jores and Steynte-Steynte.
Apr. 18. Coevert, Piter and Marya-Haermpe.
June 5. Hegemaen, Magiel and Jaennete-Magiel.
Wiellemse, Piter and Ecyna-Aelte.
Vaennist, Piter and Catreynte-Bernaerdes.
Sebering, Roelof and Catlyna-Jaennete.
Haerdenberg, Jacob Ruts and Dyna-Jacob Ruts.
Sebering, Jaen and Nelte-Jaen.
Aug. 14. Hutsen, Jaen and Elisebet-Aente.
Witnesses: Willem and Abigelte Oelden.
Laen, Willem and Jaennete-Tunes.
Seberina, Derck and Madlena-Marya.
Houts, Johannes and Safya-Magrite.
Oct. 23. Trael, Wiellem Jorese and Marya-Marya.
Dec. 4. Vaenniest, Jores and Catlyete-Peteris.
Dec. 25. Vaendervoert, Tomes and Aeryaente-Aente.
Teneyck, Jacob and Mergrita-Jaemeyte.
Vaendoren, Wiellem and Catleyte-Wellem.
Vaen Neste, Derck and Sara-Maergrite.

1764.
Jan. 29. Coevert, Luykes and Anate-Marya.
Mar. 4. Vaennist, Johaennes and Aelte-Johaennes.
Smack, Jaen and Neele-Jaen.
Mar. 18. Hoef, Bergoen and Nelte-Jaen.
Apr. 8. de Vrest, Johannes and Marya-Eysack.
Ate, Aerry and Lisebet-Piter.
----, Wiellem and Magrita-Piter.
Meller, Taemme and Arete-Magrita.
Ate, Pouwel and Marya-Voelkert.
Apr. 21. Malaenge, Eide and Elisebet-Aente.
Apr. 23. Vaen Nist, Piter and Elisebet-Yaen.
June 17. Lot, Corneles and Henderike-Marya.
July 15. Vaen Noert Weyck, Wellem and Blaendina-Magrita.

	Tuenese, Fliph and Debera-Aberaem.
	Witnesses: Aberaem and Aente Teunese.
	Tuenese, Coerneles and Aente-Vemmete.
July 22.	Teneyck, Tewes and Nelte-Marya.
Aug 12.	Vaen Middelswaert, Tunes and Jaennete-Cristevaen; also Jaen.
	Merel, Neclaes and Elidea-Matewes.
	Messelaer, Corneles and Marya-Gerret.
	Schenck, Henderick and Lena-Vrereck.
Sept. 23.	te neyck, Konrat and Eisse-Jacob.
Oct. 14.	Haerdenbrock, Lodeweyck and Catryna-Jacob.
Nov. 25.	Berca, Isack and Treynte-[child's name omitted].
Dec. 17.	Coevert, Dael and Marya-Tunes.
1765.	
Feb. 10.	Coevert, Piter and Marya-Peteris.
	Vaen aersdalen, Jaen and Reses-Eddem Smit.
Mar. 31.	Sebering, Jores and Marya-Willem.
	Coevert, Bergoen and Seyte-Saerte.
Apr. 21.	Sebering, Johennes and Gerte-Saerte.
	Wecoef, Jacob and Catleyte-Nelte.
	Coevert, Bergoen and Vemmete-Josewa.
May 12.	Hutsen, Jaen and Belisebet-Marya.
	Witness: Begelte Oelden.
	Vaen Saent, Rueyaent and Aente-Nelte.
	Erresmit, Josep and Gerte-Reynier.
May 26.	Aersse, Mattewes and Marya-Eysack.
	Vaen Voeres, Jaen and Marya-Jores.
	Speder, Wellem and Marya-Wellem.
	Vaen Voerhes, Aberaem and Maryria -Staynte
	Aense, Jaen and Johaena-Roseta; also Sofaena.
June 30.	Vaendoren, Willem and Catleyte-Wellem.
	Streyker, Jacobes and Gerte-Aberaem.
Aug. 18.	Bries, Johannes and Lea-Jacob.
	Witnesses: Jacob Breys and Ecye.
Sept. 15.	Smack, Teys and Gerte-Marya.
	Berca, Jaen and Mareya-Vernaendes.
	Boelmer, Aberaem and Bette-Aberaem.
	Witness: Mareyte ----.
Sept. 23.	Sebering, Aberaem and Madlena-Madlena.
Dec. 23.	Haerdenberg, Jacobrues Ruts and Deyna-Ragel.

Witness: Loura de Vroemberge.

1766.

Jan. 2. Vaen Veghte, Derck and Sara-Magiel.

Feb. 6. Reyke, Henderick and Nente-Magrite.

Convert, Luykes and Anate-Peteris.

de Vrest, Johannes and Marya-Catlyte.

Mar. 10. Vaen nist, Johaennes and Deyna-Aberaem.

Mar. 23. teneyt, Jacob and Maergrita-Magria.

Welsel, Peteres and Anate-Anate.

Apr. 12. Boelmer, Robbert and Sery-Maryte.

Apr. 27. Loth, Coernelis and Henderickte-Isack.

Vaen aersdalen, Henderick and Jaennete-Maya.

June 15. Bogert, Sameel and Catrina-Catlyna.

Witness: Coernele Bogert.

Coevert, Bergoen and Seyte-Luckes.

Merel, Necklaes and Elidea-Welhelme.

June[?]12. Stryker, Jaen and Cosia-Piter.

July 21. Vaennist, Jores and Catleyte-Wellem.

Nov. 11 . [Name omitted-Aten?]. Pouwel and Marya-Pouwel.

Demoen, Derck and Raget-Vemmete.

Nov. 24 . Matanye, Ide and Elisebet-Anate.

Beekmaen, Sameel and Elisebet-Sameel.

Sebering, Jacob-Gerte.

Dec. 10. Vaenaersdalen, Jaen and Anate-Phelep.

Dec. 25. Teunese, Pelep and Debera-Benardes.

Coevert, Daenel and Marya-Helena.

1767.

Jan. 18. Teunese, Coerneles and Aente-Aberem.

[One baptism cut out here].

Feb. 8. Scenck, Henderick and Magdelena-Magdelena.

Witness: Piter Scenck.

Coevert, Bergoen and Vemmete-Ana.

Erresmet, Joseb and Gerte-Gerte.

Mar. 29. Berca, Jaen and Marya-Benyemaen.

Apr. 19. Aersse, Jaen and Johaenna-Johaennes.

Voen Saent, Weyaent and Aente-Isack.

Apr. 20. Vaen Middelswaert, Tunes and Jaennete-Jaennete.

May 3. Dote, Corneles and Hellete-Jaen.

[One baptism cut out here].

Bedeyn, Jaen and Vemmete-Lena.

May 23.	Vaen malene, Ederjaen and Elisebet-Jan.
June 5.	Dele, Willem-Enne.
	Coevert, Luykes and Anate-Vrerick.
	Boelmer, Robbert and Selle-Pelye.
	Coevert, Aberaen and Beleye-Johaennes.
	Streyker, Johaennen and Elideya-Johaennes.
	Coevert, Bergoen and Vette-Jaennete.
	Bueys, Jaen and Lena-Eide.
July 17.	Berck, Benjemaen and Sara-Marya.
	Messelaer, Jacobes and Jaennete-Gerte.
	Haerdenberg, Jacobes Ruts and Dyna-Jacobes Ruts.
	V. arsdalen, Hend'k and Jannetje-Wilmpje.
Aug. 7.	Beekman, Sameal and Eliesebet-Eliesebet.
Aug. 28.	Sebering, Aberaem and Cristina -Jaennete.
	Sebering, Derck and Madlena-Derck.
Sept. 8.	Cadner, Aenderis and Vemmete-Derck.
Oct. 29.	van Veghten, Dereck and Sere-Elisebet.
Nov. 13.	Vaenderver, Verdinaendes and Rabecka-Corneles.
Dec. 9.	Mataenje, Eide and Elisebet-Jacobes.
	Borca, Jaen and Maria-Migael.
1768.	
Jan. 8.	Coevert, Bergon and Vemmete-Bergoen.
Feb. 19.	Sadaem, Henderick and Nelte-Catring.
Mar. -.	Coevert, Dael and Marya-Calyna.
	Sebrija, Jaen and Nelte-Elisebet.
	Rolaent, Tomaes and Resel-Tomaes.
Apr. 28.	Aerse, Matewes and Marya-Aelte.
June 18.	Aten, Pouwel and Marya-Jaen.
	Aten, Are and Elisebet-Are.
	Voerhes, Aberaem and Elisebet-Elisebet.
	Luckes, Jurya and Lisebet-Gerte.
Aug. 6.	Teneyck, Jacob and Magrita-Treynte.
	Aersse, Jaen and Johanna-Deyna.
Sept. 3.	Sebering, Jacob and Jaennete-Leffert.
	Meller, Toma and Peeje-Peter.
Sept. 17.	Teneyck, Anders and Vemete-Matewes.
Oct. 22.	Coevert, Luykes and Cornelena-Aerret.
Oct. 26.	Weycoef, Jacob and Catleyte-Aberaem.
Dec. -.	Seberina, Volckert and Treynte-Marya.

1769.
[No record for this year].
1770.
Jan. -. Neuse, Welhelme and Aeryaente-Nelte.
Jan. 14. Van Derveer, John and Mareya-Wilemte.
Feb. 11. Conraet [Ten Eick?] and Else-Hendrick.
Teneyt, Conrades and Elsse-Henderick.
[Above two entries probably relate to same party].
Witnesses: Jacob Bergen and Raelte.
Feb. 18. Bries, Leukes and Anate-Johannes.
Apr. 1. Vaen niest, Johaennes and Deyna-Sara.
Coevert, Aberaem and Bette-Madelena.
Borck, Beniemen and Sara-Aberaem.
Apr. 29. Streyker, Jaen and Leidea-Henderick.
Weintersten, Jacob and Marya-Jacobes.
Vaen Saent, Weyaent and Aente-Belete.
June 15. Coevert, Luykes and Anate-Anat.
Coevert, Piter and Marya-Catrina.
Coevert, Bergoen and Seyte-Marya.
July 1. Middelswaert, Tunes and Sara-Nelte.
Aug. 26. Wenterstein, Cobes and Aeryaente-Aente.
Sept. 16. Beekman, Semwel and Elisebat-Cernelea.
Vaen mulener, Aderyaen and Elisebet-Maria.
Boelmer, Robbert and Saerte-Madlena.
Berca, Eelck and Jaennte-Isack.
Oct. 7. Berck, Jaen and Marya-Vemmete.
Boeremaen, Semwel-Gertruy.
Mataenye, Eide-[mother's and child's names omitted].
1771.
Feb. 3 Sebring, Abraham and Styna-Mira.
Apr. 7. Aten, Tomas and Saerte-Fraenseyte.
Sebering, Jacob and Jenneke-Aberaem.
Sept. 1. Teunese, Vellip and Debera-Debera.
Sept. 22. Vaen mulene, Eide and Leisebet-Maria.
Oct. 6. Vaen oerstrent, Jaen and Marya-Jenneke.
Nov. 3. Vaennest, Jores and Catleyte-Reynier.
Nov. 17. Aten, Are and Lisebet-Tomas.
Dec. 15. Berca, Bensemen and Sara-Jaen.
1772.
Jan. 5. Sebring, Jan and Neltee-Jan.

	Waldron, Johannes and Annate-Elesebet.
Jan. 19.	[Ten Eyck?) Koenrades and Elsse-Anate.
	Vaen Der Veer, Jaen and Marya-Henderick.
	Luckes, Oreya and Elisebet-Saerte.
Feb. 17.	Smit, Benjemeen and Biejette-Ragel.
	Sedam, Henderick and Nelle-Henderick Visser.
	Beemaen, Jaen and Aeriate-Coerneles.
	Coevert, Bergoen and Seyte-Johannes Smack.
May 16.	Vaennoest, Casparis and Eva-Johannes Vrelinhuysen.
May 17.	Aten, Pouwel and Marya-Marya.
July 4.	Demoen, Derck and Ragel-Sara.
July 26.	Nefser, Wellem and Aeryaente-Elisebet.
	Vaen niest, Johaennes and Deyna-Jores.
	Kep, Neclaes and Lea-Treynte.
Sept. 7.	Coeyemaen, Samewell and Aeryante-Aenderis.
	[Two baptisms cut out here.]
	Dote, Coerneles and Hellete-Vemmete.
	Boerom, Johaennes and Jaennete-Johannes.
	Clark, William and Sarah-Maria.
	Sebring, Derick and Madlena-Cornelius.
June -.	Haerdenberg, Jacob Rutsen and Deyna-Lewis.
	Voerhes, Jaen and Mareyte-Jaen.
	Vaenderbelt, Jacob and Veyte-Neys.
	[Two baptisms cut out here].
Dec. 15.	Deavits, Isaac and Jannetie-Jores.
	Coevert, Peter and Maria-Henderick.
Dec. 25.	Vechter, Rynier and Catrena-Hendereck.
	Cadmus, Andries and Fammetie-Abraham.
	Coevert, Luykes and Cornelya-Antie.
	Cosart, Jacobes and Elizabet-Catlintie.
1773.	
Jan. 1.	Winterstien, Jacobes and Ariantie-Maria.
	Montanye, Eiden and Elizabet-William.
	Wykof, Jacob and Catlyntie-Jannitie.
Feb. 19.	Dowe, Dirick and Giertie-Johannes.
	Arsen, Matheus and Maria-Osela.
	Vanderbilt, Jacob and Safiya-Hilletie.
Mar. 25.	Vandom, Jacob and Jannetie-Nelltie.
	Detmas, Frederick and Femmetie-Abraham.
Apr. 16.	Brocaw, Jan and Maria-Peter.

May 14. Vanmidelswart, Teunes and Sara-Henderick.
Ferly, Calap and Jannetie-Abraham.
June 3. Ten Eyck, Jacob and Maregrita-Jacobus.
Beekman, Samuel and Elizabet-Martan.
July 5. Stats, Abraham and Maregrita-Jannetie.
July 25. Bishop, Samuel and Antie-Elizabet.
Aug. 22. Dumon, Peter and Sara-Adreaun.
Sebring, Abraham and Cristena-Abraham.
Borem, Johannes and Jannetie-Anne.
Oct. 13. Snedeken, Jacob and Catlintie-Gerret.
Nov. 13. Coevert, Lukes and Annatie-Elizebet.
Vanduin, Jacobus and Annatie-Cornelius.
Nov. 27. Tunison, Cornelius and Elizabet-Neeltie.
1774.
Feb. 5. Neefius, Wilhalmes and Areantie-Johannes.
Feb. 26. Stewart, John and Lidia-Marigrita.
Mar. 26. Vandorn, Jacob and Jannetie-Maria.
Deavets, Isaac and Jenne-Maria.
Apr. 16. Deavets, Petres and Jenneke-Petres.
Coevert, Peter and Mary-Abraham.
Detmas, Frederick and Femmetie-Femmetie.
June 25. Vanvorhees, Abraham and Catriena-Margrit.
Sebring, George and Phebe-George.
1771.
Apr. 7. Sebring, Thomas and Sara-Franseyntie.
[Foregoing entry probably inserted out of place].
1775.
Mar. 26. Vanmidelswart, Teunes and Sara-Jannetie.
Stryker, Barnt and Lena-Peter.
July 30. Auten, Powel and Maria-Roelf.
Aug. -. Vennist, George and Lenake-Phebe.
Vanderbilt, Jacob and Saphiah-Sara.
Vannist, Joris and Catlyntie-Joris.
Vermeulen, Adriaum and Elizebeth-Elizebeth.
Oct. 8. Staats, Abraham and Marigrita-Femnietie.
1776.
Jan. 20. Roseboem, Garrit and Geertry-Marigrita.
Mar. 10. Vannostrant, John and Maria-Isaac.
May 5. Frelingheisen, Fredrich and Geertie-John.
Sebring, Thomas and Sara-Roelef.

Dowe, Dirick and Geertie-Davit.
Brocaw, John and Maria-Maria.

[The years of some of following entries mixed and uncertain].

1775 [?].
Nov. 12. Sebring, Abraham and Cristina-Jan.

1776 [?].
Nov. 21. Brokaw, Benjemin and Sara-Annatie.
Vannostrant, John and Maria-Jacob.
Dec. 12. Striker, John and Sara-Geertie.
Arrosmith, Barnt and Debora-Maria.

1777 [?[.
Apr. 3. Smith, Benjamin and Abigel-Elizabeth.
Ten Eyck, Andries and Maregrita-Jores.
Vandorn, Abraham and Neeltie-Cornelius Tunison.
Witness: Jannetie Brower, wife of Cornelius Tunison.
Apr. 17. Vermeulen, Frederick and Aaltie-Cornelius.
Staats, Peter and Susanna-Jan.
Vannostrant, Cristopher and Maria-Crisparis.
May 15. Ten Eyck, Conrad and Elsie-Petres.
Beekman, John and Arrientie-Marta.
Vansickler, John and Nelah-Reynier.
Vermulen, Eden and Elizabet-Elizebet.
June 5. Vannostrant, Caspares and Eva-Dina.
Clark, William and Sara-Sara.
June 26. Sebring, Jacob and Jenneke-Mettie.
Vannise, John and Aaltie-Martie.
July 10. Brokaw, John and Maria-Antie.
Arrismith, Joseph and Geertie-Nensey.
July 31. Tunison, Folkert and Antie-Rebecka.
Sebring, Aaltie-William Vanduyn.
Sept. 18. Vannest, Johannes and Dina-Cristofel.
Sebring, Thomes and Sara-Maria.
Dowe, Dirick and Geertie-Catlyntie.
Millen, Thomes and Marigrita-Elizabet.
Oct. 24. Cadmus, Andries and Fammetie-Cornelius.
Goltrey, Olever and Lena-Maria.

1777.
May 19. Vannostrant, Crespares and Eva-Geerte.
Tunison, Philep and Debra-Philep.
Vanarsdalen, Hendrek and Catrina-Magdalena.

	Ten Eyck, Cornelius and Anna-Maria.
Aug. 4.	Sebring, Jacob and Jannetie-Cornelius.
	Sebring, Jacob and Jannetie-Abraham.
	Aten, Aron and Elizabet-Isaac.
	Arrismith, Joseph and Geertie-Joseph.
Sept. 7.	Miller, Thomes and Margrita-Oliver.
Nov. 4.	Deavets, Isaac and Jannetie-Jude.
	Vermeulen, Fredrick and Aeltie-Jacob.
	Stewart, John and Ledia-Hanna.
1776 (?).	
Nov. 17.	Tunison, Cornelius and Elizabeth-Jenneka.
1777.	
June 1.	Vannest, Jores and Catlyna-Abraham.
	Vannest, Johannes and Dina-Cristofel.
Aug. 24.	Bolmer, Robbert and Sara-Robbert.
Sept. 14.	Smith, Benjamin and Abigal-Adam.
Dec. 7.	Brown, Jacob and Fytie-Olever.
	Vorhees, Jacobes and Maria-Maria.
1778.	
Jan. 1.	Vandyke, Cornelius and Maria-Maregrite.
Jan. 26.	Vanasdalen, Philip and Aeltie-Abraham.
Feb. 23.	Clark, Wm. and Sara-Susanna.
1779.	
Mch. 7.	Sebring, Abraham and Cristina-Jacob.
Apr. 11.	Vermeulen, Frederick and Aeltie-Jannetie.
	Veghte, Ryneir and Catrine-Catrine.
	Sebring, Gorge and Phebe-Jacobes.
May 9.	Brokaw, Calip and Jannetie-Antie.
May 29.	Bolmer, Robberd and Sara-William.
July 25.	Ten Eyck, Cornelius and Antie-Corneleya.
Aug. 8.	Vermeulen, Eden and Elizabeth-Cornelius.
	Deavets, Petres and Jenneke-Judick.
Oct. 3.	Frelinghuysen, Frederick and Geertie-Dina.
	Beekman, John and Ariaentie-Gerret.
Oct. 31.	Ten Eyck, Andries and Elizabeth-Andries.
	Sudam, Henderic and Marea-Abraham.
Nov. 21.	Sebring, Jacob and Jannetie-Mettie; Jannetie.
1780.	
Jan. 14.	Sebring, Thomes and Sara-Jannetie.
	Miller, Thomes and Maregrita-William.

Apr. 23.	Auten, Aaron and Elizabeth-Anna.
	Dumon, John and Ariaentie-Annatie.
May 14.	Vannest, Joris and Catlyna-Jacob.
	Middag, Jan and Steyntie-Sara.
	Beem, Elizebeth (mother)-Jacobes Vandeveer (child).
July 2.	Hardenberg, John and Nency Walace-Dina.
	Stewart, John and Lidea-Thomes.
	Miller, Maria (mother)-Rebecka.
Sept. 10.	Sebring, John and Abegel-Tomson
	Powlson, Abraham and Lammet-Johannes.
	Davetson, Isaac and Jenny-Nency.
Oct. 15.	Vanmiddelswart, Andries and Sara-Neeltie.
Dec. 10.	Low, Peter and Hanna-Cornelius.
	Vannest, Joris and Lammertie-Sara.
	Dowe, Folkert and Elizabeth-Maria.
I781.	
Feb. 11.	Dowe, Dirick and Maria-Geartie.
	Tunison, Cornelius and Elizabeth-Jennekie.
Mch. 4.	Ven Nest, Abraham and Catrina-Femmetie.
	Vannostrant, Crisparis and Eva-Maria.
Mch. 9.	Chandler, John and Elizabeth-Isaac.
Mch. 18.	Goltrey, Olever and Neome-Maria.
	Brokaw, Crispares and Neeltie-Neeltie.
Apr. 8.	Frelinghuysen, Fradrek and Geertie-Theodorus Jacobus.
	Lane, Mathies and Lowra-Catryntie.
	Vandeveer, Jacobes and Maria-Dina.
	Middagh, Cornelius and Antie-Diricke.
June 3.	Voorhees, Folkert and Maregrieta-Elizabeth; Abraham. (witnesses) Abraham Bolmer and Elizabeth Sexen (?)-.
Sept. 30.	Vermeulen, Fredrek and Aeltie-Marca.
Oct. 21.	Bekman, John and Ariaentie-Johannes.
	Kozeboom, Hendrek-Andries.
	Ten Eyck, Andries and Elizabeth-Elizabeth.
	Clauson, Neeltie (mother) Sara.
1782.	
Jan. 6.	Davetson, Peter and Jenneke-Magdelena.
Apr. 21.	Sebring, Abraham and Cristina-Maria.
	Sebring, Thomes and Sara-Ariaantie.
	Vansant, Peter-Neeltie.
Sept. 8.	Defreast, John and Maria-Larance.

Sebring, John and Abegel-John.
Oct. 6. Bolmer, Robert and Sarah-Isaac.
Chandler, John and Elizabeth-Sarah.
Brokaw, Calab and Jannetie-Maria.
Tunison, Cornelius and Elizabeth-Garret.
Traphagen, Roelef and Phenne-Roelef.

1783.
Jan. 12. Vannest, Jores and Catlyno-Jannitie.
Dowe, Dirick and Maria-Patres.
Vanpelt, Roelef and wife-Aaltie.
Apr. 20. Vermeulen, Cornelius and Elizabeth-Dirick.
June 8. Keder, Wielder and Maragrite-Calvinies Middagh (born July 29, 1782).

1784.
Jan. 4. Tunison, Garret and Sara-Jenneke Davese.
April 18. Davis, Peter and Jannitie-Jannitie.
Bennet, Hendrick and Jannitie-Johannes.
Cornel, William and Sara-Jacob.
May 23. King, John and Agnes Barclay-Elizabeth.
Deforest, Johannes and Maria Vanneste-Johannes.
Rooseboom, Hendrick and Rachel Smalley-Garret.
Sebring, Joris and Fammetje Voorhees-Geertje Tertits.
Aug. 5. Brokaw, Dirck and Jenny Hoff-John.
Hardenbergh, John and Nancey Wallace-John Wallace.
Sebring, Folkert and Maria Sebring-Neeltje.
Steward, John and Lydia Douw-Maria.
Aug. 8 Van Dyck, Corn. and Maria Brokaw-Jannetje.
Oct. 3. Van Pelt, Roelof and Cathrina Ten Eyck-Peter.
Van Neste, Abraham and Sarah Boerem-Anna.
[This child was born the 29th Aug., 1784.]
Oct. 17. Tunison, Cornelius, Hannah Louw (witness)-Elizabeth.
Messelaer, Cornelius and Maria Stryker-Magdelena.
Vroom, Peter D., Elsie Bogart (witness)-Johannes.
Oct. 31. Ten Eyck, Frederick and ---- Field-Richard.
Suydam, Cornelius and Antje Rapalje-Antje.
Aug. 4. [Here occur certain repetitions].
Nov. - Van Neste, Abraham and Cathrina Sebring-Maria.
Van Neste, Joris and Lummetje Staats-Jan.
Wintersteen, Jacobus and Ariantje Vander Beek-Jacobus.
Dec. 5. Hardenbrook, Isaac and Willempje Buys-Henry Deware.

Dec. 29. Goltrie, Oliver and Anna Van Tuyl-Abraham.

1785.

Jan. 16. Sexton, William and Elizabeth Bolmer-Robert.
Van Middleswaart, And. and Sarah Bogart-Cathrina.

Feb. 20. Stryker, Abraham and Geertje Jobs-Elisabeth.

Feb. 27. Tunison, Dirck and Maria Sutphen-Anna.
Sebring, Thomas and Sarah Auten-Thomas.
[Young] Elizabeth Kerr, wife of George Young-Philip.

Mch. 20. Van Doren, Brogun and Neeltje Voorheese-Willem.
Douw, Folkert and Elizabeth Bodine-Peterus.

Apr. 24. Sebring, Johannes and Abigail Thompson-Tammage Ross.

Apr. 30. Bolmer, Robert and Sarah Van Tuyl-Sarah.

May 15. Ver Meule, Cornelius and Elizabeth Middagh-Dinah.

June 16. Ten Eyck, Andris and Elizabeth La Grange-Margaret.
Stewart, John and Lydia Douw-Abraham.

June 19. Hart, James and Hannah Mapes-James.
Montanje, Eda and Cathrina Young-Maria.

July 10. Louw, Dirck and Dorothea Ten Eyck-Rebechka.
Van Noordstrand, Jan and Maria Brokaw-[Sarah, crossed out].
[Crane] Maragrietje Van Veghten, wife of Joseph Crane-Sarah.

July 31. A full grown slave of Teunis Van Middleswaert-Diaan.

Sept. 11. Tunison, Hendrich and Nancy Boerem-Jannetje.
Van Duyn, William and Dinah Van Neste-Abraham.

1786.

Feb. 26. Amerman, Abraham and Peggy Suydam-Caty.

Mch. 26. Hardenbergh, John and Nancey Wallace-Frederick Frelinghuysen.
Bennet, Abraham and Mary Arrowsmith-James.
Bennet, John (witness) and Aeltje Bennet-Letty.
Van Middleswaert, John and Hannah Lane-Jenny.
Perrine, John and Sophia Burges-Gitty.
Elmendorf, John and Margaret Zabriskie-William Crooke.
Roseboom, Rendriclz and Rachel Smalley-John.
Perrine, Peter and Elizabeth Burges-Elizabeth.
Van Nordwyck, John and Elizabeth Auten-Sarah.
Van Nordstrand, Matteus and Mary Phillips-Matteus.
Ten Eyck, Jacob and Jannetje Lane-Teunis.
[Crane], Maragrietje Van Veghte, wife of Joseph Crane-Dirck Van Veghten.

1787.
Mch. 18. Sebring, Folcard and Mary Sebring-Catherine.
May 20. Van Neste, Abm. and Catharine Sebring-Cornellious.
Vechter, Ryneer and Catharine Wagener-Garret.
Messler, Cornelious and Marea Stryker-Lamettie.
Bergird, Jacobus and Antye Voorhees-Marea.
[Young], Elizabeth Carr, wife of Joris Young-Joris.
1786.
June 27. Derye, Johannes and Marea Lee-Hendrick Brinkelhoof.
Lane, Mathies and Geertie Sutfen-Aaron.
V. Voorhees, Abraham and Catrina Doty-Catrina.
1787.
Apr. 15. Venness, Peter and Phebe Braca-Catherin.
May 27. Sebring, Jacob and Janeca Ventyle-Phebe.
Aug. 12. Vroom, Peter D. and Elsie Bogart-Maria.
Tennick, Andres and Elizabeth Lagrange-Jacob.
Aug. 26. Middleswart, Andres and Sara Bogert-Johannes Bogert.
Dow, Folcard and Elesebeth Bodine-Anna.
Aug. 7. Wagener, Coanroad V. and Sarah Bogert-Cora Jemima.
Nov. 18. Broca, Isaac and Meria Boise-Abraham.
Dec. 2. Maslor, Cornelious and Marea Stryker-Denise.
Ryker, Cornelious and Anne Rapleyea-Crestina.
Dec. 25. Lefrees, Isaac and Laneerche Wortmen-Peter.
1788.
Jan. 13. Abraham Vennest and Catlyntye Sebring-Altye Suydam.
Mar. 30. William Parish and Elizabeth Beekman-Henry.
Apr. 12. Jacob Tennick and Jenne Lane-Peter.
Apr. 13. John Elmondorf and Margert Zabriskie-James.
Apr. 20. John Vorhase and Margert Vensant-Nicolas.
May 25. William Wilson and Christena Auten-Marea.
Rynier Veghte and Catherine V. Wagennen-Rynier.
June 1. Michel Van Veghten and Elisabeth Legrange-Dirick.
June 29. Derick Low and Doryty Tennick-Nelly.
Aug. 10. Peter Quick and Altye Peterson-Naltye.
Aug. 17. Bengemen Arysmith and Mary Hont-Mary.
Sept. 21. Garet Tunison and Sara Tenick-Naltye.
Garet Bulmore and Nancey Colyar-Elizebeth.
Peter Low and Hanna Tenick-Andres Tenick.
Hendrick Tunison and Nansey Burck-Sally Lane.
Hendrick Bennet and Jenney Lane-Aron Lane.

Sept. 29.	Bergon Vendornt and Naltye Vorhas-Naltye.
Oct. 12.	George Vrom and Willemtve Vennasdale-Philip.
	Benardes Bennest (Van Nest?) and Catherine Sharp-Elizebeth.
	Whitehead Leonerd and Atche Harrison-Sary Harrison.
Oct. 18.	Black women of widow Middleswart.
	Daughter of Jorge Rolend-Hannah.
1789.	
Feb. 22.	John Miller and Elizebeth Sebring-Thomas.
Apr. 19.	John Durye and Mary Lee-Elizebeth.
Apr. 26.	Abraham Tinnick and Lane Simoson-John Simoson.
	Roeloff Venpelt and Catherine Ten Eyck-Marea.
Apr. 15.	Willit Taylor and Jenney Bogert-Elezebeth.
May 17.	James Tunison and Marget Tomson-Jennet.
May 24.	Coanroad V. Wagnen and Sary Bogert-Garret.
	William Wilson and Christina Auten-William.
June 28.	Jacob V'dorn and Jenney Vorhase-Elezebeth.
	Jacob Vannostrant and Phebe Macdonald-Richard.
July 12.	Cornelius Vmulinder and Elezebeth Middagh-Margret.
July 19.	Jacob V'nest and Anney fasor-Peter.
Aug. 2.	Isaac Harrison and Nancy-John.
	[Mathias Harrison is named with above; reason unknown].
Aug. 30.	Peter Doty and Catherine Pouelson-Sarah.
Sept. 20.	John Stuard and Lydia Dow-Rabacca.
	Isaac Daves and Jane Dunnem-Jane.
1788.	
Jan. 15.	John Hardenbargh and Nancey Wallas-William Wallas.
Sept. 20.	John Hardenbarih and Nancey Wallas-Joshua Maddox.
1789.	
Feb. 15.	Pellep folccardson, and Deborah Tunison-Phillip.
Nov. 14.	Abraham V. nest and Catherine Sebring-Catherine.
Nov. 29.	Folcard Dow and Elezebeth Bedine-Dina.
	Gisbert W. Lane and Rebacca Betron-Rebacca.
Dec. 6.	Powel Auten and Mary Sebring-Catherine.
Dec. 20.	Peter B. Demont and Susannah Middleswart-Tuness.
Dec. 6.	Isaac Brokaw and Mary Boyse-Neeltye.
1790.	
Jan. 24.	Isaac de freese and Kaneerche Wortman-Marea.
Mar. 21.	Peter Daves and Jenney Tennick-Phebe, born Feb. 20.
May 2.	Cristofel Vennasdala and Sarah Ademont-Sarah.
May 9.	Abraham V. Vorhase and Elche Tennick-Jacob.

Mar. 4. Jeames Barger and Annache Vorhase-John.
May 29. Jacob Tennick and Jeane Lain-James.
---- Vrom and Sarah Lain-Jacob.
June 14. ---- and Roxene Fause-Tunis; also John.
Cornelious Tunison and Mary Olward-Henry; also Elezebeth
Henry Post and Margret Cock-Tunis.
Josepth Howel and Catherine Sebring-Roeleff Sebring.
July 25. Coonrand Tennick and Elezebeth Tomson-Hendrick Barge.
Thomas Cooper and Mary Bedine-Cornelious, born May 28, 1785; Jacob, born Nov. 9, 1787; Catheline, born June 7, 1790.
Sept. 26. Wighthead Leonerd and Alche Harrison-John.
Oct. 17. Cornelius Suydam and Anne Rappleye-Phebe, born Sept. 11.
Nov. 28. John Rosebome and Phebe Van Neste-Guysbert, born Sept. 27.
Dec. 19. Joseph Crane and Peggy Van Veghte-Catelina, born Nov. 7. 1791.
Jan. 2. Hendrick Douw and Kezia Johnson-Sarah, born Oct. 10, 1790.
Jan. 30. Michiel Van Veghte and Elizebeth La Granza-Elizebeth Munsenrow (?).
Feb. 6. Borgun Van Doran and Neltie Voorhies-Garet T.
Feb. 27. Benjamin Arrasmith and Polly Hunt-John Hunt.
Mar. 20. Caleb Fulkerson and Deborah Thunison-Margret.
Apr. 3. John Miller and Elezebeth Sebring-Nelly.
Apr. 17. James Wintersteen and Adderantie Van Derbeek-Elezebeth.
David Cox and Rachel Lisk-Dorkas.
Apr. 30. John Borkaw and Arraantie Van Northwick-Simon.
John Van Middlesworth and Hannah Lane-Guysbert Lane.
Andrus Tartisus (Ten Eyck?) and Elizibeth Lagranse-Neltie.
May 22. Corad Teneyck and Sarah Bogart-James Stryker.
May 22. Andrew Van Middelswart and Sarah Bogart-Neltie.
James Hart and Hannah Mapes-Nancy.
John Brokaw and Caty Defrest-Maria.
John Poulison and Sophia Barber-Anna.
Cornelius Thunison and Mary Alwood-Nelly.
Garret Rosebome and Charity Compton-Garret.
May 29. Abraham Van Neste and Caty Sebring-Jane.
William Parish and Elizebeth Beekman-Phebe.
June 12. ---- Clark and Elizebeth Sebring-Sarah.
Paul Galtrie and Elizebeth Morphet-Margret.
June 19. Peter Wortman, Jun. and Anne Field-Mary Field.

July 3. Abraham Ten Eyck and Lena Swaison (?)-Jeremiah Field.
Burgun Borkaw and Hendrick Buys [evidently an error]-Isaac.
July 17. Robert Bolmore and Mary Allen-Abraham.
July 31. John Sebring and Maria Wintersteen-John.
July 31. Peter Rosebome and Catherine Van Arsdalen-Catherine.
Aug. 21. Garret Thunison and Sara Ten Eyck-Matthew Teneyck.
Peter Miller and Sophia Pane-Margret.
Aug. 28. John Hardenbergh, Esq., and Ann Wallace-Ann Wallace.
Sept. 11 . Isaac Davis, Esq., and Jane Dunn-Cathrine.
Sept. 18 . Cornelius Ver Mulener and Elizebeth Middagh-Fredrick.
Oct. 9. John Ten Eyck and Dorkis Lish (?)-John, born July 17.
Jacob Van Neste and Anne Frasher-John, born Aug. 21.
Joshw Borkaw and Caty Borkaw-John, born Aug. 22.
John Smith and Caty Hortwack-John Hardenbergh.
Isaac Harrison and Anne ---- - Hester.
John Stuard and Lidia Douw-Lidia, born July 2.
Oct. 30. Wallet Taylor and Jane Bogart-John, born Sept. 24.
Nov. 20. Rev. John Duryee and Mary Lee-Jane Lee, born Oct. 27.
Isaac Defrest and Knerchie Wortman-Dinah.

1791.

Nov. 27. Van Neste, Peter and Phebe Borkaw-Mary, born Oct. 30.

1792.

Jan. 15. Douw, Hendrich and Keziah Johnson-Phebe Borkaw, born Sept. 12, 1791.
Jan. 29. Vroom, Peter D. and Elsie Bogert-Peter Dumont, born Dec. 12, 1791.
Auter, Paul and Mary Sebrint-Folkert.
Jan. 30. Dumont, Peter B. and Susannah Van Middelswart-Jane, born Dec. 1, 1791.
Feb. 19. Van Louw, Frederick and Garretie Ten Eyck (deceast)-Jeremiah, born Jan. 25, 1792.
Van Nostrant, John and Margret Handkerson-Mary Mattax.
Apr. 1. Van Pelt, Rulif and Caty Ten Eyck-Andrew Ten Eyck.
Hatt, John and Mary Stout-Benijah.
Apr. 6. Hammersly, Susannah Brierson (wife of Abraham)-Elezebeth.
Apr. 17. Molener, Leah Mac Collum (wife of Phililp)-Mary Mac Collum; also John.
Arrasmith, Benjamin and Mary Hunt-John.
May 11. Low, Derick and Dority Ten Eyck-Anne Van Derveer.
Quick, Peter and Altie Peterson-Maria.

June 17. Voorhees, John and Peggy Van Sant-Gashey.
Smith, Frankey Sebring (wife of John).
Aug. 8. Low, Hannah Ten Eyck (wife of Peter)-Rebechah.
July 1. Van Arsdalen, Christoffer and Sarah Dumont-Hendrick.
Douw, Folkert and Elezebeth Bodine-Lidia, born June 14, 1792.
July 8. Borkaw, Burgun-Peter.
Aug. 5. Drake, Derick and Sarah Messlaer-Elezebeth.
Aug. 11. Hegamon, Adrian and Elezebeth Hegamon-Jane.
Aug. 12. Brown, Jacob and Sophia Galtrie-Jacob.
Galtrie, Thomas and Elezebeth Cole-James.
Aug. 19. Borkaw, Isaac and Mary Buys-Isaac, born July 26, 1792.
Ten Eyck, Andries Tartitus and Elezebeth Lagrange(?)-Caty.
Willemson, Arth and Nelly Van Middelswart-Sally.
Thunison, Hendrick and Nancy Burck-Mary Fulkerson.
Sept. 30 . Lott, John and Mary Young-Mary, born July 24, 1792.
Borkaw, Derick and Jane Ove-Isaac.
Oct. 7. Voorhees, James and Fransaje Vroom-James.
Oct. 27. Compton, Richard and Arriantic Thunison-Jane Brower, born May 16, 1792.
Nov. 22. Berger, James and Nancy Voorhees-Zaccheus, born Oct. 1, 1792.
Dec. 9. Leonard, Whitehead and Altie Arrison-Elener Field.
Dec. 30. Lisk, David and Mary Van Derhoof-Margret, born Nov. 24, 1792.

1793.
Jan. 1. Thunison, Abraham and Abigail Wortman-Hardenbergh.
Feb. 5. Galtrie, Albert and Amme Van Tuyl-Peggy, born Nov. 26, 1792.
Feb. 10. Hardenbergh, John and Anne Walace-Hans(?) Van Bergh.
Wortman, Peter and Anne Field-Sarah, born Dec. 21, 1792.
Mar. 7. Davis, Peter and Jane Ten Eyck-Theodorus Romyn, born Jan. 21, 1793.
Mar. 30. Vroom, Hendrick and Sarah Lane-Sarah.
Apr. 7. Van Neste, Abraham and Caty Sebring-Elezebeth and Simon.
Apr. 21. Voorhees, Abraham and Elsie Ten Eyck-Cornelius.
Dumont, Albert and Cornelia Hogeland-John.
Cox, David and Rebeccha Cox-Jane Taylor.
May 11. Van Veghte, Michael and Elezebeth La Gransie-Sarah.
Roseboom, Peter and Caty Van Arsdalen-Gertry.

May 12. Arrasmith, Benjaman and Mary Hunt-Jane.
Galtrie, Paul and Elezebeth Morphet-Anna.
June 9. Crane, Margreth Van Veghte (wife of Joseph)-Elezebeth Van Veghte.
Stuart (?) Lidia Douw (wife of John)-Jane.
Borkaw, Abraham and Phebe Rappelyea-Anne.
June 16. Douw, Hendrick and Caziah Johnson-Margret.
Suydam, Cornelius and Anne Rappelyea-Mariah.
Aug. 18. Hart, James and Hannah Mapes-Peter Dumont.
Sept. 8. Sebring, John, Jr., and Maria Winterseen-Arrantie.
Sept. 15. Webster, James and Rebeccah Thunison-Anne, born Aug. 3.
Ten Eyck, Abraham and Lanah Symonson-Catherine.
Oct. 12. Van Middelswarth, Andrew and Sarah Bogert-Andrew, born Sept. 22.
Hartwick, Caty (wife of Johnersen?)-Laurance.
Nov. 10. Bogert, Jacob and Mary Borkaw-Peter Borkaw.
Nov. 17. Van Doren, Jacob and Jane Voorhees-Gitthrud Coynman.
Auter, Peter and Hannah ---- -Anne.
Dec. 15. Cowenhoven, Peter and Sarah McDonel-Elezebeth, born Oct. 12.
Vermiilen, Cornelius and Elezebeth Middagh-Isaac Davis.

1794.

Jan. 5. Van Wagenen, Conrad and Sarah Bogert-Huybert, born Nov. 11.
Clyn, David and Mary Harriot-David Harriot.
Sebring, Folkert and Mary Sebring-Ellanor, born Nov. 28.
Jan. 26. Dumont, John and Mary Polyea-Rebecha, born Dec. 21, 1793.
Miller, John and Elezebeth Sebring-Margret, born Dec. 18.
Mar. 16. Dumont, Peter B. and Susannah Van Middleswarth-Mary.
Apr. 20. Defrist, Isaac and Anertie Wortman-John.
Van Neste, Jacob and Anne Fasher-Christian Fasher.
Apr. 27. Berger, James and Nancy Voorhees-Jane, born Mar. 13, 1794.
Van Nostrant, John and Margret Handkerson-Nancy Hardenbergh.
May 11. Auten, John and Mary Sebring-Mary.
Van Dyck, Cornelius and Mary Borkaw-Cornelius.
May 28. Demarest, Nicolas and Mary Banta (Warwick)-Samuel, born Feb. 11, 1794.
Vanhotiten, Isaac and Mary Pott-Jacob, born Oct. 30, 1794 (sic).

Demarest, Cornelius and Elezebeth Whortendyk-Sarah, born Apr. 19, 1794.
Post, Gerret and Martentie Bartolf-Elezebeth, born Feb. 3, 1794.
Teneyck, John and Dorkas Lisk (Warwick)-Mary, born Mar. 28, 1794.
July 6. Borkaw, Burgon and Hindic Buys (sic)-Mary.
July 6. Borkaw, Casparus and Caty Borkaw-Anne, born Apr. 23, 1794.
July 27. Borkaw, John and Caty Defrest-Antie, born May 1, 1794.
Aug. 3. Borkaw, Abraham and Mary Stryker-Jane, born July 6, 1794.
Aug. 10. Vanarsdalen, Philip H. and Sarah Wortman-Elezebeth, born June 12, 1794.
Smith, William and Sarah Bird-Gaster(?), born June 7, 1794.
Lane, Mathew and Maria Johnson-Maria.
Drake, Derick and Sara Messlaar-Maria.
Low, Derick and Dorty Ten Eyck-Peter Ten Eyck.
Quick, John and Lena Van Neste-Margret, born July 28, 1794.
Oct. 30. Davis, Isaac and Jane Dunnam.
Nov. 2. Hageman, Adrian and Elezebeth Hageman.
Nov. 17. Van Middelsworth, Thomas and Rebecka Brobasho.
Nov. 30. Berger, Jacob and Mary Borkaw.
Van Arsdalen, Christpher and Sarah Dumont.
Dec. 28. Thunison, John and Elezebeth Miller.
Dunn, Nelly Van Pelt (wife of Jonathan).

1795.
Feb. 8. Borkaw, Borgun and Jane Suydam.
Feb. 12. Howel, Joseph and Caty Sebring.
Mar. 1. Wortman, Peter and Anne Field.
Mar. 29. Thunison, Abraham and Abigal Wortman-Philip, born Jan. 18, 1795.
Apr. 19. Taylor, Willet and Jane Bogert-Benjamin; also Cornelius.
Apr. 26. Ten Eyck, Andrew Tartus and Elezebeth Lagrave(?)-Susanna Dumont.
Smith, Franky Sebring (wife of John)-Thomas, born Apr. 16, 1795.
June 7. Van Neste, Abraham and Caty Sebring-John Elmendorf.
June 21. Stuard, Lidia (wife of John)-Sarah Drake.
Van Devere, Cornelius and Anne Van Devere-Rebecka.
July 19. Voorhees, Abraham and Rebecah Perry-Jacob Ten Eyck, born

June 7, 1795.

Aug. 16. Van Neste, Rynier and Anne Borkaw-George, born July 13, 1795.

Quick Peter and Anne Peterson-Peter Peterson, born June 17, 1795.

Aug. 30. Borkaw, Borgun and Altic Post-Cornelius Stryker.

Van Neste, Peter and Phebe Borkaw-George.

Dumont, Albert and Cornelia Hogeland-William.

Codmas, Derick and Percilla Elston (not baptized)-Andrew. Witness: Deborah Codmas.

Sept. 6. Van Doren, Borgun and Nelly Voorhees-Peter.

Sept. 20. Vroom, Hendrick and Sarah Lane-Elezebeth, born Aug. 6.

Oct. 25. Brown, James and Deborah Van Duyn-Cathrine, born Sept. 15.

Nov. 14. Ten Eyck, Jacob and Anne Prine-Cathrine, born Oct. 17.

Roseboom, Peter and Caty Vanarsdalen-Mary Dumont.

Van Nostrant, Jacob and Phebe Mac Donald-Jane Van Stay.

Dec. 25. Thunison, Garret and Sarah Ten Eyck-Garret.

1796.

Jan. 3. Voorhees, Abraham and Elshe Ten Eyck-Abraham, born Nov. 25, 1795.

Jan. 31. Van Veghte, Machiel and Elezebeth Lagrange-Mary Lagrange, born Dec. 25.

Sebring, John and Mary Winterstein-James Winterstein.

Feb. 7. Vermulen, Corenlius and Elizabeth Middagh-Judith Middagh.

Feb. 21. Van Middleswarth, Andrew and Sarah Bogert-Sarah, born Dec. 18.

Harris, Israel and Altic Schenk-Hendrick Schenk, born Dec. 6.

April 3. Ten Eyck, Abraham and Lena Simonson-John, born Mar. 6, 1796.

Mar. 13. Van Leuwen, Fridrich and Idow Perine- Janitye, born Feb 1, 1796.

April 5. Mollenar, Philip and Lena Betron-Sara Betron.

April 12. Smock, George and Peggy Van Devanter-Jacob.

April 23. Voorhees, John and Altie Wortman-Jacobus, born Mar. 11, 1796.

Davis, Peter and Jane Ten Eyck-Cathrine, born Mar. 15, 1796.

April 24. Van Pelt, Rulif and Caty Ten Eyck-Jane White.

May 29. Auter, Paul and Polly Sebring-Jacobus Van Dyn.

June 12. Douw, Folkert and Polly Bordine-Judith.

Stull, John and Sarah Carroll-Ann.
Roseboom, John and Caty Van Arsdalen-Mary.
July 11. Borkaw, John and Mary Van Nothwick-Johanas.
July 31. Howel, Joseph and Caty Sebring-David.
Dehart, John and Hannah Mapes-Hannah Van Middlesworth.
Aug. 14. Dumont, Peter B. and Susannah Van Middlesworth-Antie Van Duyn.
Cook, William and Mary Van Wagonen-Isaac, born Mar. 3.
Aug. 28. Crane, Joseph and Margret Van Veghte-John.
Sept. 25. Borkaw, Christopher and Caty Borkaw-David, born Aug. 19, 1796.

1797.
Jan. 8. Douw, Henry and Keziah Johnson-Cathrine Duryee.
Jan. 13. Taylor, Willet and Jane Bogert-Mary.
Feb. 12. Beekman, Cornelius and Rebecah Sharp-Sarah.
Mar. 11. Rosekrans, Alexander and Mary Wortman-Peter, born Mar. 3, 1795.
Van Dyke, Cornelius and Mary Borkaw-Benjamin.
May 7. Teneyck, Matthew-Thunis Coock.
Borkaw, John and Caty Deforest-Nancy Van Dyn, born Mar. 3.
May 26. Bergen, James and Ann Voorhees-Jane, born Apr. 12.
Ten Eyck, John - Peter, born, Mar. 28.
July 2. Douw, John and Catherine Van Neste-Catherine.
Drake, Derick and Sarah Messelaar-Matilda.
July 23. Van Neste, John P. and Fanny Smith-Elezebeth, born June 17.
Voorhees, Abraham-Marthin.
Brown, James and Deborah Van Dyn-Ann.
Huff, Dennis and Elizabeth Prine-Eliner, born Mar. 25.
July 30. Van Arsdalen, Christopher and Sarah Dumont-Antie.
Aug. 27. Dumont, Albert and Caty Hogeland-Albert Stothuff.
Spader, Abraham and Mary Quick-William.
Montanyae, William and Sarah Clawson-Hannah.
Bennet, John and Jane Van Middelsworth-Jane De Camp.

1798.
Jan. 14. Whiteknegh t, John and Charity Striker-John.
Smock, George and Peggy Van Deventer-Garret.
Cooper, Isaac and Leanah Whitehead-Abraham.
Jan. 28. Voorhees, John and Ally Worttnan-Mary.
Hogeland, Christopher and Sarah Wicoff-Lucas Voorhees.

Feb. 4. Van Nostrand, Jacob and Phebe McDonald-Sarah Cowenhoum.
Cock, David and Rachel Cock-Mariah born Jan. 4, 1798.
Rosekrans Alexander and Caty Wortman-Cathrine Van Neste.
Thunison, John and Elezebeth Miller-Thomas.
April 8. Sebring, Fulkert and ---- Harrison-Cornelius.
April 28. Van Leuw, Frederick and Ida Prine-Daniel Prine.
Howel, Andrew and Maria Hardenbergh-Ann Maria Wallace, born Nov. 23, 1798.
Borkaw, Isaac and Lena Van Leuw-Cornelius.
June 10. Beekman, Martin and Matilda Borkaw-Peter.
July 22. Van Doron, Burgun and Nelly Voorhees-Cathrine.
Aug. 12. Voorhees, John and Margret Van Sant-Hendrick, born May 5, 1798.
Aug. 19. Mollener, Philip and Magdalen McCollem-Elezebeth Ten Eyck, born July 23.
Cojeman, Andrew and Jane Van Doren-Samuel Staats, born June 11.
Sept. 2. Ten Eyck, Abraham and Lena Simonson-Abraham.
Sept. 23. Webster, James and Rebecka Thunison-Margaret, born June 20.
Oct. 14. Sebring, John and Mary Winterstein-Nelly.
Van Neste, Jacob and Anne Fraser-Jacob.
Nov. 11. Van Veghte, Michael and Elezebeth Lagrans-Margret (?).
Dec. 29. Van Middlesworth, Thunis and Rebecah Brobasgo-Mary Ditmass.
Van Duyn, James-Styntie.

1799.
No dates. Welsh, John and Jaine Todd-William Wolsh, born Aug. 26, 1799.
Montenye, William and Sarah Clauson-William Montony, born Mar. 6.
Spader, Abraham and Mary Quick-Elisebeth Wortman, born July 10.
Dumon, John and Mary Perlee-Abraham, born June 15.
Taylor, Willet and Jaine Bogart-Gilbert Bogart, born June 2.
Davis, Peter and Nancy Welien-Jaine Davis, born Dec. 8.
Bergen, James and Hannah Voorhese-James Bergen, born Aug. 30.
Brokaw, John and Ariant V. Notwick-Metie Brokaw, born

	July 5.
	Whiteknaght, John and Gertrude Stryker-Abraham, born Sept. 20.
	V. Arsdalen, Christopher and Sarah Dumon-Chaterine, born Oct. 20.
1800.	
----	Dumon, Abraham and Judith Davis-Sarah, born Apr. 5.
July 6.	Rosekrants, Alexander and Mary Wortman-Ann.
	Van Devanter, Cornelius and Susan Talmage-James.
July 13.	Van Dervere, Henry and Ellenor Sutfin-Ferdinand.
July 20.	Covert, Lucas and Mary Post-Peter Post.
Aug. 3.	Voorhees, John and Letty Wortman-John Wortman.
	Rosebome, Gilbert and Ann Brokaw-Benjamin Brokaw.
Aug. 24.	Cojeman, Andrew and Jane V. Doren-Jacob V. Doren.
	Crane, Joseph and Margaret V. Veghten-Michael V. Veghten.
Sept. 7.	Howel, Andrew and Mary Maddox Hardenburgh-Josiah Burt.
	Beekman, Martin and Matte Brokaw-Elizabeth.
	Davis, Peter, Jr., and Nancy Welling-Thomas Welling.
Nov. 30.	Cooper, Isaac and Lana Whitehead-Maria.

READINGTON CHURCH BAPTISMS FROM 1720

The introduction and records begin in Volume IV (1915) of the Quarterly, page 142.

[Note.-The Readington Reformed Church, formerly known as "The Church over the North Branch," and the "North Branch Reformed Dutch Church," was organized in 1717, or 1718, and began separate worship in a log building Feb. 21, 1719-20, located nearly opposite to the then residence of Andrew Ten Eyck (recently that of the late Mr. John Vosseller), its first pastor being the Rev. Theodorus J. Frelinghuysen. It was at this period collegiate with three other churches, Raritan, Six-Mile Run and Three-Mile Run. In 1739 the building was abandoned for a new frame building erected at Readington, about three miles west of the former site. This latter building was used for ninety-four years, or until 1833, when another church was built, and stood until 1864, at which time it was accidentally burned down. The present church building dates from 1865. The pastors have been as follows: Rev. T. J. Frelinghuysen, 1720-'48; Rev. John Frelinghuysen, 1750-'54; Rev. Dr. Jacob R. Hardenbergh, 1758-81; Rev. Simeon Van Arsdalen, 1783-87; Rev. Peter Studdiford, 1787-1826; Rev. Dr. John Van Liew, 1828-69; Rev. Dr. J. G. Van Slyke, 1869-'70; Rev. John H. Smock, 1871-'83; Rev. B. V. D. Wyckoff, 1884 to present. The early baptismal records of the church were admirably kept and in an excellent handwriting, believed to have been that of Elbert Stothoff. The record now given is from the copy made by the present pastor, Rev. Mr. Wyckoff, by whose courtesy we are enabled to publish it. -Editor, *Quarterly*.]

1720.

Feb. 21. Ten Eyk, Andries and Adriaentje-Mattheus.
Witness: Jacob Ten Eyk.

Apr. 9. DuBois, Abraham and Maria-Margarietje.
Witness: Andries Ten Eyk.

Pursel, John and Henah-Thomas.
Witnesses: Jacob Sebring and Ceitjen Van Neste.

Chrison, Josua and Catharina-Aaltje.
Witnesses: Daniel Sebring and Catharina, his wife.

Hendericksen, Jan and Weyntje-Jennekc.
Witnesses: Koenraed Ten Eyck and Catheryntje, his wife.

Oct. 2. Van Veghten, Dirck and Barbara-Margrietje.
Witnesses: Michael Van Vegten and Jannetje, his wife.

MacDowal, Alexander and Margaret-George.
Witnesses: Benjamin Burt and Henah Hall.

Oct. 30. Van Sickelen, Jan and Lena-Johannes.
Witnesses: Coert Jansen and Geertje, his wife.
Stol, Jacob and Annatje-Hendericus.
Witnesses: Teunis Middleswaert and Susanna, his wife.
Hall. George and Oetje-Mary.
Witnesses: Albert Lou and Susanna, his wife.
Nov. 27. Rosa, William and Elizabeth-Elizabeth.,
Dec. 26. Butner, Paulus and Elizabeth-Thomas.
1721.
Mar. 19. Schermerhoorn, Lucas and Elizabeth-Sara.
Van Neste, Pieter and Magdalena-Jacob.
Krom, William and Weintje-Neeltje.
Apr. 14. Lou, Cornelius and Judick-Marytje.
Witnesses: Albert Lou and Susanna, his wife.
Cock, John and Geertruy-Catherina.
Witnesses: Joris Van Neste and Marytje, his wife.
Lou, Jan and Jannetje-Weintje.
Witnesses: Emanuel Van Etten and Ceitjen Van Neste.
May 18. Moor, Michael and Elizabeth-Christiaen.
Witnesses: Johannes Grau and Antje, his wife.
Nov. 5. Pursle, John and Henah-John,.
Witness: Cere Doot.
Dec. 3. Jansen, Coert and Geertje-Adriaen.
Clothry, Casper and Jannetje-Paulus.
Witnesses: Daniel ----; Antje Van Etten.
Du Bois, Abraham and Maria-Maria.
Witness: --- Dubois.
Emmens, John and Rachel-Nicholaes.
V. Neste, Henderik and Avice-Neeltje.
V. Middleswaert, Theunis and Susanna-Theunis.
Witnesses: Jacob Stol and Annatje, his wife.
1722.
Mar. 25. Dildein, Georg and Christiana-Elizabeth.
Apr. 29. Reading, John and Marritje-Johannee.
Van Neste, Jan and Gerritje-Jan.
May 20. Van Vliedt, Gerrit and Judick-Dirck.
Ten Eyk, Andries and Adriaentje-Janneke.
Witness: Coenraed Ten Eyk.
Aug. 17. Roseboom, Henderick and Debora-Gerrit.
Sept. 23. Van Sickelen, Cornelius and Mary-Marytje.

Witnesses: David Cussard and Christina, his wife.
Oct. 21. Aersen, Jan and Barbara-Mattheus.
Witnesses: Ouke Jansen and Catherina, his wife.
Nov. 17. ten Eyk, Coenraed and Catherintje-Cathereintje.
Witness: Jeronimus Van Neste.
Dec. 16. Clasen, Johannes and Elizabeth-Elizabeth.
Witnesses: Jacob Sebring and Adriaentje Jansen.
Waldron, Frans and Cathelina-Elizabeth.
Witnesses: Henderick Van Neste and Avice, his wife.
Botner, Paulus and Elizabeth-Catherina..
Witnesses: Jan Lou and Catherina Corsen.

1723.

Jan. -. Peter, Godfried and Anna Margretha-Philip.
Witnesses: Philip Peter and Anna Kinnianta, his wife.
Mar. 3. Van Etten, Emanuel and Antje-Samuel.
Lou, Cornelius and Judick-Cathelyntie.
Witnesses: Adriaen Aten and Jacobje, his wife.
Moor, Michael and Elizabeth-Johannis.
Witnesses: Johannis Lucas and Elizabeth, his wife.
Van Sickelen, Jan and Lena-Abrabam.
Witnesses: Reinier V. Sickelen and Henah, his wife.
Mar. 31. Rosa, William and Elizabeth-Jan.
May 23. Cock, Johanes and Antje-Annatje.
Witness: Margrietje V: Neste.
June 16. Subair [Joubert?), David and Elizabeth-Susanna.
July 21. Reading, John and Marritje-Anne.
Aug. 18. Bodyn, Isaac and Engeltje-Jacob.
Witnesses: Jacob Ten Eyk and Jacomyntje, his wife.
Lou, Jan and Jannetje-Metje.
Witnesses: Paulus Butner and Catherina Corsen.
Sept. 15. Broca, Abraham and Maria-Abrabain.
Witnesses: Isaac Bodyn and Engeltje, his wife.
Cock, John and Geertruy-Anne.
Nov. 17. V: Sickelen, Reinier and Henah-Reinier.
Dec. 13. V: Middleswaert, Theunis and Susanna-Abrabam.
Witness: Peterneeltje Boogaert.

1724.

Jan. 26. Van Neste, Pieter and Maria-Joris.
Mar. 1. Pursle, John and Henah-Styntje.
May 3. Clothry, Casper and Jannetje-Magdalena.

Jager, Peter and Catherina-Anna Maria.
May 24. Dearch, Robert and Mary-Coy.
Sept. 13. Pauwelse, Cornelius and Jannetje-Hendrick.
Van Neste, Pieter and Magdalena-Catherina.
Witnesses: Jacob Stol and Annatje, his wife.
Nov. 8. Middagh, Cornelius and Ike-Blandina.
Witnesses: Adriaen Aten and Jacobje, his wife.
1725.
--- 21. Buttner, Paulus and Elizabeth-Jannetje.
Witness: Antje Van Etten.
Cock, Johannis and Antje-Maria.
Ten Eyk, Andries and Adriaentje-Petrus.
Mar. 21. Reading, John and Marritie-George.
May 16. Emmens, Nicholaes and Ceitjen-Rebecca.
June 13. Van, Neste, Pieter and Magdalena-Johannes.
July 18. Van Neste, Pieter and Maria-Hendericus.
Nov. 14. Lou, Cornelius and Judick-Gysbert.
V: Neste, Jeronimus and Susanna-Petrus.
Visher, Pieter and Maria-Anthoy.
1726.
Jan. 23. Broca, Abraham and Maria-Joris.
Mar. 20. Jager, Peter and Catherina-Hendrick.
May 19. Van Etten, Emanuel and Antje-Benjamin.
Oct. 2. Bogaert, Cornelius and Cornela-Nathaniel.
Bries, Hendrick and Antje-Hanna.
Pursle, John and Henah-Margareth.
Oct. 30. V: Middleswaert, Theunis and Susanna-Annatje.
Dec. 26. Botner, Paulus and Elizabeth-Elizabeth.
1727.
Jan. 22. Van Neste, Jeronimus and Susanna-Johannes.
Allen, Ananias and Henah-Jonathan.
Mar. 19. Van Neste, Pieter and Magdalena-Antje.
Reading, John and Marritje-Daniel.
Wimmer, Johannes and Weintje-Johannes.
Witnesses: Barent Simonsen and Apolonia, his wife.
Ten Eyk, Andries and Adriaentje-Andries.
Apr. 16. Vischer, Pieter and Anna Mari-Johan Wilhelm.
Aug. 6. Van Neste, Jan and Marytje-Isaac.
Van Neste, Pieter and Magdalena-Joris.
Sept. 3. Emmens, Nicholaes and Ceitjen-Abraham.

Bodyn, Isaac and Engeltje-Petrus.
Oct. 5. Pursle, Daniel and Elisabeth-Jan and Elisabeth.
Laurents, Georg William and Maria-Elizabeth.
Dec. 3. Van Neste, Pieter and Maria-Pieter.
Lou, Cornelius and Judick-Cornelius.
Witnesses: Cornelius Middagh and Eyke, his wife.
1728.
Jan. 28. ten Eyk, Jacob and Jacomyntje-Janneke.
Hoogland, Hendrick and Anne-Jan.
Witness: Dirck Hoogland.
Feb. 25. Vanderbeek, Burger and Annetje-Wilhelmyntie.
Witnesses: Lourens Kinne and Catherine, his wife.
Jaager, Pieter and Catherina-Elizabeth.
Aten, Adriaen and Jacobje-Marytje. [Inserted by another hand: "Wife, Jacobje Middagh, born. Oct. 24, 1693, according to family records"].
Witnesses: Cornelius Lou and Judick, his wife.
Mar. 24. De wit, Paulus and Catherina-Paulus.
Apr. 20. Subair (Joubert?), David and Elisabeth-Elisabeth.
Aug. 11. Ten Eyk, Coenraed and Catherientje-Coenraed.
Nov. 17. Van Stuck, Johan Diederik and Margaretha-Andries.
1729.
Jan. 1. Van Dyk, Hendrik and Margrietje-Jannetje
Reading, John and Marritje-Joseph.
Wimmer, Johannes and Weintje-Maria.
Apr. 20. Cock, Johannis and Annaatje-Jacobus.
Witnesses: Jacob Goewee and Cathereintje, his wife.
Woertman, Andries and Jannetje-Theunis.
Feb. 1. Woertman, Jan Everse Bouth and Beelitje-Jan.
June 8. V:Aersdaalen, Philip and Jannetje-Hendrick.
Vischer, Peter and Anna Maria-Elizabeth.
Lourens, Georg Willen and Mary Keth-Johan Willem.
1730.
May 24. Barculo, Jaques and Jannetje-Barent.
June 21. Pickeltzinier, Johannis and Maragretha-Abraham.
Witnesses: Abraham De la Mater and Sara, his wife.
Aug. 2. Clason, Isaiah and Elizabeth-Elizabeth.
Van Neste, Pieter and Magdalena-Elizabeth.
Aug. 29. Aten, Adriaen and Jacobje-Cathelina.
Witnesses: Cornelius Middagh and Eyke, his wife.

Dec. 20. Ten Eyk, Jacob and Jacomyntje-Annatje.
Bethy, Thomas and Maria-Charles.

1731.

Jan. 31. V:Dyk, Hendrick and Maragrietje-Domenecus.
Emans, Johannis and Theuntje-Jan.
Reading, John and Marritje-Elizabeth.
Harney, Walter and Elizabeth-Mary.

Feb. 28. Van Aersdaalen, Jan and Jannetje-Johannis.
Butner, Adam and Elizabeth-Elizabeth.

Mar. 28. Warfoot, Job and Sara-Elizabeth.
Witnesses: Abraham d'la Meter and Sara, his wife.
Butner, Paulus and Elizabeth-Metje.
Witnesses: Jacob Corsen and Adriaentje, his wife.
Lourens, Georg and Martje-Adam.
Eyk, Georg and Anna Eva-Georg.
Hansen, Johannis and Neeltje-Elizabeth.

Oct. 10. Traphagen, Roelof and Cornelia-Hendrick.
Van Etten, Jacobus and Elizabeth-Samuel.
Van Hoorn, Abraham and Antje-Abraham.

Nov. 7. Snyder, Christoffel and ---- -Elizabeth.
Witnesses: Lodewyk Smit and Elizabeth Smit.

1732.

Jan. 1. Barculo, Jaques and Jannetje-Jaques.
V: Aersdaalen, Philip and Jannetye-Maria.

Jan. 30. V:Schaak, Nicholas and Marytje-Annatje.

Mar. 26. Haff, Lourens and Marritje-Picter.
Loth, Abraham and Peternelletje-Geertje.
Jansen, Petrus and Catherina-Catherina.
Witnesses: Myndert Jansen and Catherina, his wife.

Apr. 23. d'la Montagne, Joseph and Marytje-Abraham.
Butnaer, Adam and Elizabeth-Catrina Lea.
Rounseval, Richard and Rebecca-Henry.

May 10. Emans, Nicholaes and Ceitjen-Neeltje.

June 11. Hoogland, Cornelius and Lena-Cornelius.
Witness: Neeltje Kinne.
Middagh, Pieter and Marritje-Gerrit.
Vroom, Christiaen and Debora-Catherina.
Corsen, Jacob and Adriaentie-Geertruy.
Witness: Elizabeth.
Aten, Jan and Lybetje-Antje.

Sept. 7. Losie, John and ___ -Cornelius.
Ten Eyk, Andries and Adriaentje-Johannis.
Oct. 15. Cock, Johannis and Antie-Cornelius Bouman.
Witnesses: Cornelius Jorisse Bouman and Antje, his wife.
1733.
Jan. 7. Brouwer, Jurrie and Elizabeth-Jurrie.
Kinne, Jacobus and Neeltje-Jacobus.
Emans, Johannes and Theuntje-Anna.
Feb. 4. Aten, Adriaen and Jacobje-Jan and Geradus.
Witnesses: Dirck De Moth and Christina, his wife.
Lou, Cornelius and Judick-Jan.
Witnesses: Theunis Middagh and Neeltje Lammersen.
Reading, John and Marritje-Richard.
Mar. 4. Van Neste, Pieter and Margrietje-Judick.
Apr. 1. Warfoot, Job and Sara-Abraham.
Van der Bilt, Jacob and Neeltje-Jacob.
Witnesses: Abraham Van Hoorn and Antje, his wife.
May 13. Dircksen, Folkert and Dina-Johannes.
Gulick, Dirck and Geertje-Hendrick.
Witness: Cathelyntje Gulick.
June 10. Lourens, Georg Willem and Maria Catherina-Georg.
Witnesses: Jacob Eyk and Elsje.
Tieds, Christiaen and Eva-Antje.
Witnesses: Johannis Hof and Else Maria.
Engel, Jacob and Elizabeth-Willem.
Witnesses: Willem Engel and Eva, his wife.
Hobbach, Hendrick and Geertje-Pieter.
Witnesses: Pieter Hobbach and Marytje, his wife.
July 8. Amerman, Dirck and Leena-Albert.
Witnesses: Albert Amerman and Frances, his wife.
Aug. 5. Van Etten, Jacobus and Elizabeth-Margriet.
Sept. 9. Aten, Paulus and Marytjen-Marytje.
Oct. 7. Jewel, William and Catherina-Cornelia.
Nov. 11. Ten Eyk, Jacob and Jacomyntje-Jacob.
Robert, Vincent and Annatje-Antje.
Botner, Paulus and Elizabeth-Maria.
Van Neste, Pieter and Magdalena-Jan.
Dec. 9. Jansen, Myndert and Catherientje-Annatje.
Jansen, Hendrick and Catryn--Abraham.
Witnesses: Jan Jansen and Geertje Kortreght.

Polemus, Daniel and Margrietje-Johannis.

1734.

Feb. 17. Haff, Lourens and Marritje-Abraham.

Mar. 17. Vander Veer, Jacob and Femmetje-Joseph.

J----, W---- and Catherientje d. lameter-Catherientje.

Witness: Abraham d- la Meter.

Scherfenstein, Matthys and Anna Geertruy-Johan George.

Witnesses: Johan Georg Eyk, Jacob Eyk and Eva Thomasse.

Mar. 17.Vroom, Christiaen and Debora-Neeltje.

Witness: Neeltje Simonsen.

Apr. 14. Riemer, Pieter and Wyntje-Petrus.

Witness: Catherina Riemer.

V:Aersdaalen, Simon and Antje-Maria.

V:Aersdaalen, Philip and Jannetje-Isaac.

Berculo, Jaques and Jannetje-Jan.

Jansen, Petrtis and Cathrina-Willem.

polhemus, Hendrick and Margrietje-Neeltje.

Van Hoorn, Abraham and Antje-Neeltje.

Witnesses: Jacob Van der Bilt and Neeltje, his wife.

Hall, George and Blandina-Anne.

May 12. Biggs, George and Lena-Jan.

Klyn, Heriiianus and ---- -Hermanus.

Witnesses: Pieter Tills and Eva, his wife.

De wit, Paulus and Cathrina-Petrus.

Middagh, Pieter and Marritje Middagh-Cathelyntje.

Woertman, Andries and Jannetje-Elizabeth.

Witness: Elizabeth Post.

V: der Veer, Hendrick and Antje-Jan.

June 9. Monfoort, Pieter and Margrietje-Jacobus.

Aug. 4. Kinne, Adriaen and Kniertje-Pieter.

Brouwer, Pieter and Susanna-Abraham.

Witness: Elizabeth Titsoort.

Hobbach, Teunis and Antie-Johan Georg.

Witnesses: Johan Georg and Anna Maria.

Hansel, Johannis and Neeltje-Johannis.

Sept. 1. Pittenger, Daniel and Elisabetti-Elizabeth.

Pieterse, Harpert and Antje-Roelof.

Nov. 3. Dumon, Jan and Annatje-Petrtis.

Nov. 3. Selover, Daniel and Leena-Isaac.

Witness: Maria Schermerhoorn.

Bodyn, Frederick and Saartje Bodyn-Saartje.
Reading, John and Marritje-Thomas.
Dec. 1. Hall, Henry and Neeltje-George.
1735.
Jan. 12. Loth, Abraham and Pieterneltje-Aeltje.
Mar. 9. Van Aersdaalen, Jan and Jannetje-Jannetje.
Van der Bilt, Jacob and Neeltje-Yda.
Apr. 6. Amerman Nicholaes and Neeltje-Neeltje.
Witness: Neeltje Polhemus.
Apr. 7. Post, Theunis and Annatje-Annatje.
May 4. Beekman, Pieter and Neeltie-Helena.
Witness: Antje Stot.
Mesacre, Evert and Lena-Isaac.(Born 8 Jan., 1735).
June 1. Wykhof, Nicholaes and Marytje-Annatje.
June 20. Riemer, Pieter and Weintje-Weintje.
Aug. 3. Aten, Adriaen and Jacobje-Judick. [Born July 9, 1735. Married Joseph Morehead. Had 4 children. Died July 22, 1819].
Lou, Cornelius and Judick-Gerrit.
Witness: Joris Middagh.
Beekman, Marten and Elizabeth-Annatje.
Witness:: Susanna V:Middelswaert.
Van Etten, Arie and Elizabeth-Elizabeth.
Warfoot, Job and Sara-Rachel.
Jansen, Andries and Elizabeth-Thomas.
Witnesses: Thomas Bouman and Neeltje, his wife.
Oct. 26. Selover, Abraham and Sophia-Lucas.
Witness: Cornelia Traphagen.
Teunissen , Teunis and Adriaentje-Cornelius.
Emans, Johannis and Teuntje-Jacobus.
Vroom, Christiaen and Debora-Maria.
Witnesses: Nicholaes Van Schaak and Annatje.
Dec. 21. Ten Eyk, Andries and Adriaentje-Abraham.
1735/36.
Feb. 1. Haff, Lourens and Marritje-Jacob.
1736.
Mar. 28. Hall, George and Blandina-George.
Witness: Engeltje V:Neste.
Van der Bilt, Ryk and Geertje-Yda.
Witnesses: Jan Van der Bilt and Yda, his wife.
Van Etten, Jacobus and Elizabeth-Samuel.

Dumon, Jan and Annatje-Dirck.
May 23. Brouwer, Elias and Lena-Judick.
Brouwer, Pieter and Susanna-Annatje.
Pittenger, Daniel and Elizabeth-Maria.
Witness: Maria Biggs.
July 11. Van Neste, Pieter and Magdalena-Magdalena.
Jewel, William and Catherina-Tabitha.
Hall, Henry and Neeltje-John.
Witnesses: John Cock and Geertruy, his wife.
Aug. 8. Barculo, Jaques and Jannetje-Cornelius.
Reading, John and Marritje-Mary.
Winterstien, Jacobus and Antje-Judick.
Sept. 5. Robert, Vincent and Annatje-Magdalena.
Witness: Anna Van Gelden.
Oct. 3. Aten, Paulus and Marytje-Joris.
Oct. 31. De Wit, Paulus and Catherina-Sara.
Nov. 28.Housel, Johannis and Neeltje-Pieter.
1736/37.
Jan. 1. Jansen, Andries and Elizabeth-Neeltje.
Marlet, Dirck and Jannetje-Elizabeth.
Feb. 28. Jansen, Hendrick and Neeltje-Dirck.
Van der Veer, Jacob and Femmetje-Femmetje.
1737.
Mar. 27. Van der Bilt, Jacob and Neeltje-William.
Freeman, John and Martyntje-Maria.
Apr. 25. Daily, Charles and Neeltje-Nathan.
Van Etten, Arie and Elizabeth-Emanuel.
York, Daniel and Geertje-Lena.
Witness: Lena Selover.
May 29. Wykhof, Nicholaes and Marytje-Jacobus.
Van Duyn, David and Yda-Maria.
Jansen, Andries and Maria-Rachel.
Brouwer, Jacob and Marike-Dirck.
June 26. Messecre, Evert and Lena-Antje. (Born Dec. 12, 1736).
July 24. V:Aersdaalen, Simon and Antje-Johannis.
Van Sickelen, Gerrit and Margrietje-Margretha.
Witness: Henah Van Sickelen.
Elling, John and Susannah-Moses.
Aug. 21.Hall, William and Dorothea-Andreas.
Witnesses: Folkert Douwe and Lidia Douwe.

Vroom, Christiaen and Debora-Apolonia.
De Riemer, Isaac and Geertje-Isaac.
Oct. 23. Beem, Georg and Elizabeth-Elisabeth.
Witness: Lodewyk Smith.
Van der Bilt, Ryck and Geertje-Angenietje.
Nov. 20. Salomonse, Pieter and Jora-Willem.
Dec. 18. Aten, Adriaen and Jacobje-Adriaen.
Jansen, Coert and Geurtie-Hendericus.
Goes, Harpert and Jannetje-Cornelia.
1737/38.
Jan. 15. Van Aersdaalen, Jan and Jannetje-Johanna.
Feb. 12. Laan, Hendrick and Margriet-Hendericus.
Mar. 12. Emans, Johannis and Theuntje-Catheryn.
1738.
Apr. 9. Winterstein, Jacobus and Antje-Judick.
May 14. Rappalie, Joris and Lena-Lena.
Laan, Abraham and Annatje-Rebecca.
Andriese, Dirck and Henah-Femmetje.
Beekman, Pieter and Neeltje-Annaetje.
Witnesses: Marten Beekman and Elizabeth, his wife.
Brouwer, Pieter and Susanna-Margrietje.
Brouwer, Elias and Lena-David.
Correll, Emanuel and Sara-Abraham.
June 9. Van Sickelen, Reynier and Christina-Ferdinandus.
Hall, George and Blandina-Mareytje.
Witness: Mary Reading.
Reyersen, Marten and Catherina-Marytje.
Jewel, William and Catrina-Cornelius.
July 9. Loth, Abraham and Pieternelletje-Cornelius.
Middagh, Pieter and Marritje-Elisabeth.
Aug. 5. Hall, Henry and Neeltje-Hendrick.
Witnesses: Frederick Mourisse and Elizabeth, his wife.
V: Neste, Barnardus and Cathelyntje-Elizabeth.
Boerum, William and Henah-Henderick.
Oct. 3. Brouwer, Jan and Lena-Marytje.
Oct. 29. Van Etten, Arie and Elizabeth-Samuel.
Witness: Hanna Robert.
Simonsen, Simeon and Elizabeth-Jan.
Cock, Thomas and Marytje-Jooris.
Jansen, Hendrick and Neeltje-Hendrick.

de Wit, Barent and Neeltje-Saertje.
Reading, John and Marritje-Sara.
Dec. 24. Jansen, Andries and Marytje-Koert.
Wykhof, Nicholaes and Marytje-Marytje.
Hanselt, Matthys and ----, -Christienje.
Witness: Judick Engel.

1739.
Jan. 21. Lou, Cornelius and Judick-Antje.
Jansen, Andries and Elizabeth-Thomas.
Haff, Lourens and Marritje-Dirck.
Witness: Styntje De Mot.
Schamp, Joris and Kniertje-Margrietje.
Ten Broeck, Johannis and Catheryntje-Johannis.
Witnesses: Jacob Ten Eik and Elizabeth Ten Broek.
Feb. 18. Aree, Adam and Susanna-Isaac.
Freeman, John and Martyntje-Samuel.
Wykhof, Jan and Aelfje-Dirck.
Mar. 18. Van Nuys, Isaac and Catharyntje-Isaac.
Marlet, Dirck and Jannetje-Jannetje.
Apr. 15. Bouman, Cornelius and Marytje-Neeltje.
Robert, Vincent and Annatje-Vincent.
Witnesses: Arie Van Etten and Elizabeth, his wife.
Schermerhoorn, Jan and Femmetje-Marcytje.
May 27. Ten Eik, Andries and Adriaentje-Adriaentje.
Witness: Neeltje Van Middelswaert.
V:Neste, Abraham and Saartje-Joris.
Witnesses: Joris Van Neste and Marytje, his wife.
Bodyn, Frederick and Saartje-Isaac.
Van der Bilt, Jacob and Neeltje-Yda.
V:Deventer, Wynand and ----, -Jan.
Witnesses: Jan Van Deventer and Antje Van Deventer.
June 17. Laen, Cornelius and Neeltje-Gysbert.
Selover, Daniel and Lena-Maria.
Salomonse, Peter and Jora-Elizabeth.
Witness: Susanna Aree.
Aug. 12. de Riemer, Pieter and Weyna-Antje.
Sept. 9. Goewee, Jacob and Catherina-Antje.
Iselstyn, Isaac and Rachel-Sara.
Witnesses: Abraham de la Meter and Sara, his wife.
Hanselt, Jacob and Catherina-Pieter.

Witnesses: Pieter Liffelaer and Antje Hanselt.
Aten, Paulus and Marytje-Antje.
Witness: Styntje de Moth.
Philips, John and Antje-Marytje.
Dec. 25.Hall, William and Dorothea Douwe-Thomas.
Hall, John and Magdalena Gouverneur-Jacomyntje.
Witness: Elizabeth Hall.
Nov. 4. Brouwer, Jacob and Marike-Elizabeth.
Witness: Elizabeth Folkersen.
Dec. 2. Stol, Jan and Janneke Ten Eik-Magdalena.
Witness: Annaatje Stol.
de Hart, Gysbert and Jannetje Reed-Antje.
Witnesses: Dirck Gulick and Geertje Gulick.
1740.
Feb. 10. Van Sichelen, Gerrit and Margrita V: Leuven-Gerrit.
Korsen, Benjamin and Catherina-Jacob.
Hoppach, Teunis and ___ -Cornelius.
Witnesses: Deymant Scherpstien and Cornelius Hoppach.
Mar. 9. Van Oughern, Hendrick and Rachel Bogaert-Cornelius.
Witnesses: Cornelius Bogaert and Jannetje Van Ste.
Andriesse, Dirck and Hanna-Samuel.
Van Sickelen, Reynier and Styntje-Ryck.
Bon, Gerrit and Mary-Laurentz.
May 18. Jansen, Andries and Mary-Maria.
Dirckson, Folkert and Dina Van Leeuwen-Abraham.
June 15. Laad, Richard and ____ -Edward.
Witness: Maria Jansen.
Dayly, Charles and Neeltje-Joris.
Aug. 10.Jansen, Hendrick and Neeltje Symonsen-Barent.
de Wit, Barent and Neeltje-Maria.
Brouwer, Pieter and Susanna Tietsoort-Maria.
Tromm, Philip and Maria Catherina-Johan Philip.
Nov. 23.Jansen, Andries and Elizabeth Bouman-Pieter.
Dec. 25.Brouwer, Elias and Lena Willemsen-Elias.
Van Duin, David and Yda Monfoort-Saertje.
Schamp, Jooris and Kniertje Monfoort-Femmetje.
Witnesses: Jooris Schamp and Margrietje, his wife.
Simeonsen, Simeon and Elizabeth-Saertje.
Middagh, Pieter and Marrietje D: Moth-Antje.
Van der Bilt, Ryck and Geertje Messelaar-Jeremias.

Witnesses: Jeremias V: der Bilt and Saartie.

1740/41.

Jan. 11. D: Moth, Johannis and Elizabeth Davids-Dirck.
Van Etten, Arie and Elizabeth Chrison-Jacobus.

Feb. 8. Freeman, John and Martyntje Jansen-Jonathan.
Korsen, Douwe and Jannetje Conyn-Cornelius.
Arree, Adam and Elizabeth-Wilhelmus.

Mar. 8. Bodyn, Frederick and Saertje Rappalie-Saertje.
Salomonse, Pieter and Jora-Jacob.
Witnesses: Adam Arree and Mary Dey.
Woertman, Abraham and Annaetje Smith-Andries.
Bouman, Pieter and Margrietje Scholl-Debora.

1741.

April 12.Arree, Adan and Susanna-Isaac.
Middagh, Teunis and Elizabeth Tietsoort. (Born Oct. 15/26, 1740).

May 10. Hall, Henry and Neeltje Cock-Oetje.
Laan, Cornelius and Neeltje-Styntje.

June 4. Pettinger, William and Eva Henneschal-Hendrick.
Witnesses: Hendrick Thomson and Catheryn Bodyn.
Emans, Johannis and Teuntje-Sara.
Knoo, Philip and Maria-Catheryn.

June 4. Woertman, Mary.

June 6. Marlett, Dirck and Jannetje Schamp-Joost.
Van Meteren, Isaac and Elsje Scholl-Johannis and Margrietje.
Witness: Cathelyntje Broca.
K. D., and Jannetje Korsen-Yda.
Witness: Jacob Korsen.

July 12. Bercelo, Jaques and Janetje-Lena.
Ryersen, Marten and Catheryntje Cock-Elenar.
Robert, Vincent and Annaetje V: Etten-Samuel.
Hall, John and Magdalena Gouverneur-Annaetje.
Witnesses: David Ogden and Geertruy, his wife.

Aug. 8. Hall, George and Blandina Ryersen-Joseph.

Aug. 9.Messecre, Evert and Lena Tietsoort-William. (Born May 17, 1741).

Sept. 6. Middagh, Dirck and Engeltje Hall-Elizabeth.
----, and Elizabeth-Antje.
Van der Bildt, Jacob and Neeltje-Margreta.

Oct. 4. Van Neste, Jan and Kniertje De Moth-Saertje.
Aten, Paulus and Marytje Van Neste-Antje.
Van Neste, Peter and Grietje Ariaense-Tanneke.

Witnesses: Jan Ariaense and Tanneke, his wife.
V: Neste, Barnardus and Cathelyntje Bodyn-Pieter.
Witnesses: Jeremias Doaty and Marytje Van Schaak.
Oct. 4. Schermerhoorn, Jan and Femmetje-Antje.
Nov. 1. Ten Eyk, Mattheus and Neeltje Teunisse-Rebecca.
De Wit, Paulus and Catheryn-Isaac.
Nov. 29. Van Sickele, Rynier and Styntje-Gysbert.
1741/2.
Andriesse, Dirck and Johanna-Maria.
Witnesses: Nicholaes Wykhof and Maria.
Stol, Jan and Jenneke Ten Eyk-Jacob.
Reading, John and Marritje Ryersen-Samuel.
Mainor, Samuel and Annaatje Douwe-William.
Witnesses: Elihu Mainor and Catherina Douwe.
Feb. 14. Stevens, Hendericus and Cathelyntje Hof-Cathetyntje.
Mar. 14. Laine, Richard and Sara Jansen-Albert.
Witness: Mary Johnson.
1742.
May 27. Maters, John and Catheryn-Johannis.
Polon, William and Sara-Nicholaes.
de Wit, Barent and Neeltje-Antje.
Goewee, Jacob and Trientje Bouman-Maria.
Witnesses: Andries Jansen and Elizabeth, his wife.
July -. Kool, Teunis and Sara Biggs-Jesaias.
Witnesses: Mordechai Mac Kinny and Mary Mac Kinny.
Van Deventer, Isaac and Sara-Pieter.
Witnesses: Dirck Jansen and Sara Van Dyk.
Van Deventer, Wynant and ---- -Sara.
July 18. Van Etten, Johannis and Neeltje-Maria.
Korsen, Benjamin and Catherina-Sara.
Hoppagh, Teunis and Antje-Lena.
Bullisvelt, William and Catherina-Johan Georg.
Jewell, William and Catherina Bogaert-Neeltje.
Oct. 31. Hall, John and Magdalena Gouverneur-Jooris.
Hoed, Lucas and Johanna-Aaron.
Buys, Arie and Elizabeth Herman-Maria.
Witnesses: Cornelius Van Aughem and Maria, his wife.
Jansen, Andries and Maria-Jan.
Tietsoort, Abraham and Geertruy Hof-Abraham.
Middagh, Teunis and Elizabeth Tietsoort-Elizabeth. (Born July

30/Aug. 10, 1742).
Arree, Adam and Elizabeth-Susanna.
Dec. 26. De Mott, Johannis and Elizabeth Davids-Catherina.
1743.
Jan. 23. V: der beek, Burger and Annaetje-Jacobus.
V: der Belt, Jacob and Neeltje-Aaris.
De Hart, Gysbert and Jannetje Reed-Gysbert.
Jan. 24. Jansen, Hendrick and Neeltje Symensen-Johannis.
Cock, Thomas and Mary Hall-Thomas.
Mar. 20. Schamp, Joris and Kniertje Monfoort-Saertje.
April 17. Salomonse, Pieter and Jora-Annaetje.
Jansen, Andries and Lybetje Bouman-Abraham.
Bitten, Philip and Marytje-Agnietje.
May 15. Bodyn, Abraham and Marytje Lou-Jan.
Middagh, Pieter and Marritje De Moth-Saertje.
June 16. V:Campen, Cornelius and Catherina Hall-Catherina.
June 19. Pettinger, William and Eva Henneschul-Marytje.
July 16. Van Etten, Petrus and Jannetje Ariaense-Samuel.
Witnesses: Vincent Robert and Annaetje, his wife.
Aug. 14. Jansen, Jan and Catherientje-Abraham.
Younglove, Isaac and Maria-Johannis.
Korsen, Jan and Geertje-Jacob.
Lewis, Daniel and Geertje-Philip.
Sept. 11. Brouwer, Pieter and Susanna Tietsoort-Dirck.
Oct. 9. Voorhees, Jan and Maria-Cornelia.
Wykhof, Nicholaes and Maria-Jan.
Andriessen, Dirck and Hanna-Barent.
Nov. 6. Willemsen, Nicholaes and Rachel-Cathelina.
Lou, Benjamis and Neeltje Van Neste-Pieter.
Witnesses: Pieter Van Neste and Magdalena, his wife.
Van Neste, Jacob and Elizabeth Bodyn-Joris.
Stol, Jan and Jenneke Ten Eyk-Andries.
Witnesses: Andries Ten Eyk and Adrianetje, his wife.
Dec. 4. Van Neste, Jan and Kniertje De Moth-Marytje.
1744.
Jan. 1. Laan, Cornelius and Neeltie-Marytje.
Marlet, Dirck and Jannetje Schamp-Dirck.
Van Duin, David and Yda Monfort-Denys.
Freeman, John and Martyntje Freeman-Jonathan.
Van Etten, Arie and Elizabeth Chrison-Johannis.

Jan. 29. Emans, Johannis and Teuntje-Abraham.
Zutphen, Adriaen and Elizabeth-Jacob.
Tietsoort, Marcus and Aegje Hof-Cathelina.
Feb. 26. Hall, Henry and Neeltje Cock-Mary.
Witness: Antje Hall.
Ryersen, Marten and Catherina Cock-Catherina.
Wykhof, Cornelius and Maria-Cornelius.
Mar. 25. Beekman, Pieter and Neeltje Lammertz-Marytje.
Bogaert, Isaac and Neeltje Van Neste-Sara.
Holshart (Kohlshaat?), Anthony and Marytje-Benjamin.
Schermerhoorn, Jan and Femmetje-Elizabeth.
Willense, Dirck and Sara-Bartholomeus.
Roes, Johannis and Merse-Rachel.
Post, William and Yda Probasco-Yda.
June 10. Wyknof, Pieter and Marytje-Annaetje.
Witnesses: Nicholaes Wykhof and Marytje.
Bodyn, Abraham and Adriaentje Janse-Maria.
Hall, William and Dorothea Douwe-John.
July 8. Robert, Vincent and Annaetje V: Etten-Johannis.
Brouwer, Elias and Helena Willemse-Helena.
V:Deventer, Isaac and Sara Kouwenhoven-Cornelius.
Jewel, William and Cathrina Bogaert-Sara.
Pettinger, Johannis and Sara Stevens-Saertje.
Witness: Geertruy Vroom.
Messico, Evert and Lena Tietsoort-Reuben. (Born Feb. 8, 1744).
De Hart, Gysbert and Jannetje Reed-Cornelius.
Middagh, Teunis and Elizabeth Tietsoort-Cornelius. (Born Apr. 13, 1744).
D----, I. and Lena Williamson-James.
Aug. 5. Monfort, Jan and Kniertje-Pieter.
Sept. 2. ----, Richard and Saertje-William.
Tietsoort, Abraham and Geertruy Hof-Pieter.
Lucas, Frans and Jannetje Aten-Hilletje.
Oct. 28. Stol, Hendericus and Annetje V:Middelswaert-Jacob.
Witnesses: Jan Stol and Jenneke, his wife.
De Moth, Johannis and Elizabeth Davids-Saertje.
Polen, William and Saertje-Adriaentje.
Jansen, Andries and Mary Knowls-Geertje.
Nov. 25. V: der Zaal, Hendrick and Maria-Maria.
Bullisvelt, Willem and Catherina-Johannis.

Houselt, Jacob and Catherina-Martein.
V:Sickelen, Andries and Lea Krom-Jan.

1745.

Jan 7. Brouwer, Jacob and Marike-Antje.
Feb. 3. Ryersen, Lucas and Elizabeth-Elizabeth.
Witnesses: Martin Ryersen and Catherine.
Hood, Lucas and Johanna V: Stockholm-Jan.
Witnesses: Rynier Van Sichelen and Mersere.
Kool, Thomas and Marytje-Saertje.
Witnesses: Theunis Kool and Saertje Biggs.
Laan, Hermanus and Elizabeth-Cornelius.
Feb. 3. Arree, Adam and Elizabeth-David.
Mar. 3. Schamp, Joost and Kniertje Monfoort-Kniertje.
Jansen, Andries and Elizabeth Bouman-Elizabeth.
Mar. 31. Bodyn, Abraham and Marytje Lou-Judick.
Dey, William and Elizabeth-Eva.
May 5. Kinne, Jacobus and Neeltje Hoogland-Neeltie.
Zutphen, Adriaen and Elizabeth-Anne.
V:Middleswaert, Henricus and Neeltie Ten Eyk-Susanna.
V:Campen, Cornelius and Catherina Hall-Isaac.
Hall, Edward and Catherina Cock-Anne.
Cock, Thomas and Mary Hall-Hendrick.
Botiman, Joris and Jannete Scholl-Elsje.
May 26. Hoppagh, Peter and Catherina-Anna Maria.
June 23. Pettinger, William and Eva Henneschul-William.
Jansen, Hendrick and Neeltje Symonsen-Neeltje.
Korsen, Jan and Geertje-Isaac.
Salomonse, Pieter and Jora-Pieter.
July 28. Korsen, Benjamin and Catherina-Elizabeth.
Aug. 25. Van Duin, David and Yda Monfoort-Kezia.
Douw, Johannis and Annatje Barentse-Andreas.
Witnesses: Volkert Douw and Lidia Douw.
Goewee, Jacob and Catherina Bouman-Maria.
Younglove, Isaiah and Maria-Elizabeth.
Button, Philip and Maria-Hendrick.
Witnesses: Abraham Messalaer and Rachel Jorisse.
Sept. 22. De Wit, Titus and Elizabeth Weatherly-Antje.
Oct. 20. Wykhof, Pieter and Marytje-Nicholaes.
Van Etten, Petrus and Jannetje Ariaense-Jan.
Mainer, Samuel and Annaetje Douwe-Samuel.

Witnesses: Volkert Douw and Lidia Douw.

1746.

Feb. 23. Andriese, Dirck and Hannatje-Nicholaes.
V:Sickelen, Rynier and Christina-Hendrick Zudam.
Douw, Volkert and Aeltje Polhemus-Andreas.
Witness: Johannis Douw.
Mainer, Samuel and Annatje Douwe-Lidia.
Witness: Lidia Douw.
Barkelo, Jaques and Jannetje-Hermanus.
V:Deventer, Barent and Jannetje-Pieter.
Witnesses: Jan Schermerhoorn and Femmetje.
Wykhof, Cornelius and Maria-Sara.
Ten Eyk, Mattheus and Aaltje Woertman-Jacomyntje.

Mar. 23. Lou, Benjamin and Neeltje Van Neste-Jan.
Laan, Cornelius and Neeltje-Cornelius.
de Hart, Gysbert and Jannetje Reed-Jacobus.
Ten Eik, Andries and Antje-Dirck.
Ryersen, Marten and Catherina Cock-Catherina.
Emans, Johannis and Teuntje-Jacob.
Van Neste, Jacob and Elizabeth Bodyn-Jacob.
Witnesses: Isaac Bodine and Engeltje.

April 27. Cock, William and Cornelia Van den Bergh-William.
Middagh, Teunis and Elizabeth Tietsoort-Margrietje. (Born Nov. 11/22, 1745).
Witnesses: William Tietsoort and Margrietje Tietsoort.
Bogaert, Isaac and Neeltje Van Neste-Hendrick.
Witnesses: Johannis Bogaert and Petronella, his wife.
Hall, Henry and Neeltje Cock-Thomas.
Rose, Johannis and Merse-Dina.
Stol, Jan and Janneke Ten Eik-Adriaentje.
V:Deventer, Wynant and Martyntje-Rebecca.

June 20. Schermerhoorn, Jan and Femmetje-Femmetje.
Van Etten, Arie and Elizabeth Chrison-Arie.

Aug. 17. Vroom, Jacob and Elizabeth-Debora.

Oct. 19. De Riemer, Abraham and Jannetje-Antje.
Stevens, Henricus and Cathelyntje Hof-Henricus.
Bodyn, Frederick and Saertje Rappalie-Marytje.
Tietsoort, Abraham and Geertruy Hof-Isaac.
[Following bapt. by Fryenmoet, V. D. M., of Minisink].

Dec. 10. Van Neste, Abraham and Sara Bergen-Joris.

Witness: Hendrick Van Neste.
Laan, Hermanus and Elizabeth-Abraham.
Middagh, Pieter and Marritje De Moth-Pieter.
Brouwer, Jan and Lena-Elsje.
Poling, William and Sara-William.
Witnesses: Pieter Wykhof and Marytje Dildyn.
Schamp, Joost and Kniertje Monfoort-Annaetie.
Witnesses: David Van Duyn and Yda Monfoort.
Aten, Jan and Elizabeth Zutphen-Maria.
Beekman, Pieter and Neeltje Lambertsz-Petrus.
Witnesses: Hendrick Stol and Annaetje V:Middelswaert.
Hall, William and Dorothea Douwe-Henry.

1747.
May 3. V:Wagenen, Gerrit and Catherientje Ten Eyk-Catherientje.
Witnesses: Coenraad Ten Eyk and Catherientje.
[Following in 1747 bapt. by T. J. Frelinghuysen, Jr., date not given].
Hall, Edward and Catherina Cock-George.
Lucas, Frans and Jannetje Aten-Hilletje.
Jobs, James and Rachel Smith-John.
Robert, Vincent and Annatje Van Etten-Jacobus.
Arree, Adam, Jur., and Elizabeth-Adam.
Engel, Nicholaes and Marytje-Judick.
Smack, Jacobus and Margrietje-Henricus.
Jansen, Andries and Elizabeth Bouman-Cornelius.
Buys, Arie and Elizabeth Herman-John.
Amerman, Isaac and Jannetje-Jannetje.
Williamsen, Dirck and Sara-Antje and Sara.
Oct. 3. Kinne, Jacobus and Neeltje Hoogland-Simeon.
Witness: Simeon Kinne.
Gulick, Joachim and Cornelia-Petrus.
Wykhof, Marten and Elizabeth-Jacob.
Wykhof, Peter and Marytje-Jan. (marr. Altje Lane).
Hall, George, Jr., and Blandina Ryersen-Joseph.
Tremmer, Johannis and Elsje-Hendrick.
Witness: Hendrick Beem.
Douw, Volkert and Aaltje Polhemius-Aaltje.
Witnesses: Daniel Polhemeus and Aaltje.
Wykhof, Nicholaes and Marytje-Elizabeth.
Chips, John and Jannetje-Thomas.

1748. [Baptisms by Ericksen].
Mar. 31. Lou, Benjamin and Neeltje Van Neste-Janneke.
Lou, Dirck and Rebecca Emans-Maria.
Stryker, Denys and Lena-Barent.
[Baptisms by Ericksen].
July 10. ten Eik, Andries and Antje Ryersen-Berendina.
Bogaert, Isaac and Neeltje Van Neste-Cornelius.
Kaalsie, Matthys and Albertina-Styntje.
Middagh, Teunis and Elizabeth Tietsoort-Cathelyntje. (Born Nov. 26, 1747).
Witnesses: Cornelius Lou, Jr., and Judick Lou.
Stol, Jan and Jenneke Ten Eik-Jan.
Roes, Johannes and Mercy-Molly.
Nov. 27. V:Noordwyk, Wilhelm and Blandina Middagh-Elizabeth.
Van Aughem, Hendrick and Rachel Bogaert-Abrahain.
Sept. 29. Laan, Dirck and Saertje-Maria.
Monfoort, Jan and Kniertje-Grietje.
Jansen, Andries and Maria-Phebe.
Laan, Arie and Elizabeth-Maria.
Bounaan, Cornelius and Marytje-Releeke.
Nov. 27. Middagb, Peter and Marritje De Mott-Peter.
Laan, Cornelius and Neeltje-Abraham.
Stevens, Hendrik and Cathelyntje Hoff-Sarah.
Bouwman, Pieter and Grietje-Antje.
Ryersen, Marten and Catherine Cock-Marten
1748/9.
Jan. 8. Sickelse, Jan and Maria-Maria.
V:Sickelen, Rynier and Styntje-Maria.
Van Wagenen, Gerrit and Catherietje Ten Eyk-Gerrit.
Witnesses: Huybert V:Wagenen, Teuntje V: den Bergh, and [wife of ?] Gerrit V:Wagenen.
Jobs, James and Rachel Smith-Adam.
Feb. 5. V: der Veer, Jacobus and Femmetje- ----.
Mar. 19. Hall, Richard and Elisabeth Ten Eyk-Rebecca.
Tietsoort, Abraham and Geertruy Hoff-Jan.
V:Deventer, Isaac and Sara-Jacob.
Engel, Nicholaes and Marytje-William.
Schamp, Joost and Kniertje Monfoort-Joost.
Jansen, Hendrick and Neeltje-Zaccheus.
Aree, Adam and Elisabeth-Jonathan.

April 30. Andrise, Dirck and Hannaetje-Elisabeth.
Jansen, Andries and Elisabeth-Maria.
Witnesses: Jan Stol and Maria.
Salomonse, Peter and Joora Aree-Sara.
Scbermerhoorn, Jan and Femmetje-Antje.
May 8. Baem, Hendrick and Cornelia Engel-Elisabeth.
Lucas, Frans and Elizabeth-Femmetje.
June 11. Wykhof, Marten and Elisabeth-Marten.
Laan, Harmen and Elizabeth Dildein-Annaetje.
July 23. Van Neste, Jacob and Cathereintje T: Eyk-Jacob.
Kouwenhoven, Gerrit and Sara Traphagen-David.
Voorhees, William and Alieda-Steven.
Bowman, Thomas and Rachel-Neeltje.
Pettinger, William and Eva Henneschul-Elizabeth.
D:Hart, Gysbert and Jannetje Reed-Wilhelmus.
Laan, Arie and Sara-Neeltje.
Sept. 3. Smock, Jacobus and Margrietje-Adriaentje.
Bodyn, Abraham and Marytje-Cathelyntje.
Witnesses: Teunis Corsen and Metje Corsen.
Oct. 8. Brouwer, William and Margrietje-Catherina.
Williamson, Johannis and Angenietje-Maria.
Stol, Hendrick and Annaetje V:Middelswaert-Annaetje.
Witnesses: Jan Stol and Annaetje Stol.
Nov. 22. Van Sickle, Jan and Lena Van Sickle-Maria.
Dec. 26. Brouwer, Jan and Lena-Johannis.
Ten Eyk, Mattheus and Aeltje-Coenraed.
Wykbof, Pieter and Marytje-Elizabeth.
----, Joris and Marytje-Joris.
Jansen, Jan and Cathelyntje-Elisabeth.
Hoff, Isaac and Catherina V: Neste-Catheleintje.
V:Sickelen, Andries and Lea Krom-Lena.
Lou, Dirck and Rebecca Emans-Dirck.
Schamp, Nicholaes and Antje Aten-Adriaen.
Witness: Jacobje Aten.
[Baptisms by Fryenmoet; exact date not given].
1750.
May --. V. Voorhees, Albert and Catherina-Koert.
Witnesses: Zacharias V: Voorhees and Maria Van Voorhees.
Hegeman, Adriaen and Maria-Garie.
Witnesses: Adriaen Hegeman and Sara Hegeman.

Middagh, Joris and Elisabeth Allen-John.
V:Hoorn, Abraham and Antje-Antje.
Witnesses: Mattheus Van Hoorn and Nelly Van HoortL
V:Hoorn, Abraham and Antje-Antje.
Witnesses: Tobias Ten Eyk and Antje Ten Eyk.
Brewer, Matthias and Elizabeth-Elizabeth.
Witnesses: John Egbert and Metje Egbert.
Kinne, Jacobus and Neeltje Hoogland-Lea.
Witness: Maria York.
Hardenbroeck, Lodewyk and Catheryn Bodyn-Abraham.
Wykhof, Cornelius and Elisabeth-Elizabeth.
Witnesses: George Andrieson and Metje Andrieson.
Polling, William and Sary-Elisabeth.
Zutphen, Adriaen and Elisabeth-Phebe.
Myer, Marten and Ionia-Christophel.
Lou, Benjamin and Neeltje Van Neste-Cornelius.
V:Campen, Cornelius and Catherina Hall-Elisabeth.
Witnesses: Jacobus Alte and Elisabeth Alte.
V:Sickelen, Rynier and Maka-Rynier.
V:Neste, William and Margriet-Geertje.
Witnesses: Johannis Null and Geertje Null.
Null, Hendrick and Sara-Geertje.
Witnesses: Johannis Null and Geertje Null.
Van Sickelen, Abraham and Antje Rosa-Elisabeth.
Witnesses: William Rosa and Elisabeth Rosa.
Vroom, Hendrick and Gerritje Staats-Catherina.
Witnesses: Daniel Sebring and Catherina Sebring.
Rectmeier, Lodewyk and Elisabeth-Coenraed.
Witnesses: Johannis Speder and Elisabeth Jonghbloedt.
V: Neste, Abraham and Saertje Bergen-Abraham.
Witnesses: Abraham de Mont and Femmetje.
Staatsz, Jan and Femmetje Broca-Lammetje.
Witness: Gerritje Vroom.
June 24. Sickelse, Jan and Mareytje-Johannes.
Witness: William Rettensen.
Kaelsitt, Matthys and Albertina Wagenaer-Marytje.
Van Neste, Jan and Saertje Vroom-Jan.
Witness: Jan Van Neste.
V:Aughem, Hendrick and Rachel Bogaert-Maria.
Aug. 12. Nevius, Lucas and Metje-Martinus.

Krom, Gysbert and Metje-Maria.
Wykhof, Nicholaes and Margrietje-Nicholaes.
Witnesses: Nicholaes Wykhof and Marytie.
Sept. 9. Rose, Jan and Mary-Jan.
Brady, John and Eleanor-Eleanor.
Sept. 30. Jansen, Andries and Jannetje-Cathrina.
Aten, Dirck and Adriaentje Langestraat-Judick.
Lou, Cornelius and Annaetje Dildein-Cornelius.
Ten Eyk, Andries and Marytje Vroom-Andries.
V:Middelswaert, Teunis and Jannetje Le Gransie-Christiaen.
Witnesses: Yellis Le Gransie and Chateleintje Le Gransie.
Nov. 4. Van Wagenen, Gerrit and Chatrientje T: Eyk-Teuntje.
Witnesses: Jacob Van Wagenen and Aeltje Van Wagenen.
Nov. 25. Amack, Andries and Teuntje Amack-Jan.
Witnesses: Jan Stol and Marytje Stol.
Chips, John and Jannetje-Elizabeth.
Dec. 16. Stryker, Denys and Lena-Chatelina.
Veghten, Hendrick and Petronella V: Middelswaert-Petronella.
Witness: Jan Van Middelswaert.
Jobs, James and Rachel Smith-Geertje.
1751.
Jan. -. Wykhof, Cornelius and Marytje-Chaterina.
Monfoort, Jan and Kniertje- ----.
Feb. 17. Engel, Nicbolaes and Marytje-Margrietje.
April. 7. Lane, Cornelius and Neeltje Langestraat-Jan.
Wykhof, Samuel and Geertje-Geertie.
D:Mott, Michael and Femmetje-Dirck.
Schamp, Joost and Kniertje Monfoort-Pieter.
April. 8. Hall, Edward and Chaterin Cock-Henry.
Witness: Neeltje Hall.
Hoogland, Martinus and Annaatje-Hermanus.
Davids, Isaac and Agnietje Bries-George.
Emans, Abraham and Margrietje-Neeltje.
Erbert, Jan and Metje-Cathrina.
Ten Eyk, Tobias and Antje Van Hoorn- ----.
April 28. Andriesse, Dirck and Annaetje-Annaetje.
DeMott, Johannis and Elizabeth-Abraham.
Bouman, Cornelius and Maria-Maria.
Tietsoort, Abraham and Geertruy Hoff-Margrietje.
Hardenbroeck, Lodewyk and Catryn Bodine-Hendrick.

May 19. Fein, William and Eva-Elizabeth.
Herton, Edward-William.
June 30. V: der Beeck, Jaques and Marytje Ten Eyk-Rem.
Witness: Debora Van Der Beeck.
Van Campen, Arie and Sara-Gerrit.
Hall, Richard and Elizabeth Ten Eyk-Elizabeth.
Pettinger, Johannis and Sara Stevens-Joseph.
July 21. Lou, Dirck and Rebecca Emans-Johannis.
Jansen, Hendrick and Neeltje-Jonathan.
Van den Berg, Goosen and Jennet-Annaetje and Jennet.
Salomonse, Pieter and Jora-Jooris.
Aug. 11. Van der Beek, Burger and Antje-Elizabeth.
Witnesses: Johannis Cock and Antje.
Jansen, Abraham and Maria-Catrina.
Sept. 1. Kool, Thomas and Leentje V: Van Etten-Thomas.
Laan, Adriaen and Sara-Mattheus.
Marlet, Jan and Maria Marlet-Margrietje.
Sept. 29. Marlet, Jan and Maria-Gideon.
D:Mont, Pieter and Breghje Vroom-Jeseintje.
Witnesses: Hendrick Van Ste and Jeseintje Vroom.
Middagh, Pieter and Marritje D:Mott-Johannis.
V:Hoorn, Cornelius and Geertje-Sara.
Witnesses: Simeon Wykhof and Geertje.
Bishop, Aaron and Annaetje-Johanna.
Oct. 20. Swart, Johannis and Elizabeth-Jannetje.
Witnesses: Jacobus Swart and Jannetje Swart.
De Mott, Lourens and Dorothea V: D: Beek-Saertje.
Krom, Abraham and Aeltje Pieterse-Aelte.
Van Neste, Jacob and Cathereintje T: Eyk-Jacomyntje.
Witness: Jacomyntje T: Eyk.
Nov. 10. Pietersen, Pieter and Catrien-Maria.
Witnesses: Adam Broch and Annaetje.
Kinne, Jacobus and Lena-Lena.
De Hart, Gysbert and Jannetje-Gysbert.
Schamp, Nicholaes and Antje Aten-Joost.
Witnesses: Joost Schamp and Margrietje.
V: Vliedt, William and Marytje Aten-Jan.
Lou, Cornelius and Annaetje Dildein-Cathelyntje.
Ryersen, Marten and Catherine Cock-Johannis.
Dec. 8. Van Vliedt, Thomas and Margrietje Wykhof-Maria.

Witnesses: Nicholaes Wykhof and Marytje.
Ten Eyk, Mattheus and Neeltje-Johanna.
Smock, Jacobus and Margrietje-Jan.
Witnesses: Jacob Korsen and Adriaentje.
Laen, Hermanus and Elizabeth Dildein-Abraham.
V: Sichelen, Rynier and Margery-Jan.
V: Sichelen, Andries and Lea Krom-William.
Witness: Jan Van Sichelen.
Baem, Hendrick and Cornelia Engel-Cornelia.
Dec. 28. Monfoort, Pieter and Johanna Langestraat-Styntje.
Kouwenhoven, Gerrit and Sara Traphagen-Abraham.
Louw, Lourens and Geertje Rosa-Elisabeth.
Dec. 29. Jansen, Jan and Chatrientje-Catrientje.
1752.
Jan. 1. V: Neste, Abraham and Saertje-Seitje.
Feb. 16. Brouwer, William and Margrietje-William.
Witness: Margery.
Zutphen, Pieter and Chatelyntje-Geertje.
Hoff, Jan and Antje Van Neste-Margrietje.
Mar. 8. Schamp, Hendrick and Margreta-Joost.
Witnesses: Joost Schamp and Margrietje.
Kip, Isaac and Hillegont Rosa-Elisabeth.
Stryker, Jan and Judick Van Neste-Barent.
Wykhof, Nicholaes and Margreta-Isaac.
May 10. V: Sichelen, Rynier and Maayke Langestraat-Annaetje.
Witnesses: William Brouwer and Margrietje, his wife.
May 13. Lou, Cornelius and Johanna Jansen-Jan.
Witness: Jannetje Lou.
Hoff, Isaac and Chatrina V: Neste-Magdalena.
Witness: Magdalena Van Neste.
Van Neste, Jan and Saertje Vroom-Jannetje.
Aug. 2. Van Pelt, Teunis and Geertje-Agnietje.
Egberts, John and Metje-Jan.
Van Campen, Cornelius and Catherine Hall-Thomas.
Lou, Teunis and Maayke Hall-Jan.
Aug. 23. Krom, Cornelius and Rebecca-Metje.
Jansen, Hendrick and Neeltje-Marytje.
June 12. Van Aughem, Hendrick and Rachel Bogaert-Rachel.

["New style is begun the 3rd day of Sept., 1752. In place of the 3rd of Sept., we reckon the 14th"].

1752.
Oct. 1. Emans, Abraham and Margrietje Schenk-Nicholaes.
Oct. 22. Van Sichelen, Abraham and Antje Vos-Wilhelmus.
Wykhof, Pieter and Elizabeth-Willemtje.
Van der Veer, Jacobus and Femmetje Stryker-Jannetje.
Bouwman, Thomas and Rachel-Jan.
Bogaert, Martin and Maria Cock-Maria.
Ten Eyk, Tobias and Antje Van Hoorn-Abraham.
Stol, Jan and Jenneke Ten Eyk-Annaetje.
Hoogland, Elbert and ---- Gulick-Eva.
Nov. 12. Wykhof, Samuel and Geertje-Maria.
Wykhof, Cornelius and Elizabeth-Annaetje. (m. George Anderson).
Van der Beek, Jaques and Marytje Ten Eyk-Adriaentje.
Witness: Adriaentje Ten Eyk.
Dec. 18. Hogeboom, Pieter and Neeltje-Dirck.
Schenk, Gerrit and Marytje Van Sichele-Roelof.
1753.
Jan. -. Jansen, Andries and Neeltje-Elizabeth.
Jan. 28. Van Sichelen, Arie and Maria Laan-Maria.
Lou, Dirck and Rebecca Emans-Teuntje.
Krom, Gysbert and Metje-Abraham.
Kaelsche, Matthys and Albertina Wagenaer-Jannetje.
Witness: Jannetje Hoes.
Van Wagenen, Gerrit and Catherientie Ten Eyk-Koenraed.
Feb. 18. De Mott, Michiel and Femmetje-Saertje.
Mar. 11. Bouman, Cornelius and Marytje-Cornelius.
Kool, Benjamin and Geertje-Saertje.
Apr. 1. Krom, Abraham and Aeltje-Weintie.
Witnesses: Cornelius Kron and Rebecca.
Van Sichelen, Abraham and Saertje-Rachel.
De Mott, Johannis and Elizabeth Davids-Elizabeth.
Kool, Jan and Marytje Lou-Jan.
Witnesses: David Kool and Metje Lou.
Apr. 22. Aten, Dirck and Adriaentje Langestraat-Adriaen.
Monfoort, Jan and Kniertje-Lourens.
Bogaert, Isaac and Neeltje-Elizabeth.
Apr. 23. Roes, Johannes and Mercy-Mercy.

Baem, Hendrick and Cornelia Engel-Hendrick.
Engel, Nicholaes and Marytje-Nicholaes.
June. 3. Brouwer, Mattheus and Elizabeth-Maria.
Van Vliedt, William and Marytje Aten-Judick.
July 3. Van den Berg, Gosen and Jannetje-Goosen.
July 1. Laan, Cornelius and Neeltje Langestraat-Jacob.
July 22. De Mott, Lourens and Dorothea Van der Beek-Dirck.
Sept. 16. Amack, Andries and Tietje V:Bosck-Kerk-Thomas.
Emans, Andries and Saertje Van Duyn-Anna
Vroom, Pieter and Jannetje Dumont-Jannetje.
Witnesses: Andries Ten Eyk and Marytje, his wife.
Van Duyn, Roelof and Susanna Pettinger-William.
Witnesses: William Van Duyn and Sibrech.
Stryker, Teunis and Lena-Elizabeth.
Oct. 7. Bodyn, Pieter and Marytje-Elizabeth. ("Born Sept. 18, 1753; d. Nov. 18, 1825; m. Dec. 23, 1779, Folkert Douw").
Witness: Judick Bodein.
Waldron, Samuel and Catherina Hegeman-Adriaen.
Hall, Edward and Catherina Cock-Geertruy.
Pietersen, Pieter G. and Catherina Hegeman-Gerbrandt.
Marlett, Jan and Jannetje Van Sichelen-Abraham.
Witness: Helena Van Sickelen.
Swart, Johannis and Elizabeth-Annaetje.
Chrison, Adolphus and Saertje-Saertje.
Witnesses: William Wood and Alida.
Oct. 9. MacKinny, Mordechai and Agnietje Bodein-Johannis.
Oct. 28. Van Vliedt, Thomas and Grietie Wykhoff-Grietie.
Lou, Cornelius J. and Johanna Jansen-Benjamin.
Van Deventer, Isaac and Sara-Abraham.
Witnesses: Nicholaes Wykhoff and Margrietje Wykhoff.
Stol, Hendrick and Annaetje Van Middleswaert-Magdalena.
Nov. 21. Jansen, Abraham and Maria-Maria.
Dumont, Petrus and Breghje Vroom-Petrus.
Dec. 9. Stryker, Jan and Judick Van Neste-Hendrick.
Laan, Arie and Sara-Elizabeth.
Dec. 30. Ryerson, Marten and Chatherina Cock-Thomas.
Jansen, William and Rebecca-Sara.
Van Hoorn, Cornelius and Geertje-Simeon.
Kinne, William and Eva Schirts-David.

1754.

Jan. 19. Bodeyn, Frederick and Elsje Bogert-Jan.

Mar. 3. Wykhof, Cornelius and Maria-Annaetje.
Krom, Cornelius and Rebecca-Thomas.
Wykhof, Pieter and Marytje-Pieter.
("Captured by Indians. Returned").
Polen, William and Sara-Martha.
Wykhoff, Nicholaes and Grietje-William.
Witnesses: Isaac Van Deventer and Saertje Van Deventer.
Zutphen, Dirck and Neeltje-William.
Pouwelse, Cornelius and Maria-Maria.
Phenix, John and Maria Woertman-Sara.

Mar. 24. Lou, Dirck and Rebecca Emans-Cathelina.
Ten Eyk, Tobias and Antje Van Hoorn-Neeltie.
Hogeboom, Pieter and Neeltje - Maria.

April 14. Hoff, Isaac and Catherina Van Neste-Elizabeth.

May 5. Kouwenhoven, Gerrit and Sara Traphagen-Lena.
Quick, Petrus and Johanna-Petrus.
Kinne, Jacobus and Neeltje-Dirck.

May 26. Zutphen, Pieter and Cathelyntje-Margrietje.
Witness: Margrietje Woertman.
Van Zandt, Barnardus and Magdeleentje-Barnardus.
Witness: Barnardus Van Zandt.

June 16. Stol, Jan and Annaetje-Magdalena.
Jansen, Jan and Annaetje-Magdalena.
Pettinger, Johannis and Sara Stevens-Maria.
Tietsoort, Marcus and Aeghje Hoff-Marcus.
Johnson, ---- and Sary Lane-John.
Witness: Abert Janson's wife.
D'Haryet, Charles and Anna-Charles.
Wykhof, Samuel and Geertje-Jan.
Cooper, Jan and Martha-Jan.
Marlat, Abraham and Martha Veal-Pieter, Nelly and Gideon.
Witnesses: Penelope and Elizabeth Slecht.

Sept. 8. Egbert, John and Metje-Elizabeth.
Schamp, Hendrick and Margrietje Cock-David.
Witnesses: David Cock and Marya.
Symonse, Symon and Anne-Symon.
Van Sichele, Reynier and Margery-Marytje.
Lou, Cornelius C. and Annaetje Dildein-Judick.

Oct. 10. Egbert, Nicholaes and Maria-Chaterina.
Emans, Abraham and Margrietje-Anne.
Algert, Benjamin and Chatelyna-Elizabeth.
Dec. 26. Van Sichelen, Rynier and Maayke-Elsje.
Polen, Samuel and Lena-William.
Wykhoff, Cornelius and Elisabeth-Cornelia. ("Born July 16, 1754; m. David Traphagen").
Witness: Geertje Van Hoorn.
Van Aughem, Cornelius and Maria-Christina.
Van Sichelen, Andries and Lea Krom-Maria.
Van Neste, Petrus and Cathelyntje Davids-Jan.
Macilvene, Thomas and Antje-Eesje.
Kool, Teunis and Elizabeth-Sara.
Brady, John and Elizabeth Chrison-Catherina.
Witnesses: Christoffel Braziel and Elizabeth Slecht.
Britain, Abraham and Sarah Forster-[child's name not given].

1755.
Feb. 6. Monfoort, Jacob and Jannetje Nevius-Margretha.
Van Vliedt, William and Adriaentje Wykhoff-Maria.
Louw, Teunis and Maayke Hall-Thomas.
Lane, William and Jannetje-Jannetje.
Monfoort, Pieter, Jur., and Johanna Langestraat-Sara.
Van der Beek, Jaques and Maria Ten Eyk-Dorothea.
Sturges, James A. and Margretha-Pieter.
Heath, Samuel and Anna Maria-Maria.
Powelsen, Jacob and Margretha-Johannes.
Apr. 13. Ten Broeck, Cornelius and Maria-Johannes.
Witnesses: Daniel Sebring and Catherine Le boy Teaub.
Van Neste, Pieter and Elizabeth-Pieter.
De Mott, Michael and Femmetje-Elizabeth.
Louw, Benjamin and Neeltje Van Neste-Jannetje.
Van Stee, Hendrick and Ruth Blackford-Wyntje.
Witness: Wyntje Ten Eyk.
Bogaert, Marten and Maria-Cornelius.
Kool, Jan and Marytie Louw-Teunis.
Doaty, Jeremias and Harmtje Koevers-Jan.
Hoff, Jan and Antje Van Neste-Pieter.
Witness: Margriet Van Neste.
Wykhoff, Marten and Elizabeth-Joseph.
Van den Berg, Goosen and Jane Heryard-Margretha.

Tietsoort, Abraham and Gertruy Hoff-William.
Van Sichelen, Jan and Christina Sebring-Helena.
Witness: Helena ---
Tarett, David and Catherina-Pleter.
April 27. Stol, Jan and Jenneke Ten Eyk-Annaetje.
June 6. Jansen, William and Annaetje-Barbaraetje.
De Mott, Lourens and Dorothea V:D:Beek-Lourens.
Hardenbroek, Lodewyk and Catheryn Bodyn-Lodewyk.
V:Middelswaert, Abraham and Maria-Hendericus.
Aug. 10. Cock, Jacobus and Christina Schamp-Grietje.
Witnesses: Joost Schamp and Grietje Schamp.
Korsen, Teunis and Henah-Mally; Metje.
Witnesses: Jacobus Smack and Margriet Smack.
Bouman, Thomas and Rachel-Thomas.
Ten Eyk, Tobias and Antje Van Hoorn-Tobias.
Middagh, Pieter and Marritje De Mott-Rebecca.
Bodyn, Abraham and Marytie-Saertje.
V:Middleswaert, Hendicus and Neeltje Ten Eyk-Femmetje.
Van Neste, Jan and Saertje Vroom-Sara.
Vroom, Jacob and Elisabeth Schoonmaek-Catherina.
Sept. 30. Van Sichelen, Arie and Maria Laan-Abraham.
Van der Bilt, Jan and Angenietje-Jacob.
Witnesses: Jacob Van der Bilt and Neeltje Van der Bilt.
Jansen, Hendrick and Neeltje-Ezekiel.
Nov. 27. Marlet, Jan and Jannetje Van Sichelen-Thomas.
Hegeman, Joseph and Niesje Waldron-Maria.
Waldron, Samuel and Catherina Hegeman-Frans.
LeGrange, Yellis and Antie LeGrange-Antje.
Mackinny, Mordechai and Agnietje Bodyn-Marytje.
Nov. 30.Bouman, Cornelius and Marytje-Elizabeth.
Bogaert, Isaac and Neeltje Van Neste-Ruthje.
Dec. 28. Stol, Teunis and Elizabeth-Magdelena.
Ryersen, Marten and Catherine Cock-William Assilby.
Smock, Jacobus and Margriet-Matthys.
Hardin, Thomas and Priscilla-Sarah.
Middagh, Teunis and Jannetje Broca-Cornelius. ("Born Sept. 17, 1755.
Baptized Sept. 29, 1755, by Johannis Henricus Goetschius").

1756.

Jan. 11. Descher, Wilhelm and Yda-Geertje.
Vander Veer, Jacobus and Femmetje-Cathrina.

Jan. 18. Louw, Dirck and Rebecca Emans-Cornelius.
Cock, William and Cornelia Van den Bergh-Henry.
Van Vliedt, Thomas and Margrietje Wykhoff-Lea.
Stryker, Jan and Judick Van Neste-Pieter.
Jansen, Abraham and Elizabeth-Adriaen.
Feb. 1. Laen, Arie and Sara-Mattheus.
Kouwenhoven, Pieter and Neeltje-Joris.
Cooper, John and Martha-[name of child omitted].
Feb. 8. Dumont, Rynier and Annaetje Brouwer-Margrietje.
Pietersen, Lucas and Cathryntje-Isaac.
V:Vliedt, Frederick, Jur., and Rebecca Dubois-Abraham. ("Born July 19, 1755").
De Mott, Johannis and Elizabeth Davis-Maria.
Cornelis, Cornelis and Antje-[name of child omitted].
Broca, Jan and Geertje Kaelsche-Dina.
Witness: Albertina Wagenaer.
Van Campen, Cornelius and Maria-Maria.
Witnesses: David Cock and Maria Cock.
Feb. 22. Van Vliedt, William and Adriaentje Wykhof-Gerrit. ("Died 1860").
Witnesses: Gerrit Van Vliedt and Judick Van Vliedt.
Emans, Andries and Sara Van Duyn-Catheryn.
Witnesses: Cornelius Lou and Catherine, his wife.
Van Duyn, Roelof and Susanna Pittengen-Hendrick.
Mar. 21. Van Tuyl, Jan and Marytje-Abraham.
Kleyn, Godfried and Yda-Jacob.
Kool, David and Margrietje-David.
Louw, Teunis and Maayke-Metje.
Witnesses: Lourens Louw and Geertje, his wife.
Liest, Pieter and Catherina-Johannes.
Witnesses: Coenradus Van der Beek and Annetje.
Kouwenhoven, Gerrit and Sara Traphagen-Cornelius.
Mar. 28. Smack, Gerrit and Jannetie-Aeltje.
Apr. 4. Miskorn, Nicholaes and Antje De Mott-Antje.
Wykhoff, Samuel and Geertje-Nicholaes.
Witnesses: Nicholaes Wykhoff and Marytje.
Hoff, Isaac and Catherina Van Neste-Pieter.
Apr. 26. Aten, Dirck and Adriaentje Langestraat-Christina.
May 2. Arree, Abraham and Eva-Catherina.
Wykhof, Nicholaes and Margrietje-Sara.
Witnesses: Isaac Van Deventer and Sara.

Van der Bilt, Jacob and Aeltje-Jacob.
Pietersen, Pieter and Maria Pettinger-Thomas.
Witnesses: Thomas Pieterson and Antje, his wife.
June 6. Dumont, Pieter and Breghje Vroom-Hendrick.
Witnesses: Jan Van Neste and Saertje, his wife.
Bodyn, Frederick and Elsje Bogert-Elsje.
Van Zandt, Gerrit and Magdalena-Marritje.
Witnesses: Barnardus V:Zandt and Marritje.
Kool, Banjamin and Geertje-Rachel.
Witness: Metje Korsen.
Algert, Benjamin and Cathelina-Maria.
Van Vliedt, Dirck and Rachel-Rachel.
Stryker, Denis and Lena Hoglandt-Christafel.
Ten Eyk, Mattheus and Neeltje Teunisse-Janneke.
June 7. Jansen, Jan and Cathelina-Sara.
Witness: Pieter Wykhoff.
June 13. Schoemaker, Daniel and Anne-Henricus.
Witnesses: Arie Van Kampe and Sara.
Swart, Johannis and Elisabeth-Femmetje.
Witnesses: Ram Hegeman and Femmetje.
June 27. Same, Hendrick and Anna Catherina-Andries.
July 18. Van pelt, Teunis and Grietje-Pieter.
Egberts, Nicholaes and Marytje-Lena.
Witness: Lena Biggs.
Polen, William and Sara-Sara.
Stol, Jan and Anne Bonny-Joseph.
Witness: Jan Stol, Sr.
Aug. 1. Hoff, Jan and Antje Van Neste-Jan.
Schermerhoorn, Jacob and Neeltje-Jan.
Aug. 8. Rass, Jacobus and Elizabeth-William.
Aug. 15. Pettinger, Richard and Rebecca Griggs-Hendrick.
Jansen, Andries and Jannetje-Aefje.
Witnesses: Arie Jansen and Elisabeth Jansen.
Emans, Abraham and Margriet-Saertje.
Aug. 29. Ten Broeck, Cornelius and Maria-Dirck Wesselse.
Simson, Gershom and Cathrina-Jacobus.
Witness: Jacobus Brink.
Hofman, Johannis and Rebecca-Maria.
De Mott, Jacob and Nelly-Saertje.
Doaty, Jeremias and Harmtje-Jannetje.

Oct. 24. V:Vliedt, Frederick and Rebecca DuBois-Frederick.
Hegeman, Rem and Femmetje-Joseph.
Witnesses: Joseph Hegeman and Adriaentje.
Louw, Cornelius and Annaetje-Gysbert.
Nov. 14. Egberts, John and Metje-Maria.
Van Sichelen, Rynier and Mary-Lena.
Witnesses: Jan Van Sichelen and Lena.
Bergen, Evert and Jannetje Hegeman-Evert.
1757.
Jan. 9. Wells, Thomas and Elizabeth-Sary.
[Handwriting changes here. New clerk].
Van Sickle, Jan, (Sr.?), and Maregrietta-Jan.
Van Sickle, Jan, Jur., and Steintge-Maria.
Witnesses: Dirck Sebring and Maria.
McCane, Thomas and Antge-Neiltge.
Van fliedt, Jeromes and Annatie-Maregrietta.
Witnesses: Jost Schamp and Maregrietta.
Van fliedt, Willim and Ariantge-Cornelius.
Witnesses: Cornelius Wyckoff and Maria.
totterson, Hendrick and Maregrietta-Elizabeth.
Witness: Antge Hall.
Cole, Jan and Maria (Low?)-Jenneia.
tietsoort, Marcus and Esge-Isack.
Lou, Abraham and Ida (widow of Albert Stothoff)-Abraham.
Van Nest, Petrus and Catleintge-Jores.
----, and Maregrietta-Antge.
Witnesses: William Polen and Saartge.
Aten, Hendrick and ----, -Hendrick.
Witnesses: Adrian Aten and Jacpge.
Wortman, Jan and Saartge-Johannes.
Witness: Elsje Wortman.
Jansen, William and Annatie-Jacob.
Sutfin, Peter and Catelina-Geisbert.
Apr. 17. Vroom, Peter and Jannetje-Hendrick.
Witnesses: Jan Vroom and Sara V:Nest.
May 2. Wyckoff, Peter and Maria-Maria.
D'mont, Petrus and Arriantie-Jan.
Witnesses: Jan D'Mont and Annatie.
May 22. Kinney, Willem and Eva-Willem.
Witness: Peter Kinney.

Cozyn, Cornelius and Antje-Elizabeth.
Monfort, Peter and Johanna-Peter.
Dister, Willem and Ida-Willem.
Lane, Cornelius and Neiltje-Neiltje.
Low, Jan and Catrina-Johannes.

June 13. Amack, Andries and Tietje-Abraham.
V:Vliedt, Willem and Maria-Cateleyntie.

July 24. V:Horn, Cornelius and Geertje-Maregritta.
Low, Cornelius and Catrina-Catrentje.
Krom, Hendrick and Maregrietta-Isaack.

Aug. 6. Sebring, Johannes and Geertje-Neiltje.
Witnesses: Teunis Teunison and Aeltje V:Nest.
Haal, Edward and Catrine-Thomas.
D:Mott, Lowrence and Doritie-Martha.
Douw, Jan and Anna-Marigrittie.
V:Derbilt, Willem and Maria-Davidt.
Woortman, Willem and Maragrietta-Samuel.

Sept. 11. Stoll, Jan and Jenneia-Abraham.
Olleger, Benjamen and Catleina-Benjemin.

Dec. 20. Monfort, Abraham and Neiltje Peter.
D:Mott, Johannes and Elizabeth-Dirck.
Herden, Thomas and Prissilla-Samuel.

Dec. 26. Low, Benjamin and Neiltje-Benjamin.
D:Wit, Jacob and Jannetie-Cornelius.
Cock, Samuel and Annatie-Teunis.
Cock, Jacobus and Cristina-Cristina.
Witnesses: David Cock and Maria.
Vanderbeek, Jakes and Maria-Maria.
Lane, Willem and Jannetie-Gisbert.

1758.

Feb. 12. McKinney, Martegay and Egnes-Catrina.
Lane, Harmanes and Elizabeth-Jurrey.
Striker, Jan and Judick-Jan.
D:Mott, Michael and Femmitie-Steyntie.
Terret, Davidt and Catrina-Cornelius.
Biggs, Jan and Maregrietta-Johannes.
V: Sickle, Jacobes and Saara-Abraham.
Stout, Thomas and Jannetie-Mergit.
V:Stee, Hendrick and Ruth-Catrina.
Low, Dirck and Rebecca-Rebecca.

V:Vliedt, Thomas and Grietje-Annatie.
Low, Garret and Rachael-Cornelius.
Apr. 12. V:Vliedt, Dirck and Rachael-Lidea.
Aug. 27. D:Mott, Jacob and Nelle-Dirck.
V:Nest, Jan and Saertje-Fredrick.
Corsen, Teunis and Hanna-Maregriet.
Oct. 29. Hicks, Hugh and Maregriet-Pieter.
D:Mott, Isaac and Molley-Dirck.
V:Zant, Garret and Magdelena-Magdelena.
Bodine, Fredrick and Eisje-Catteleyntje.
Bries, Hendrick and Ruth-Ruth.
Broca, Jan and Geertje-Maria.
Ten Eyck, Matthewes and Neiltje-Femmetie.
Ten Eyck, Jan and Maria-Andries.
Teunissen, Teunis and Adriantie-Teunes.
Dec. 17.Stoll, Hendrick and Annatie-Femmetie.
Bogert, Isaac and Neiltie-Maria.
1759.
Jan. 7. Arrey, Jacob and Catriena-Jacobes.
Egbert, Nicholas and Maria-Abraham.
Feb. 4. Striker, Denies and Lena-Denies.
Mar. 4. Kinney, Pieter and Sara-Maria.
Ten Eyck, Andries and Maria-Hendrick.
Low, Cornelius and Annatie-Maria.
Apr. 5. Monfort, Abraham and Neiltje-Steintie.
Emans, Abraham and Marregrieta-Catriina.
Apr. 29. Van Sichelen, Jan and Steyntie-Jannetie.
Hofman, Jan and Rebecca-Maregrietta.
Cole, Ezekiel and Steintie-Obedia.
Witnesses: Teunes Cole and Elizabeth.
Herrington, Edwart and Jannetie-Geertie.
Smack, Jacobus and Maregrieta-Elizabeth.
Bogert, Martein and Maria-Johannes.
Aten, Jan and Elizebeth-Elizebeth.
May 24. Jansen, Arye and Maregrietta-Jacob.
Cole, Jan and Mara-Elizabeth.
June 17. V:Nest, Isaac and Elizabeth-Elizabeth.
Witness: Jan V:Nest.
July 15. V:Derbilt, Willem and Maria-Neiltie.
Low, Jan and Catriena-Abraham.

Aug. 12. Egbert, Jan and Metie-James.
Low, Gerret and Rachel-Judith.
Bowman, Jores and Maria-Jacob.
Teiler, Benjamin and Mareitie-Willet.
Witness: Willet Teeler.
Sept. 9. Dow, Jan and Annatie-Folkert.
Jansen, Thomas and Annatie-Andries.
Oct. 14. V:Nest, Jan and Saartie-Jores.
V:Pelt, Teunes and Grietie-Elsie.
Stool, Jan and Anna-Maria.
Nov. 11. D:Mott, Lourence and Dorithe-Pieter.
V:Nest, Jan and Saartie-Lena.
Aten, Gerret and Dina Johnson-Maria.
Low, Dirck and Rebecca-Gisbert.
V:Vliedt, Willem and Maria-Adrian.
Nov. 23. V:Nest, Pieter and Treintie-Petrus.
Dec. 9. Monfort, Pieter and Johanna-Johanna.
Cozyn, Cornelius and Antie-Femitie.
1760.
Mar.2. McKinney, Marteghai and Angenietie-Johannes.
Cock, Samuel and Annatie-Samuel.
Mar. 30. Striyker, Jan and Judick-Abraham.
V:Zant, Bernardes and Neiltie-Belitie.
Zuylinger, Phillip and Hanna-Rachael.
Apr. 27. Herden, Thomas and Priscilla-Mary.
V:Nest, Jeromes and Petience-Hendrick.
June 8. Stool, Jan and Jennike-Hendrickes.
Cole, Teunes and Elizabeth-Elizabeth.
Witnesses: David Cole and Marget.
Cole, Thomas and Leintie-Teunes.
Stoll, Hendrick and Annatie-Hendrickes.
Egbert, Nicholas and Maria-Maritie.
V:Derbeek, Jakes and Maria-Andries.
Omack, Andries and Tietie-Willem.
1760.
July 6. Jansen, Andries and Jannetie-Antje.
Aug. 31. D:Mott, Jacob and Nelle-Maria.
Polen, Samuel and Jannetie-Willem.
Oct. 5. Sebering, Dirck and Leintie-Jennike.
Hall, Jan and Jannetie-Henry.

Ten Eyck, Matheues and Alida-Catrientie.
Laen, Willem and Jannetie-Sara.
McKinney, Willem and Annatie-Willem.
Teunisen, Teunes and Ariantie-Neiltie.

1761.

Feb. 15. Monfort, Abraham and Neiltie-Isaack.
Apr. 12. Bogert, Isaack and Neiltie-Abraham.
Hofman, Johannes and Rebecca-Sarrie.
Broca, Jan and Geertie-Abraham.
V:Nest, Jan and Saartie-Rosina.
Dorlant, Johannes and Catrina-Johannes.
Aten, Gerret and Dina-Rebecca.
June 21. Dumont, Petrus and Adriantie-Elbert.
Low, Cornelius and Annatie-Rebecca.
July 19.Bowman, Jores and Maria-Elizabeth.
Aug. 16.Trop Hagel, Hendrick and Annatie-Cornelia.
Wortman, Pieter and Saartie-Maregrietta.
Oct. 11. Jansen, Arie and Grietje-Jan.
Egbert, Jan and Metje-Saertje.
Nov. 15.Van Nest, Vernandes and Mareitje-Susanna.
Van Middleswart, Abraham and Maria-Jacobes.
Cock, Samuel and Annatie-Annatie.
Lane, Harmanes and Elizabeth-Johannes.

1762.

Feb. 21. Van Vliedt, Willim and Maria-Rachael.
Tailer, Benjamin and Matje-Ariantie.
Striker, Denies and Lena Hooglandt-Maria.
Witness: Maria Van Neuis.
Mar. 21.Bodine, Isaack and Maregrietta-Vredrick.
Van Stee, Hendrick and Ruth-Hendrick.
Van Arsdalen, Ares and Elizabeth-Johannes.
Apr. 4. Jansen, Andries and Jannetie-Johannes.
Jansen, Thomas and Annatie-Maria.
May 16. Mettes, Jan and Catrientje-Jannetie.
May 23. Saams, Hendrick and Anna Maregrietta-Maregrietta.
June 13. Fanger, Willem and Cristena-Lea.
Sweesey, Amos and Ida-David.
June 27. Sutfin, Peter and Catleintie-Geisbert.
July 25. Bowman, Cornelius and Mareitje-Saartje.
Streiker, Jan and Judick-Isaack.

Oct. 3. Teunisen, Teunes and Ariantje-Ariantje.
Cole, Jan and Maria-Benjamin.
Cuilinger, Phillip and Hanna-Phillip.
Stoll, Jan and Jennike-Neiltje.
Nov. 14. V:Middleswart, Hendrick and Neiltje-Jennike.
Stein, Andries and Angenietje-Johannes.
1763.
Jan. 9. McKinney, David and Rebecca-Abraham.
30. V:Zant, Garret and Magdelena-Johannes.
Mar. 20. Bodine, Vredrick and Elsje-Geisbert.
Apr. 2. Schits, Willem and Debora-Pieter.
Aten, Gerret and Dina-Adrian.
June 8. Jansen, Andries and Jannetie-Andries.
Monfort, Abraham and Neiltje-Marregrietje.
Merlatt, Jan and Jannetie-Jan.
Hofman, Johannes and Rebecca-Rebecca.
Endersen, Jacob and Rachael-Catrientje.
Herrington, Edward and Jannetie-Edward.
Valentine, Hendrick and Nencey-Pieter.
26. Aten, Adrian and Elizabeth-Adrian.
Dorem, Daniel and Hester-Elizabeth.
July 24. V:Nest, Johannes and Judith-Jores.
Nov. 6. Bogert, Isaack and Neiltje-Willem.
Arrey, Jacob and Catriena-Maria.
27. V:Arsdalen, Cornelius and Sara-Jan.
Arrey, Isaac and Annatie-Adam.
Sept. 11. Egbert, Jan and Metje-Nicholas.
1764.
Jan. 15. V:Enden, Cornelius and Annatie-Maria.
Feb. 19. Trophagen, Hendrick and Annatie-Annatie.
Bodine, Isaac and Maregrietje-Saara.
Mar. 25.D:Mott, Isaac and Molley-Saara.
Apr. 15. Aten, Jan and Elizabeth-Jan.
McKinney, Martichay and Angenetje-Martichai.
V:Derveer, Verdinandes and Rebecca-Matthews.
Wortman, Pieter and Sara-Maria.
Sweesey, Amos and Ida-Amos.
Jansen, Thomas and Annatie-Abraham.
June 10. McKinney, David and Rebecca-Maria.
Pittenger, Hendrick and Tietie-Catriena.

Nuel, Pieter and Dirckje-Elizabeth.
11. Laws, Richard and Maria-Willem.
24. Bowman, Thomas and Rachael-Cornelius.
Brouer, Daniel and Maria-Daniel and Maria.
Hoff, Steven and Eva, Maria.
Jansen, Andries and Jannetie-Cornelius.
July 29. Britten, Richard and Eva-John, Molley, Elizabeth, Frenkje.
Governeur, Elenor-Barent, Reinders.
Witness: Marten Reirson.
Couenoven, Gerret and Antje-Elizabeth.
Aug. 19. Britten, Abraham and Sara-Abraham.
Lane, Gisbert and Matje-Geisbert.
Sept. 1. V:Derbilt, Willem and Maria-Maria.
V:Vliedt, Willem and Maria-Lea.
Oct. 7. Cozyn, Cornelius and Antje-Maria.
Mettes, John and Catriena-Daniel.
28. Cole, Ezekiel and ----, -Jacob.
Witness: Jannetie Herrenton.
Nov. 28. Teunisen, Teunes and Ariantic-Teunes.
V:Nest, Vernandes and Maria-Jeromes and Johannes.
Sutfin, Pieter and Catlina-Judick.
Stoll, Jacob and Sara-Johannes.
Dec. 30. Monfort, Jacobes and Lea-Rachael.
1765.
Jan. 13. Cernel, Allebertes and Antje-Barent.
Merlatt, Mark and Sovia-Enoch.
Stine, Andries and Angenietje-Cornelius.
Feb. 17. Striker, Denies and Lena-Pietel.
Striker, Jan and Judick-Elizabeth.
Mar. 13. Lane, Aaron and Lidea-Annatie.
Apr. 7. Monfort, Abraham and Neiltje-Neiltje.
Egbert, Nicholas and Maria-Anna.
May 16. Hofman, Jacob and Steintje-Johannes.
Fanger, Willem and Cristeina-Johannes.
June 2. Cole, Thomas and Lena-Thomas.
Kuilinger, Phillip and Hanna-Maria.
Merlatt, Jan and Jannetie-Jacob.
Aten, Jan and Maria-Jacobes.
16. V:Derbilt, Jacobes and Elizabeth-Catriena.
Middagh, Dirck and Elizabeth-Elizabeth.

V:Sickle, Jan and Steintje-Dirck.
21. Hofman, Johannes and Rebecca-David.
Sept. 1. Kerkhoff, Abraham and Hanna-Maregrietta and Maria.
22. V:Sickle, Andries and Annatie Schamp-Andries.
Oct. 13. Low, Jan and Catrina-Teuntje.
Arrey, Isaac and Annatic-Isaac.
Nov. 10.Miller, Jan and Femmetie-Maria.
24. Ditmas, Johannes and Servieja-Johannes.
Vanende, Corneleus and Anathe-Elesabet.
Vanderbilt, Corneleus and Stenthe-Mariya.
Kinne, David M. and Rebecka-Johannes.
Dec. 25.Demott, Isaac and Mariya-Stenthe.
1766.
Jan. 5. Demon, Peter and Adreyana-Jories.
Meinders, Williem and Catrena-Samuel.
Feb. 23. Auten, Jan and Elisebet-Comeleus.
Willemse, Jores and Kaseya-Mariya.
Janse, Abraham and Elisebet-Elesebet
Mar. 16.Green, John and Elisebet-Mary.
----, and Mary Vastbender-Margret.
Stout, Thomas and Jannethe-Catrena.
Bretten, Richert and Eva-Richert.
31. Hoff, Jan and Catrena-Rebecka.
Wortman, Peter and Sara-Petres.
Sebring, Dirck and Lana-Jan.
Apr. 20. Vanarsdalen, Hendrick and Catlina-Mariya.
Neul, Peter and Derickye-Hana.
May 18. Demott, Jacob and Nelle-Mariya.
M'Kinne, Martegai and Angenetie-Angenetie.
Janse, Peter and Anatie-Peter.
Bogert, Marten and Mariya-Marten.
Aten, Adreyaen and Elesebet-Jaepye.
June 8. Brower, Daniel and Mariya-Elesebet.
Clickner, Jurrey and Elsye-Diena.
22. Stoll, Jan and Jannetie-Mariya.
July 20. Lane, Geisbert and Matje-Comeles.
Van midelswart, Teunes and Sara-Antye.
Vantein, Charrel and Elisebet-Mariya.
Aug. 24. Vannest, Johannes and Yudick-Catlyna.
Sept. 7. Coul, Simon and Mariya-Williem.

Pettenger, Hendrick and Catrena-Williem.
24. Cole, Jesaja and Sara-Tiunes.
Oct. 5. Cownover, Necasai and Catrina-Petres.
Van Sickle, Rinier and Mayake-Peter.
Stoll, Jacob and Sara-Jenneke.
Tine, Andries and Angenietie-Marja.
Gerresse, Gerret and Sara-Stientie.
Nov. 15. Casine, Coneles and Antye-Gerret.
Van Viet, Willem and Mariya-Elesebet.
16. Bowman, Thomaes and Ragel-Petres.
30. Haff, Steven and Eva-Elisebet.
Dec. 21. Van Sicklen, Jan and Stintje-Catlyna.
Shets, Williem and Debera-Williem.
Hoffman, Jacob and Stintje-Jacob.

1767.
Feb. 15. Tenick, Abrabam and Sara-Begeltie.
Vanhorn, Jemes and Elesebet-John.
Merlett, Marck and Serviya-Sara.
Vanarsdalen, Isaac and Lammetie-Gerret.
Mar. 1. Hardenberg, Gerardes and Nensey-Johannes Reierse.
Apr. 5. Bigs, Peter and Elesebet-Frederick.
Hall, John and Sara-Willem.
Aten, Jan and Marya-Jacobes.
26. Lesk, Peter and Caetie-David.
May 17. Vannest, Fernandes and Marya-Jacobes.
31. Egbert, John and Metye-Tiunes.
June 7. Vanderbelt, Corneles and Stintie-Jacob.
14. Keilingger, Phillep and Henne-Ragel.
Merlett, Jan and Jannetie-Nieltie.
July 5. Egbert, Necolas and Marya-Elesebet.
Lefever, Simon and Marya-Anathe.
19. MecKenne, David and Rebecka-Isaac.
Aug. 23. Setven, Peter and Catlina-Elesebet and Neeltie.
Tenbrock, Jan and Gerritje-Johannes.
Sept. 13. Cole, Ezekiel and Lena-Marya.
Teunesse, Teunes and Arejaentie-Hendrickes.
Oct. 24. Post, Abraham and Stientie-Johannes. (Born Sept. 23, 1767; d. Sept. 2, 1769).
25. Hofman, Johannes and Rebecka-Jacob.
Striker, Jan and Judick-Jacob.

Nov. 8. Vannetten, Jan and Maregreta-Catrena.
Dec. 13. Monfort, Abraham and Neeltie-Sara.
Striker, Denise and Lena-Antye.
Aten, Jan and Elesebet-Madelena.
27. Janse, Abraham and Elesebet-Elsye.

1768.

Jan. 31. Meinders, Willem and Catrena-Hendrick.
Feb. 3. Bedine, Isaac and Marigreta-Elsye.
Mar. 6. Brower, Daniel and Mariya-Sara.
Apr. 10. Bigs, Peter and Elesebet-George. (Born blind).
Arey, Jacob and Catrina-Jacob.
May 29. Meller, Jan and Febe-Ebbe.
Queck, Petries and Johanna-Johannes.
June 12. Low, Jan and Catrena-Judick.
Callshet, Martice and Dina-Pieter.
Vannostrant, Johannes and Antie-Anatie.
July 10. Waldren, Corneles and Sara-Ida.
Clickner, Joris and Elsye-Catrena.
11. M'Kinne, Martecaii and Angeneitie-Willem.
24. Salemon, Jacob and Sara-Anatie.
Aug. 14. Swese, Emas and Ida-Jannetie.
Bretten, Richard and Eva-Enne.
Sept. 4. Trophagen, Hendrick and Annatie-Hendrick.
Simonse, Jan and Catlina-Lena.
Demon, Peter and Adreyana-Wilhelmus.
Oct. 16. Demott, Isaac and Molle-David.
Aten, Gerret and Dina-Willem.
Neul, Peter and Dirckje-Johannes.
Vanende, Corneles and Annatie-Corneles.
Nov. 6. Demott, Jacob and Nelle-Neeltie.
Tine, Andries and Angenetie-Andrias.
---- and Henne Keilenger-Sara.
Dec. 11. Vanarsdalen, Hendrick and Catlina-Hendrick.
Devore, Daneel and Mary-Obediah.
25. Vanderbilt, Jacobes and Elesebet-Andries.
26. Hafman, Jacob and Stentie-Lena.

1769.

Feb. 5. Hall, Tobeies and Sara-Elesebet.
Hall, John and Sara-Cornelis Wickoff.
Stout, Thomas and Jannetie-Gerret.

Lane, Corneles and Sara-Hendrick.
Mar. 12. Stoll, Jan and Jannetie-Antie.
Cornel, Alber and Antie-Elesebet.
Vanetten, Arie and Jacemantie-Sara.
Bogert, Isaac and Neeltie-Annatie.
Vlerboom, Servase and Femmetie Schamp-Knertie.
May 21. Vansickle, Rinier and Mayeke-Sameel.
Vanhuis, Isaac and Neeltie-Jan.
June 4. Monfort, Jacobes and Leya-Petres.
Collshit, Matiees and Nensey-Peter.
5. Green, John and Elesebet-Ellener.
Vansickle, Jan and Maregreta-Henrey.
25. Cock, Thomas and Ida-Thomas.
Egbert, Nicolas and Mariya-Nicolas.
Fanger, Williem and Cerstena-Jemes.
Vansickle, Jan and Catrena-Mariya.
July 30. Egbert, Jan and Metye-Peules.
Hafman, Johannes and Rebecka-Joseph.
Cole, Ezekel and Lena Shipman-Ezekeel.
Lane, Aron and Ledeya-Rebecka.
Sept. 10. Van Veet, Willem and Mariya-Hendrickes.
Bogert, Corneles and Nelle-Isaac.
Oct. 29. Clickner, Jurrey and Elsye-Johannes.
Vansickle, Corneles and Anne-Mariya.
Biggs, Peter and Elesebeth-Elesebeth.
Mackenne, David and Rebecke-Sara.
Dec. 17. Cole, Jesaija and Sara-Mariya.
Post, Abraham and Stientie-Johannes. (Born Nov. 9, 1769; d. Feb. 21, 1772).
Hall, Georgs and Elesebet-Jan.

1770.

Jan. 7. Vansickle, Jan and Stientie-Abraham.
28. Tenbrock, Jan and Trientie Vrome-Gerret.
Feb. 18. Monfort, Abraham and Neeltie-Saerthe.
Mar. 4. Brower, Daneel and Marya-Eva.
Apr. 8. Cule, Simon and Mariya-Fredrick.
May 6. Janson, Peter and Antye-Mariya.
20. Vanderbilt, Corneles and Stintie-Sara.
June 24. Van horn, Jemes and Elesebet-Jemes.
July 7. Setven, Peter and Catlina-Johannes.

Vanderbilt, Ares and Angenetie-Geertye.
Cupper, Thomas and Mariya-Isaac.
8. Striker, Jan and Judick-Eva.
Co Zine, Peter and Wilemtie-Corneles.
Meckdennel, Collen and Geertie-Jacob.
Minders, Willem and Catrena-Johannes.
29. Kenney, Michel and Mariya-Welliem.
Aug. 12. Vannest, Johannes and Judick-Lena.
McKenne, Martegaie and Angnetie-Antie.
Bedine, Isaac and Maregreta-Maregreta.
Devore, Daneel and Sara-Mariya.
Demon, Peter and Adryana-Welhelmes.
Sept. 9. Traphagel, Hendrick and Annatie-Jonathan.
Lane, Corneles and Sara-Elesebet.
23. Neul, Peter and Dirckje-Jacob.
Arrey, Jacob and Annatie-Isaac.
Oct. 14. Arrey, Isaac and Annatie-Peter.
Hall, Tobies and Sara-Ann.
Prusse, Cristofel and Mariya-Hariya.
Lane, Geisbert and Matye-Elesebet.
Janson, Abraham and Elesebet-Mariya.
Nov. 25. Decker, Johannes and Sara-Femmetie.
Dec. 16. Vrome, Hendrick and Jacominthe-Sores.
Tine, Andres and Angenetie-Catrena.
Teunesse, Teunes and Areyatie-Altie.
1771.
Jan. 27. Counover, Gerret and Antye-Gerret.
Cole, Ezekeel and Lena-Sara.
Cineer, Henrey and Mariya-Femmetie.
Mar. 24. Vandevere, Fernandes and Rebecka-Fernandes.
Waldren, Corneles and Sara-Geertye.
Vlerebome, Serevase and Femmetye-Peter.
Hofman, Jacob and Stintye-Isaac.
Apr. 14. Sweley, Amos and Ida-Elesebet.
Dow, Andries and Mariya-Crestofel.
Cossaat, David and Jannetie-David.
Simonse, Gerret and Areyantie-Corneles.
21. Callshet, Mattheies and Nensey-Dina.
Slagt, John and Catrena-Mattie.
May 26. Vanhuis, Isaac and Neeltye-Mattye.

Stevens, Henry and Magdelena-Catrena.
June 9. Egbert, Necolas and Mariya-Gorge.
July 14. Vanetten, Jan and Maregreta-Janetye.
Wene, Peter and Jannetie-Antye.
Aug. i8. Demott, Jacob and ____ - Jacob.
Biggs, Peter and Elesebet-Derick.
Wickoff, Marten and Geertye-Hendrick.
Vansickle, Rinier and Maieke-David.
Sept. 29.Bretten, Abraham and Sara-Sara.
Nov. 10. Hall, Gorge and Elesebet-Magdalena.
Van Clef, Isaac and Dorkes-Mariya.
Cleckner, Jurrey and Elsye-Jannetie.
Dec. 22.Copper, Thomas and Mariya-Sara.
Kenne, Michel and Mariya-Andries.
Green, John and Elesebet-Richard.
Vandick, Jacobes and Jenneke-Maregreta.
Vansickle, Jan and Mariya-Cate.
29. Ditmas, Johannes and Servya-Williem.
Tenbroock, John and Annatie-Andries.
1772.
Jan. 26. Lane, Arey and Ledeya-Nelle.
Vansickle, Andries and Annatic-Annatie.
Steen, Michel Crigel and Annatie-Gorge.
Feb. 23. Emmens, Abraham and Annatie-Jacbes.
Mar. 8. Wickoff, Necolaes and Altye-Catrena.
Egbert, John and Mettye-Jacob.
29. Stout, Thomas and Jannetie-Elesebet.
Apr. 12. Snedeker, Jacobes and Annatie-Lea.
Wickoff, Peter and Jannetie-Albert.
Wickoff, Williem and Molle-Edward.
May 10.Van horn, Abraham and Geertie-Corneles Wickoff.
Witnesses: Corneles Wickoff and Elesebet Wickoff.
More, John and Catrena-Abraham.
Witnesses: Abraham Vanhorn and Geertie Vanhorn.
June 28. Bogert, Isaac and Elesebet-Neeltie.
Vanderbilt, Jacobes and Elesebet-Hendrick.
Aug. 9. Tomson, John and Judick Bodine-John. (Born July 3, 1772; d. Mar. 9, 1947) (John Tomson was b. Apr. 15, 1730. "Killed and scalped by ye Tory and Indians at Shemokem," June 9, 17-8. See "Hazard's Penn. Archives," VII, p. 589). (Judick Bodine

was b. Mar. 17, 1735; bapt. Apr. 20, 1735, at Raritan Ch.; d. July, 1796).

23. Vanarsdale, Joseph and Elesebet-Lucresya.
Meinders, Williem and Catrena-Wilhelmus.
Amack, Jan and Catrena-Titye.

Sept. 27. Wickoff, Simon and Jacameintye-Mettye.

Oct. 31. Vansickle, Jan and Catrena-Williem.
Miller, Jan and Febe-Jan.

Nov. 1. Johnson, Ellicksander and Cattina-Johannes.

22. Daley, Williem and Margret-Jan.
Vanetten, Arey and Jacemientie-Geisbert.
Striker, Jan and Judick-Marya.
Cownover, Peter and Nelle-Nelle.

Dec. 13. Vanderbilt, Jan and Angenetie-Corneles.
Swart, Corneles and Maregreta-Geertie.
Blankinberg, Christeyaen and Mariya-Antye.
Cole, Ezekeel and Lena-Lena.

27. Cule, Simon and Marya-Elesebet.
Devore, Daneel and Sara-Margret.

1773.

Feb. 14. Wickoff, Jan and Maregreta-John.
Janson, Abraham and Elesebeth-Jan.

15. Messelaar, Corneles and Mariya-Sara. [Wife of Richard Drake. Died in Ovid, N.Y., Sept., 1826.]

Mar. 14. Van Clef, Isaac and Dorkes-Lowerence.
Hall, Williem and Rebecka-Samuiel.
Hall, Tobies and Sara-Richard.
Tenbroock, Jan and Annatie-Sara.

28. Egbert, Necoles and Mariya-Jemes.
Arrey, Isaac and Annatie-Johanna.
Vanhorn, Abraham and Geertie-Anta.

Apr. 18. Simonse, Gerret and Areyantye-Abraham.

May 2. Pettenger, Jan and Annatie-Annatie.
Hoffman, Jacob and Stintie-Blandena.
Vliet, Jan and Jacamientie-Maregreta.
Decker, Johannes and Sara-Micheel.

23. Wene, Peter and Janntie-Sara.
Wickoff, Johannes and Mariya-Antie.

June 6. Henderson, Jemes and Sara-Robert.

27. Sutven, Peter and Johanna-Neeltie.

Stoll, Jacob and Sara-Sara.
July 11.Cownover, Abraham and Rebecka-Joris.
Aug. 15.Van Horn, Abraham and Eva-Baltes Pickel.
Vrome, Hendrick and Jacemientie-Jacob.
Van Vliet, Jan and Elsebet-Catrena.
Vansickle, Gerret and Nensey-Gerret.
Cule, Peter and Elsye-Fredrick.
Bennet, Peter and Elsebet-Arreyantie.
16. Vansickle, Direck and Mariya-Rineir.
29. Simonse, Jan and Ledeya-Jan.
Sept. 19. Pettenger, Hendrick and Mariya-Abraham.
Demon, Peter and Adrayana-Isaac.
Vlereboom, Serrevase and Femmetie-Femmetie.
Oct. 17. Monfort, Abraham and Neeltie-Mariya.
Wickoff, Jan and Aeltie-Peter.
Sweesey, Emos and Ida-Mariya.
Van nest, Joris and Lemmtie-Abraham.
Janson, Peter and Anne-Elesbet.
Nov. 14. Couper, Thomas and Mariya-Jannetic and Mariya.
Daley, John and Anntie-Jenneke.
Dec. 19. Clickner, Jeurey and Elsye-Lena.
1774.
Jan. 2. Smack, Martice and Geertie-Abraham.
23. Snedeker, Jacobus and Annatie-Helletye.
Mar. 20. Van horn, James and Elesebet-Elesebet.
May 29. Green, John and Elesebeth- Metthew.
Waldren, Corneles and Sara-Mariya.
Mattison, Joseph and Catrena-Mariya.
Neul, Peter and Dirckye-Ealtie.
30. Trophager, John and Geertie-Hendrick.
June 11. Kempel, Chriteyaer and Frenkye-Williem.
12. Smack, Jan and Sara-Jacobas.
July 17. Vorhees, Johannes and Rebecka-Mariya.
Van Vliet, Williem and Mariya-Rebecka.
Teunesse, Teunes and Areyantie-Susan.
Stillewel, Richard and Antta-Tobies.
Aug. 21. Bigs, Gorge and Jannetie-Mariya.
Sept. 24. Tenbroock, Jan and Annatie-Counrate.
Post, Abraham and Stintye-Abraham. (Born Aug. 27, 1774.)
Sharp, Mathias and Sara-Antye.

Cornel, Albert and Antye-Neeltie.
Nov. 2. Cownover, Gorge and Nensey-Gerret.
Herreton, Williem and Petiance-Mariya.
Hunt, Jacob and Nensey-Daneel.
Arnack, Jan and Catrena-Andries.
20. Slaght, John and Cate-John.
Vansickle, Dirick and Mariya-Gabereel.
21. More, John and Catrena-Elesebet.
Witnesses: Corneles Wickoff and Elesebet Wickoff.
Dec. 4. Low, Jan and Aeltie-Catlintie.
Hunt, Daneel and Elesebet-David.
Biggs, Peter and Elesebet-Peter.
1775.
Jan. 8. Wickoff, Simon and Mariya- ---- and Geertie.
Buckelow, Jan and Mariya-Egness.
Devore, Daneel and Sara-Peter.
Mannen, Samuel and Catrena-Maregreta.
9. Vleet, Jan and Jacamientie-Geertie.
Witnesses: Abraham Vanhorn and Geertie Vanhorn.
Feb. 12. Cole, Ezekeel and Lena-Sara.
Arrey, Isaac and Annatie-Jacob.
Mar. 5. Meinders, Williem and Catrena-Mariya.
Apr. 2. Borca, Evert and Cornelya-Isaac.
3. Biggs, Jan and Maregreta-David Kenne.
23. Wickoff, John and Catrena-Jacob.
May 7. Counover, Peter and Neeltye-Albert.
---- and Elesebeth Willmott-Sesle.
Vrome, Hendrick and Jannetie-John.
27. Tine, Andries and Jacameintie-Casper.
July 2. Egbert, Nicklaes and Mariya-John.
Vansickle, Gerret and Nensey-Mariya.
Egbert, John and Elesbet-John.
16. Hall, Williem and Rebecka-Isaac.
Demont, Derick and Ragel-Philipes.
Aug. 20. Wickoff, Marten and Geertie-Marten.
Trophager, John and Geertie-John.
Vanhorn, Abraham and Eva-Simon Wickoff.
Daley, Williem and Margret-Catrina.
Mattison, Joseph and Cate-Hester.
Daley, John and Annatie-Elesebet.

21. Mattison, Jemes and Cate-Williem.
Sept. 10. Lane, Aurey and Ledeya-Aurey.
Prine, John and Serviya-Elesebet.
24. Cole, David and Margret-Margret.
Blue, Mickhel and Febe-Elesebet.
Hall, Tobies and Sara-Begeman.
Oct. 15. Ween, Peter and Jannetie-Jannetie.
Counover, Abraham and Elesebeth-Jacob.
Vanhorn, Abraham and Elesebet-Abraham.
29. Monfort, Abraham and Neeltie-Maragretja.
Wickoff, Simon and Jacameintie-Elesebet.
Witnesses: Corneles Wickoff and Elesebet Wickoff.
Janson, Corneles and Leija-Elesebet.
Vrome, Hendrick and Jacamentie-Gerretie.
Bretten, Richard and Eva-Ragel.
Nov. 20. Messelar, Corneles and Mariya-Jacob.
1776.
Jan. 7. Tuler, Bengemen and Catlina Bogert-Mariya.
Striker, John and Sara-Peter.
28. Cole, Jesaya and Sara-John.
---- and Maregreta Wellemse-John Peyet.
Mar. 3. Bowman, Corneles and Mariya-Corneles.
8. Lane, Abraham and Mary Hufman-Rebecca.
17. Bennet, Peter and Elesebet-Elesebet.
Janson, Abraham and Elesebet-Andries.
Defrest, Abraham and Maragreta-Jacameintie.
Apr. 7. Tenick, Abraham and Sara-Teunes.
Wickoff, Jan. and Altje-Mattaeis.
Vanhorn, James and Elesebet-Abraham.
Vrome, Peter and Elyse Bogert-Gerretye. (Born Mar. 26.)
21. Clickner, Jurrey and Elsye-Juries.
May 26. Vanhorn, Abraham and Geertye-Geertie.
Green, John and Elesebet-Ledeya.
Van Vlet, Andries and Elesebet-Andries.
26. Coper, Thomas and Marya-Abraham.
V:Middelswart, Andries and Sara Bogert-Henderieks.
June 23. Ten Brock, Jan and Annatie-Jacob.
Bogert, Guisbert and Willemtie Niefis-Petris.
Vlerebome, Serrevens and Femmetie-Geertrui.
July 7. Krusse, Jan and Blandena-Gerret.

28. Simonse, Gerret and Aryantie-Jacobes.
Sept. 1. Blankenberg, Christejane and Marya-Corneles.
25. Kenne, Adreyaan and Elesebet-David.
Oct. 7. Wickoff, Gorge and Rebecke-Elesebet.
19. Vanderbelt, Corneles and Stentie-Corneles.
20. Berka, Bergon and Lena-Bergon.
Blue, Ezekeel and Marta-Isaac.
Nov. 10. Cole, Ezekiel and Lena-Elesebet.
Van Vliet, Jan and Elesebet-Williem.
Schamp, Jose and Marya-Hendrick.
1777.
Jan. 19. Voorhees, Johannes and Rubecka-Isaac.
Smack, Martice and Geertie-Geertie.
Mar. 9. Bowman, Thomas and Lena-Corneles.
Apr. 30. Anderson, Gorge and Anne-Gorge.
Willimsen, Sammul and Judick Bodine-Naomi.
Yorcks, Willim and Elesebet-Catlinthe.
31. Vansickle, Gerret and Nensey-Margret.
Mienders, Williem and Catrena-Englebort.
May 4. Bowman, Cornelius and Marya-Catie.
Armstrong, William and Cattrena-Thomas.
Vandeventer, John and Sarah-Caleb.
18. Stillawill, Richard and Antie-Mattie.
Brocaw, Evert and Cornelya-Sara.
19. Schamp, Peter and Maregreta-Joeste.
June 8. Gist, Peter and Cate-Rachal.
Vanzant, Bernardes and Neeltje Beeckman-Annatie.
Biggs, Peter and Elesebet Middagh-Helena.
Witnesses: Gorge Biggs and Helena Kenney.
22. ---- and Elesebet Mackinne-Sara.
July 13. Cole, David, Jur., and Baleche Van zant-Margret. Born June 21, 1777.
27. Counover, Peter and Nelle-Samuel.
Aug. 1. Bogert, Isaac and Elesebet-Johannes and Isaac.
31. Vrome, Hendrick and Jakemientie-Trientie.
Teunessen, Teunes and Aryaentie-Jan.
Sept. 21. Daley, William and Maregreta-Edward.
Biggs, Gorge, Jr., and Janethe-Peggy and Betsey.
Oct. 5. Greggs, Bengeman and Nelle-John.
Dec. 5. More, John and Catrena-Jacobas.
1778.

Jan. 8. Daley, John and Annathe-Neeltie.
Mar. 1. Bogert, Gisbert and Willimtie-Johannes.
Apr. 19. Monfoort, Abraham and Neeltie-Annatie.
Simonson, John and Elesebet-Denies.
Wickoff, Joachem and Anathe-Catlienthe. (Born Nov. 30, 1777).
May 3. Vanhorn, James and Elesebet-Janetie.
17. Walderom, Cornelus and Sara-Cornelus.
Nief Veis, Johannes and Debora-Amee.
---- and Maria Vanderspegel-Herrerutta.
Ditmars, Fradrick and Femetit Dumon-Sietie. (Born May 19).
Dugen, Danel and Elesebet-Michal.
[Some doubt about above. Note says, "Born April 20, 1780"].
June 14. Lou, Bengeman and Elesebet-Elesebath.
Witness: Geertye Newberry.
Tine, Andries and Angenietye-Angenietye.
July 19. Lane, Arey and Lidea-John.
19. Cuper, Thomas and Marya-John.
Schamp, Joest and Marya-Sara.
Aug. 3. Gist, Peter and Catrena-Abraham.
26. Voorhees, John and Rubecka-Stientye.
Wickoff, Simon and Jacemientye-Jacamientye.
Janson, Adryaen and Hester-Marya.
Oct. 25. Vlereboom, Serevaes and Femetye-Maregreta.
Tunison, Cornelius and Elesebeth-Angenietye.
Swesey, Emus and Ida-Aaron.
6. Lane, Abraham and Mary Hufman-Elizabeth.
Nov. 22. Wickoff, John and Catrena-Ealtye.
Clickenger, Jurrey and Elsye-Maticus.
Dec. 6. Stevens, Joseph and Ealtye-Catrena.
27. York, William and Elesebeth-Bengemen.
1779.
Jan. 3. Wickoff, Joachim and Annatye-Jacobas.
5. Messelaar, Cornelius and Arreiantye-Marya.
Davis, Joris and Marya-Janetye.
Taylor, Bengeman and Cattlina-Geisbert Bogert.
Feb. 28. Schamp, Peter and Maregreta-John.
Griggs, Bengeman and Neeley-Sara.
Apr. 4. Post, Abraham and Stienthe-Johannes. (Born Feb. 16, 1779.)
Egbert, Jemes and Sara-Jemes.
Vannest, John and Sara-Jacob.

Lion, Henry and Marya-Michel.
25. Mienders, Williem and Geertie-Cattrana.
Johnson, Abraham and Elesbet-Antie.
Lane, Matieus and Altie-Aron.
May 16. Wickoff, Gorge and Rebecka-Johannes.
Anderson, Gorge and Annatie-Elesebet. [Married Geo. P. Schomp.]
Brocaw, Evert and Corneleya-Marya.
June 6. Bowman, Thomas and Lena-Marya.
27. Ramsey, Joseph and Rachel-James.
Aug. 15. Cole, David, Jr., and Baleche-Nelly.
Cole, Ezekiel and Lena-Tuenes.
Sept. 19. Bodine, Cornelius and Maragrita-Abraham.
Simonson, Jan and Elesebet-Lamethe. (Born Sept. 13).
Oct. 24. Covenhoven, Gerret and Antie-Arey.
Vanfleet, Jan and Elesebet-Isaac.
Nov. 28. Vansickle, Andries and Annatie-Sara.
Dec. 12. Vroom, Hendrick and Jacamientie-Jores.
1780.
Feb. 6. Niefvies, Johannes and Debera-Petres.
Wickoff, Niclas and Marya-Marya.
9. Tenick, Jacob and Jannetie-Sara.
Mar. 26. Tenick, Abraham and Nelly-Tobies.
Apr. 16. Beckman, Samuel and Elesebet-Enne.
Wickoff, John and Ealtye-John.
30. Stillwell, Richard and Antye-Rachel.
Smith, John and Catrena-Elesebet Bowdish.
June 19. Dugen, Danel and Catrena-Margret.
July 8. Blankenberg, Cristeaen and Marya-Cornelia.
9. Mitchel, Edward and Catrena-Jannetye.
Teuneson, Teunes and Arreaentye-Sara.
Lane, Cornelius and Sara-John.
Aug. 13. Biggs, Gorge and Jannetye-Jannetye.
Lion, Henry and Marya-Jane.
28. Low, John and Altye-Bengemen.
Oct. 12. Monfore, Peter and Altye-Nelley.
Cooper, Thomas and Marya-Margret.
Jonson, Cornelius and Lea-Marya.
Vroom, Peter and Elsye Bogert-Elesebet.
Stevens, Joshep and Altye-Henry.
Ramsy, Joseph and Rachel Van Sickel-James.

Nov. 26. Griggs, Bengemen and Nelley-Aron.
1791.
Feb. 1. Waldren, Jacobas and Maragreta-Bengemen.
18. Mac Clow, Thomas and Febe-Catrena.
Wickoff, Simon and Jacamientye-Gertie.
Mar. 3. Lane, Abraham and Mary Hufman-Mary.
11. Huff, Peter and Marya-Abraham.
Vlereboom, Serevase and Femmetye-Sara.
25. Bodine, Cornelius and Maregreta-Peter.
Cole, Ezekiel and Lena-Josiah.
Egbert, James and Sara-Mary.
York, William and Elesebeth-Mary.
Prine, Daniel and Elizebeth-Daniel; Elesebeth; James; Tobias Hall.
Cleckner, Jurey and Elsje-Abraham.
Apr. 29. Wickoff, Thou and Catrena-Simon.
Lane, Mathew and Altye-Antje.
Schamp, Peter and Margret-Rebecca.
May 20. Mainders, William and Gertje-Susanna Hall.
June 10. De freest, Abraham and Maragreta-Catlina.
Brocaw, Evort and Cornelia-Johannes.
July 8. Voorheese, Johannes and Rubecka-Rubecka.
Sept. 23. Simonson, John and Elisebeth Stryker-Elesebeth.
Oct. 22. Van Vleet, William and Antye-Marja.
28. Decker, Johannes and Sara-Johannes.
Teunisson, Dirick and Marya-Neeltye.
Stillwill, Richard and Enne-Richard.
Vandeventer, John and Sara-Sara.
1782.
Jan. 11. Lane, Jacob and Susanna-Hannah.
Teunison, John and Peggy-Cornelius.
12. Vanhorn, James and Elizebeth-Mary
Apr. 14. Brocaw, Bergon and Lena-Nelly.
Tenick, Abraham and Nelley-Siteye.
Wickoff, Gorge and Rubecka-Maregreta.
Wyckoff, Nicklas and Marya-Cornelius Van Cleef.
Sickles, Garret and Phebe-Marya.
Cline, John and Jannetie-Enne.
Mitchel, Edward and Catrena-John.
Aug. 13. Van Vleet, John and Elesebeth-John.
Monfore, Peter and Altye-Abraham.

Lane, Arey and Ledeja-Andries Vansickle.
Sept. 29. Griggs, Bengemen and Nelley-Daniel.
Oct. 12. Vanarsdale, Philip and Margret-Isaac.
Smock, Matthias and Hannah-Gertye. (born Sept. 19, 1782).
Dec. 22. Low, Cornelius and Sara-Sara.
Vanhorn, Abram and Geertye-Mathies.
Vanhorn, Simon and Sara-Marya.
1783.
Mar. 2. Simonson, Stofel and Cristiena-Garrett.
Lane, Mattieus and Altje-Cornelius.
Anderson, Gorge and Enne-Mettie.
Johnson, John and Sara-Aron.
Venselius, Aandrew and Lenah-Gorge Andres.
---- and Marya Arrey-Jacob.
May 18. Lane, Abraham and Mary Hufman-Margerett.
July 27. Voorhees, Johonis and Rebekan-Johonis.
Lane, Cornelius and Stientic-Liedea.
Navius, Johonis and Debora-Martan.
Vanhorn, Abraham and Elesebeth-Liedea.
Johnson, Samuel and Corneleja-Jemime.
Hunt, William and Enne-Cete.
York, William and Elesebeth-Jan.
Sept. 28. Monfort, Abraham and Neelije-Abraham.
Huff, Peter and Maria-Cete.
Low, Cornelius and Catlina-Lena.
Cinne, John M. and Elesebet Wyckoff-John.
Dumont, Elbert and Corneleja-Adryana.
Jansen, Adreajaen and Stintje-Abraham.
Striker, Peter and Lena-Jan.
Tenick, Jacob and Jannethe-William.
Lane, Matties and Geerthe-John.
---- and Jenne Keerhart-Abraham. (Born Sept. 19, 1783).
Nov. 9. Wickoff, John and Altje Lane-Nicolas.
23. Vandorn, Cristean and Jehanna-John.
25. Fardimwort, Henery and Elizebath-Jacob Demot.
Dec. 7. Vrome, John and Nancy-Catrena.
Van sickle, John and Rachel-John.
Aray, Isaac and Annatje-Jacobes.
11. Simonsen, John and Elesebet-Femmethe.
Schamp, Peter and Margret-Margret.

18. Wickoff, Simon and Jacamienthe-Anne.
28. Guelick, Johones and Elesebeth-Johanas.
Demott, Denick and Marta-Leah.
Van middleswart, John and Hannah-Hendrickes. (Born Dec. 20th).

1784.

Feb. 8. Davis, Gorge and Maria-Bergun.
Williams, Gorge and Maria-James Melven.
Minders, William and Gerthe-Elesebeth.
22. Stout, Thomas and Jannethe-Jannethe.
Mar. 7. Manning, Samuel and Catrina Cole-Leah.
8. Amack, John and Catharina Dennis-Isaac.
21. Berry, Abraham and Maria-Cetje.
29. Shits, Williem and ____ - Cornelius.
Witness: Marya Bowman.
Apr. 4. Wyckoff, Nicklas and Marya-Barbaratie.
11. Stevens, Joseph and Ealtje-Amaleja.
18. Griggs, Daniel and Margret-Barnet.
25. Huff, Isaac and Catrena-Lues.
Defrest, Abraham and Marregretje-Annatje.
May 9. Cline, Gorge and Rebecke-Frenkje.
Vlerrebome, Serrevase and Famitje-Gorge.
Tenick, Abraham and Nelly-John Rue.
Burger, Casper and Antje-Jasper. (Born May 1).
Cline, John and Jannetje-Rachel. (Born May 9, 1784).
15. Cole, Ezekiel and Lena-Charity.
16. Taylor, Bengemen and Catlina-John and Bengemen.
June 20. Pettenger, Daneel and Geerthe-Antje.
27. Verselies, Andrew and Lana-Sara.
Dugan, Daniel, and Elesebeth-Eva.
27. Bennet, Peter and Elesebeth-Peter.
July 18. Demont, Peter and Marya-Marya.
Slaght, Abraham and ---- -James.
Aug. 1. Wickoff, John and Catrena-Joseph.
29. Lane, Corneleus and Stientie-Neeltie.
Kenney, Adriejaan and Maregrieta-John.
Oct. 17. Grigs, Barent and Nelly-Gorge.
Dilly, Tunes and Elesebeth-Elesebeth.
Bowman, John and Rebecka-Cristenna.
Nov. 7. Monfore, Peter and Aeltye-Gerret.
Waldron, William and Marya-Samuel.

9. Carte, Jemes and Liedeja-Antone Hesel.
Witnesses: Anton Hesel and Ellener, his wife.
28. Smock, Mathias and Hannah-Jannetye.
Dec. 19. Vrome, Hendrick and Jemime-Jannetje. (Born Nov. 13, 1784). Baptized by Dr. Vanasdel.
Wickoff, Nicolas and Leah-Hendrick.

1785.
Jan. 1. Bedine, Cornelius and Maregretje-John.
Cole, Obidiah and Rebecka-Esekiel.
3. Johnson, Andrew and Margret-Margret.
Mitchel, Edward and Catrena-Andries.
23. Scamp, David and Lena Hoffman-Gorge.
30. Vansickle, William and Maria-Hendrick.
Feb. 6. Voorhees, Abraham and Wilmtje-Geertje.
13. Cowenhoven, Daniel and Maria-Catriena.
20. Johnson, John and Sara-Elesebeth.
27. Alleger, Bengeman and Sisley-Sisley.
---- and Marya Alleger-Jeremiah.
Covenhoven, Abraham and Rebeckah-Abraham; Sarah; Elisabeth.
Mar. 20. Wickoff, Gorge and Rebecke-Marya.
Lane, Matthias and Aeltje-Sara.
Demont, John and Anathe-Areanthe.
Vandick, Jacobes and Jannethe-Jannethe.
Apr. 17. Demont, Elbert and Cornelia-Maria.
Bowman, Thomas and Jannethe-Ragel.
Mitchel, Edwar, was baptized on making confession of his faith before the Rev. Simon Van Asdalen and the Consistory.
May 29. Vroom, John and Nancey-Jannetye.
Leturatt, David and Lenah-John.
June 12. Monfort, Isaac and Hannah-Lidia.
Mucklow, Thomas and Phebe Farly-Isaack. (Born Mar. 14, 1785).
19. Wickoff, Denise and Elesebet-Corneleus.
Cimble, Cristefer and Frinkje-Margret.
Hall, Isaac and Jude Van Fleet-Elesebet.
July 10. Cerkoff, Arrebanes and ____ -Maregreta.
Vandeventer, John and Sarah-Margret.
Voorhees, John and Rebekah-Isaac.
Johnson, Arean and Catlantie Vorhais-Mary.
Aug. 1. Cornell, Tunos and Mary Williamson-Janetie; Barholomew; Catherine; Aulida.

7. Van Dorn, Isaack and Sarah Appie-Abraham.
14. Rockafalla, David and Margaret Resler-Henry.
21. Lane, Abraham and Mary Hufman-Harmon.
Sept. 4. Cutter, Samuel and Mary Cole-Leanah.
18. Haas, John and Lydea Rue-John.
Van Atten, Aaron and Jacemima Hall-Isaack Goveneer.
Triphagen, Rulif and his wife-Henry.
Nov. 6. Schamp, Peter and Marget Hufman-Peter.
Van Sickle, Garret and Nance Conon-Garret.
Titsort, Peter and Catherine Huff-Levi. (Born Sept. 6, 1785).
Boman, Thomas and Lenah Tufen-John.
Pearse, Thomas and Else Harsoh-Mary.
Ramsy, Joseph and Rachel V: Sickel-Alexander.
Emans, Jaromes and Caty Van Campen-Rebacah.
Yorks, William and Elizabeth Alleger-Hannah.
Aumock, Abraham and Suffiah McCarn-Andrew.
Van Sickle, Andrew and Magdelena Lane-Sarah.
Wickoff, Peter and Caty Van Atten-Sarah. (Born Sept. 27, 1785).
The Rev. Simon Van Asdalen's Black Tone. Baptized on making Confession of his faith Before the Minister and the Consistory.
Guleck, John and Elizabeth Dumott-Joacem.
Dec. 18. Field, Jeremiah and Jane Ten Eyk-Ritcherd.
1786.
Jan. 8. Williamson, Cornelius and Staintie Demott-John.
Feb. 7. Powesa, Cornelius and Catrintie Sutphin-Elizabeh.
Vorhees, Folkard and Marget Galtry-Rulf.
19. Covenhoven, Cornelius and Nealtie Monfort-Sarah.
Mar. 6. Neueus, John and Deborah Mount-Anne.
---- and Catherine Vandeventer-Tunes.
Anderson, Gorge and Anne Wickoff-Jamime.
Rosaborn, Robert and Syntie Dumont-Patres.
Matthews, John and Mary Berry-Catherine.
Wickoff, Joseph and Army McKinny-Jese.
Mannen, Samuel and Catherine Cole-Catherine.
Stout, Thomas and Jannite Van Stay-Rachel.
Johnson, Samuel and ____ -Sarah.
Blew, Ezekle and Martha Voorhais-Elizabeth.
Cole, Tunes and Mary Cock-Jacobes.
---- and Lucretie Cock-Lydya.
Apr. 17. McKinny, John and Elizabeth Wicaff-Isaack.

July 2. Low, Cornelius and Catlina Striker-Catlina.
Lane, Cornelius and Sarah Stevens-Sarah.
Cornel, William and Sarah Wyckoff-Catlanty.
Minor, William and Charity Proos-Christean.
Dumott, John and Caty Vroom-Hendrick Vroom.
23. Stryker, Barent and Hannah Jinnings-Jeremiah.
Jobes, Adam and Caty Covenhoven-Elizabeth.
Aug. 22. Hogeland, Dirick and Judah V: Vleat-Dirrick.
Ramsy, Joseph and Rachel Vansickel-John.
Dec. 26. Simason, John and Elizabeth Striker-Simeon Van Astdalen. (Born Dec. 4, 1786).
Van Vleat, John and Elizabeth Huff-Mary.
Davis, George and Mary Brokaw-Abraham.
V: Sickel, John and Rachel V: Vleat-Mary.
Ammerman, Dannel and Lenab Nafews-Caty.
Stull, Joseph and Caty Sutphin-Anny.
Waldron, Rinear and Nelly Aumerman-Cornelius.
M'Clo, Thomas and Phoby Farley-William.

1787.

Mar. 11. V: Vleat, George and Martha Voorhais-Margreat.
Johnson, Andrew and Elizabeth Johnson-Natie.
Post, Abraham and Caty Dumott-Peter. (B. Feb. 5, 1787; d. Mar. 15, 1788).
Waldron, William and Mary Waldron-John.
Cole, Obadiah and Rebacca Hufman-John.
Emmans, John and Trintie Ten Brook-Garritie.
Apr. 10. Wyckoff, Denys and Elizabeth Ten Eyck-Anne. (Born Oct. 3, 1786).
Mitchel, Edwar and ____ -Mary.
Lane, Matthias and Altje Covenhoven-William.
Stevens, Joseph and Altje Henderson-John.
Stout, Thomas and Jannetje Van Stee-Brachje.
Post, Peter and ____ -Cornelius.
July Jinnings, Peter and Elizabeth Van Vleat-Isaack.
Witness: Mary Aughter.
Simason, Christopher and Cerstena Snadacer-Hannah.
Sept. 2. Cutter, Samuel and Mary Cole-Susanah.
Manen, Samuel and Catherine Cole-Molly.
Oct. 28. Dumott, Dirrick and Martha Snadiker-Martha.
Schamp, Peter and Margret Huffman-Sarah.
Nov. 4. V: Dorne, Abraham and Jahanah-Abraham.

Gulick, Joachim and Sinne Wickoff-Cornelian.
11. Verselias, Andrew and Lenah Van Sickel-Rachel.
18. Covenhoven, Rulef and Sarah Vansickle-David.
Huff, Peter and Mary Brokaw-Elizabeth.
Dumont, Albert and Cornelian Hogelant-John.
25. Wickoff, John and Mary Johnson-Cornelious.
Wickoff, George and Rebeckah V: Cleaf-Cornelian.
Dec. 30.Hall, Richard and Jannetie Vroom-Elizabeth. (Born Sept. 17).
Wickoff, Simon and Jamima Anderson-Cornelian.
Voorhaise, Abraham and Wallimtie Wickoff-Lucas.
Field, Jerimah and Jannetie Ten Eyk-Jacob.
Van Dorne, Isaack and Sarah Oppy-Margret.

1788.
Jan. 28. Mackeinny, John and Elizabeth Wickoff-Rebecah.
Sutphin, Geisbert and Elizabeth Proos-Catlintie.
Aumerman, Abraham and Margret Sudam-Danel.
Apr. 13. Monfort, Peter and Altje Covenhoven-Peter.
Covenhoven, Cors. and Nelly Monfort-Nelly.
Lane, Abraham and Marry Hufman-Jacob.
Voorhase, John and Rebecah Williamson-Nelly.
Merlat, George and Hannah Vansickel-Jannetie.
Emmans, John and Traintje Ten Brook-Andrew.
Van Tine, Rinear and Nelly Mecolm-Elizabeth.
May 21. Vroom, John and Ann Bunn-Edward Bunn.
June 29. Minor, William and Gartji Proos-Sarah.
July 23. V: Horn, Wil'm and Elizabeth Van Horn-Garritje.
Titsort, Peter and Caty Huff-Rebecah.
Johnson, Andrew and Elizabeth Johnson-Mary.
Low, Wil'm and Franky Huff-Abraham Huff.
Huff, Isaack and Cathrine Waldron-Elisha.
27. Laquear, Jannetic (widdow of John Kline, dec'd)-John.
Aug. 3. Voorhais, Folkert and Peggy Goltry-Caty.
Sept. 14. Ditmas, John and Mary Smock-Saphyah.
21. Bogert, John and Antje Schank-John. (B. Aug. 26).
Oct. 26.Van Vleat, John and Elizabeth Huff-Elizabeth.
Latturat, Peter and Margaret Stout-Thomas Stout.
Dec. 14. Williamson, Cornelius and Staintje Demott-Anne. (Married Geo. D. Schomp).

1789.
Jan. 25. Stout, Thomas and Jannitie Van Stay-Sarah.

28. Stryker, Isaack and Mary Slaht-Elizabeth.
19 Cutter, Samuel and Mary Cole-Ephrem.
Apr. 26. Anderson, George and Anne Wickoff-Anne.
Waldron, Rinear and Nelly Amerman-Dannel.
May 3. Cole, Obadiah and Rebacah Hufman-Rebacca.
Maclo, Elizabeth Bruer (wife of Cornelius)-Joseph. (B. Feb. 6).
22. Labtulix, Peter and Margret Van Vleat-Abraham.
Simonson, John and Elizabeth Striker-Mary. (B. Apr. 29).
Brocaw, Isaack and Mary Wickoff-Margret.
July 26. Dally, William and Margret Bunn-Margret.
Aug. 9. Waldron, William and Mary Waldron-William.
Low, Cornelius and Yane Allen-Garret. (B. July 13).
17. Kroesen, Derrick and Abigal Ten Eyke-Sally.
23. Van Dorn, Christean and Jahannah Hogeland-Jahannah.
Nov. 15. Sutphin, Gaisbert and Elizabeth Proos-Peter.
Dec. 6. Ramsy, Joseph and Rachel Van Sickel-Sarah.
Covenhoven, Rulef and Sarah Van Sickel-James.
25. Aumerman, Abraham and Margret Sudam-Hendrick.
1790.
Jan. 13. Dumont, Albert and Cornelian Hogelant-Audreyans.
Van Sickel, Andrew and Rebecah Van Sickel-Hannah.
Mar. 21. Jinnings, Elizabeth Van Vleat (wife of Peter)-Mary.
Apr. 4. Monfort, Peter and Altje Covenhoven-David Covenhoven.
May 8. Amerman, Daniel and Lenah Naves-Elizabeth.
Voorhaise, Abraham and Williamtje Wickoff-Sarah.
Brokaw, Abraham and Judah Van Vleat-Abraham. (B. Mar. 11).
June 13. Monfort, Isaack and Hannah Lane-Nelle.
Aug. 1. Ditmas, John, Jr., and Mary Smock-Charrity.
15. Hall, Richard and Jannetie Vroom-Richard.
Stout, Thomas and Jannetje Van Stay-Cornelius.
Mucklow, Phoby Farley (wife of Thomas)-Cornelus. (B. May 25).
Oct. 31. Demott, Abraham and Hannah Van Horn-John; Cornelius.
Demott, Derrick and Lanah Van Sickle-Leah.
Johnson, Andrew and Elizabeth Johnson-Elizabeth. (B. Feb. 16).
Nov. 21.McKinny, John and Elizabeth Wickoff-Peter Studaford.
Hall, Isaack and Judah Van Vleat (dau. of Thomas) -Hannah.
28. Wickoff, Simon and Jamime Anderson-Gerdina.
Dec. 26. Lane, Abraham and Mary Hufman-John.
1791.
Feb. 6. Williamson, Cornelius and Staintje Demott-Abraham.

May 1. Mac Cloc, Elizabeth Bruer (wife of Cornelius)-Mary. (B. Feb. 21).
7. Cuters, Samuel and Mary Cole-Sarah.
22. Brocaw, Isaack and Mary Wickoff-Bergun.
29. Verseles, Andrew and Lenah Van Sickel-Abraham.
June 12. Vroom, Hend'k D., and Elizabeth Demott-Michael DeMott. (B. May 18).
Sutphin, Gisbert and Elizabeth Proos-Mary; Judah.
Simason, John and Elizabeth Striker-Anne. (B. May 14).
26. Low, Wil'm and Franke Huff-Hannah. (B. June 8).
Waldron, Wil'm and Mary Waldron-Ritchard. (B. Mar. 20).
July 3. Cole, Obadiah and Rebecah, his wife-Mary.
Sept. 18.Studaford, Rev. Peter and Phebe V:Der Vare-Jacobes Van Der Vare. (B. Aug. 20).
Stryker, Abraham and Anne Lapordus-Peter.
Demont, Abraham and Jane Van Cleaf-Margret; Adriannah. (B. Oct. 21).
Oct. 2. Williams, George and Mary Latteret-John. (B. Aug. 27).
Stryker, John and Elizabeth Kinny-John. (B. Aug. 5).
V: Dorne, Abraham and Mary Covert-Mariah. (B. May 14).
Wyckoff, Hendrick and Fammetje Dacker-Joannes Dacker. (B. Aug. 31).
Nov. 6. Bogart, John, Jr., and Anne Schank-Martan Schank. (B. Sept. 30).
Striker, Christopher and Jude Low-Garret. (B. Mar. 16).
Wickoff, Cornelius and Elizabeth Cornal-Cornelias. (B. Oct. 14).
14. Mates, John and Mary Berry-Anne. (B. Oct. 18).
Covenhoven, Garret and Margret Reger-David. (B. Sept. 24).
Ten Brook, Gabrel and Caty Bodine-Peter Bodine.
16 Low, Cornelius and Jane Allen-Robert Allen. (B. Sept. 1).
Edger, Nathaniel and Elizabeth Bogart-Isaack Bogart. (B. June 13, 1790).
Low, Abraham and Phobe Bodine-John; Easter. (John was b. Sept. 20, 1789; Phobe [Easter?] Jan. 2, 1791).

1792.
Feb. 5. Amerman, Danel and Lenah Nafey-Sarah.
26 Jinnings, Elizabeth Van Vleat (wife of Peter)-William. (B. Nov. 14, 1791).
Broon, Elleck and Joannah Stout-Rebecah. (B. Jan 12).
Mar. --. Stout, Thomas and Inatie Van Stay-Ritcherd.
Apr. 8. Johnson, Adrian and Tine Voorhees-Elizabeth. (B. Mar.11).
Breur, Wil'm and Catherine Bodine-William. (B. Feb. 15).

Hall, George and Margret Huff-Catherine. (B. Feb. --.)
Demott, Derrick and Martha Snadecer-John.
Stevens, Henry and Elizabeth Bockoven-Joseph.
29. Cole, Tunas and Rebecah Smith-Sarah. (B. Jan. 8).
Field, Jeremiah and Jannetje Ten Eyk-Jeramiah. (B. Feb. 17).
May 6. Emans, Leah Van Sickel (wife of Isaac)-John; Jacob. (John, born Feb. 12, 1791; Jacob, born May 5, 1787).
Tunason, Tunas and Margret Covenhoven-John Covenhoven. (B. Feb. 12).
Hall, George and Elizabeth Butner-Jannitie. (B. Oct. 15, 1791).
Yong, Peter and Phobe Buram-Peter. (B. Oct. 15, 1791).
Ernens, John and Traintje Ten Brook-John Ten Brook. (B. Apr. 8).
Scamp, David and Lenah Hufman-David. (B. Jan. 13).
Emans, Cornelius and Sarah Low-Caty. (B. Aug. 5, 1791).
Hall, Ritchard and Jannitje Vroom-Catherine. (B. Mar. 14).
Van Sickel, Andrew and Rebecah Lane-Nelly. (B. May 1).
June 3. Johnson, Henry and Agness Jinnings-Abraham. (B. Apr. 4).
Nimrod (Himrod?), William and Elizabeth Sutphin-Mariah. (B. Apr. 22).
Sheats, Peter and Jinny Savage-Fradrick Biggs. (B. Mar. 12).
Ten Brook, Derrick and Mary Bodine-Cornelius. (B. Mar. 3).
7. Merlat, Jost and Hannah V: Siccle-Polly. (B. June 7).
15. Johnson, Peter and Hannah Null-Sarah. (B. Nov. 15,1791).
Vorhess, Abraham and Williamtje Wickoff-Elias Wickoff. (B. May 14).
Huff, Peter and Mary Brocaw-Anne. (B. Apr. 1).
Monfort, Peter and Altje Covenhoven-Sarah. (B. Apr. -.)
Spader, Wil'm and Catrena V: Der Veer-Phobe. (B. Mar. 12).
William, Servant of Joseph Vandorn, and Elizabeth, Servant of Peter Quick- Mary.
July 15. Ditmas, John and Mary Smock-John. (B. June 22).
Edger, Nathaniel and Elizabeth Bogart-Moses (B. June 24).
Aug. 5. Emens, Jeromas and Sarah Emens-Elizabeth. (B. Mar. 13).
Sept. 9. Vroom, Hend'k D., and Elizabeth Demott-Jacamintie. (B. Aug. 11).
Low, Laurance and Hannah Latturat-Caty. (B. July 11).
Van Nest, Peter and Phobe Hardenbrook-Peter. (B. Apr. 8).
Kinny, Andrew and Areantje Bennet-Mary. (B. July 25).
Brocaw, Peter and Elizabeth Low-Mary; Jinny. (Mary, b. Aug. 2, 1792; Jinny, b. Jan. 19, 1790).
23. Stull, Joseph and Catrena Sutphen-Ann. (B. Aug. 22).

Ten Eyke, Andrew and Sarah Berger-Ann. (B. Aug. 20).
Dener, Matthies and Mary Amerman-Albert Amerman. (B. July 10).
Stryker, Peter and Sarah Low-Sally; Lenah. (Sally, b. Feb. 4, 1788; Lenah, b. May 21, 1792).

Oct. 14. Latturet, Peter and Margret Stout-Elizabeth. (B. Sept. 3).
Striker, Jacob and Hannah Labertux-Cathrin. (B. July 12).
Demont, John and Elizabeth Smally-John Hardenbergh.
Post, Abraham and Catrena Demott-Peter. (B. Sept. 12, 1792; d. Jan. 11, 1877).
Maclo, Phobe Farly (wife of Thomas)-Peter.

27. ---- and Jane Van Camp-Catherine. (B. Aug. 14).
---- Cate, a free Wench-Samuel.

Nov. 4. Stillwill, Nicholes and Catheline Van Nest-Richard. (B.Sept. 29).
V.Nest, Bernardus and Caty Sharp-Sarah. (B. Oct. 15).
Hamer, Cor's and Mary Veal-John. (B. Sept. 20).

11. Tremley, John and Mary Pool-Ann. (B. Sept. 10).

18. Van Houten, John and Charity Hall-Nelly. (B. Oct. 15).
Titsort, Peter and Caty Huff-Elizabeth. (B. Nov. 7).
V:Vleat, Garret and Catlantje Hagaman-Rebecah. (B. Oct. 23).

Dec. 9. Lane, Cornelius and Judah Van Vleat-Elizabeth. (B. Nov. 24).

1793.

Jan. 1. Wickoff, Cornelius and Elizabeth Cornell-Jacobus. (B. Nov. 27, 1792).

7. Williamson, Cornelius and Staintje De mott-Mary.
Lane, John and Nelly Berger-Harmen; Susannah. (Harmen, b. Aug. 16, 1790; Susannah, Dec. 14, 1792).
De Mott, Abraham and Hanah Van Horn-Cerstena.

Mar. 17. Hall, John and Ann Stryker-William. (B. Dec. 28, 1792).
Egbert, Nicles and Elizabeth Lane-Cornelius Lane. (B. Nov. 11, 1792).
Emens, Andrew and Elizabeth Lane-Dinah. (B. Nov. 1, 1792).
Sutphin, Gaisbert and Elizabeth Proos-John. (B. Dec. 17, 1792).
Wyckoff, Henry and Fammetje Dacker-Martin. (B. Jan. 21).

Apr. 14. Sutphin, Peter, Jr., and Caty Ten Eyk-Peter; Margret Ten Eyk. (Peter, b. Apr. 20, 1791; Margret Ten Eyk, Feb. 14, 1793).

May 5. Hall, Joseph and Catherine Mackinney-Hannah.
Dunkin, William-Mary; Hannah; Gitty; Sally. (Mary, b. Feb. 29, 1786; Hannah, June 29, 1789; Gitty, May 18, 1791; Sally, Jan. 14, 1793).
Brocaw, Abraham and Judah Van Vleat-William. (B. Feb. 9).
Voorhes, John and Rebecah Williamson-Kort. (B. Mar. --.)
Scamp, Peter and Margret Hufman-David; Mary. (David, b. Feb. 10).

19. Blew, Fradrick and Effe Titsort-Martba. (B. Mar. 28).
Simason, John and Elizabeth Striker-Denise. (B. Apr. 5).
Mitchel, Edward and Cathrine Mates-Peter. (B. Apr. 8).
Varseles, Andrew and Lenah Vansicle-James. (B. Feb. 17).
Tume, Rebecah Van Vleat (wife of David)-John. (B. Jan. 22).
June 15.Van Vleat, Adrean and Elizabeth Switsor-Ann. (B. Apr. 21).
Titsort, William and Alshe Van Nest-Mary. (B. Apr. 16).
30. Ditmas, William and Keziah Tunason-John. (B. Jan. 28).
July 7. Cole, Ezekiel, Jr., and Mary Wickoff-Catherine. (B. June 6).
Emens, Cornelius and Sarah Low-Garret Low. (B. Oct. 28, 1792).
Vroom, John and Ann Bunn-Peter. (B. May --.)
---- and Mary Stryker-John Striker. (B. Feb. 2).
Aug. 5. Brocaw, Isaack and Mary Wickoff-John Wickoff. (B. July 14).
Kinny, William and Phobe Van Daventer-Mary. (B. July 21).
Van Vleat, John and Elizabeth Huff-Abraham. (B. May 9).
Cutter, Samuel and Mary Cole-John.
Sept. 1. Roberson, William and Mary Bogart-John. (B. June 22).
8 Ten Eyke, Andrew and Mary Ten Eyke-Abraham. (B. July 21).
22 Bogart, John and Ann Schank-Sarah. (B. Aug. 20).
Oct. 6. Ten Eyke, Jacob and Ann Perine-Danniel. (B. Sept. 23, 1792).
13. Low, Wil'm and Franke Huff-Hendrick. (B. July 6).
22. Hall, Isaac and Judah Van Vleat-Mary. (B. July 31).
Wickoff, Cornelius and Sarah Van Vleat-Ann. (B. June 30).
26 Van Sickel, Wil'm and Christenah Cole-Mary. (B. Jan. 20).
Hutnet, Lenah Biggs (wife of David)-Elijah. (B. July 15, 1792).
---- and Tuntah Emens-Leah. (B. Mar. 13, 1792).
27 Ten Eyke, Cor's and Elizabith Johnson-Leah. (B. Sept. 26).
Nov. 17.Low, Larance and Hannah Lattaret-Gilbert. (B. Oct. 18).
Van Nest, Peter and Phobe Hardenbrook-Rebecah. (B. July 24).
Dally, William and Margret Bunn-Nathan. (B. Aug. 21).
V: Vleat, Henry and Doroty Tume-William. (B. Aug. 30.)

1794.

Jan. 19. Quick, Teunis and Altje Voorhees-Jaques. (B. Nov. 10, 1793).
Feb. 20. Sullivan, Margaret-John (surname Pantlern). (B. May, 1789; godfather Jerome Van Der Bilt).
Mar. 2. Cole, Obadiah and Rebekah-David. (B. Jan. 3).
9 Stout, Thomas and Jane Van Stay-Cornelius. (B. Dec. 23, 1793).
23 Pesbaco, Christopher and Caty Schank-Maica. (B. Feb. 12).
Apr. 13.Mackinney, John and Elizabeth Wickoff-Mary. (B. Mar. 7).
Beakman, John and Eave Bruer-Mary. (B. Jan. 26).

Himrod, Wil'm and Elizabeth Sutphin-Peter. (B. Feb. 25).
20. Hall, Richard and Jannetje Vroom-John Vroom.
Hamer, Corn's and Mary Veal-Elizabeth. (B. Mar. 23).
Stryker, Jacob and Hannah Laberulix-Jane. (B. Sept. 3, 1793).
27. Cole, Jacob and Sarah Cool-Christopher. (B. Mar. 19).
Hunt, Wil'm and Ann Johnson-Jacob. (B. Mar. 18).
May 11.Clickenger, John and Caty Karkhuff-Elizabeth. (B. Feb. 12).
24. Amerman, Danel and Lenah Neves-Jacobes. (B. Mar. 27).
Du mont, Abraham and Jane Van Cleaf-Jahannah. (B. Apr. 12).
June 22. Cole, Tunas and Rebecah Smith-Jamima. (B. Dec. 1793).
29. Williams, Mary Latturet (widow of George)-Keziah.
July 13. Stout, Garret and Jane Wickoff-Thomas. (B. June 3).
27. Aray, Isaack and ---- -Isaack.
Aug. 3.Vroom, Hend'k D. and Elizabeth De mott-Mary. (B. June 29).
17. Mesena, Peter and Mary Harrimon-Mary. (B. June 1).
Johnson, Hendrick and Agnes Jinnings-John. (B. June 25).
Hicks, Hugh and Lenah-Mary. (B. Oct. 6, 1793).
Aug. 31.Studdiford, Rev. Peter and Phobe Van Der Veere-Aleta. (B. July 20).
Van Vleat, Wil'm and Cornetje Flerebome-Phobe. (B. June 20).
Sept. 28.Beeakman, Cornelius and Rebecah Sharp-John. (B. Aug. 16).
Oct. 5. Van Debesreh, Peter and Phobe Dumont-Rachel. (B. Aug. 17).
19 V: Sickle, Andrew and Rebecah Lane-Sarah (afterward wife of Janney Dawes).
Thomson, John and Hannah Van Sickle-Andrew. (B. Sept. 23).
---- and Mary Labytux-Elizabeth. (B. July 11).
31. Jinnings, Elizabeth Van Vleat (wife of Peter)-Sarah. (B. Aug. 29).
Slaves of John Wickoff-Joe and Susan, his wife.
Nov. 30.Wickoff, Hend'k and Fammatje Dacker-Gartje. (B. Oct. 18).
Dec. 7. Mattis, John and Mary Berry-Sarah. (B. Oct. 14).
De mott, Derick and Martha Snadaker-Elizabeth. (B. Oct. 5).
14. Hall, John and Ann Stryker-Denes Stryker. (B. Sept. 18).
28. Tunason, Tunes and Margret Covenhoven-Tunes. (B. Sept. 25).
Van Horn, James and Elizabeth Hall-Danel.

1795.

Feb. 16. V: fleet, William and Ann Huff-Rebeckah. (B. Aug. 30, 1794).
16. Cock, Jacob and Dinah Jeraleman-Tunas. (B. Sept. 10, 1794).
Williamson, Aaron and Nelle Middlesworth-John Brocaw. (B. Oct. 3, 1794).
Low, Gaisbert and Margret Emry-Mary. (B. Jan. 29).
Mar. 30.Quick, Abraham and Cathrine Beakman-Elizabeth. (B. Feb. 4).

Apr. 5. Van Sickel, John and Rachel Van Vleat-Abraham. (B. Jan. 1).
12. Ditmas, John and Mary Smock-Abraham. (B. Feb. 9).
23 Cole, David and Beletge Van Sant-Lydia. (B. Sept. 1, 1794).
May 3. Blew, Fradrick and Effe Titsort-Ezekiel. (B. Apr. 12).
31 Voorhees, Abraham and Williamtje Wickoff-Williamtje. (B. Apr. -).
Lane, Cornelius and Jude Van Vleat-Andrew. (B. Jan. 10).
Cole, Ezekiel and Mary Wickoff-Elanah. (B. Jan. 19).
Egbert, James and Elizabeth Cool-John Cool. (B. Mar. 27).
June 6. Kinny, Andrew and Areantje Benet-Peter. (B. Nov. 5, 1794).
Hudnet, Lenah Biggs (wife of David)-(child's name omitted; born Nov. 25, 1794).
Bruer, William and Cathrine Bodine-Fradrick. (B. Mar. 29).
Servents of John Wickoff, (Joseph and Susan)-Benjamin; Nance; Joseph; Antony.
--- and Catherine Van Vleat-Antje V: Vleat. (B. Oct. 4, 1794).
7 Arrasmith, Benjamin and Mary Hunt-Benjamin. (B. Apr. 17).
14 Scomp, David and Lenah Hufman-Jacob. (B. Apr. 11).
28 Van Vleat, Adriane and Elizabeth Swicer-William. (B. May 12).
July 12. Hogland, Isaack and Margret Meshet-Andrew Lyle. (B. Apr. 22).
Aug. 16.Stout, Thomas and Jantje Van Stay-Garritje. (B. Apr. 27).
Sept. 6. Stilwill, Nicles and Catheline Van Nest-John. (B. July 29).
Brocaw, Isaack and Mary Wickoff-Jane. (B. Aug. 7).
Van Campen, Cor's and Leah Smock-Thomas. (B. July 5).
Oct. 4. Tine, Andrew and Charity Johnson-John. (B. Aug. 8).
Nafues, Rulef and Mary Van horlagen-Johannah. (B. Aug. 25).
Van Sickel, Garret and Nance Conon-Caty. (B. Aug. 19).
Spader, Abraham and Mary Quick-Jacob Quick. (B. July 23).
Kinny, Will'm and Phobe V:Daventer-John. (B. June 10).
V:Vleat, Henry and Doraty Tuma-Elizabeth. (B. July 30).
Nov. 8. Williamson, Cornelius and Stintje Demott-Cornelius. (B. Oct. 9).
Dec. 6. Higgs, Hugh and Lena, his wife-Samuel. (B. Nov. 5).
25. Low, Cor's and Catlintje Stryker-Barent. (B. Aug. 27).
Amerman, Abraham and Margret Sudam-Abraham. (B. Sept. 28).

1796.

Jan. 24. Hall, Richard and Fransintje Huff-Elizabeth. (B. Nov. 4, 1795).
Anderson, John and Elizabeth Johnson-Hannah. (B. Sept. 30, 1795).
31 William (servant of Abraham Dumont) and Elizabeth (servent of Peter Quick)-Rachel.
Feb. 21.Hamer, Cornelius and Mary Veal-Margret. (B. Jan. 12).
25. Cutter, Samuel and Mary Cole-Agnas. (B. Apr. 4, 1795).

17. Ten Eyk, Andrew and Sarah Berger-Mathew. (B. Jan. 12).
Mar. 27.Roberson, William and Mary Bogart-William. (B. Feb. 29).
Sutphin, Gisbert and Elizabeth Proos-Elizabeth. (B. Feb. 7).
Hunt, Will'm and Ann Johnson-William. (B. Jan. 11)
29 Servents of John Wickoff (Joseph and Susan)-Dinah. (B. Feb. 13).
Apr. 3. V: Sickele, Henry and Mary Eal-Isaack. (B. Jan. 8).
18. Benet, Peter and Elizabeth Stout-John. (B. Nov. 21, 1795).
Seiner, Danel and Isable Todd-Ann. (B. Feb. --).
19. Cole, Obadiah and Rebeccah Hufman-Elijah. (B. Feb. 20).
20. Cole, Tunas and Rebecah Smith-Ann. (B. Sept. 19, 1795).
Bowman, Cor's. and Mary Eggbet-Mary. (B. Nov. 1795).
May 1. Ditmas, William and Kezia Tunason-Mariah. (B. Jan. 2).
22. Ten Eyk, Andrew and Mary Ten Eyk-Sarah. (B. Apr. 24).
Wickoff, Henry and Famatje Dacker-Henry. (B. Apr. 16).
Van Hoorn, Cor's. and Nelly Covenhoven-Eliza. (B. Apr. 3).
Kinny, Andrew and Areantje Benet-Elizabeth. (B. Apr. 10).
28. Mates, Andrew and Ann Weean-Mariah. (B. Apr. 5).
Krusen, Derrick and Abbegal Ten Eyk-Tunas Ten Eyk. (B. Feb. 12).
July 3. Vroom, Hend'k D. and Elizabeth Demott-Hendrick Dumont, (B. May 15).
Simason, John and Elizabeth Striker-Bragtje. (B. June 2).
Van Desbareh, Peter and Phobe Dumont-Margret. (B. May 21).
17 Stryker, Adrian and Sarah Pipenger-Peter Quick. (B. June 18).
24. Beeakman, John and Effe Bruer-Phobe. (B. Apr. 14).
Egbert, Niclius and Elizabeth Lane-Sarah. (B. Feb. 24).
31. Stedaford, Rev. Peter and Phobe Van Dervare-Waintje Van Stay. (B. June 20).
Merlat, George and Hannah Van Sickel-George. (B. Apr. 28).
Hall, Joseph and Caty Mac Kinny-William.
Aug. 7. Himrod, William and Elizabeth Sutphin-Catherine Sutphin. (B. July 8).
Cole, Jacob and Sarah Coule-Henelat. (B. June 22).
Case, Philip and Henelat Cole-Ezekiel. (B. June 12).
21. Tomson, John and Hannah Van Sickel-Jude. (B. July 17).
Low, Cornelius and Yane Allen-Elizabeth. (B. July 20).
Spader, William and Catherine Van Dervear-Sarah. (B. June 29).
28. Lane, Aaron and Caty Demott-Eliza. (B. July 30).
Lane, John and Nelly Berger-Casper Berger. (B. Aug. 2).
Sept. 11.Hall, Richard and Jane Vroom-Elizabeth. (B. Apr. 4).
Oct. 2. Voorhees, Isaack and Lenah Ditmas-Caty. (B. Aug. 21).
9 Emens, Lenah V:Sickel (wife of Isaack)-Andrew. (B. Oct. 7, 1794).

23 Johnson, Andrew and Elizabeth Johnson-Abraham. (B. Sept. -).
30 Sull, Joseph and Catlintje Sutphin-Judah Sutphin. (B. Sept. 18).
Nov. 6. Dacker, Machael and Fametje Crimer-Mary. (B. Aug. 12, 1795).
Van Vleat, Will'm and Cornertje Vlerebome-Mary. (B. Oct. 13).
Demott, Richard and Elizabeth Smith-Nelly; Christian. (Nelly, b. Jan. 20, 1790; Christian, b. Jan. 6, 1796).
Dec. 9. Voorhees, Fulkerd and Margret Goltre-Margret. (B. Oct. 20).
1797.
Jan. 1. Wickoff, Corn's and Elizabeth Cornal-Albert. (B. Oct. 6, 1796).
22 Demont, Phillip and Ann Calshet-Dirrick. (B. Nov. 11, 1796).
Covert, Luces and Mary Post-Margret Ten Eyk. (B. Nov. 10, 1796).
Feb. 5. V: Dervear, Hend'k and Nelly Sutphin-Rebecah.
12 Nafues, David and Mary Addis-Simon Addis. (B. Dec. 17, 1796).
26 Weeaton, Charity Wickoff, (wife of Samuel)-Jacob Wickoff. (B. Dec. 25, 1795).
Mar. 5. Quick, Abraham and Catherine Beeakman-Mary. (B. Dec. 7, 1796).
26 Cole, Ezekiel and Mary Wickoff-Nickles. (B. Dec. 10, 1796).
Apr. 9. Low, Gaisbert and Margret Emre-Cornelius. (B. Mar. 9).
30 V: Sickele, Andrew and Rebecab Lane-Andrew. (B. Mar. 23).
Biggs, John and Elizabeth Slaght-George. (B. Nov. 25, 1796).
May 7. Van Vleat, Joseph and Charity Flerabome-Catlinte. (B. Mar. 14).
14 Porter, Ann Nafues (wife of Jonathan)-Mary Eles. (B. Feb. 11).
Smock, Abraham and Jane Van Compen-Altje. (B. Feb. 10).
28 .---- and Elizabeth V: Vleat-Elizabeth. (B. Dec. 7, 1796).
Cole, David and Belitse, his wife-Lydeah; Elizabeth. (Lydeah, b. Sept. 5, 1794; Elizabeth Kinny, b. May 1).
July 2. V: Vleat, Aaddrian and Elizabeth Switser-Judah Brocaw. (B. Apr. 27).
Arrismet, Benjamin and Mary Hunt-Ann. (B. May 20).
Ditmass, John and Mary Smock-Lenah. (B. June 8).
9 Jinnings, Elizabeth V:Vleat (wife of Peter)-Dezire. (B. Feb. 13).
Johnson, Peter and Hannah Nule-Catherine. (B. Jan. 21).
23 Mac Kinny, John and Elizabeth Wickoff-Nickles Wickoff. (B. June 25).
30 Cornish, Elisha H. and Helenah Biggs-Elizabeth Biggs. (B. May 15).
Hall, Isaack I. and Judah V: Vleat-John. (B. Mar. 5).
Aug. 6. Demont, Abraham and Jane V: Cleaf-Isaack Van Cleaf. (B. June 21).
20 Smock, Jame and Leah Smith-John. (B. May 16).
Egbert, James and Elizabeth Cool-Benjamin. (B. May --).
Emens, Cornelius and Sarah Low-Cornelius. (B. Nov. 28, 1796).
V: Vleat, Abr'm and Nelly Lane-Rebecah V: Sickle. (B. July 21).

Smith, Jacob and Grose Stout-Christian. (B. Dec. 25, 1796).
Stout, Benjamin and Elizabeth Anderson-Mary.
27 Howsel, Mary V: Sickel (wife of Jacob Howsell)-John V:Sickel. (B. Feb. 11).
Van Compen, Corn's and Leah Smock-Mathies, (B. July 19).
Brocaw, Isaack and Mary Wickoff-Isaack. (B. July 26).
Sept. 10. Tume, Rebecah V: Vleat (wife of David)-Mary Van Vleat. B. Apr. 20.
18 Van Vleat, Henry and Doraty Tume-Elias. (B. Aug. 3).
22. ---- and Sarah Huff-Tunes Huff. (B. Mar. 2).
24 Biggs, Mary Carehart (wife of William)-Margret. (B. Nov. 17, 1796).
Oct. 29. Lisk, David and Mary Vanderhoof-Gartry. (B. Sept. 25).
Scomp, Peter and Margret Hufman-Jacob. (B. Sept. 19).
Tunason, Henry and Agness Johnson-Jacob. (B. Mar. 1).
Nov. 19. Tunason, Tunas and Margret Covenhoven-Abraham. (B. July 23).
26. V: Vleat, John and Susanah Burger-Ann. (B. Oct. 25).
Orr, William and Jane Wickoff-Catlintje. (B. Oct. 6).
1798.
Jan. Brocaw, Peter and Elizabeth Low-Cathrine. (B. Nov. 5, 1797).
Kinny, Andrew and Areantje Benet-Eave. (B. Nov. 24, 1797).
Anderson, John and Elizabeth Johnson-Elshe. (B. Sept. 21, 1797).
Kinny, Will'm and Phobe V: Deventer-Sarah. (B. May 22, 1797).
Biggs, John and Elizabeth Slaght-Abraham. (B. Aug. 12, 1797).
28 Bogart, John and Ann Schank-Mary. (B. Dec. 15, 1797).
Feb. 4. Stout, Garret and Jane Wickoff-Abraham Prole. (B. Dec. 1797).
Striker, Adrean and Sarah Pipenger-Margret. (B. Dec. 27, 1797).
16 Cuter, Samuel and Mary-Charity. (B. July 10, 1797).
18 Stillwill, Nicles and Catlintje Van Nest-Ann. (B. Jan. 17).
Mar. 4. Servents of Peter Quick, William and Elizabeth-Antong.
Apr. 1. Tomson, John and Hannah V: Sickel-John. (B. Jan. 3).
Demott, Derrick and Martha Snadecar-Michael. (B. Nov. 30, 1797).
Tomson, Will'm and Elizabeth Voorheeas-Maryah Voorhees. (B. Feb. 12).
8 Ditmas, Will'm and Kezeah Tunason-Cornelius Tunason. (B. Nov. 7, 1797).
15 Case, Philip and Lenah Cole-Elizabeth. (B. Jan. 20).
22. Hamer, Cor's and Mary Veal-Susanah. (B. Feb. 25).
Williamson, Corn's and Staintje Demott-Richard. (B. Dec. 14, 1797).

29 Ten Eyke, Andrew and Sarah Berger-Phobe. (B. Mar. --).
May 9. Demott, Richard and Elizabeth Smith-Margret. (B. Nov. 11, 1797).
13 Van Sickle, John and Rachel Van Vleat-William. (B. Mar. 6).
Laturet, Peter and Margret Stout-Garret. (B. Mar. 17).
20 Spader, Jonathan and Staintje Voorheesi-John. (B. Mar. --).
27 Van Desberah, Peter and Phobe Dumont-Sarah. (B. Apr. 19).
Cole, Benjamin and Lenah Cole-Jacob.
Cole, Isaiah and Jane Biggs-Sarah.
June 17.Cole, Tunis and Rebecah Smith-Mary Smith. (B. Apr. 21).
Wickoff, Marten and Mary Voorhees-Cornelius. (B. May 15).
July 1. Cole, Obediah and Rebecah Hufman-Jacob. (B. May 9).
22 Ten Eyke, Cornelius and Elizabeth Johnson-Cornelius. (B. June 14).
Aug. 12.Anderson, Ann Johnson (wife of Joseph)-Hannah. (B. June 23).
19 Navues, David and Mary Addas-Areantje. (B. July 31).
26 Hall, Joseph and Caty MacKinny-Magdalin. (B. May 12).
Striker, Sarah Low (wife of Peter)-Derrick Low. (B. Jan. 29).
Sept. 2. Yorks, Henry and Elizabeth Cozine-Hannah. (B. Aug. 3).
21. Pipenger, John and Catherine Stevens-Little. (B. July 15).
Quick, Abraham and Catherine Beeakman-Christopher.(B. Aug. 21).
30 Porter, Ann Nafues (wife of Johnathan)-Ann Voorhees. (B. July 13).
Hufman, Jacob and Margret Biggs-Rebeckah. (B. July 19).
Oct. 14. Higgs, Hue and Lenah Manen-John.
Servents of John Wickoff, (Joseph and Susanah)-Susanah. B. Aug. 28.
28 Aray, Isaack and Mary Mackentier-John. (B. Aug. 22, 1797).
Nov.4. Lane, John and Nelly Berger-Jacob. (B. Oct. 1).
Smock, Abraham and Jane Van Compen-Catherine V: Camp. (B. Sept. 28).
11 .--- and Caty Bowman-Ruben. (B. June 23).
Dec. 16.Beeakman, John and Effe Bruer-Henry. (B. Oct. 23).
25 Vroom, Hend'k and Elizabeth Demott-Richard. (B. Oct. 1).
1799.
Jan. 6. Dally, John and Jane Davis-William.
Weeaton, ---- and Charity Wickoff-Samuel. (B. Nov. 5, 1798).
Lockwood, ---- and Naltje Wickoff-John Wickoff. (B. Nov. 16, 1798).
Mar. 8. Alliger, Benjamin and Sisly-Cathrine; David; George.
10 Hall, Richard and Jane Vroom-Peter. (B. Sept. 19, 1798).
Apr. 14. Huff, Denise and Elizabeth Perine-Elizabeth; Nelly. (Elizabeth, b. Nov. 25, 1798; Nelly, b. Mar. 25, 1797. Baptized at Ratiton by the

Rev. Duryea).
Van Vleat, Adrean and Elizabeth Swiser-Henry Swiser. (B. Jan. 3).
Apr. 21. Studaford, Rev. Peter and Phobe Van Derveer-Peter Ogelbee.
May 5. Orr, William and Jane Wickoff-Hannah. (B. Oct. 26, 1798).
Johnson, John and Elizabeth Anderson-Benjamin Anderson. (B. Feb. 21).
12 Van Horn, Cor's and Nelly Covenhoven-Mary. (B. Feb. --).
19. Smock, James and Leah Smith-Jacob. (B. Mar. 4).
Mattes, John and Mary Berry-Garret. (B. Feb. 9).
26 Lane, Aaron and Catherine Demott-Catherine. (B. Apr. 24).
June 1. Waldron, Nelly Amerman (wife of Rinear)-Mary. (B. Jan. 13).
2 Dunn, Nell V: Pelt (wife of Johnathan)-Cathy Mildrom.
Williamson, Mathew and Altje Hall-Cornelius. (B. Apr. 18).
9 Bowman, Cornelius and Sarah Hamer-Nathan. (B. Apr. 18).
Voorhees, Isaack and Lenah Ditmas-Isaack. (B. Feb. —).
Garrabrant, Cor's and Sarah Smith-John. (B. Nov. 1798).
Smith, Jacob and Grace Stout-Benjamin. (B. Apr. 14).
Cole, Ezekiel and Mary Wickoff-Ezekiel and Jacob, twins. (B. Mar. 7).
23 Amerman, Abraham and Margret Sudam-Cornelius. (B. Mar. 23).
30 Cole, John and Elizabeth Sciner-Franke. (B. Dec. 18, 1798).
Hall, John and Mary Hall-Elizabeth. (B. Feb. 17).
July 7. Scomp, George P. and Elizabeth Anderson-Ann. (B. May 4).
14 Van Pelt, Rulef and Catrintje Ten Eyk-Abraham. (B. Mar. 16).
Aug. 25.Ten Eyke, Andrew and Mary Ten Eyke-Peter. (B. Apr. 2).
Sept. 13.Clickner, George and Marth Dead-Elshe.
15 Ten Eick, Matthew and Cornelia Post-John. (B. July 7).
Ditmas, John and Mary Smock-Altje. (B. July 12).
Johnson, Andrew and Elizabeth Johnson-Peter. (B. June 2).
22. Wickoff, Cor's and Elizabeth Cornal-Ann. (B. July 19).
Nov. 3. Spader, Wil'm and Catrena Van Derveer-James Van Derveer. (B. Sept. 14).
10 Case, Philip and Helenah Case-Mary. (B. Oct. 7).
Cole, Jacob and Sarah Cole-Paul Kuhl. (B. Sept. 20).
Pipenger, Peter and Elizabeth Lane-Mary. (B. Oct. 7).
22. Van Compen, Cor's and Leah Smock-Cornelius. (B. Oct. 1).
Ten Eyke, Jacobes and Easter-Margaret Hagaman. (B. Oct. 8).
1800.
Jan. 26. Van Der Barch, Peter and Phobe Dumont-Peter. (B. Nov. 16, 1799).
Feb. 2. Scomp, Peter and Margret Hufman-Hannah. (B. Oct. 15, 1799).
Van Vleat, Henry and Doraty Tume-Henry. (B. Oct. 25, 1799).

11 Kinny, William and Phobe Van Daventer-Ann. (B. June 26, 1799).
Apr. 13. V: Derveer, Cornelius and Anne V: Derveer-Michael. (B. Dec. 24, 1799).
20 Ten Eyke, Cor's and Elizabeth Johnson-Abraham, (B. Jan.).
Wickoff, Martin Z. and Mary Voorhees-John. (B. Feb. 23).
Low, Isaack and Elizabeth Hall-Mary. (B. Dec. 25, 1799).
Mar. 2. Stryker, Adrian and Sarah Pipenger-James. (B. Dec. 8, 1799).
May 4. Hamer Cors and Mary Veal-Sarah Van Doren. (B. Mar. 20).
11 Cole, John and Elizabeth Sciner-Abraham. (B. Oct. 23, 1799).
Cole, Tunas and Rebecah Smith-Elizabeth. (B. Oct. 22, 1799).
16 Egbert, Nicles and Elizabeth-Henry. (B. Feb. 18).
Egbert, James and Elizabeth Cool-George. (B. Nov. 19, 1799).
June 8. V: Sickle, Andrew and Rebecah Lane-Lediah. (B. Apr. 30).
Le fever, Adam and ----, -William, (B. Jan. 28).
July 6. Thomson, John and Hannah V: Sickel-Peter. (B. May 25).
Fusler, Luke and Ann Smith-Luke. (B. June 10).
Hufman, David and Caty Wickoff-John. (B. Apr. 22).
27 Bogert, John and Ann Schank-Marten Schank. (B. June 16).
Brocaw, Isaack and Mary Wickoff-Peter Quick. (B. June 19).
Aug. 24. V: Vleat, Joseph and Catlintje Flerabome-Peter. (B. June 21).
Blare, Jame and Jane Mitchel-Edward Mitchel. (B. May 31).
Sept. 28. Cole, Isaiah and Jane Biggs-Jane Biggs. (B. Nov. 23, 1799).
Cole, John and Mary Biggs-Jacob. (B. Nov. 16, 1799).
Cole, Benjamin and Lanah Cole-Sarah.
Oct. 5. V: Sickle, John and Rachel V: Vleat-Jane. (B. Aug. 4).
Porter, Johnathan and Ann Nafues-Peter Nafues. (B. July 14).
---- and Lenah Hunter-Margret. (B. Apr. 3).
Hufman, Jacob and -, -Jane Biggs. (B. Apr. 19).
Jinnings, Peter and Elizabeth V:Vleat-Jamime. (B. July 6).
12 Striker, Peter and Sarah Low-Elizabeth. (B. Feb. 15).
26. Trimer, Andres and Tuntje Emens-James. (B. Feb. 26).
Nov. 2. Naves, David and Mary Addes-Nelly. (B. Oct. 3).
9 Sutphen, John and Trintje Vroom-George. (B. Sept. 23).
Cole, Ezekial and Mary Wickoff-Leah. (B. Sept. 9).
16 Anderson, Joseph and Ann Johnson-Mary. (B. Oct. 22).
Cornish, Elisha and Henalar Biggs-Peter. (B. Aug. 14, 1799).
30 Kinny, And'w and Areantje Benet-Sarah. (B. Oct. 12).
Hicks, Hue and Lenah Manen-Caterine. (B. Mar. 28).
1801.
Jan. 11. Tomson, Will'm and Elizabeth Van Voorhaes-Abraham Voorhaes. (B.

Dec. 15, 1800).
23. Orr, Will'm and Jane Wickoff-Sarah. (B. Oct. 21, 1800).
T: Eyke, Cornelius and Elizabeth Johnson-Abraham. (B. Jan. 22, 1800).
Mar. 8 Ditmars, WIll'm and Kozia Tunason-Sophia. (B. Dec. 30, 1800).
May Huff, Denise and Elizabeth Perine-Hettiam. (B. July 25, 1800).
V: Vleat, Wil'm and Cnearcha Flerebone-Margre. (B. Oct. 28, 1800).
June 14. Bowman, Cor's and Sarah Hamer-Michael. (B. Dec. 31, 1800).

HILLSBOROUGH (MILLSTONE) REFORMED CHURCH BAPTISMS BY THE PASTOR, REV. ANDREW HANSEN

These records begin in Volume VII (1918) of the Quarterly, page 199.

This church was organized August 11, 1766, as the church of "New Millstone." On April 6, 1775, it was incorporated under the name of "Hillsborough" (the name of the township), to distinguish it from the Harlingen church, then called "Millstone," that is, "the church op de Millstone." The pastors have been: 1766-'74, supplies; 1774-9, Christian F. Foering; 1780-'6, Solomon Froeligh; 1787-'95, J. M. Van Harlingen; 1797-1807, James S. Cannon; 1807-'09, John Schureman; 1811-'50, John L. Zabriskie; 1850-'63, John DeWitt; 1863-'88, Edw. Tanjore Corwin; 1889-1904, Theodore Shafer; 1904-l912, Floris Ferwarda; 1913-present, Andrew Hansen.--Editor *Quarterly*.

1767.
Apr. 3. Vanbeuren, Abraham and Eva-Eva.
Dec. 27. Van Lewe, Cornelis and Antye-Deneys.
1768.
Jan. 10. Smit, Eldert and Elschi-Deyna.
Hogelandt, Willem and Marigrityi-Marityi.
June 19. Smack, Jan and Neeltyi-Cornelis.
Lott, Corneles and Hendrico-Benyemen.
Cool, Symon and Mariya-Sara.
Wilson, Peter and Annatye-Eeva.
Probasco, Hendrick and Antye-Jacob.
July 10. Smack, Teys and Gertyi-Jan.
1769.
Feb. 26. Kroesen, Dirreck and Elisabeth-Cornelis.

	Pouwelson, Pouwel and Leya-Eva.
	Van Aersdalen, Crisstoffel, Junr., and Catrina-Cristoffel.
Apr. 30.	Bennet, Johanis and Mariya-Piter.
July 2.	Rynierson, Ouke and Elschie-Crisstoffel.
	Stryker, Jacobus and Gertyi-Antye.
Aug. 20.	Sekely, Jan-Johan, and Adolphus Wievor and his wife (compeer and godmother for this child).
Nov. 17.	Van Harlengen, Ernestus and Maria-Maria.
	Weler, James and Lena-Antje.
	Stryker, Jan and Laah-Jacobus.
1770.	
Jan. 22.	Garrison, Barnardus and Sarah-Janatah.
Feb. 18.	Gerrison, Jacobus and Lena-Rem.
Mar. 18.	Wyckoff, Piter and Jacamayntye-Hendrick.
	Van Cleef, Isack and Derkis-Janitye.
	Stryker, Piter and Mariya-Piter.
May 6.	Gerritson, Steven and Femitye-Petrus.
July 8.	Lott, Cornelis and Hendrikie-Nelli.
Aug. 5.	Van Noonstrant, Johanis and Antye-Piter.
	Van Leuwe, Cornelis and Antyi-Johanis.
	Van Doorn, Jacob and Janitye-Teunis.
	Covert, Johannis, Junior, and ---- -Eldert.
	Leshlee, James and Marigritye-Willem.
Sept. 2.	Smack, Teys and Gertye-Leya.
Dec. 31.	Stryker, Peter and Famaya-Famaya.
1771.	
Feb. 21.	Coverts, Brogun and Femmetie-Katriena.
Apr. 7.	Covert, Teunes and Lena-Ryneir.
	Hogelandt, William and Maregritje-Jan.
	Bennet, Johannes and Maria-William.
May 5.	Buyse, Folkert and Henderschen-Henderieke.
	Blouw, Peter and Marieya-Peterus.
July 26.	Hegelen, Ouke V. and Elsie-Jochom.
28.	Krosen, Derrick and Elasabet-Jacob.
	Van Arsdalen, Hendrick and Ketrina-Isaac.
	Van Arsdalen, Christophel and Catrina-Maria.
Sept. 22.	Stryker, John--- Eva (Eva Perrine, wife of Peter Perrine godmother).
Oct. 27.	Stryker, Baerant and Elesabet-Elesabet.
	Hageman, Elesabet-Maria.

Dec. 1.	Probasco, Hendrick and Antie-Cristujaannes.
	Hoff, Isaac and (name omitted)-Francintie.
22.	Stryker, Peter and Maria-Simon.
26.	Addes, Simon and Noullie-Maria.
1772.	
Feb. 2.	Van Arsdalen, Ouke and Maria-Isaac.
	Staats, Pieter and Susanna-Nellie.
	Gerritson, Jacobus and Lana-Sara.
Mar. 1.	Arrosmith, Joseph and Gertie-Lowra.
June 7.	Lot, Cornelius and Hendrica-Gertie.
	Gerritsen, Rem and Maria-Annie.
July 5.	Van Norstand, John and Annie-William.
Aug. 1.	Van Lewe, Cornelius and Annie-Helena.
Sept. 6.	Bergen, Johannis and Altie-Mariea.
1773.	
Jan. 3.	Weler, James and Lana-Abraham.
Feb. 7.	Staats, Riniere and Sitie-Jan.
Apr. 4.	Covert, Tunis and Magdelena-Jannitie.
	Bennit, Johannis and Maria-Maria.
July 4.	Hogelandt, William and Margrietie-Marigrietie.
Oct. 2.	Stryker, Peter and Maria-Annie.
3.	Probasco, Jacob and Dina-Johannis.
Nov. 7.	Rinerson, Rinere and Marta-Ouke.
1774.	
Apr. 3.	Gerritson, Jacobus and Lena-Helena.
	Van Doren, Abraham and Elezabet-Jan.
	Van Arsdalen, Christopher and Catrina-Cornelius.
May 1.	Lott, Cornelius and Hendrikca-Pieter.
June 5.	Stryker, John and Lediea-Antje.
	Covert, Abraham and Beletie-Beletie.
	Willson, Pieter-Margrita (about 17 mos. old).
12.	Christopher, John and Maria-Joseph.
16.	Powelson, Powel and Lena-Elsie and Charles (Elsie about 5 yrs.).
Oct. 9.	Wycoff, Pieter and Catrina-Elezabeth.
Nov. 27.	Detmers, Abraham and Catrina-Helena.
Dec. 25.	Wycoff, Jacob and Catlina-Jacob.
	Van Clefe, Isaac and Dorcuss-Peter.
1775.	
Feb. 19.	Van Englen, Ouke and Elsie-Geertie.

	Stryker, Simon and Altie-Jacobus.
Mar. 5.	Blauw, Pieter and Maria-Abraham.
Apr. 2.	Stryker, Pieter and Maria-Maria.
16.	Bennit, John and Maria-Gerrit.
	Merrill, Adriyaan and Jane-William.
May 17.	Folkerson, Fillip and Maria-Maria.
June 2.	Dynah, negro woman of John Stryker.
9.	Brokaw, Benjamen and Sarah-Eva.
16.	Van Deveere, Gerrit-John.
Aug. 20.	Covert, Tunis and Lana-Brogun.
	Weler, James and Lana-Lana.
Oct. 27.	Jack, negro of Lana Detmars.
29.	Rynerson, Rynere and Marta-John.
Nov. 19.	Schank, Pieter and Sara-Nellie.
Dec. 16.	Bennit, Hendrick and Betsie-Williem.
24.	Covert, Lucas and Cornelia-Magdalena.
1776.	
Feb. 11.	Terhunah, Gerrit Jur. and Williamtie-Catrina.
Mar. 10.	Staats, Peter and Susannah-Marilantie.
31.	Gerritsen, Jacobus and Leentie-Samuel.
	Van Doren, Abraham and Bedtjie-Abraham.
Apr. 28.	Stryker, John and Liedea-Liedea.
	Mercer, Archibald and Maria-[name not given], b. Mar. 2.
June 16.	Lott, Cornelius and Hendrica-Sara.
	Van Nuyse, Isaac and Neltie-Peterus.
21.	Mesces, Archeble and Maria-Pieter Schenk.
July 14.	Anderson, Annatie, wife of William Anderson-Charritie.
28.	Vorheese, Cort and Margretie-Lacries.
Aug. 4.	Stryker, Pieter and Femmetie-Gerrit.
18.	Smock, John and Nellie-Rynier, b. Aug. 1.
	Bennit, Hendrick and Ennie-Hendrick.
Sept. 15.	Faring, Cristayaan Fredrick and Margrietie-Fredrick.
Oct. 6.	Blaw, John and Catrina-Catrina.
	Ditmars, Abraham and Catrina-(Name of child not given).
20.	Low, Cornelius and Catrina-John.
27.	Vaghte, Rynier and Catrintie-Peternelly.
1777.	
Nov. 25.	Beekemen, James I. and Sarah-John Coch.
1778.	
Feb. 3.	Brocaw, David and Annache-Magdalena.

17. Schenck, Abraham and Eva-Hendrick.
25. Van Cleef, Garrit and Blandena-Urias.
Aug. 2. Lott, Cornelius and Hendrica-Banjame.
Sept. 22. Thompson, Cyrenius and Rebecca-Garret.
1779.
Feb. 1. Mercer, Archibald and Maria-Archibald, b. Dec. 1, 1778.
Mar. 28. Faring, Cristiyan Fradrick and Margrietie-Abraham P.
July --. Mercer, Archibald and Maria-Eliza., b. June 14, 1777.
Oct. 10. Neuius, Albert and Nelly-Joseph.
Nov. 10. Probasco, Jacob and Sarah-Johanes Stryker.
1780.
Apr. 9. Thompson, Cyrenius and Rebeckah-Ellener.
June 25. Van Der Veer, Garrit and ____ -Elizabeth.
July 2. Rynearson, Rynear and Marta-Charles.
Anderson, Amatie, wife of William-Peter.
16. Garritson, Garrit R. and Anne-Garrit.
Aug. 6. Ross, Levi and Sarah-Nehlche.
Oct. 19. Elmendorf, John and Margaret Zabriskie-Maria, b. Sept. 24.
29. Van Brunt, Nicholus and Katrinche-Gerrit.
Nov. 19. Stryker, John and Ledea-James.
Van Doren, John and Catryneha-Jan.
Rynearson, Gerret and Janache-Ouke.
24. Wyckoff, Peter and Jacominiche-Sara.
Dec. 10. Van Cleef, Gerret and Blandina-Anche.
1781.
Feb. 18. Veighte, Rynear and Caty-Peternelly.
Cock, William and Tuneke-Elezebeth.
Jan. 14. Stryker, Peter and Maria-John.
Mar. 11. Lott, Cornelius and Hendricka-Hendrick.
Davis, Samuel and Caty-Mary.
Stryker, Simon and Allche-Elsey.
18. Magell, John and Mary-Sarah.
Hoagland, John and Feben-Cornelius Hatfield.
Bennet, John and Maria-Jacob.
Apr. 16. Nevius, Martinus and Gertche-Cornelius.
May 13. Gerretsen, Jacobus and Magdelena-Stephanus.
June 10. Covert, Brogun and Feben-Jacob.
Cornell, Joseph and Elezebeth-Joseph.
Nov. 18. Waldron, Benjamen and Helen-Samuel.
25. Garritson, Garret R. and Anna-Court.

Dec. 16. Staats, Peter and Susanna-Hendricks.
Blaw, John and Cattlyna-Abraham.
Mercer, Archabal and Maria-Gertrude.

1782.
Jan. 13. Terhune, Garret and Willimche-Magdelena.
Thompson, Cyrenius and Rebecca-Mary.
27. Willson, Jan Joseph and Catrina-Isaac.
Williamson, Annache-Annache Ten Eyck.
Feb. 17. Van Zant, John and Rachel-Catrina.
24. Probasco, Jacobus and Sara-Margritta.
Mar. 10. Waldron, William and Maria-Samuel.
Van Zant, Janache-Teunis Covert.
17. Hoagland, Abraham and Maria-Henery.
31. Dun, Nelechi and Van Jonaton-Marea.
Brocaw, Joses and Janyche-Sara.
Dumont, Albert and Cernelea-Peter.
Nortewick, John and Elezebeth-Philip.
Apr. 25. Van Norstrand, Marea and Jan-John Decamps.
June 16. Van Cleef, Michal and Tanache-Marea.
30. Schenk, Hennery and Nelly-Hendrick.
Van Nest, Abraham and Sara-Johanes.
Van Dine, William and Dina-Jacobus.
July 14. Runnion, Mary-Lennice.
Aug. 4. Van Der Veer, John and Tanache-Teunis.
Nevius, Martines and Anche-Lucas.
Oct. 6. Veighte, Reynear and Caty-Jan Van Medleswart.
Rynearson, Reynear and Margretta-Elsey.
13. Freleigh, the Rev. Domini Solomon and Rachel-Peter Ditmars.
24. Stryker, John and Feben-Janneche.
27. Thompson, Cyrenius-(baptized).
Dec. 8. Dumont, Peter A. and Sara-Peter.
Nov. 24. Powelson, Abraham and Lanache-Maria.
Van Doren, In. and Teyne-Gerret.
Dec. 15. Welson, Catrena and Van Joseph-Maria.
29. Williamson, Nicholus and Arayche-Arayanche.
Van Nest, Abraham and Catrina-Jacob and Sara.

1783.
Jan. 12. Covert, Jacob and Lutuche-Anna.
Post, Abraham and Catrina-Hendrick.
Dumont, Peter P. and Susana-Maria.

26.	Middleswart, Andrees and Sara-Hendrick.
Feb. 2.	Davis, Isaac and Tanache-Elezebeth.
23.	Wyckoff, Peter and Janchamyneche-Jacob Deryea.
Mar. 30.	Van Nuyse, Isaac and Nilche-Nileche.
	Lane, John and Lena-Catrynche.
Apr. 6.	Van Doren, Abraham and Elezebeth-Edmund.
20.	Voorhees, Lucas and Hanna-Lucas.
June 9.	Van Norstrand, Jan and Maria-John.
Aug. 3.	Garretson, Jacobus and Lena-Peter.
	Willson, William and Catrena-Myndort.
10.	Garretson, Gerret R. and Anna-Anna.
	Bennet, Johanes and Janaca-John.
24.	Billson, William and ---- -Peter.
31.	Stryker, John and Ledea-Daniel Perrine.
31.	Brocaw, John and Adrayana-Sara.
Sept. 14.	Terhune, William and Maria-Jan.
	Van Brunt, Nicholus and Catrynche-Isaac.
	Hoagland, Abraham and (Name of wife not given)-Gorge.
Oct. 26.	Voor, Abraham L. and Elsey-Conorate Ten Eyck.
Nov. 24.	Thompson, Cyrenius and Rebecka-Caty.
Dec. 7.	Staats, Peter and Susana-Peter.
Nov. 24.	Van Derbett, John and Janache-Janache.
Dec. 11.	Van Der Veer, Cornelius-Tyche and Garret.
25.	Davis, Samuel and Caty-Jacobus.
1784.	
Feb. 1.	Van Lewen, Johannes and Madalenche-Schyche.
Apr. 12.	Mercer, Arcbabald and Maria-Charlott.
	Arrowsmith, Benjamin and Maria-Edward.
May 2.	Davis, Isaac and Janache-Isaac.
	Van Der Beek, Andreas and Allche-Maria.
31.	Hoagland, John and Feben-Elezebeth Miller.
June 6.	Bergen, Johannes and Allche-Schytche.
	Veighte, Rynear and Caty-Allche.
July 11.	Powelson, Abraham and Janache-Magdalen.
18.	Suydam, Hendrick and Allche-Adrayanche.
	Brocaw, Wert and Cornelia-Peter.
Aug. 8.	Monfort, Peter and Marea-Johannes, b. June 11, 1784.
Oct. 10.	Hoagland, Abraham and Marea-Johanes.
	Van Doren, Peter and Frenche-Peter and Abraham.
Nov. 21.	Van Cleef, Garret and Dyna-Maria.

Dec. 5. Voorhees, Garret and Mareche-Garret.
Quick, Garret and Anche-Jehoacem.

1785.
Jan. 9. Stoothuff, Cornelius and Gerche-Cattlynche.
30. Van Zant, John and Rachel-Johanas.
Feb. 27 Van Der Veer, Cornelius and Sara-Jacaobus.
Williamson, Nicholus and Adrayanche-Gertche.
Voor, Isaac and Altche-Joseph.
Apr. 29. Cornell, Joseph and Elezebeth-Catrina.
Ditmars, Abraham and Catrina-Peter.
May 15. Northwick, Hendrick and Nancy-John.
29. Van Doren, John and Cattlynche-Abraham.
Hoagland, Johannes and Sara-Marea.
July 10. Van Nuyse, Isaac and Niliche-Katrynche.
17. Van Lewe, Peter and Syteche-Maria.
Aug. 7. Van Cleef, Isaac and Darkes-Abraham.
Freleigh, the Rev. Domine Solomon and Rachel-Isaac Van Der Beeck.
21. Stryker, Peter and Maria-Margreta.
Probasco, Peter and (Name of wife not given)-Hendrick.
Bennet, Johannes and Janache-Neleche.
23. Van Zant, Barnardus and Maria-Catrina Wortman.
Sept. 18. Smith, Benjamen and Begel-Anna.
Nov. 11. Wyckoff, Peter and Jacamynche-Reynear Veighte.
Blaw, Gerret and Catrina-Maria.
13. Spader, Johannes and Janache-Peter.
Voor, Abraham and Else-Nielche.
Bennet, Hendrick and Jannache-John.
Dec. 11. Ditmars, Peter and Margreta-Cornelius.
Ten Eyck, Cunarate and Elezebeth-William Thompson.
26. Frulenhuysen, Fredrick and Gertrude-Hendrick Schenk.

1786.
Jan. 8. Thompson, Cyrenius and Rebecca-Peter Brower.
22. Lott, Cornelius and Hendrica-Femmitie.
29. Van Nuyse, Cornelius and Maria-Isaac.
Feb. 19. Davis, Isaac and Janache-Peter Brocaw.
Mar. 12. Terhune, Stephen and Althe-Hendrick Stryker.
July 30. Davis, Samuel and Caty-Katrina Wever.
Dec. 3. Terhune, William and Maria-William.
McKinney, Cornelius and Madalena Covert-Anna.

	Waler, Simon and Mattys-Maghdalena.
24.	Van Cleef, Isaac and Durkas-John.
	Bennet, Abraham and Maria-John.
	Hoagland, Johanis and Sara-Charles Van Tyne.
1787.	
Feb 4.	Staats, Peter and Susana-Maria.
Mar. 4.	Cornell, Barant and Katrina-Albert.
	Omnfort, Peter and Maria-Peter, b. Feb. 5.
	Van Zant, John and Rachel-Adam Jobs.
11.	Christopher, John and Maria-Maria.
Sept. 16.	Voorhees, Lucas and Jahanna-Adrayana.
Nov. 11.	Brocaw, Simon and Maria-Metche.
	Brocaw, John and Adrayana-Brogun.
25.	Stryker, John and Feben-Sara Martinse, b. Oct. 23, 1787.
Dec. 9.	Wyckoff, Peter and Jaeamimethe-Jan Van Medelleswart.
1788.	
July 20.	Cornell, Barant and Catrina-Peter Stotehuff.
Apr. --.	Davis, Samuel and Caty-Abraham.
Aug. 17.	Ditmars, Peter and Margreta-Fredrick.
Oct. 11.	Stryker, John A. and Lamithe-Hendrick.
Nov. 9.	Bennet, Abraham and Maria-Joseph Arrosmith.
	Garretson, Jacobus. (Nothing more given).
1789.	
Jan. 18.	Rynearson, Rynear and Marta-Gerthe.
Feb. 15.	Terhune, William and Maria-Matche.
Mar. 15.	Smylie, Robert and Annie-Gennie.
May 10.	Staats, Peter and Susana-Abraham, b. Mar. 19.
	Monfort, Peter and Maria-Cornelius, b. Mar. 30.
July 19.	Ditmars, Abraham and Catrina-Nicholus William.
Aug. 2.	Van Lew, Peter and Sythe-Dynah, b. July 1.
30.	Cornell, Joseph and Elezebeth-Joseph, b. July 22.
Sept. 27.	Nevius, Peter and Maria-Metje, b. Sept. 5.
Oct. 11.	Van Arsdalen, Myndert and Caty-Sarah, b. Sept. 6.
Dec. 6.	Wyckoff, Peter and Jacmeintie-Abraham Duryee, b. Nov. 12.
1790.	
Jan. 17.	Meserol, Charles and Caty-Helena, b. Oct. 26, 1789.
31.	Garretson, Garret R. and Anna-Derick Heagaman, b. Dec. 27, 1789.
Feb. 27.	Wilson, Hendrick and Nelly-John, b. Jan. 7.
28.	Bennet, Johnes and Janche-Neleche.

Apr. 25. Davis, Samuel and Caty-Elezebeth, b. Mar. 13, 1790.
July 4. Clark, Andrew and Betsy Elezebeth-Andrew, b. Apr. 1, 1788; and Elezebeth, b. Feb. 24, 1790.
16. Mercer, Archabald and Maria-John Richard, b. May 9.
Terhune, Gerret and Willemphe-Rachel.
Aug. 15. Frelinghuysen, Fredrick and Gertrude-Gertrude, b. July 16.
Willson, Minedert and Janache-William, b. July 11.
Wyckoff's, Peter-Servant named Prince.
Cortelyou's, William-Servant named Peg.
Cornell's, Cornelius-Servant named Jude.
Cornell's, Joseph-Servant named Lyna.
Hoff's, Peter-Servant named Nelly.
Aug. 1. Thompson, Cyrenius and Rebecca-Cyrenius, b. July 1.
Sept. 26. Van Lewe, Johannes and Leanche-Gertche, b. Aug. 22.
Nelly (servant maid to Peter Huff)-James and Dina.
Dec. 5. Bainbredge, John and Adrayaha-Mary, b. Nov. 4.
19. Wheeler, Simon and Martha-Martha, b. Nov. 10.
25. Brocaw, Isaac and Lena-Mary.
1791.
Jan. 16. Gulick, Joakim and Jenny-Peter, b. Oct. 29, 1790.
Gordon, Charles and Nelly-Christopher, b. Nov. 7, 1790.
30. Van Doren, William and Lea-John, b. Dec. 25, 1790.
Feb. 13. Stryker, Peter and Maria-Magdalen and Sarah, b. Jan. 4, 1791.
27. Meserol, Charles and Catrina-Jenny, b. Jan. 2I.
Mar. 13. Jude (servant of Cornelius Cornell)-Thomas, b. Feb. 12.
Gano, Abraham and Jenny-Jenny, b. Jan. 7.
Apr. 10. Hoagland, Johanes and Sara-Johannas, b. Feb. I5.
May 8. Sutphen, John and Alche-Ann, b. Mar. 21.
Totten, Joseph and Anna-Levy, b. Feb. 1.
June 5. Hoagland, Teunis and Alche-Cornelius, b. Apr. 13.
13. Garretson, Jacobus and Lena-Dyna, b. May 10.
Stryker, Peter J. and Magdalena-Allche, b. May 10.
July 1. Quick, Jacobus and Maria-Catrina, b. June 12.
Stryker, John and Maria-John, b. June 14.
17. Probasco, Jacob and Sara-Peter.
Aug. 14. Stryker, John A. and Lameche-Abraham.
Oct. 22. Voorhees, Reoluf ? and Gertrude-Teunis, b. Sept. 4.
Garritson, Garret R. and Anna-Garret Remson, b. Sept. 2.
Nov. 6. Stryker, John and Feben-Peter, b. Oct. 5.
20 Stryker, Peter and Elezebeth-Hendrick Van Northwick, b.

Oct. 5
Brocaw, David and (Name of wife not given)-Stynche, b. Oct. 14.

Dec. 8. Terhune, Cornelius and Jenney-Margaret, b. Nov. 15.

1792.

Jan. 15. Monfort, Peter and Maria-Abraham Hoagland, b. Dec. 10, 1791.

Feb. 12. Garretson, Garret and Elezabeth-Jeremiah, b. Jan. 5.
Probasco, Peter. (Name of wife and child not given).

26. Van Lewen, John and Cornelia-Dorraty, b. Jan. 4.
Nelly, servant maid to Peter Huff-Polly.

Mar. 11. Frelenhuysen, Fredrick and Gertrude-Catharine, b. Feb. 1.

Apr. 22. Van Lewen, Peter and Sythe-Fredrick, b. Mar. 13.

(Record here begins in English)

May 6. Doty, Joseph and Anna-Jonathan.
Van Doren, William and Leah-Maria.

18. Ditmars, Peter and Maria-Garret, b. Apr. 5.

July 1. Van Doren, John (Name of wife not given)-Minne, b. Apr. 25.
Van Cleef, Isaac and Dorcas-Van Martera.
Davis, Samuel and Caty-Ellanor, b. May 25.

Aug. 12. Van Arsdalen, Mynedert and Caty-John, b. July 14.
Bainbridge, John and Adrayanche-Nicholas William, b. July 19.
Gorden, Barnardus and Mary-Peter, b. May 24.

22. Lott, Isaac and Anna-Abraham, b. July 22.
Sekly, John and Sarah-James Alley, b. July 21.

Sept. 9. Thompson, Cyrenius and Rebecca-Lowara, b. July 27.

23. Garritson, Jacobus and Martha-Hendrick Veighte, b. Aug. 8.

Oct. 21. Wyckoff, Peter and Jakeminete-Isaac, b. Aug. 29.
Cornell, Barent and Catrina-Anche, b. Sept. 21.

Nov. 4. Sarah, servant to Garret Terhune-Sarah.
Sarah, servant to John Wyckoff (baptized).

18. Ditmars, Abraham and Catrina-Joseph, b. Oct. 4.
Willson, Minedert and Janache-Douwe, b. Oct. 23.

Dec. 2. Bennet, John and Jenny-John, b. Oct. 28.

16. Lewe, John and Polly-Lanah, b. Nov. 16.
Brocaw, Isaac and Lenah-Caleb, b. Oct. 12.
Schenk, Martin and Margaret-Garret Cowenhoven, b. Nov. 16.

30. Wortman, Abraham and Anna-Mary, b. Nov. 8.

1793.	
Jan. 27.	Christopher, John and Maria-Cornelius, b. Dec. 1792.
Feb. 10.	Wheeler, Simon and Martha-James , b. Jan. 1.
	Van Cleef, Garret and Blandyna-Jacob Suydam, b. Dec. 31, 1792.
27.	Broach, David and Anna-Gartrude, b. Sept. 26.
Apr. 7.	Stryker, Peter and Magdalen-John, b. Jan. 30.
	Sarah (servant to John Wyckoff)-Mary.
May 19.	Simon Stryker and Maria-Elezebeth, b. Feb. 7.
June 16.	Sutphen, John and Alatty-Jahannah, b. May 24.
	Stryker, John J. and Polly-Dorcas.
July 28.	Reynearson, Catrina, wife of Isaac-Oke, b. June 1.
	Harris, Israel and Alatty (Schenk)-Margaret Pearson, b. May 3.
Sept. 22.	Terhune, Cornelius and Jenny-Susannah, b. Aug. 26.
	Garretson, Jacobus and Lena-Idah, b. Sept. 1.
	Probasco, Geoge and Jahannah-Jacob, b. Aug. 3.
	Probasco, Peter and Martha-Simon.
	Meserol, Charles and Cattina-Elizabeth, b. July 24.
Oct. 7.	Van Doren, William and Leyah-Janache, b. Sept. 5.
20.	Wilson, Hendrick and Nelly-Nelly, b. Aug. 23.
	Reynearson, Jehoakim and Tyne-Oke, b. Sept. 8.
Nov. 3.	Garretson, Garret R. and Anna-Maria, b. Sept. 26.
1794.	
Jan. 27.	Parrish, William and Elezabeth-John Waldron, b. Sept. 25.
Mar. 9.	Cornell, Barant and Catrina-Wilhelmus Stoothuff, b. Mar. 24.
24.	Nell, servant to John Van Doren, Jr.-Rachel, b. Feb. --.
Apr. 20.	Sekly, John and Sarah-John, b. Mar. 15.
	Stryker, Peter and Elezebeth-Elezebeth, b. Feb. 26.
May 4.	Garretson, Jacobus Jr. and Martah-Jawbus, b. Apr. 4.
	Schenk, Abraham and Eve-Abraham Van Buren, b. Apr. 8
July 20.	Van Leuwen, John and Mary-Sarah, b. June 29.
	Sarah, late servant to John Wyckoff-Jane, b. May 22.
Aug. 17.	Stryker, Peter and Maria-Ledia, b. July 12.
	Davis, Samuel and Caty-Cathelina, b. July 19.
Sept. 28.	Nortwick, Johanas and Nancy-Nicholas Bodine, b. July 28.
	Bainbridge, John and Adrayanche-Jahannah, b. Aug. 27.
Nov. 9.	Stryker, Simon and Mary-Maria, b. Aug. 14.
Dec. 7.	Bennett, John and Jeny-Febe.
25.	Van derbilt, John and Jenny-Ida.

1795.
Jan. 16. Bennett, Abraham and Maria-Abraham Hall.
Mar. 1. Quick, Hennery and Nelly-Abraham, b. Jan. 15.
Apr. 6. Van Doren, William and Leah-Jacob, b. Mar. 1.
26. McDonald, George and Peggy-Maria, b. Mar. 10.
Willson, Hendrick and Nelly-Sally, b. Jan. 11.
May 4. Sarah, late servant to John Wyckoff-Jude.
July 12. Covenhoven, Cornelius and Dinah-Cornelius, b. May 19.
26. Schenk, Martin and Margaret-Sarah, b. July 8.
Sept. 20. Brocaw, Abraham and Mary-Peter, b. Aug. 6.
Monfort, Peter and Maria-Garret Probasco, b. July 7.
Sutphen, John and Allatty-Reoluf, b. Aug. 15.
Probasco, Peter and Martha-Maria, b. Aug. 6.
Doty, Joseph and Anna-Jonathan, b. July.
Ditmars, Peter and Maria-Margaret, b. Aug. 1.
Schenk, Abraham and Eve-Catharine, b. July 20.
Sarah, late servant to John Wyckoff-Dyne, b. June 25.
Nov. 1. Voorhees, Garadus and Maria-Ann, b. Sept. 30.
Dec. 20. Bell, William and (Name of wife not given)-William.
1796.
May 13. Van Der Veer, Garret and Deborah-John.
Sept. 14. Garretson, Jacobus Jr. and Doraty-Doraty, b. Aug. 8.
Stryker, Dr. Peter and Magdalen-Maria Magdalen.
Oct. 16. Nevius, John and Febe-Charity, b. Aug. 25.
Van Doren, John Jr. and Nelly-Peter Voorhees, b. Sept. 11.
Frelinghuysen, Fredrick and Ann-Sarah, b. June 19.
21. Van Brunt, Reoluf and Betsey-Sarah, b. Sept. 23.
Nov. 20. Suckley, John and Sarah-Archabald, b. Sept. 26.
Bainbridge, John and Adrancha-Margaret Schenk, b. Nov. 5.
1797.
Mar. 19 Stryker, Peter and Maria-Ann Williamson, b. Dec. 29, 1796.
Willson, Hendrick and Nelly-Jacob, b. Oct. 6, 1796.
Dumont, Rynear and Jane-Catarin, b. Dec. 15, 1796.
June 18. Van Doren, William and Leah-Cornelius, b. Dec. 10, 1796.
July 2. Davis, Samuel and Caty-Magdalen, b. May 22.
30. Lowe, Jacob and Martha-Rebecah, b. July 12.
Sept. 10. Covenhoven, Cornelius and Dinah-Denise.
1798.
Jan. 14. Fulkerson, Derrick and Caty-Reoluf Van Dorne, b. Dec. 20, 1797.

Feb. 11. Merrill, William and Maria-Liza Reed, b. Jan. 8.
Stryker, Simeon and Mary-Jeremiah Van Devener, b. Dec. 21, 1797.
20. Stryker, Dr. Peter and Magdalen-Lidia Cornell, b. Jan. 18.
Mar. 11. Brocaw, Abraham and Maria-Caleb, b. Dec. 8, 1798 (1797?).
Apr. 7. Schenk, Abraham and Eva-Abraham Van Buren, b. Jan. 25.
Wyckoff, Cornelius and Cathrin-Cornelia, b. Jan. 22.
Davis, Mary, dau. of Samuel Davis-John Newman, b. Feb. 7.
May 6. Voorhees, Garadus and (Name not given of wife)-James Quick, b. Mar. 27.
Sutphen, John and Alatty-John, b. Mar. 21.
20. Ditmars, Abraham and Maria-Ellener, b. May 5.
June 3. Smock, Cornelius and Maria-Nelly Wyckoff, b. Mar. 5.
Bennett, John and Dinah-John, b. Mar. 18.
Lott, Isaac and Anna-Nelly, b. Apr. 19.
17. Frelinghuysen, Fredrick and Anna-Elizabeth Yard, b. Aug. 12.
Aug. 12. Terhune, Cornelius and Jeny-Allaty.
Bainbridge, John and Adrayana-Elezibeth. b. July 31.
Sept. 22. Sarah, late servant of John Wyckoff-Francis, b. Aug. 4.
Dec. 2. Schenk, Martin and Margaret-Ellenor, b. Oct. 22.
16. Baraclow, Farington and Hannah-James Bennet, b. Oct. 6.
Stryker, Peter and Maria-Hendrick Cornell, b. Nov. 16.
Van Doren, John and Nelly-Caty, b. Nov. 19.
Van Doren, William and Leah-Isaac, b. Nov. 17.

1799.

Jan. I3. Quick, Hennery and Nelly-Mary, b. Dec. 15, 1798.
Feb. 10. Probasco, Geoge and Anna-Phebe, b. Jan. 12.
24. Garretson, Jacobus and Martha-Magdalen, b. Jan. 13.
Cornell, Barant and Catrin-Jane P. Quick, b. Jan. 6.
Apr. 21. Covenhoven, Cornelius and Dinah-Nicholas, b. Feb. 8.
Bogert, Jacob and Maria-John b. Mar. 23.
Wyckoff, Cornelius and Caty-Elizabeth Krosen, b. Mar. 24.
Metler, Samuel and Rebecca-Rachel, b. Nov. 3.
Prawl, Samuel and Jane-John, b. Mar. 13.
June 2. Blow, Jacob and Martha-Jacob, b. Mar. 21.
Sarah, late servant to John Wyckoff, Sr.-Else, b. May 6.
30. Schenk, Josiah and Allaty-Josiah.
July 23. Cornell, John and Maria-Margaret Schenk, b. June 21.
Aug. 11. Merrel, William and Maria-Rynear Smock, b. July 12.
25. Fulkerson, Derrick and Jane-John Brown, b. Jan. 5.

Sept. 22.	Christopher, John and Mary-Lanah, b. July 28.
	Nevius, John and Phebe-Cornelius Cornell, b. July 8.
Oct. 6.	Fulkerson, Derrick and Caty-Richard, b. Sept. 12.
Dec. 1.	Wyckoff, Peter and Febe-Peter, b. Nov. 4.
15.	Stryker, Simon and Mary Van Deventer-Cornelia, b. Oct. 19.
	Sarah, dau. of Black Woman, b. Nov. 10.
1800.	
Jan. 1.	Staats, John Jr. and Maria Dechter-John, b. Nov. 24, 1799.
Apr. 18.	Stillcock, Jeremiah and Margaret Dumont-Rachel, b. Jan. 23.
20.	Cornell, Joseph and Jane Van Nuys-Maria, b. Mch. 8.
	Brokaw, Abraham and Maria Stryker-Simon, b. Feb. 22.
May 17.	Van Nostrand, Jacob and Rachel Smith-Benjamin Smith, b. Mch. 26.
June 29.	Terhune, Cornelius and Jane Middleswart-Mary, b. May 17.
	Frelinghuysen, Fredrick and Ann-Ann, b. Apr. 1.
July 27.	Dumont, Rynier and Beeltie Bogert-Rynier.
Sept. 20.	Van Doren, William and Leah Sutphen-Joseph, b. July 19.
Oct. 31.	Calden, James and Elenor Buis-Jacob Buis, b. Sept. 3, 3 A.M.
	Whitenegt, Abraham and Gertrude Van Nuys-Cornelius, b.
Sept. 19.	Voorhees, Gerardus and Mary Quick-John, b. Sept. 23.
	Stryker, John A. and Lanatty Probasco-Mary. b. Aug. 20.
Nov. 2.	Bainbridge, John and Ariantie Dumont-Abigail.
16.	Garretson, Garrit and Anna Smock-John Voorhees.
30.	Staats, Peter and Altie Cornell-Maria, b. Oct. 26.
	Barcalow, Farington and Hannah-George Washington, b. Oct. 1.

SIX-MILE RUN DUTCH REFORMED CHURCH

These records begin in Volume VIII (1919) of the Quarterly, page 124.

On Nov. 15, 1710, Rev. Paulus Van Vlecq, a Hollander, who had been a schoolmaster at Kinderhook, N. Y., organized the Six-Mile Run church at (present) Franklin Park, N. J. According to a "Journal" kept by him the members admitted on April 17, 1711, were these:

Willemse, Eytye, wife of Pieter Kinne.
Wymants, Antye, wife of Gysbert De Hart.
Hooglandt, Marritye, wife of Lammert Van Dyck.
Strycker, Lammetye, wife of Jacob Wyckhof.

He then states under an entry of the following October:

"1711, the 23 October. At 6 Myl Run a church council was elected in the place of the outgoing elders, Adrien Bennet, Baerent De Wit; and left Carl Fonteyn ruling elder, and in the place of the outgoing deacon, Baerent De Wit, Gysbert De Hart is elected, leaving Abraham Bennet the ruling deacon, and they were established on the 24 Oct. 1711.

"The members at 6 Myl Run:
Bennet, Adrien
Fonteyn, Charles
De Wit, Baerent
Bennet, Abraham
Van Dyck, Lammert
Kinne, Pieter
Van Dyck, Isaac and his wife Barbara Reyniersen
Van Hooren, Jannetje, wife of Adrian Laeru
Kinnen, Adriaen Pietersen
Wyckhof, Jacob
De Hart, Gysbert
Van Dyck, Angenetye, wife of Adriaen Bennet
Van Festen, Sara, wife of Baerent De Wit
Reynierse, Helenae, wife of Charles Fonteyn
Larue, Cattelyntie, wife of Elias De Hart
Folkers, Jannetye, wife of Abraham Bennet
Vanderlinden, Jeytye, wife of Jan Vliedt
Bennet, Angenetye, wife of Johannis Folckers

As it is noticed that no names on the two lists are duplicated, we infer that the list given Oct. 24, 1711, reverts back to the original list (in Nov. 1710) and supplements it, although the matter is not clear.

The Six-Mile Run Dutch Reformed church, in Franklin township, Somerset County, was organized Nov. 15, 1710, but no baptismal records of it are known to exist prior to 1743, except about a dozen baptisms by the organizer, Paulus Van Vlecq. For that year and then for 1749-53 a few loose leaves exist; otherwise the original baptismal book, deposited in 1894 in the Sage Library, at New Brunswick, continues the entries until 1804. From a careful copy of these entries the following baptisms have been transcribed by the Editor of the *Quarterly*. Spellings have been preserved as written. In a few cases we have transposed the names so as to make the dates consecutive. Some breaks in years will be noticed.

The pastors of the church during the period named were Theodorus J. Frelinghuysen, 1720-47; Johannes Arondeus, acting at times, 1747-54; Johannes Leydt, 1748-83; John M. Van Harlingen, 1787-95; James S. Cannon, 1797-1826. The present pastor is the Rev. Eugene H. Keator, to whom and to the Consistory of the Church we are indebted for the loan of the record of which we now commence publication. [Editor]

1743.

July 13. Van Voorhees, Court and Nelle-Femetia. Witnesses: Isaac Hagamen and Pryn.

Cornel, Corneleus and Annecke Van Voorhees-Petrus. Witness: Rynear Merill.

Van Doren, Christian and Alche-Joseph.

Schenck, Peter-Maria. Witnesses: Garret Veghten and Elizabet.

Symese, Isaac and Neltie-Aris.

Van Dyke, Hendrick and Maragritie-Cornelius; Helena.

Van Voorhees, Jocobus and Maria-Abraham.

Nevius, Tobias and Rebecca-Petrus.

Van Arsdalen, Aris and Sarah-Antie.

Stryker, Jacobus and Gertie-[Child's name not given].

Van Arsdalen, Cornelius and Mary- [Child's name not given].

Douty, Jeremias and Armya-[Child's name not given].

Monfoo [Monfort?],--odoris and Altie [Child's name not given].

Oct. 1. Van Liew, Frederick and Maricke-Jaques.

Pyet, John and Joenkie-William.

Van Arsdalen, Jurrie and Altie-Johannes.

22. Gulick, Jochem and Cornelia-Abraham.
Nov. 5. Stothoff, Elbert and Ida-Anecke.
Tunison, Cornelus and Jenneke-Cornelus.
Stryker, Johannes and Cornelia-Jacobus.
per C (?), Frederick and Grietie-Altie.
Dec. 4. Wik, Jakobus and Maritie- ---us(?).
Van Voorhees, Lucas and Nelltie-Antie.
Polen, Martin and Sarah-Petrus.
Vonk, Johanes and Geertie-Catrinche.
Van Arsdalen, John and Debora-Christoffel.
1749.
Jan. 29. Davids, Christian and Debora-Antie.
Hagamen, Nys and Mayke-Sara.
Fyn, John and Antie-Jacob.
Feb. 26. Stothoff, Cornelius and Maria-Maria.
Van Doren, Abm. and Maria-Femmetje.
Oct. 23. Failor, Benjamin and Marriche-Benjamin.
Van Arsdalen, Christoffel and Neltie-Helena.
Voorhees, Martynus and Lebeche-[Child's name not given].
Veghten, Nicholas and Neltie-Nuys.
Vliet, Daniel and Geertie-Jan.
Nov. 6. Polen, Samuel and Jacamintie-Eva.
Schenk, Albert and Catelyntie-Maria.
Williamson, Dirck and Sara-Petrus.
Sitfin, John and Neeltje-Catrena.
23. Schenk, Hendrick and Lena-Maria.
Dec. 10.Suydam, Engelty-Joseph.
1750.
Jan. 1. Bennet, Johannes and Geertye-Jannitye.
Fulkerson, Joseph and Altie-Johannes.
Emans, Benjamin and Antje-Andrias.
Wytknegt, Johannis and Neeltje-Petrus.
21. Boerum, Niclaes and Antje-Catrinche.
Williamson, Niclaes and Ragel-Willem.
Feb. 19. Dorlant, Lammert and Styntje-Gerrit.
Mar. 4. Poulse, Johannis and Harmje-Jannetje.
Cornel, Willem and Greitje-Eliesabet.
Witnesses: Adriaen Cornel and Eliesabet Van Enden.
Hegeman, Nys and Aaltje-Jakobus.
18. Van Aersd[alen], Jan and Lena-Abraham.

Apr. 1. Vechten, Gerrit and Eliesabet-Petrus.
Van Arsda[len], Cornelius and Femmitje-Maritje.
Jansen, Nicklaes-Antje.
15. Van Zant, Pieter Pra and Marytje-Jakobus.
Pryn, Jeems and Neeltje-Neeltie.
29. Hegeman, Andreas and Marya-Andreas.
Vonk, Johannis and Geertje-Dallius.
Lott, Abraham and Jannitje-Sara.
May 13. Broka, Bregon and Jannitje-Abraham.
Broka, Abraham and Eliesabet- ----tje(?).
June 1. Van Houten, Cornelus and Maytje-Johannis.
3. Van Nest, Pieter and Eliesabet-Maria.
24. Hogelant, Martynis and Femmitje-Cornelus.
July 1. Walderom (Waldron], Leffert and Ida-Saertje.
Van Pelt, Johannis and Catryna-Christoffel.
Sperling, Jan and Geertje- ----rtje(?).
29. Pouwelse, Cornetus and Marytje-Jannetje.
Sept. 2. Gerritse, Rem and Catryntje-Barbera.
Hogelant, Dirck and Maria-Dirck.
(Witness: Anaetje Hogelant.)
Oct. 6. Hout, Jonetan and Jannitje-Anaetje.
Vanderveer, Jan and Sytje-Gerrit; Cornelus.
Nov. 4. Folkerse, Folkert and Maria-Folkert.
18. Van Voorhees, Lucas and Neeltje-Jannitje.
Stoothoff, Johannis and Sara-Johanna.
Hagewouwt, Isack and Catlyntje-Petrus.
Riemer, Abraham and Jannitje-Catriena.
Dec. 2. Leek, Jakobus and Styntje-Dyna.
Speerling, Petrus and Maria-Joris.
Polen, Samuel and Jakemyntje-Samuel.
16. Snedeker, Isack and Catriena-Gerrit.
Wykhoff, Jakobus and Catalyntje-Willemje.

1751.

Feb. 14. Bennet, Jan and Annaetje-Isack.
Feb. -. Wyckoff, Cornelius and Martentje-Willimje. [Bapt. by Johannis Frelinghuysen].
Mar. 3. Corteljou, Hendrick and Catriena-Lena.
Berrieen, Pieter and Annaetje-Johannis.
Pommieeje [Pumyea], Pieter and Mallie-Bettie.
Herresen, Hen-- and Nensie-Johannis.

Van Tilburgh, Willem and Kesya-Johannis.
17. Nevius, Petrus and Johanna-Martynus.
Voorhees, Petrus and Sefya-Jakobus.
Apr. 7. Voorhees, Jan and Eliesabet-Koert.
Leydt, Domene Johannis and Tryntje-Catlyntje.
21. Derje [Duryea?], Joost and Maria-Helena.
Van Aersdalen, Jan and Debora-Magdelena.
June 2. Veghten, Nicholas and Neltie-Lucas.
15. Willemse, Jakobus and Marya-Jannetje.
July 28. Van Kleef, Jurryas and Ida-Eliesabet.
Van Bueren, Mychiel and Jannitje-Marya.
Beert, Alksander and Eliesabet-Jannitje.
Aug. 18. Voorhees, Jan and Maitje-Lucas.
25. Simson, Abraham and Maragrietje-Jan.
Terheunen, Jan and Neeltje-Jan.
Sept. 21. Van Pelt, Jan and Sarah-Aris.
Dec. 8. Hogelant, Abraham and Anaetje-Sara.
Bergen, Jacop and Grietje-Frederik.
Symese, Isack and Neeltie-Deborah.
Willemse, Dirck and Sara-Abraham.
Fyn, Jan and Antje-Marya.
Oct. 6. Van Leeuwe, Frederik and Marytje-Dyna.
Van Dyk, Henderikus and Marregrietje-Albert.
Pouwelse, Johannis and Harmje-Catrynje.
Nov. 3. Van Dyk, Jan and Gerritje-Frederick.
DeHart, Cornelus and Maike-Antje.
Dec. 15. Veghte, Gerrit and Eliesabet-Marya.
Henderikse, Daniel and Ida-Johannis.
Gerritse, Samuel and Jannetje-Gerrit.
Dannelson, William and Doeritie-Eester.

1752.
Jan. 12. Hegeman, Nys and Mayke-Gerrit.
Cornel, Jakobes and Jannitje-Annaatje.
26. Van Aarsdalen, Christoffel and Neeltje-Grietje.
Feb. 9. Van Dyke, Matys and Neeltie-Matius.
Gulick, Geertje-Dana Barkelo.
23. Van Aersdalen, Jurrie and Aaltje-Roeloff.
Mar. 22. Williemse, Jacobis and Maria-Willyem.
Bennet, Joannis and Gertye-Jacob Detwede (the second).
Apr. 5. Willemse, Jakobes and Liedea-Geertie.

Vandervoortd, Jakobes and Metje-Helena.
19. Kinne, Syme and Margrietje-Geertje.
Gulick, Jochem and Corneliea-Willem.
May 3. Stoothoff, Ida, wid. of Elbert-Elbert. Witness: Elbert Stoothoff.
Gerritse, Rem and Catryntje-Gerrit.
Menlie, Jan and Geertje-Eliesabet.
Van Hengelen, Cornelus and Maria-Arenout.
Boerem, Nicklaes and Antje-Neeltje.
14. Schenck, Pieter and Maria-Johannis.
Groenendyk, Johannis and Sara-Mayke.
June 14. Van Pelt, Pieter and Maria-Teunis.
Van Aersdalen and Sara-Chrisstoffel.
July 26. Gulick, Jochem and Rebecka-Antje.
Witnesses: Benjemen Emans and wife Antje.
Gulick, Jakobus and Maria-Jakobus.
Aug. 9. Beert, Alksander and Eliesabet-Elsje.
Vliet, Geertje, wife of Daniel Vliet-Daniel.
Oct. 1. Van Leuwe, Nys and Ida-Cornelus.
15. Van der Veer, Jan and Sytje-Jan.
Wykhoff, Jakobus and Catlyntje-Evaetje.
29. Hogelant, Henderick and Marya-Henderik.
Brouwer, Josip and Antje-Eliesabet.
Nov. 26. Snedeker, Isack and Catriena-Catrina.
Dec. 10. Cornel, Josip and Jannitje-Josip.
24. Van Kleef, Jurryas and Ida-Gerrit.
1753.
Jan. 1. Van Voorhees, Lucas and Neeltje-Neeltje.
Stryker, Pieter and Marya-Barent.
14. Corteljou, Henderick and Catriena-Maria.
Feb. 15. Hogelant, Johannis and Matje-Tuenis.
Mar. 25. Hogelant, Chrisstoffel and Sara-Catlyna.
Folkerse, Folkert and Marya-Flippus.
Apr. 8. Voorheese, Abraham and Marya-Minne.
Van Dyke, Symon and Anna-Hendrick.
Van Buren, Machil and Yannethe-Magdelena.
22. Leek, Jakobus and Styntje-Gerrit Stryker.
Herreson, Henry and Antje-Antje.
Polen, Samuel and Lena-Sara.
Jansen, Marten and Marya-Marten.
May 6. Van Dyk, Jan and Gerritje-Abraham.

20. Denelse, Wilem and Dorite-Johannis.
June 8. Pauluse, Johannes and Harmie-Antje.
Voorhees, Abraham and Geertje-Luykas; Abraham.
10. Provost, Jonathan and Ariantje-Marya. Witness: Catje Provost.
17. Jurcks, Pieter and Anaetje-Catriena.
July 1. Willemse, Wilhelmus and Antje-Antje.
Aug. 10. Emans, Benjemen and Evaatje-Benjamen.
Coevert, Johannis and Marta-Bregon.
Sept. 23. Snedeker, Isack and Catriena-Gerrit.
Vandervoort, Magiel and Marya-Anna.
Oct. 7. Hegeman, Dallius and Catryntje- ----derick.
21. Aarsdalen, Jan and Helena-Helena.
Van Dyk, Mattys and Neeltje-Anna.
Nov. 4. Beent, Alexander and Lybe-William.
Dec. -. Stoethoff, Johannis and Sara-Jenneke.
Dehart, Cornelis and Maeik-Willem.
30. Hegeman, Syme and Aeltje-Geertje.
Willemse, Jakobus and Maria-Luekresie.

1754.
Jan. 20. Schuerman, Fernandus and Neeltje-Anna.
Kinne, Syme and Margrietje-Eva.
Gulick, Jochem and Rebecke-Jackmyntje.
Mar. 31. Berrien, Pieter and Anna-Sara.
Van Nist, Henderik and Henne-Eliesabet.
Apr. 14. Foord, Tomas and Catryntje-Sara.
28. Van Kleef, Johannis and Grietje-Rebekka.
Van Aarsdalen, Jurry and Aaltje-Antje.
Hegeman, Jakobus and Eliesabet-Adrieaan.
Van Leuwe, Nys and Ida-Helena.
May 12. Van Pelt, Pieter and Maria-Jannitje.
23. Cornel, Willem and Grietje-Willem.
Voorhees, Jan and Anna-Antje.
Wykhoff, Jakobus and Catlyntje-Antje.
June 2. Williamse, Jacobus and Marytje-Hendrick.
9. Simson, Abraham and Marregrietje-Catriena.
July 7. Vechte, Gerrit and Eliesabet-Johannis.
Gulick, Jochem and Corneliea-Johannis.
Groenendyk, Johannis and Sara-Chrisstoffel.
21. Gulick, Fernandus and Neeltje-Neeltje.
Sept. 8. Neuius, Jakobus and Eegje-Annitje.

Oct. 6. Vanderveer, Jan and Sytje-Jakobus.
Miserol, Pieter and Femmitje-Marya.
Slover, Lucas and Neeltje-Jakobus.
Boerom, Nicklaes and Antje-Jannitje.
Pouwelse, Pouwell and Lena-Paulus.
Willemse, Abraham and Hendrikje-Neeltje.
26. Vliet, Geertje, wife of Daniel Vliet-Margrietje.
Blauw, Frederik and Marya-Neeltje.
Nov. 3. Van Aersdalen, Jan and Debora-Marleentje.
Hogelant, Martynus and Femmetje-Abraham.
Moor, Henderik and Ida-Johannis.
Gulick, Jakobus and Maria-Johannis.
17. Van Carlaer, Arent and Marya-Marya.
Gerritse, Rem and Catryntje-Barbera.
Van Aersdalen, Jakobus and Alieda-Jacop.
Dehart, Gysbert and Jannitje-Jan.
Van Aersdalen, Cornelus and Sara-Margrietje.
Dec. 1. Schenk, Henderik and Helena-Catyna.
15. Van Deventer, Abraham and Maria-Geertje.
29. Kroese, Dirck and Liesabet-Isack.
1755.
Jan. -. Van Dyk, Roeloff and Catryna-Jan.
Hegeman, Dallius and Catryntje-Geertje.
Van Doorn, Jan and Marytje-Aeltje.
Jan. 9. Hogelant, Henderik and Maria-Antje.
26. Blauw, Pieter and Maria-Aaltje.
Van Dyk, Jan and Gerritje-Jacop.
Feb. 23. Van Kleef, Jurryas and Ida-Isack.
Hegeman, Simon and Aeltje-Adriaen.
Mar. 15. Voorhees, Cornelus and Lena-Marya.
30. Van Voorhees, Lucas and Neeltje-Abraham.
Van Pelt, Henderik and Sara-Jan.
Apr. 20. Van Leuwe, Frederick and Marytje-Geertje.
Terheunen, Jan and Neeltje-Magdelena.
Stryker, Abraham and Catriena-Ida.
Quick, Teunis and Helena-Petrus.
Van Voorhees, Jan and Jannitje-Abraham.
Neuius, Johannis and Catriena-Gerrit.
May 4. Hogelant, Christoffel and Sara-Ida.
Pouwelse, Johannis and Harmje-Abraham.

Bennet, Johannis and Geertje-Annaetje.
Witnesses: Jakobus Van Duyn and wife Annaetje.
24. Stout, Annaetje, wife of Samuel Stout-Abraham
25. Leek, Jan and Margrietje-Chrisstoffel.
June 13. Perbesko, Jan and Dyna-Jacob.
Van Aersdalen, Ouke and Maria-Chrisstoffel.
29. Beerd, Willem and Elsje-Johannis.
Sutten, Catriena, wife of Hu Sutten-Jacop.
Menlie, Jan and Geertje-Marya.
Willemse, Wilhemus and Antje-Lena.
Voorhees, Agyas and Marya-Johannis.
July 13. Ten Broeck, Cornelius and Maregrieta-Eliesabet.
Kehaert, Tomas and Marya-Tomas.
27. Stryker, Pieter and Marya-Eliesabet.
Broka, Jan and Antje-Abraham.
Aug. 17. Vanderbilt, Nys and Sara-Saertje.
Leek, Jakobus and Styntje-Grietja.
Voorhees, Ouke and Neeltje-Jakobus.
Wykhof, Jakobus and Catalyna-Janathe.
Voorhees, Abraham and Gerthe-Isack.
Oct. 19. Gulick, Samuel and Maria-Tuenis.
Willemse, Jakobus and Maria-Ida.
Janse, Marten and Maria-Sara.
Kinne, Syme and Maria-Jakobus.
Schuerman, Fernandus and Neeltje-Neeltje.
Nov. 2. Van Dyk, Mattys and Neeltje-Neeltje.
Foord, Tomas and Catriena-Henderik.
17. Kertener, John Jurri and Maria-Hanna.
Witnesses: Henderick Deetloff, Biegel Meyer.
Voorhees, Aron and Maria-Ouke. Witness: Jan Voorhees.
Herreson, Henneri and Antje-Cornelus.
Dec. 25. Van Pelt, Aert and Sara-Jacop.
1756.
Jan. 11. Merrell, Roger and Sara-Sara.
25. Dehart, Cornelus and Mayke-Sara.
Coevert, Johannis and Marta-Isack.
Feb. 8. Skilman, Johannis and Antje-Jacop.
22. Speerling, Jan and Catryntje-Johannis Magiel.
Jansen, Pieter and Rebecka-Willem.
Van Sant, Wynant and Ragel-Sara.

Mar. 14. Van Kleek, Johannis and Grietje-Marya.
Van Deventer, Jacoubus and Elizabet-Jan.
Apr. 25. Ditmarse, Rem and Helena-Marritje.
Bennit, Jan and Atinaetje-Johannis.
Hegeman, Jakobus and Eliesabet-Geertje.
Van Buren, Machiel and Jannitje-Ida.
Witnesses: Daniel Henderikse and wife Ida.
May 9. Bergen, Joris and Marya-Metje.
Willemse, Abraham and Engelje-Dirck.
July 4. Van Leuwe, Nys and Ida-Frederick.
Bries, Jurrie and Catriena-Henderik.
Kroese, Henderik and Eliesabet-Cornelus.
Nevius, Petrus and Marya-Cattelyntje.
Aug. 1. Bergen, Jacop and Grietje-Jacop.
15. Kroese, Dirck and Lybetje-Catriena.
Van Pelt, Pieter and Marya-Neeltje.
Cortejou, Albert and Lena-Antje.
Terhuenen, Stefanus and Margrieta-Gerrit.
29. Corteljou, Henderick and Catriena-Johanna.
Tamsen, Aetsebel and Coba-Anna.
Van Noortwyk, Marten and Pieternel-Alksander.
Feler, Frederick and An Mari-Frederik.
Sept. 12. Wykhoff, Jacop and Angenietje-Fransyntje.
Stoothoff, Johannis and Sara-Sara.
Dehart, Gysbert and Jannetje-Wynant.
Fyn, Jan and Antje-Antje.
26. Gulick, Jakobus and Marytje-Abraham.
Van Deventer, Abraham and Marya-Ferrenton.
Oct. 10. Groenendyke, Johannis and Sara-Johannis.
Gulick, Jochem and Cornelia-Jannitje.
24. Van Aersdalen, Ouke and Marya-Louwerens.
Van Aersdalen, Henderick-Henderick. Witness: Eliesabet Delie.
Willemse, Jakobus and Marya-Marya.
Vander Veer, Jan and Sytje-Petrus.
Van Hengeten, Ouke and Elsje-Barent.
28. Schenk, Henderik and Helena-Aeltje.
Nov. 21. Stoothoff, Jakus and Catlyna-Cornelus.
Blauw, Frederik and Marya-Marya.
Blauw, Willem and Margrietje-Marya.
Dec. 5. Gulick, Joghom and Rebekca-Eliesabet.

Hooms, Obadya and Marya-Johannis.
Hegeman, Simon and Aeltje-Maria.
19. Sitfen, Aert and Jannitje-Jakobus.
Van Leuwe, Frederick and Marytje-Johannis.
Hogelant, Martynus and Femmitje-Ariejaentje.
1757.
Jan. 16. Voorhees, Albert and Neeltje-Albert.
Brouwer, Josip and Antje-Pieter.
30. Voorhees, Jan and Anna-Rem.
Gerritse, Gerrit and Sara-Gerrit.
Van Cleef, Juryas and Ida-Juryas.
Feb. 20. Astursens(?), Jakobus and Margrietje-Johannis.
Apr. --. Kinne, Syme and Grietje-Petrus.
Hegeman, Benjamin and Geertje-Arijaen.
Snedeker, Isack and Catriena-Marya.
Brown, And'w and Hannah-Hannah.
Van Doorn, Jan and Marya-Jan.
Jurcks, Pieter and Annaltje-Jannitje.
Quick, Tuenis and Lena-Femmitje.
May 1. Gulick, Samuel and Maria-Jochem.
15. Boerem, Nicklaes and Antje-Antje.
Stilwil, Josip and Peesjens-Neeltje.
30. Van de Water, Henderick and Eliesabet-Henderik.
June 30. Wykoff, Jakobus and Catlytje-Cornelieus.
July 3. Polen, Samuel and Jackemyntje-Eliesabet.
Van Aersdalen, Gerrit and Marya-Helena.
Wykhoff, Symon and Aeltje-Eliesabet.
Van Waglom, Jan and Eliesabet-Marya.
Blau, Jan and Eliesabet-Dyna.
17. Van Arsdalen, Jurrie and Aeltje-Maregrietje.
Simson, Abraham and Margriteje-Abraham.
Stols, Pieter and Eliesabet-Marytie.
Aug. 21. Van Voorhees, Lucas and Neeltje-Anna.
Hagelant, Chrisstoffel and Sara-Jannetje.
Van Aersdalen, Cornelieus and Catlyntje-Cornelus.
Sept. 4. Terhunen, Albert and Maria-Jan.
Foordt, Tomas and Catriena-Tomas.
Oct. 1. Van Aarsdalen, Gerrit and Ariaenje-Lena.
23. Gerritse, Samuel and Jannetje-Johannis; Lucas.
Voorhees, Koert-Jan.

Hikbie, Eliesa and Catriena-Obadia. Witness: Henderik Stols.
Nov.6. Hogelent, Dirck and Marta-Willem.
20(?). Sedam, Petrus and Femmitje-Ryk.
Terhunen, Steven and Margrietje-Willem.
Quick, Abraham and Matje-Jackmyntje.
Van Dyk, Jan and Gerritje-Jannitje.
Dec. 4. Voorhees, Isaac and Helena Barkelow-David.
Vandorn, Willem and Catlintje-Christean.
Golder, Nicholas and Maria-Abraham.
Willemsen, Willem and Angenietye-Willem.
Broca, Jan and Magdalena-Jan.
Grigs, Barent and Jackemintye-Ferdenandus.
18. Voorhees, Abraham and Geertje-Nellie.
1758.
Jan. 1. Leydt, Dom. Johannis and Tryntje-Johannis.
Jansen, Marten and Marya-Pieter.
22. Wykoff, Jacop and Sara-Pieter.
Wykoff, Jan and Maria-Jan.
Feb. 5. Stryker, Abraham and Catriena-Annaetje.
Kroese, Henderick and Eliesabet-Elsje.
Denyk, Coenraet and Elsje-Coenraet.
Misserol, Isack and Catriena-Maregrieta.
10. Van Aersdalen, Ouke and Marya-Ouke.
Mar. 5. Stryker, Pieter and Marya-Ragel.
Apr. 2. Van Doorn, Jacop and Femmitje-Femmitje.
Janse, Pieter and Rebecke-Sytje.
Bennet, Johannis and Marya-Jannetje.
Hegeman, Dallius and Catryntje-Marya.
Beert, Alhsander and Lybetje-[Child's name not given].
Willemse, Wilhelmes and Antje-Johannis.
16. More, Hendrick and Yda-Rynire.
Hogelant, Ouke and Lenthe-Femmethe.
Schurman, Fernandes and Nelthe-Yacobes.
Brise, Jurrye and Maryya-Maryya.
May 7. Van Dyk, Matys and Neeltje-Tuentje.
Noortwyk, Filippus and Sara-Chrisstoffal.
Witnesses: Chrysstoffal Perbasko and wife Lena.
Smak, Leendert and Antje-Femmetje.
Folkerse, Folkers and Marya-Jannitje.
15. Nevius, Jakobus and Pieterneltje-Eliesabet.

Van Aersdalen, Henderik and Jannitje-Douwe.
Willemse, Jakobus and Maria-Gerrit.
June 4. Voorhees, Gerrit and Neeltje-Petrus.
Kehaert, Tomas and Marya-Eliesabet.
Van Deventer, Jakobus and Eliesabet-Abraham.
18. Nevius, Petrus and Anaetje-David.
Koevert, Johannis and Marta-Daniel.
Van Nist, Hederik and Johanna-Henderikus.
Groenendyk, Johannis and Sara-Abraham.
July 2. Veghte, Gerrit and Eliesabet-Jannetje; Magdelena.
Nevins, Petrus and Marya-Neeltie.
Broka, Abraham and Eliesabet-Pieter.
Demon, Pieter and Ariejaentje-Johanna.
16. Leek, Tomas and Mayke-Nicklass.
Sept. 10. Venderveer, Jan and Sytje-Jannitje.
Voorhees, Albert and Neeltje-Jeremias.
Van Sant, Wynant and Ragel-Geertje.
24. Davits, Tomas and Catrina-Willem.
Snedeker, Isack and Catriena-Jannitje.
Kouenoven, Cornelius and Anaetie-Jacop; Abraham; Isack.
Vanderveer, Demenicus and Marya-Johannie.
Blauw, Wilhelmus and Margrietje-Neeltje.
Oct. 29. Van Pelt, Pieter and Maria-Roeloff.
Corteljou, Elbert and Helena-Roeleff.
Vonk, Jan and Geertje-Henderik.
Gulick, Ferdenandus and Marleentje-Peterus.
Sedan, Jacip and Antje-Elsje.
Nov. 12. Schenk, Henderik and Helena-Johannis.
Voorhees, Pieter and Sara-Petrus.
Prevoost, Jonetan and Ariejaantje-Ariejaantje.
Bokeloe, Joneton and Eliesabet-Jaaers.
Gulick, Jocghem and Rebecke-Johannis.
Hooms, Obadijah and Marya-Willem.
Van Aersdalen, Henderik and Catlynje-Annaetje.
Witnesses: Christoffel Van Aersdalen and wife Marleentje.
Dec. 17. Wykhoff, Jacobus and Catlyntje-Sarah.
1759.
Jan. 21. Hogelant, Abraham and Johana-Johana.
Van Aersdalen, Corneles and Sara-Corneles.
Feb. 4. Speerling, Johannis and Catryntje-Abraham; Isaac.

Monvoort, Petrus and Cornelia-Sara.
Witnesses: Christoffel Prebasco and wife Sara. ["These names have been carried over in the church book of Suerland"].
Hoglant, Henderik and Marya-Sara.
18. Sturkes, Marregrieta-Myndert.
Hogelant, Johannis and Matje-Jannetje.
Skilman, John and Anna-Abraham.
Mar. 4. Boshart, Roelof and Barbera-Sara.
Terhunen, Albert and Marya-Daniel.
Apr. 8. Gulick, Samuel and Maria-Anna.
Van Aersdalen, Cornelus and Cathyntje-Jocghem.
22. Blauw, Jan and Catrynje-Henderik.
Gulick, Jochem and Cornelia-Lea.
Bennet, Jan and Annaetje-Neeltje.
Quick, Tuenis and Lena-Martynus.
Brouwer, Josip and Antje-Tomas.
May 6. Perbesko, Jan and Dyna-Maria.
Van Kleef, Juryas and Ida-Maria.
Willemse, Samuel and Margrietje-Willem.
20. Willemse, Marya-Marya. Witness: Willem Willemse.
31. Nevius, Petrus and Aeltje-Jannitje. Witness: Susanne Nevius.
Menlie, Jan and Geertje-Charity.
June 3. Van Aersdalen, Jurrie and Aeltje-Jurrie.
Van Devanter, Marya-Neeltje.
Hickbie, Catriena-Henderik. Witness: Henderik Stols.
Kroese, Abraham and Marta-Helena.
Pelhemus, Daniel and Willemje-Abraham and Neeltje.
4. Dehart, Cornelus and Mayke-Abraham.
July 15. Van Dyk, Jan and Gerritje-Tuenje.
Van Kleef, Johannis and Grietje-Sara.
Aug. 12. Wykof, Jacop and Angenitje-Annaetje.
Merrell, Roger and Sara-Dirck.
Herresen, Henry and Antie-Maria.
26 Wykoff, Jacip and Sara-Jan. ["Was entered in the Raritan church book"].
Sept. 9. Sedam, Petrus and Femmitje-Jannitje.
Willemse, Willem and Angenietje-Isack.
Kroese, Dirck and Lybetje-Eliesabet.
Zutfen, Jacob and Neeltje-Jacob.

23. Boreem, Nicklaes and Antje-Jacop.
Oct. 14. Gerritse, Gerrit and Sara-Dirck.
Van Aersdalen, Ouke and Marya-Jannitje.
Stols, Pieter and Eliesabet-Pieter.
Stols, Engel and Jesiena-Eliesabet.
Vanderbeek, Rem and Marta-Ruben.
Voorhees, Jan and Anna-Ida.
Snedeker, Isack-Isaack.
Nov. 11. Kroese, Henderick and Eliesabet-Helena.
25. Hegemen, Benjamin and Geertje-Annatje.
Van Aarsdalen, Jan and Lenah-Lammetje.
Van Doorn, Jan and Marretje-Cornelius.
Hogeland, Jacob and Maria-Johannes.
Hogeland, Hendrik-Abraham.
Dec. 23. Perbesco, Hendrik and Elsje-Pieter.
26. Cappey(?) Johannes and Margariet-Elizabeth.
Witnesses: Hendrick Stols and wife Geertruy.

1760.
Mar. 3. Berrien, Pieter and Anna-Anna.
Ditmarse, Rem and Helena-Marya.
30. Hegemen, Symon and Aaltje-Jan.
Apr. 13. Voorhees, Luykas and Neeltje-Teunis.
27. Fort, Tomas and Catrina-Anna.
May 11. Wyckof, Symon and Aelthe-Kresteyan.
Yurcksen, Peter and Annathe-Yohanes.
Grigs, Barent and Yacamynthe-Samuel.
June 6. Hegemen, Jakobus and Eliesabet-Maria.
Stryker, Barent and Eliesabet-Eliesabet.
Simson, Abraham and Margritje-Marleintje.
Voorhees, Koert and Catriena-Nicklaes.
15. Vanderver, Jan and Seytie-Jannethe.
Van Aersdalen, Hendrik and Catelyna-Christoffel.
Kovert, Johannes and Martha-Annathe.
Wykhof, Jacobes and Cathelynthe-Catelynthe.
Aug. 3. Van Leuwe, Jan and Doorte-Frederick.
Witness: Helena Van Leuwe.
Vecgte, Jan and Catriena-Nicklaes.
Gulick, Jakobus and Marytje-Catrina.
Brown, Andrew and Hannah-Mary.
Bergen, Joris and Maria-Christoffel; Yda (twins).

Witnesses: Christoffel Perbasco and wife Betje; Willem Post and wife Ida.
Van Noertroyk, Marte and Neeltje-Arijaentje.
17. Corteljou, Albert and Helena-Henderik.
Groenendyk, Johannis and Sara-Isaak.
Snedeker, Jan and Sara-Gerrit.
Sept. 28.Schuerman, Fernandus and Neeltje-Abraham.
Bergen, Jacop and Margrietje-Elsje.
Oct. 12. Stoothoff, Johannis and Sara-Anna.
Schenk, Henderik and Helena-Henderick.
Gulick, Pietrus and Willemje-Nicklaes.
Kreeg, Joost and Sjaerlotta-Antje.
Hooms, Obadya and Maria-Obadya.
Vechte, Abraham and Maria-Nellie.
Janse, Pieter and Rabecka-Johannis; Jannetje (twins).
Nov. 30.Koolder, Nicklaes and Marya-[Child's name not entered].
Dec. 14.Hogelant, Chrisstoffel and Sara-Sara.
Wykoff, Jakobus and Sytje-Wilemje.
Cornel, Cornelus and Willemje-Willem.
1761.
Feb. 1. Manly, John and Geertj-Maria.
Mar. 1. Rappelye, Cornelas and Mrite-Elisebet.
Vanarsdalen, Corneles and Sara [or Soval]-Myndert.
Kenne, Symen and Marragethe-Marggrethe.
Messalar, Jacobes and Yannithe-Mryya.
Voorhiese, Cornelis and Lena-Jan.
Sutven, Wellem and Wyna-Petree.
22. Vandyk, Matys and Neeltje-Margrieta.
Geritse, Stefanus and Femmitje-Rem.
Hogelant, Dirck and Marta-Grietje.
Apr. 26. Gulick, Samuel and Maria-Abraham.
Van Aerdalen, Cornelus and Cathyntje-Geertje.
Stryker, Maria-Pieter. Witness: Barent Stryker.
Snedeker, Isack and Sara-Sytje.
May 3. Melcher, Frederik and Catriena-Maria.
17. Leek, Jan and Margrieta-Jakobus.
Cornel, Albartus and Antje-Jannitje.
Gulick, Ferdenandus and Marleentje-Johannis.
Kroese, Abraham and Marta-Rachel.
Sudaem, Jacob and Aenthe-Knelis; Seymen.

Van Lewen, Deneys and Eyda-Denys.
Williamson, Samuel and Margrehthe-Cornelis.
Herresin, Hennery and Nensay-William.
June 14. Kroese, Henderik and Eliesabet-Wilhelmus.
Stols, Engel and Esiena-Jacop.
Cheerdener, Johan Jurri and Maria-Eliesabet; Christiena; Johan Jurrie.
July 5. Perbesco, Henderik and Elsje-Maria.
Van Dyk, Jan and Gerritje-Elsje.
Hikbie, Catriena-Johannis. Witness: Henderik Stols.
Hogelant, Johannis and Martje-Maria.
Gerritse, Gerrit and Sara-Sara.
19. Voorhees, Abraham and Maria-Minne.
Aug. 2. Van Pelt, Pieter and Maria-Abraham.
Wykoff, Simon and Aeltje-Eliesabet.
Wenk, Jacop and Eliesabet-Rabecka.
Terhunen, Albert and Maria-Abraham.
Van Pelt, Henderik and Sara-Josip.
16. Van Aersdalen, Gerrit and Ariejaentje-Chrisstoffel.
Hogelant, Jacop and Marya-Jacop.
Pinbroek, David and Ariejaenje-Maria.
Sept. 6. Corteljou, Henderik and Annaetje-Henderik.
12. Bogert, Nathanael and Maria-Cornelius.
Hogelant, Hederick and Jannitje-Jan.
20. Wykoff, Jan and Willemje-Marya.
Lybet; [child] may or may not be the child of Jan Wykoff and Willemje.
Gerritse, Samuel and Jannitje-Petrus; Johannes (twins).
Oct. 4. Gulick, Jocghem and Rebecka-Benjemen.
Nov. 29. Ditmarse, Rem and Lena-Catryntje.
Dec. 13. Hallenhed, Francis and Doorete Hallenhed-Leisebet.
27. Van Engelen, Cornelius and Sara-Maria.
1762.
Jan. 3. Sedam, Petrus and Femmitje-Antje.
Vliet, Geertje, wife of Daniel Vliet-Gerrit.
Biedt, Alksander and Eliesabet-Eliesabet.
17. Van Aersdalen, Henderik and Sathynje-Jan.
31. Voorhees, Johannis and Neeltje-Johannis.
Feb. 14. Van Doorn, Jan and Matje-Jacop.
Mar. 14. Williamson, Willim and Maria-Catreina.
Brower, Josuph and Enne-[Child's name not entered].

28. Wellmsen, Wellem and Angenithe-Willim.
Apr. 11. Van Klef, Johannes and Grithe-Johannes.
Quick, Abraham and Maghtel-Teunes.
June 6. Carteljou, Albert and Helena-Jakus.
Wykhoff, Jakobus and Cathyntje-Neeltje.
Van Leeuwe, Johannis and Doorte-Johannis.
20. Sitfin, Willem and Wyna-Annie.
Vechgte, Abraham and Maria-Marta.
Foord, Tomas and Catriena-Frensis.
July 18. Van Leuwen, Frederick and Marytje-Geertje.
Voorhees, Lucas and Neeltje-Lucas.
Schenk, Henderik and Lena-Maria; as witnesses for the child of Abraham Van Deventer. [So appears in the original].
Willemse, Jakobus and Marya-Antje.
Voorhees, Jan and Anna-Marytje.
Aug. 1. Vanderveer, Petrus and Jannitje-Lammitje.
Witnesses: Lucas Schenk and wife Lammitje.
Gulick, Joghem and Corneliea-Anna.
15. Skilman, Johannis and Anna-Abraham.
Sept. 9. Nevins, Petrus and Aeltje-David.
Wykoff, Jakobus and Lytje-Susanna.
12. Koevert, Johannis and Marta-Johannis.
Hegeman, Benjamen and Geertje-Benjemen.
26. Vecgte, Gerrit and Eliesabet-Eliesabet.
Hooms, Obadya and Marya-Abraham.
Oct. 10. Gulick, Peterus and Willemje-Peterus.
Stryker, Barent and Eliesabet-Antje.
17. Kinne, Syme and Margrieta-Syme.
Nov. 5. Groenendeyck, Johannes and Sarah-Neeltje.
7. Vanderveer, Jan and Sytje-Petrus; Belitje.
Willemse, Gerrit and Geertje-Nicklaas.
21. Hogelant, Chrisstoffel and Sara-Sara.
Dec. 5. Kroese, Henderik and Eliesabet-Henderika.
Voorhees, Abraham and Maria-Jacop.
Stols, Engel and Eyena-Hendrik. "Was baptized last Tuesday at Cranberry."
Catrene, wife of Elise Higbee-Joseph. "Was baptized last Tuesday at Cranberry." Witness: Hendrik Stols.
24. Dehart, Cornis and Marya-Annatie.
Hogelant, Dirrik and Marta-Dirck.

1763.
Jan. 16. Simsen(?), Abraham-Femmitie.
Van Pelt, Tuenes-Aelthe.
Yurcks, Peter-Yacobes.
30. Streyker, Yosep and Maryya-Barent.
Mar. 6. Manly, John and Gerthe-Lisebat.
Wyckoff, Symon and Aelth-Aelthe.
Apr. 3. Van Dick, Yan and Garritye-Roleff.
Geulick, Samuel and Maryya-Ysack.
Pomme, Peter and Eyda-Maryya.
17. Van Buren, Jan and Sara(?)-Taunthe.
May 1. Gerrese, Steven and Femete-Jan.
12. Wyckoff, Yacob and Catelyna-Sara.
Dettemas, Rem and Lena-Femmethe.
June 19. Corteljou, Hendrick and Johanna.(?)-Welhelmas.
Boorem, Necalas-Anthe.
Blau, Peter and Maryya-Hendrick.
Sudam, Isack and Sara-Petrus.
July 10. Blau, Jan and Trinte-Mariya.
Wyckoff, Corneleus and Lamethe-Catrina.
Van Luwe, Denis and Eyda-Johannes.
Voorhees, Corneleus and Leya-Luykas.
30. Tarhune, Albrt and Mryya-Lena.
Aug. 14. Van Dick, Matyse and Nelthe-Catrina.
Wellimse, Samuel and Grethe-Petrus.
Sept. 25. Skilman, John and Enne-John.
Skilman, Tomes and Enne-Lena.
Van Asdalen, Cornelius and Catlyna-Jan.
Onderonk, Hendrik and Ragel-Hendrik.
Hogelant, Hendrick and Maryja-Johannes.
Wedel, Robert and Maryya-Willim.
Rapelye, Joris and Stynthe-Althe.
Wyllkens, Obedyeh and Sara-Elesebet.
Oct. 23. Probasco, Jan and Dina-Dina.
Veghte, Jan and Cheti-Maryya.
Hullenhet, Francis and Dorthe-Lena.
Nov. 4. Hogeland, Yohannas and Maratye-Catrina.
Wyckof, Abraham and Arayante-Cornelis.
6. Scurmen, Fernandus and Nelthi-Anna.
Bennet, Adrian and Yanithe-Johannis.

Van Klef, Yurius and Eyda-Catrina.
Vanpelt, Peter and Mag.-Helena.
Yonsen, Peter and Rabecca-Corneleya.
Fris, Peter and Gertje-Wylhelmus.
20. Lyt, Johannes and Trynye-Petrus.
Witnesses: Peter Mesure and Trynthe Sleght.
Whitlock, James and Jannetje-Moses.
Dec. 4. Hegemen, Symon and Aelthe-Symon.
Borem, Corneles and Nelthe-Femmethe.
Gerretsen, Samuel and Yanethe-Yanethe.
Voorhees, Yagus and Neitye-Jagues.
Van Arsdalen, Gerret and Aneantye-Catelyna.
Vantyn, Charel and Lisebit-Matheus.
18. Gulick, Johannes and Lammetje-Joachim.
1764.
(No Month). Nevious, Petrus and Aulthie-Meregreta.
Jan. 1. Willemsen, Wellem and Marya-Anajae.
15. Van Lue, Cornelus and Anthe-Marya.
29. Yulick, Johannes and Lena-Johana.
Witlock, John and Althe-Gerthe.
Vlet, Geathe, wife of Dennel-Anthe.
Feb. 12. Stootof, Petrus and Anye-Sara.
Vanarsdalen, Cristoffel and Catrina-Nelthe.
26. Payat, John and Yanatye-Yanatye.
Mar. 11. Karteljou, Albert and Lena-Neeltie.
Noorstrant, Johannis and Antie-Isack.
25. Voorhees, Johannes and Neeltje-Gerret.
Apr. 8. Wickoff, Jacobus and Catlyna-Cornelus.
Davoe(?), David and Sara-David.
Hofe, Abraham and Naltje-Fransyntje.
Hogaland, Hendrick and Yanete-Marya.
22. Williamson, Gerret and Geertje-Cornelius.
May 5. Wickoff, Peter and Bregje-Elisebet.
Van Deventer, Yacobus and Elisebet-Jacobus.
Furt, Tomis and Catryntje-Neeltje.
27. Vanlue, John and Doritie-Danise.
Striker, Barant and Elesabet-Cornelus.
June 3. Homes, Obedia and Maryya-Isack.
11. Hogelant, Dearrek and Martha-Abraham.
24. Van Arsdalen, Jurrey and Aeltei-Heyltea.

Wellemsen, Yacobus and Marya-Sarte.
Crosen, Derrick and Elisabet-Derrik.
July 8. Van Palt, Yon and Catrina-Elsye.
Van Pelt, Tunes and Yanatje-Trintye.
22. Cornell, Cornelus and Elisebit-Anneye.
Wellimson, Wellim and Annaetye-Johannes.
Aug. 19. Stootoof, Johannes and Sartye-Elbert.
Sept. 2. Merel, Roger and Sara-Reahel.
Nov. 4. Gulick, Jogum and Corneleya-Jogom.
Van Palt, Jan and Marigitye-Art.
18. Dahort, Hendrick and Maryya-Cornelus.
Dec. 2. Grounendick, Johannes and Sara-Jacob.
Gulick, Johannes and Lametje-Jogom.
16. Gulick, Fernendes and Lenje-Abraham.
Hagemen, Benjemen and Gerje-Petrus.
Covert, Johannes and Martha-Martha.
25. Vaghten, Garret and Lisabet-Neclas.
30. Pommey, Peter and Eyda-Enne.
1765.
Jan. 20. Manly, John and Garthe-Anne.
Feb. 3. Hogelant, Christoffel and Sara-Chrestoffel.
Vandyck, Jan and Garty(?)-Catryna.
Vandervere, Peter and Yanatye-Luykas.
Folkersen, Phillip and Enne-Marya.
17. Cortelyou, Hendrick and Anny(?)-Jakas.
Mar. 3. Quick, Abraham and Maghtel-Reyners.
Apr. 8. Boorem, Cornelius and Neltje-Antye.
21. Voorhees, Cornelus and Magdelena-Cornelius.
Hogelant, Hondrick and Marya-Annatye.
Stolts, Engel and Esena-Johannes.
May 6. Frie, John and Anne-Harodeya.
16. Cornell, Cornelius and Mariya-Mariya.
24. Detmas, Jan and Gertye-Douwe.
June 2. Kreusen, Hendrick and Elzabeth-Alexander Lukas.
16. Arsdalen, Christopher and Catryna-Handrik.
Buren, Jan and Sartye-Jan.
30. Garritson, Stephen and Femmetye-Abraham.
Aug. 4. Sedam, Jacob and Antye-Antye.
Melger, Fradrick and Catrina-Johannes.
Harden, Mare-Marcreta.

Voorhees, Abraham and Marya-Gertye and Jagues.
Van Arsdalen, Corneitis and Catelyna-Jacobus.
Sept. 8. Maselar, Jacobus and Janatje-Jacob.
Van Klef, Johannes and Maitye-Johnna.
Sudam, Jacobus and Marya-Johannes.
Semson, Abraham and Maragritye-Maregretye.
22. Blaw, Peter and Marya-Johnnes.
Snedeker, Jan and Sara-Lamatye.
Oct. 6. Terhunen, Albert and Marya-Albert.
Booram, Necolas-Elisabet.
20. Suydam, Petrus and Femmetje-Lawrence.
Jorkse, Peter and Annatje-Maria.
Nov. 10. Hagemen, Symon and Altye-Gartye.
Manly, Tommes and Yanetye-Gertye.
Van Klef, Juryes and Eyda-Annatye.
Wedel, Robert and Mery-Mery.
Van Ostrant, Johannes and Enne-Eva.
Nov. 24. Bennet, Aarie and Jannetje-Jannetje.
Dec. 8. Gulick, Samuel and Marya-Gertye.
Cortelyou, Albert and Lena-Catrena.
1766.
Jan. 24. Van Dick, Matise and Neltye-Sara.
V. Luew, Cornelus and Antye-Antje.
Feb. 9. Vaghte, John and Catrina-Catrina.
Van Dervere, Jan and Sythe-Hendrik.
Van Dorn, Jan and Marritje-Willim.
23. Snedeker, Jacob and Catelinthe-Catelynthe.
Mar. 9. Stootoff, Petrus and Antye-Caterna.
Willimson, Samuel and Marigritye-Mayeke.
Furt, Thomes and Catrina-Mari.
Apr. 4. Speder, Johannes and Antenette-Antenette.
6. Gulick, Jogom and Rabeke-Hendrik.
Homs, Obediea and Mere-Elesebet.
20. Striker, Jan and Catrina-Jan.
Pumye, Peter and Eyda-Eyda.
Van Arsdalen, Okey and Marya-Marya.
Van Arsdalen, Lamotye-Jacob.
May 20. Sutfin, Williem and Wina-Williem.
Bergen, Hendrick and Cornelya-Anna.
June 7. Kinney, Symon and Maregreity-Johannis.

July 6. Vliet, Geertje, wife of Daniel-Abraham.
Voorhees, Jaques and Nellye-Altye.
13. Van Derveer, Petrus and Yanatye-Gerrit.
20. Probesco, Jan and Dina-Mattye.
Striker, Barent and Elesebet-Barent.
Van Pelt, Tunes and Yanatye-Yanatye.
Streble(?), Frans and Peshin-Hendrick.
Slover, Dennel and Gertye-Leya.
Van Pelt, Jan and Catrena-Jan.
Aug. 31. Hogeland, Johannes and Mattye-Cornelus.
Sept. 14. Hogeland, Christoffel and Sara-Helena.
28. Van Tine, Samuel and Marya-Isak.
Edder, Symon and Nelley-Richerd.
Dehart, Hendrick and Mooya-Machdelena.
Oct. 19. Wickoff, Symon and Altye-Marya.
Nov. 16. Crosen, Derrick and Elesabet-Jacobus.
30. Tymes(?), Johnnes and Altye-Neltye.
Symonsen, Jon and Catlyna-Catlyna.
1767.
Jan. 4. Lake, Jacobus and Areyantye-Aeltye.
Gulick, Johannis and Lamentye-Catryna.
18. Cornell, Cornelus and Willyimtye-Janatye.
Feb. 1. Borem, Cornelus and Nelley-Gertye.
Powelson, Powel and Lena-Cornelus.
Williemsen, Jacobus and Mary-Josep.
15. Cortelyou, Hendrick and Annaty-Sara.
Williemsen, Williem and Angenetye-Jorys.
Mar. 1. Gulick, Johnnes and Lena-Eva.
Apr. 12. Hagemen, Benyemnen and Gerty-Marya.
16. Wickoff, Jacob and Angenity-Marygrity.
Piett(?), Jan and Janatye-John.
Willisem, Peter and Catrytye-Janaty.
May 10. Langstrat, Eron and Anne-Cate; George.
28. Menley, Thomas and Janatye-John.
Aug. 8. Wilkens, Obediah and Sara-Meathem.
Gulick, Jacobus and Marya-Isack.
23. Stolts, Engel and Essina-Thomas.
Sept. 6. Menley, John and Gertye-Neltye.
Gulick, Jogom and Cornelya-Willim.
Dehart, Peter and Gerritye-Johnnis.

Stribly, Frans(?) and Pashans-Sara.
Stryker, John and Catrena-Dyna.
20. Voorhees, Abraham and Maria-Ida.
Voorhees, Johannes and Neeltje-Jacobus.
Oct. 25. Covert, John and Martha-Yannathe.
Van Dyck, Jan and Gerrity-Sara.
Sudam, Jacobus and Marya-Petrus.
Voorheese, Jan and Willymtye-Yanathe.
Nov. 22. Voorhees, Jaques and Neeltje-Abraham.
Dec. 6. Wickoff, Piter and Jacamyntye-Cornelus.
Van Buren, Jan and Sara-Annatye.
6. Jonsen, Peter and Rabeca-Peter.
20. Terhune, Albert and Maria-Elizabeth.
Fry, Anna, wife of John-Abigail.
26. Janse, Barent and Elizabeth-Nicolas.
1768.
Jan. 10. Cortelyou, Harmanus and Catharina-Hendrick.
24. Pumyea, Peter and Ida-Peter.
Voorhees, Lucas and Neltye-Teunes?
Feb. 7. Gerritsen, Samuell and Janatye-Samuel.
Slover, Dannel and Gertye-Marya.
21. Furt, Thomes and Catrena-Jogom.
Mar. 6. Gerritsen, Rem and Mercy-Mercy.
20. Bergen, Hendrick and Cornelya-Johannes.
Apr. 10. Vaghte, John and Caty-Ares.
May 8. Quick, Abraham and Maghteltye-Antye.
Eddis, Sime and Nelley-Daniel.
Van Arsdalen, Cornelius and Catlintye-Abraham; Isaac.
Snedecar, Jacob and Catlyntye-Maria.
20. Kinney, Symon and Marigrety-Abraham.
June 12. Van Leuwe, Hendrik and Marygrety-Jacobus.
July 10. Van Luev, Denice and Eyda-Eyda.
Semson, Abraham and Mregaty-Tomas.
Aug. 20. Snedeker, Isack and Sara-Anna.
Sept. 2. Borem, Cornelus and Nelley-Johonnes.
18. Van Pelt, Jan and Catrytye-Nellye.
Willisen(?), Samuel and Maregratye-Antye.
Boorem, Necolas and Janatye-Sara.
Oct. 2. Dehart, Cornelius and Maria-Jacameyntje.
Hollenshead, Angenitye, wife of John-Sarah.

16. Wickoff, Symon and Altye-Sara.
Nov. 6. Gulick, Samuel and Marya-Jacob.
Yorks, Peter and Annatye-Gertye.
Gulick, Johannes and Lamatye-Cornelus.
Borckelow, Conrat and Sartye-Enney.
Van Cleaf, Juryas and Eyda-Eyda.
1769.
Jan. 15. Dehert, Hendrick and Marytje-Jacamyntye.
Menley, Thomese and Janatye-Henniry(?).
Cortelyou, Hendrick and Anna-Albert; Petrus (twins).
29. Blaw, John and Trynty-Altye.
Mar. 12. Van Pelt, Peter and Marya-Marya.
26. Sperling, John and Catryna-Rabeca.
Hegeman, Benyemen and Gertye-Gertye.
May 14. Van Dorne, Petrus and Janatye-Jeramyas.
Snediker, Jan and Sara-Wellem.
June 3. Hegeman, Symon and Aaltje-Elizabeth.
4. Witlok, John and Aaltje-Sarah.
Gulick, Johannes and Lenah-Petrus.
Johnson, William and Elizabeth-Antie.
Vreest, Peter and Geertje-Antje; Johannes.
Slover, Jacob and Geertje-Abraham.
Aug. 27. Van Leuwen, Jan and Dorithy-Antje.
Terhune, Gerret and Neeltje-Neeltje.
Stryker, Jan and Catharina-Luykas.
Sept. 10. Williamse, Peter and Catharintje Brouwer-Wilhelmus.
Voorhees, Jan and Willemje-Cornelius.
Oct. 15. Hogelant, Christofel and Sara-Lucas.
28. Rubert, Johannes and Cornelia Slover-Mara Elizabeth.
Slover, Daniel and Geertje Gulick-Isaac.
Nov. 12. Pomyea, Peter and Ida Suydam-Sarah.
Dec. 10. Menly, John and Gertye-John.
24. Cornel, Cornelus and Willyemtye-Altye.
1770.
Jan. 14. Terhune, Albert and Maria-Gerret.
28. Sedam, Jacobus and Maria-Ryk.
Van Tien, Samuel and Maria-Maria.
Feb. 11. Nevius, Albert and Neeltje-David.
Boorem, Cornelus and Neltje-Eliesabet.
25. Willemsen, Willem and Angenithe-Antia.

Mar. 25. Kinney, Symon and Maregraty-Lea.
Willemson, Jacobus and Maria-Winte.
Miserol, Barent and Antje-Jonatan.
Apr. 8. Stolts, Engel and Essina-Petrus.
Piett, Jan and Janatye-Fransynta.
Berjen, Hendrick and Cornelia-Garritya.
May 6. Gerrise, Steven and Femete-Petrus.
24. Stryker, Jacobus and Catrina-Petrus.
Hollenshead, Angenitye Yurcks, wife of John-Peter.
27. Piett, Abraham and Anne-Cattrin.
July 22. Van Dyk, Jan and Maria-Mattheus.
Gerrisen, Rem and Maria-Gerrit.
Sept. 2. Probasco, Gerrit and Mayke-Rebacka.
23. Voorhees, Abraham and Maria-Nelley.
Jansen, Barent and Eliesabet-Jan.
Snedeker, Isack and Sara-Jacob.
Oct. 14. Hagemen, Bengemen and Gertye-Janetye.
Furt, Thomes and Catrena-Marget.
28. Johnson, William and Eliesabet-Marten.
Nov. 18.Quick, Abrabam-Hendrick.
Van Arsdawlen, Cornelus and Catlintye-Catrina.
Deremer, Abraham and Neltye-Patries.
Dec. 2. Cortelyou, Harmans, and Catharina-Antje.
16. Terhune, Gerret and Neltye-Marrity.
Berkelow, Conrat and Sartye-Dannel.
Groenendyk, Sammel and Lenah-Christoffel.
Gulick, Johannes and Lamaty-Antje.
30. Vankleef, Benyemen and Eva-Joseph.
1771.
Jan. 6. Wicoff, Peter and Gerrebregh-Catryna.
Mar. 3. Nevius, Peter and Adriantie-David.
31. Jeurksen, Peter and Annatie-Hendrick.
Apr. 7. Hogelant, Elbert and Johanna-Sara.
Leinse, Daniel and Antie-Sara.
May 19. Van Cleif, Vreyes and Eyda-Ram.
June 9. Slover, Jacob and Rebecca-Derreck.
Boorem, Necoles and Jannytie-Joseph.
23. Slover, Daniel and Ghearte-Jacobes.
Dhyetmast, Peter and Merreghriette-Peter.
July 7. Hartman, Phillep and Marya-William.

Aug. 4. Van Voorhies, Johannes and Nicalthie-Daniel.
Van Deyk, John and Lena-Catriena.
18. Dehart, Hendrick and Maryia-Maghdelena.
Reubaart, Johannes and Cornelyiea-Maryghriete.
Ghrieghs, Samuel and Jannyete-Maryia.
Phyalhersen, Phyeliph and Anna-Dhyerick.
Sept. 29.Pummy, Peter and Eyda-Johannes.
Van Voorhyes, John and Wilmte-Isaac.
Gulick, Johannes and Helena-Jonnete.
Oct. 13. Vandeveer, Peter and Jonnete-Innete(?).
Van Liew, Denyis and Eyda-Dyna.
Gulick, Abraham and Elyesabet-Cornelyia.
Nov. 10. Sedam, Peter and Femmete-Peter.
Bercaleo, Wellem and Jacameinte-Ferntown.
24. Sedam, Abraham and Jonnate-Maryia.
Sthryker, Jacobus and Catriena-Aryian.
Dec. 26.Brown, Matthews and Hana-Andriew.
1772.
Jan. 25. Barcalo, Hendrick and Leana-Daniel.
Feb. 2. Crusen, John and Blandiena-Ceteryena.
Blandiena, Andrew and Theyn-Chrystyiane.
16. Van Buren, John and Sara-Derryck.
Hogelant, Chresstoffel and Sara-Isaac.
Mar. 1. Peyat, Abraham and Anthie-Fransynthie.
15. Berrien, Hendrick and Cornelya-Elyesabet.
Wycoff, Symon and Aulthye-Peter.
Apr. 17. Dehart, Cornelius and Marya-Cornelyus.
Wykof, Peter and Jacomynte-Peternellete.
19. Terhunen, Albert and Marya-Isaac.
26. Van Deventer, Jacobus and Liesabet-Lyesabet.
May 10. Slover, Jacob and Gerrite-Saartje.
31. Hallenset, Angeniete Jurksen, wife of John-Neente.
June 28. Queck, Abraham and Gerrete-Jacob.
Lentener, Andrew and Cureynte-Antye.
July 19. Hegeman, Benjemen and Geertje-Jon.
Aug. 2. Menley, John and Geerte-Deyna.
Leinse, Danyel and Antje-Wiellemte.
Snedeker, Isaac and Sara-Femmete.
16. Welmsen, Jacobes and Maryja-Corneljus.
Nevius, Pettres, and Addrejana-Gerret.

Oct. 11. Feurt, Thamme and Cethe-Jacamynte.
Ghrjendyk, Samuel and Leena-Moyche.
Edders, Symon and Nelle-Marya.
26. Cortelyou, Hendrjck and Johanna-Johannes.
Guljck, Johannes and Lammete-Samuel.
Nov. 15.Hogelant, Elbert and Johanna-Abraham.
Schetven [Sutphen], Gheysbert and Ghjeert-Aart.
Dehart, Peter and Phegge-Corneljus.
Dec. 6. Van Voorhjes, Abraham and Maria-Marya.
Berculo, Coen and Sara-Hendrick.
Blouw, John and Catrejnte-Aalte.
Beart, Welm and Hanna-Alexander.
27. Pejet, John and Jonnjte-Wellem.
1773.
Jan. 1. Wetlock, Jacobus and Jonnyta-Deryck.
17. Grjgs, Samuel and Jannete-Samuel.
Van Liew, Hendrick and Eata-Mareyte.
Sedam, Abraham and Jannete-Joseph.
Croesen, John and Brandena-Derreck.
Feb. 28. Gulick, Samuel and Marjja-Johannes.
Terhunen, Gerret and Njelte-Aalte.
Vandeveer, Peter and Jnnette-Maryia.
Mar. 28.Dehart, Welhelmes and Antie-Catreinte.
Apr. 25. Meserol, Barent and Antje-Femmetje.
May 9. Sedam, Jacobus and Marya-Jannette.
Hartman, Fillip and Maryria-Rachel.
28. Johnson, Barent and Elesabet-Petres.
30. Cornel, Corneljus and Wellemte-Jonnete.
June 6. Cortelyou, Harmanus and Catreinte-Cotriena.
Schenk, Johnns Jr. and Anne-Anne. Witness; Peter Schenk.
18. Hogelant, Chrisstophel and Sara-Jacob.
Bercalo, Hendrick and Lena-Daniel.
Slover, Jacob and Rebecca-Maryya.
Pyejet, Abraham and Enne-Elyesebet.
Jonsen, Willyem and Eliesebet-Antye.
Van Clieaf, Benieman and Eva-Eva.
Aug. 2. Snedeker, Jon and Sara-Catriena.
4. Gulick, Johannes and Helena-Cornelius.
16. Van Voorhies, John and Willimtye-Abraham.
Hegemen, Symon and Aalte-Aaltie.

[Also a Benjamin. Not plain in the original whether this child is Gulick's or Hegeman's].

Oct. 24. Van Voorhees, Jacob and Saarte-Catriente.
Nov. 7. Mjsereul, John and Eljsebet-Peter.
Hegeman, Beniamen and Geertye-Symon.
Bercalo, Willem and Jacameynte-Cornelius.
Reubcart, Johannes and Cornelya-Pethries.
21. Wicuf, Jochum and Johana-Jacobus.

1774.

Jan. 16. Van Dike, Fernandes and Aaltie-Marregriete.
Stryker, John and Catriena-Frederick.
Vandeveer, Gerret and Elesebet?-Mary.
30. Dehart, Hendrick and Mareyte-Vryai.
Ditmas, John and Gerte-Griete.
Creytres(?), Henry and Catrien-Lena.
Feb. 13. Vliet, Symon and Antje-Jan.
Manliys, Jon and Geertye-John.
Apr 10. Quick, Abraham and Gerritie-Abraham.
Snedecar, Isaack and Sara-Abraham.
24. Bennet, Abraham and Jannate-Femmete.
May 20. Phreyn, Jacobus and Annate-Johannes.
Brouw, Mattewes and Hanna-Mery.
22. Gulick, Abraham and Bette-Maryya.
June 19. Weycoff, Gerret and Sara-Abraham.
July 1. Nevius, Albert and Nellje-Margrietje.
Groendyk, Samuel and Leana-Samuel.
3. Weycoff, Pethres and Jacamsinte-Peter.
17. Vanderveer, Jon and Jonnetje-Jon.
Manley, Richart and Marya-John.
Aug. 14. Terhunen, Albert and Marya-Jacob.
Hollenset, Anganiete, wife of Jon-Annate.
Sept 25. Pomye, Peter and Ejda-Mergriet.
Oct. 23. Yeorcksen, Peter ana Annate-Leeja.
Lentenner, Andrjew and Tein-Johannes.
Nov. 6. Nevius, Petros and Addrejaante-Petrus.
Setven, Geysbert and Geerte-Jannete.
20. Dehart, Peter and Pegge-Hendrick.
Dec. 4. Nevius, Petrus and Jenneke Stoothoff-Johanes.
Suydam, Abraham and Jannetje Voorhees-Anne.
18. Hogelendt, Elbert and Johanna-Johannis; Elbert.

1775.
Jan. 1. Cortelyou, Hendrick Jr. and Johanna-Harmanes.
15. Van Dike, Jon and Lena-Antie.
29. Sedam, Jacobus and Marya-Joseph.
Feb. 12. Dehart, Jacobus and Antie-Geisbert.
Dehart, Cornelius and Eyda-Catreinte.
26. Bercalo, Coen and Sary?-John.
Jonson, Barent and Bette-Petres.
Van Pelt, Jacob and Marya-John.
Mar. 12. Vandoren, Isaac and Selle-William.
Wicoff, Jochem and Annate-Petres.
26. Neevius, Martyn and Ann-Annate; Abraham.
Witnesses: Hendrick Cortelyou and Cotriena.
Apr. 9. Rechmyre, Jerry and Weinte-Femmete.
Wetlock, Jacobus and Jannate-John.
Van Cleef, Eva-Cattleinte.
23. Slover, Daniel and Geerte-Geerte.
Pejet, Abraham and Enne-Jacob.
May 7. Terhunen, Gerret and Neelte-Johannes.
June 18. Hogelant, Chrisstoffel and Sara-Abraham.
July 16. Feurt, Thomas and Catreinte-Catreinte.
Aug. 13. Gulick, Johannes and Leena-Johannes.
Kreitsen, Henry and Catriena-Hendrick.
Slover, Jacob and Rebecka-Daniel.
Bercalo, Willem and Jacameinte-Mareyia.
Van Liew, Hendrick and Margriette-Hendrick.
27. Wicof, Simon and Aalte-Jacob.
Edders, Simon and Nelle-Sara.
Hartman, Philip and Palle-Peter.
Oct. 8. Bercalo, Hendrick and Lena-Marya.
22. Brieas, Annate-Marya. Witness: Wellem Welmsen.
Dec. 17. Cock, John and Doorte-William.
1776.
Feb. 25. Voorhiesen, Jon and Welmtie-Johannes.
Mar. 11. Cortelyou, Harmanes and Teine-Catriente.
25. Beard, Wellem and Cateleinte-Willem.
Sperling, Joseph and Griete-Ecborts.
Apr. 7. Nevius, Martjnes and Saarte-Johanna.
8. Nevius, Petres, Jr., and Jeneca-Petres.
21. Menley, Ritchert and Marya-Lesebet.

May 5. Groendyke, Samel and Leena-Leena.
16. Hegeman, Benjamin and Geethie-Willm.
June 2. Peyeat, Jon and Jonnete-Jacob.
16. Van Leuwe, Johannes and Dorete-Hendrick.
Stryker, Jon and Catriena-Cneleia.
Meseral, Barent and Ante-Barent.
Meseral, Jan and Lesabet-John.
Wicoff, Petres and Jacaminte-Maryia.
16. Rubaart, Johannes and Catrien-Jacob.
30. Robberson, James and Caterine-Harregriete.
Quick, Abraham and Gerrete-Marregriete.
Vanheis, Welhelmus and Annate-Moycae.
Aug. 11. Nevious, Albert and Nelle-Neelthie.
Merrel, William and Elisabet-John.
Van Lewen, Cornelious and Maria-Denys.
25. Reynold, John and Catharina-Margery.
Gulick, Samuel and Maria Quick-Maria.
Laan, Jan and Lenah Johnson-Jan.
Sept. 22.Dehart, Jacobes and Antie-Cornelius.
Oct. 20. Vandevear, Peter and Jannete-Catriena.
Jansen, Marta and Syte-Joseph.
Nov. 3. Pomye, Peter and Syte-Ledeja.
Slover, Jacob and Geerte-Jacob.
24. Peiett, Abraham and Enne-Abraham.
Gulick, Peter and Gerrete-Jocom.
1777.
Mar. 9. Deremer, Derrick and Barbara Gosen-Jacob.
16. Terhunen, Gerret and Nelle-Abraham.
Cock, Hendrick and Jannete-Cornelya.
Gulick, Abraham and Bette-Marya.
Nevius, Petres and Addreiana-Johannes.
23. Cortelyou, Hendrick and Annate-Antie.
Dehart, Peter and Pegge-Gerrete.
Hallenhed, Angeniete Jorcksen, wife of John-Daniel.
30. Sedom, Abraham and Yannathe-Patris.
Apr. 13. Vandevare, John and Yannathe-Peter.
20. Sadom, Jacob and Saurchy-Jacob.
May 11. Criser, Hannery and Catriena-Hendrick.
Manley, John and Geertyes-Richard; Saurchy.
July 20. Willimsen, Somwill and Morrigriet-John.

Van Nosestront, Addriaune and Lanaw-Isaac.
Aug.31. Vandoren, Jacob and Yonnache-Yonnacha.
Sept. 14. Gulick, John and Lanaw-Marya.
Nov. 9. Slover, Daniel and Geertye-Daniel.
Barrinkloe, Coonrode and Sarah-Farrington.
Dec.21. Beert, Wellem and Catlina-Chrisstophel.
Lot, Abraham and Mary-Jurry.
Provoost, Davit and Lesebet-Marrya.
1778.
Jan. 18. Van Aarsdalen, Antie-Antie.
Mar. 1. Edders, Simon and Nelle-Daniel.
Apr. 12. Peyet, William and Jacaminte-John.
Witlock, James and Jannete-Arreiaante.
Bennet, Hendrick and Enne-Sara.
Cleindennes, Annate, wife of Isack-Catriena.
May 10. Van Doorn, Abraham and Annatje Van Diek-Jacob.
June 7. Queck, Abraham and Gerrete-Ante.
Voorhees, Gerret and Marrete-Leena.
July 5. Cock, Jon and Doorte-Marya.
Aug. 2. Wicoff, Symon and Aalte-Simon.
15. Menley, Rechert and Marya-Rechert.
30. Wicoff, Petrus and Jacomantic-Sara.
Beekman, Abraham and Anne-Gerardus.
Spencer, John (unbaptized) and Annatie-Joachim.
Sept. 13.Cortelyou, Hendrick and Johanna-The Second Jaques.
25. Peiet, Jan and Jannete Willemsen-Wellem.
Oct. 21. Snedeker, Jan and Sara Wellemson-Maria.
Griggs, Samuel and Jannete Williamson-Margritje.
Nicksen, Thomas and Elesebet Randel-Isaac.
Nov. 8. Gronendick, Samuel and Lena Probasco-Johannes.
Hartman, Phellyp and Pally Donnesen-Abraham.
12. Hegemen, Andries and Rachel-Peter.
22. Brown, Helena, wife of W. B.-Wellem.
Witnesses: Hendrick Cortelyou and Ante Stootoff.
Bergen, Jacob and Tunte-Aron.
Dec. 20.Ven Deyk, Hendrick and Elisebeth-Marya.
27. Jonsen, Barent and Elisebeth-Abraham.
1779.
Jan. 24. Van Liew, Jan and Doorte-Cornelius.
Van Liew, Cornelius and Marya-Aalte.

Feb. 7. Voorhees, Rem and Hellete--Jan.
Pornyea, Peter and Idaugh-Elisebeth.
Vaghte, Johannes and Palle-Elesebeth.
21. Hogelandt, Elbert and Johanna-Elbert.
Mar. 21. Cortelyou, Harmanes and Catrina-Simon.
Apr. 4. Slover, Daniel and Geerte-Leucrese.
12. Sperling, Joseph and Maregreta-Sara.
Guest, John and Sara-Mary.
18. Van Deyk, Jermey and Lamethie-Jannethie.
May 2. Dehart, Jacobus and Antye-Jacobus.
Gro--, Samuel and Altye-Elisabet.
16. Gilbert, Aaron and Antenettes-Wellem.
30. Beckmen, James and Sarke-Elesabet.
June 27. Dehart, Hendrick and Marya-Anna.
Beert, Wellem and Catlina-Annate.
July 11. Gulick, Johannes and Elesabet-Cornelea.
Ledenbur, Peter and Catrena-Gabreel.
25. Stoothoff, Petrus and Anthie-Johanna.
Van Klef, Isack and Dorkes-Jacohb.
Aug. 8. Slover, Jacob and Rebeca-Abrham.
Terhune, Gerrit and Nelley-Cornelus.
22. Voorhees, John and Willity-Willity.
Sept. 19. Dehart, Peter and Margretye-Jacob.
Voorheess, Isaac and Yanatye-Gerty.
Hegeman, Adreyan and Fonsyntje-Gertey.
Oct. 15. Smit, Jacob and Janatey-Marya.
Nov. 28. V. Lieuw, Fradrick and Gerritye-Eishe.
Hagemen, Benyemen and Sara-Isaac.
Dec. 9. Bergen, Jacob and Tunye-Mateus.
1780.
Jan. 9. Hollinghead, John and Net-Cotrena.
23. Rynesen, Borrent and Sarhar-Elsye.
Bennet, Hendryck and Enney-Adryane.
Hartog, Engelbort and Enney-Dyna.
Feb. 6. Backman, Abraham and Antey-Nelley.
Done, Jonathan and Neltey-John Prine.
Vandervear, Jan and Janatey-Marya.
Van Ostrand, Adryane and Lena-Folkert.
Van Cleefe, Mikel and Yonaty-Femmitey.
6. Menley, Jon and Cerrytey-Adryane.

Pervost, David and Mercy-Jonethan.
Wodue, Angenety-Janaty.
Brown, Mat and Hanney-Janaty.
Hanna (No names of parents given).
Feb. 20. Piatt, Abram and Enney-Margret.
Mar. 5. Quyck, Abraham and Gemithe-Johennes.
Hagemen, Andries and Ragil-Lesabet.
27. Sudam, Jacobes and Marya-Jacob.
Apr. 2. Lott, Abraham and Marya-Sara.
16. Sutphin, Ryck and Marya-Annatye.
Barcklow, Handrick ana Lena-Handrick.
30. V. Dick, Handrick and Elesebet-Symon.
Dreyer, Fradrick and Gertye-Cobus.
May 14. Kinney, Jacobus and Sara-Symon.
June 25. Voorhees, Gerret and Marrytie-Nelte.
Bouer, John and Hanna-Johannes.
Groves, Samnuel and Altye-Hanny or Harry.
Croysen, Harry and Catrina-Peter.
Furt, Benymen and Mary-Jacobus.
July 27. Merrel, William and Elesabet-Sara.
Aug. 20.Vaghte, Johannes and Marya-Gerret.
Oct. 1. Van Dorn, Abraham and Antye-Johannes.
Wicklock, James and Yonaty-James.
Cryson, John and Antey-Johannes.
15. Menley, Richerd and Marey-Mercy or Meraj.
29. Hunneman, John and Mary-Sara.
Nevius, Petrus and Janeka-Elbert.
Nov. 12 Cortelyou, Handrick and Annatye-Abraham.
1781.
Feb. 8. Symonsen, Cornelus and Marya-Lana.
Cock, John and Dortey-John.
Voorhees, Abraham and Elsha-Luycas.
Beackman, James and Sara-Alshe.
Mar. 4. Bert, William and Catelyna-William.
Van Arsdalen, Roluf and Lena-Altye.
18. Slover, Daniel and Gertye-Sytye.
Sperling, Joship and Marggretie-Joannes.
Griggs, Samuel and Janatye-Samuel.
Apr. 1. Bruer, Peter and Pegey-Anne.
Cock, Jacb and Abbegel-William.

Terhune, Gerret and Nelley-Gerret. [This bapt. dated Mar. 32].
15. Cock, Harry and Janathe-Harry.
28. V. Dorn, Jacob and Janatye-Halena.
29. Eddis, Symon and Nelly-John.
Gulick, Joannes and Elesabet-Elesabet.
May 13. V. Luew, Hendrick and Margretye-Janatye.
Hageland, Albert and Annatye-Jahnna.
Furt, Hennyry and Anney-Thomes.
Voorheese, Johannes and Katy-Lena.
Cornell, Peter and Nelley-Cornelus.
Pevost, Davit and Marya-Merey or Mercy; Betsey.
V. Dick, Fradrick and Lydia-John.
Cornelius, Elesabet-Margriet.
27. Nevies, Albert and Neltye-Petrus.
July 2. Dehaert, Hendrick and Marya-Hendrick.
7. Vaghte, Johannes and Polley-William.
Meshroll, Borrent and Antye-Antye.
8. Cortelyow, Harmanus and Catryna-Jaques.
22. Rogher, Henry and Sary-John.
Aug. 5. Wickoff, Jogom and Annatye-Annatye.
20. Dehart, Jacobus and Antye-Abraham.
Sept. 30. Witlock, William and Cartye-John.
Sutfin, James and Alesebet-Janme.
Dilling, Peter and Mary-Isaac.
Willemson, Handrick and Anney-Isaac.
Dec. 9. Hagemen, Bengemen and Sara-Gertye.
23. Bergen, Jacob and Tunye-Mergret.
1782.
Jan. 6. More, Reynere and Catrena-Jan Roozen.
Feb. 17. Jonsten, Borrent and Elesabet-Borrent.
Mar. 3. V. Leewen, Johannes and Lena-Marya.
Sudam, Petrus and Sara-Abraham.
Voorhees, Rolef and Leena-Leena.
Bennet, Hendrick and Enney-William.
Apr. 1. Holenhid, John and Angenetye-John. (Entry date is Mar. 32).
Beckman, Abraham and Antye-Johannes.
V. Luew, Fradrick and Gerretye-Fradrick.
Vanderveer, Gerret and Sartye-Marya.
V. Arsdalen, Jurrey and Altye-Catelyntey.
July 7. Hartog, Engelbort and Enney-Handrick.

Highens, James and Leya-Jogom.
21. Wickoff, Gerret and Sara-Corneles.
Aug. 4. Quick, Abraham and Gerrithe-Petrus.
Hagemen, Aderiane and Fransyntye-Jacob.
Regtmir, Yurry and Wintye-Wynty.
Pumye, Peter and Eyda-Abraham.
Kenney, Jacobus and Sara-Catylina.
Sept. 15. Nevins, Davet and Lesabet-Petrus.
29. Van Luew, Cornelus and Marya-Symon.
Stryker, Jan and Elesabet-Peter.
Breas, Hendrick and Selley-Yemyma; Caty.
Crysen, Heyry and Caryna-John.
Oct. 13. Piatt, John and Janatye-Catlina.
Beeckmen, James and Selley-Selley.
Broer, Peter and Peggey-Cornelus.
Nov. 10. Smit, Jacob and Yanaty-Peter.
Cryser, John and Antye-Hendrick.
1783.
Jan. 5. Stoothoff, Petrus and Antye-Marya.
Symonsen, Cornelus and Maryte-Catryna.
Williamson, Cornelus and Steyntye-Willim.
19. Whitlock, James and Janaty-Gerrit.
Mar. 16. Piatt, Abraham and Anney-Jenney.
Brow, Mat and Henney-Josep.
Menley, Richerd and Merey-Aderayene.
30. Vandorn, Abraham and Antye-Marya.
Grigs, Samuel and Yanatye-Eida.
Apr. 13. Van Ostrand, Adreyane and Lana-Isaac.
Van Ostrand, Jores and Polly-Altye.
May 11. Grofe, Samuel and Altye-John.
Campel, Fillyp and Marya-Anne.
25. Rapelye, Jaromes and Susanna-Cornelus.
Terhune, Gerret and Nelley-Elisabet.
Willemsen, William and Annay-Femmitje.
Aug. 15. Van Buren, John and Sara-Hendrick.
Wickof, Johannes and Annatje-Johannes.
Nov. 16. Dehart, Winnant and Marya-Enney.
Dehart, Jan and Enney-Abraham.
Bert, William and Catlyna-Sara?
Dec. 11. V. Dorn, William and Marya-Marya.

21. Cock, Henry and Janaty-Jantye.
Davis?, Tommes and Enne-Enne.

1784.

Feb. 15. Funck, Josep and Polley-Catrynty.
Dehart, Cornelus and Maregretye-Mayke.

Mar. 25. Beeckman, Abraham and Antye-Abraham.

June 18. Gulick, Johannis and Lametye-Marya.
Furt, Henny and Antye-Jorge.
Hogelant, Albert and Annatye-Neltye.

20. Nevius, David and Elisabet-Antye.
Bennet, Abraham and Janatye-William.
Meselol, Borrent and Antye-Necolase.
Van Dick, Handrick and Elisabet-Jan.
Prine, James? and Annatye-Gerret.
Higens, James and Lena-Nensey.

Aug. 15 Smit, Jacob and Janatye-Jacob.
Hollenbid, John and Angenetye-Elesabet.
Willisen, Hendrick and Antye-William.
Willisen, Sartye-Antye.
Covert, Jacob and Elisabet-Magdelen.

29. Coyser, Hendrick and Catrina-Annatye.
Elleson, Dennel and Elesabet-Geertye.
Furt, Thomas and Mergret-Mercy.

Oct. 17. V. Luew, Fradrick and Gerritye-Conrate.
Willisen, William and Enney-Williem.
Bennet, Hendrick and Enney-Janatye.
Jonsen, Peter and Catryntye-Necolase.
Van Deventer, Jan and Antye-Abraham.

1785.

Jan. 16. Rapya, Jeromes and Susanna-Altye.
Slover, Jacob and Rabeca-Annatye.
Veachte, Johnnes and Polley-Johannes.
Quick, Abraham and Gerritye-Elshe.
Terhun, Gerrit and Nelly-Catrena.

May 8. Withlock, William and Sartye-Symon.
V. Dorn, Cornelus and Elesabet-Cornelus.
V. Norstrant, Jorge and Marya-Josep.
Voorhees, Johennes and Barbra-Catrynty.
V. Luew, Hendrick and Margret-Hendrick.
Witlock, James and Janatye-William.

More, Reynere and Catrena-Ida.
Wickoff, Jan and Elesabet-Cornelus.
Cortelyou, Harmanes and Catreyntye-Jan.
29. Pervost, Davet and Marya-Betshe.
Van Arsdalen, Reulief and Lena-Gerrett.
Vanarsdalen, George and Aalte-Aalte.
Aug. 14. Symonson, Cornelus and Marya-Cornelus.
Merrel, Derrick and Janatye-William.
V. Lue, Cornelus and Marya-Cornelus.
Cock, John and Dortye-Conelya.
V. De Backe(?), Andrys and Altye-Gertye.
Tunyson, Gerret and Santye (or Sartye)-Cornelus.
Wickoff, Jogom and Annatye-Marya.
Brocks, Jahenne was baptized.
V. Derver, Gerrit and Sartye-Seytye.
Dec. 23. Nevius, Davit and Elisabet-Johannes.
Merrel, Derrick and Janatye-William.
V. Lue, Cornelius and Marya-Cornelus.
1786.
Mar. 1. Voorheese, Lucas and Elesabet-Lucrecy.
Beekman, Abraham and Antye-Rolf Voorhees.
Willsen, William and Lana-Samuel.
26. Perstide, William and Paggey-Anne.
Quick, Tunes and Altye-Leyda.
June 25. Johnsen, Peter and Catryntye-Johannes.
Brower, Peter and Peggey-Josey.
Hogeland, Hendreck and Gertey-Maregrety.
Sept. 3. Gulick Abraham and Marya-Abraham.
Furt, Henniry and Anne-Jacamynte.
Hertme, Phillip and Polley-Jacob.
Williamsen, Hendrick and Anne-James.
Higens, James and Lena-William.
Breas, Gerrit and Anne-Catryn; Wittim; Joshe.
Dec. 24. Van Tine, Ephrim and Anne-Ida.
Witlock, Moses and Catryna-Marya.
Fermer, Jesper and Elesabet-Marya.
Devis, Lemme (or Semme) and Anne-Jan.
1787.
Apr. 1. Voorhees, Abraham Jr. and Grace-Abraham.
Sudam, Ryck and Ragel-Peter.

Willisen, Jores and Ida-Angenetye.
Voorhees, Jacob and Lametye-Abraham.
Arsdalen, Myndert and Caryna-Abraham.
Terhune, Gerret and Nelley-Isac.
Coeycer?, Henry and Catrena-Catrena.
Terhune, Abraham and Mayeke-Albert.
Britton, Samuel and Janaty-Genny; Catryn (twins).
June 3. Nevius, Petrus and Aryyantie-Albert.
Elleson, Dennel and Elesabet-Thomas.
17. Griges, Samuel and Jenne-Willam.
Funck, Josep and Marya-Elesabet.
July. 1. Van Dorn, Jacob and Janatye-Catrena.
Vagete, John and Polley-Hendrick.
Aug. 12. Williamsen, Peter and Gertye-Geysbert.
Gulick, Abraham and Sara-Marya.
Oct. 7. Quick, Tunes and Altye (no further entry).
Nevius, Davet and Elesabet-Davet.
Dec. 30. Garner, Sarah-Eloner. Witness(?): Isaac Slover. [Uncertain if Isaac Slover a witness or otherwise].
Van Lue, Cornelius and Mary-Idaugh.
Dehart, Cornelius and Marget-Cornelius.

1788.
Jan. 1. Quick, Abraham and Gerritha-Elsher.
13. Williamson, William and Anne-Peter.
27. Wicoff, Joacam and Hany-Cornelius.
Hagaman, Adrian and Frances-Bengeman.
Feb. 10. Beckman, Abraham and Anne-Jacob.
Baker, John and Sarah-Moriah.
24. Symonsen, Abraham and Ayda-Jan.
Mar. 25. Vandorn, Abraham and Ann-Elizabeth.
Apr. 6. Whitlock, Moses and Caterine-James.
Vanderbick, Andrew and Aultye-Elizabeth.
Van Der Veer, Lucas and Ann-Sarah.
May 12. Slover, Jacob and Rebeckah-Jacob.
18. V. D. Vere(?), Tewes and wife-Peter.
Williamson, John and Margret-Isaac.
Grove, Samuel and Alche-David.
June 1. Baird, William and Catlintye-Abraham.
15. Withlock, James and Jenne-Cornelious.
29. Farmer, Jesper and Elezebeth-Nelle.

Williamson, George and Idaugh-Peter.
July 13. Coick, John and Dorthe-Areyante.
Aug. 10. Brees, Garret and Margret(?) or Mary(?)-Phebe.
Williamson, Garret and Nancy(?) or Margret(?)-Mary (or Nancy).
[Names in original so entered that it is not possible to decide who was mother or child].
Sept. 21.Gulick, Abraham-Salle.
Sudam, Rike-John.
Hogeland, Hendrick-Abraham.
Nov. 2. Funck, Joseph and Mary-Geertye.
Meserul, Abraham and Ann-Agness.
16. Terhune, Dennle and Anne-Mergrit.
Lane, Jan and Lena-Altye.
Pershed, William and Maregreta-Gette.
Hogeland, Abraham and Anne-Mary.
1789.
Jan. 11. Davis, Thomas and Anne-Margeret.
25. Voorhees, Menny and Belythe-Jan.
Voorhees, Jacob and Lammethe-Jan.
Voorhees, Jarymyes and Lena-Altye.
Feb. 22. Williamson, Peter and Charity-Samuel.
Mar. 22. Gulick, Joakim and Jinne-Cornelius Cornel.
Apr. 5. Stoothoff, Cornelius and Charity-Jaques.
Voorhies, Jaques and Dinah-Jaques.
June 14. Sansbury, Ralph and Eloner-Caterene.
Aug. 9. Furt, Henery and Anna-John Davison.
Nevius, David and Elizabeth-Willimpi.
23. Baker, John and Salley-Salley.
Baker, More and Elezebeth-Joseph.
Vantine, Ephram and Anne-Peter.
Sept. 6. Gulick, Abraham and Sarah-Williampe.
20. Brewer, Daniel and Mary-Mary.
Kitchen, Richard and Margaret-John.
Oct. 4. Gulick, Joakim S. and Caterine-Samuel.
Nov. 1. Terhune, Abraham and Margret-Samuel.
15. Davis, Samuel and Mary-Abrm. Tucker.
Van Dyke, Hendrick and Elizabeth-Anna.
Whitlock, Moses and Caterine-Daniel.
29. Wickoff, John and Johannah-Mary.
Dec. 13. Kortelyou, Hendrick and Anne-Hendrick.

1790.

Jan. 27. Simonson, Abraham and Idaugh-Abraham.

Mar. 7. Baird, Wilam and Catey-Lelah.
Vegte, John and Mary-Isaac.

21. Van Der Veer, Lucas and Anne-Abraham.
Williamson, George and Idaugh-Lydea.

Apr. 4. Simonson, Cornelious and Mary-Mary.

May 2. Vanderbick, Andrew and Aultye-Jaquish.
Van der Veer, Mathew and Meriah-George.

16. Wickoff, Garret and Sarah-Garret.
Hogeland, Hendrick and Gite-Jaques.
Vanliewe, Cornelious and Mary-Elizabeth.

30. Addis, Richard and Jememe-Elioner.

June 27. Barracklow, Henderick and Lena-William.

July 11. Williamson, William and Anne-Agness

Sept. 5. Vanpelt, Ruben and Altye-Jenne.

Oct. 7. Baird, John and wife-Elsey, b. Oct. 7, 1779; Abraham, b. Dec. 19,1781; William, b. Oct. 25, 1783; Janette, b. Oct. 21, 1785; Magdalany, b. July 19, 1790.

Nov. 14.Van Liewe, Frederick and Anne-Hendrick.
Stoothoff, Cornelius and Charity-Mary.

Sept. 20.Voorhees, Jaques and Dinah-John.
Sparlen, John and Margeret-Mariah.

Oct. 31. Hoagland, Derick and Mattie-Margeret.
Beekman, Abraham and Anne-Isaac.

Nov. 28.Hoagland, Abraham and Jehannah-Hannah.
Sedam, Rike and Rachel-Phebe.
Meserull, Abraham and Anna-John.
Farmer, Jasper and Elizabeth-Peter.

Dec. 26. Johnson, Nicolas and Margeret-Barrent.

1791.

Feb. 20. Davis, Thomas and Anna-William.
Provost, John and Eve-Ariette.
Collins, Evert and Mary-Ariette.

Mar. 15. Sparling, Isaac and Elezebeth-Caterine; John.

20. Sansbury, Ralph and Elenanor-Julia.

Apr. 25. Van Pelt, Abraham and Elenanor-Elenanor.

May 1. Bennet, Abraham and Charlote-Anne.

15. Gulick, Abraham and Mary-Peter.
Bastedo, William and Margeret-William.

June 12. Nevius, David and Elizabeth-James.
26. Veghte, John and Mary-Abraham.
Williamson, John and Mary-William.
Vandervear, Garret and Sarah-Sarah.
July 10. Vunk, Joseph and Mary-John.
Aug. 7. Vandoren, Abraham and Anne-Sarah.
Van Northwick, Hendrick and Anne-Caterine Cornell.
7. Gerretson, John and Phebe-Steven.
Voorheese, Jacob and Lameche-Jacob.
Sept. 18. Baird, William and Caty-Isaac; Jacob.
Gulick, Joachim and Caty-Ram.
Baker, John and Sarah-Jemima.
Cock, John and Dorate-Andrew.
Oct. 2. Kertelyou, Hendrick, son of Hermanus, and Elizabeth-Mary.
Dehart, Abraham and Sarah-Maacha.
Terhune, Abraham and Maalha-Mary.
Demooth, Derick and Sarah-Mary.
28. Vegte, Mary, wife of John.
Nov. 13. Williamson, Jorge and Idah-Jenne.
Terhune, Daniel and Anne-Mary.
Vanderveer, John and Rachel-Joseph.
Dec. 11. Terhune, William and Mary-Garret.
25. Voorheese, Jaques A. and Sarah-Simon.
1792.
Jan. 8. Gerretson, John and Dinah-John.
Feb. 5. Vannostrant, John and Caty-Lenah.
Vanderveer, Lucas and Anne-Anne.
Hogeland, Christopher and Nelle-Abraham.
19. Johnson, Nicholas and Margeret-William.
Apr. 1. Vanderbeek, Andrew and Alche-Cornelious.
Vanpelt, Ruben and Alche-Margeret.
Sedam, Lawrence and Abigal-Phebe.
Priest, Robert and Lenah-Sarah.
May 13. Baker, More and Elizabeth-Mary.
Skilman, Jacob and Ellenor-Isaac.
June 24. Williamson, William and Anne-Abraham.
Voorheese, Jaques and Dinah-Jaques.
Van Liewe, James and Caty-Elizabeth.
Veghte, Nicholas and Althye-Garret.
Scot, William and Ammy-Samuel.

Stryker, Lucas and Sarah-Caterine.
27. Kertelyou, Hendrick and Anne-Mary.
July 22. Van Asdalen, Roeloff-Lenah.
22. Gulick, William and Lenah-Adreaan.
Simonson, Sarah, wife of Thomas-Abraham.
Aug. 5. Williamson, Hendrick and Anne-Elizebeth; Joseph.
Oct. 14. Van Liewe, Cornelious and Mary-Helanah.
Hageman, Aaron and Francis-Agness.
14. Van Ostrant, Jacob and Anne-Abraham.
26. Simonson, Cornelius and Mary-John.
28. DeHart, Cornelius and Elie-George Hogeland.
Vantine, Ephraim and Anne-Mary.
Hogeland, Derick and Metee-Phebe.
Williamson, Peter and Charity-Margret.
Gulick, Joachim and Jenne-John.
Nov. 11. Waldron, Cornelius and Janne-Anne.
Dec. 20. Nevius, Peter P. and Jenica-Sarah.
Dehart, James and Anne-John.
23. Stoothoff, Cornelius and Geertike-Johanna.
1793.
Jan. 6. Simonson, Abraham and Idah-Cornelius.
Voorheese, Jaques and Sarah-Mary.
Meseroll, Abraham and Anne-Anne Vanherlen.
Feb. 3. Dehart, Cornelius son of Corn. and Anne-Mary.
Mar. 31. Nevius, David and Elizabeth-Martines.
May 12. Furte, Hendrick and Anne-Catharin.
Williamson, Gorge and Idah-Margret.
Sedam, Ryke and Rachel-William.
Farmer, Jasper and Elizabeth-Sarah.
June 9. Voorheese, Lucas Jr. and Johannah-Isaac.
23. Gerretson, John and Phebe-Sarah.
July 7. Powel, Archebel and Sarah-Elezebeth.
Aug. 4. Kortelyou, Hendrick and Elezebeth-Hermanes. [This child's name had been crossed out, without inserting another in the original].
Davis, Thomas and Anne-Jacob Perbasco.
Veghte, John and Mary-Mary.
Bastato, William and Margeret-Catherine.
4. Kertelyou, Wilhalmus and Mary-Hendrick.
Van Liewe, John and Magdalanah-Peter.
Van Liewe, John and Anne-Dorethe.

Sept. 29. Hegemen, Peter and Anne-Sarah.
Sedeam, Lowrence and Abbe-Anne.
Oct. 13. Garretson, Rem and Elezebeth-Hendrick.
27. Slover, John and Ellenor-Elleanor.
Nov. 10.Baker, John and Sarah-Jane.
24. Gulick, Abraham and Mary-Jaques.
Yorks, Hindrick and Elezebeth-Peter.
Williamson, John and Mary-Margeret.
Kritcher, Henry and Caty-Mary.
Dec. 22. Scot, William and Ammi-John.
Nevius, Garret and Mary-Anna.
Hogeland, William and Mary-Margeret.
1794.
Feb. 2. Dehart, Abraham and Sarah-John Van Clive.
Vanpelt, Ruben and Alchiete-Gisbert Sutphin.
Vanderbeek, Andrew and Alche-Andrew.
Mar. 2. Vandervear, Lucas and Anne-Lucas Schank.
Baird, William and Caty-Robert.
30. Barkelow, Ferrington and Hannah-William.
Voorhees, Jacob and Lameche-Isaac.
Apr. 13. Johnson, Nicholas and Margeret-Abraham.
27. Scilman, Jacob and Nelley-Jacob.
Van Nortwyck, Hedrick and Nancy-Hendrick.
Aug. 10. Wyckoff, John and Johanna-John; Johannes Van Clive.
Priest, Robert and Lenah-Catherine.
Williamson, Anne.
Sept. 21.Gerretson, Rem and Elezebeth-Phebe.
Williamson, William and Anne-Lowrance Van Clive.
Cock, John and Dorrete-Abigal.
Addes, Ritcherd and Jemimi-Mary.
Van Liewe, James and Caty-Garret.
Oct. 5. Stryker, Lucas and Sarah-Caterinah.
Sparling, Isaac and Elezebeth-Abraham.
19. Hogeland, Abraham and Anne-Abraham.
Nov. 2. Hogeland, Christopher and Nelley-Peter Wyckoff.
16. Gorden, Charles and Nelly-Sarah Statts.
30. Williamson, Peter and Charity-Cornelius.
Vannostrand, Jacob and Anne-Lenah.
Wortman, Abraham and Anne-James.
Dec. 14. Nephies, David and Elezebeth-Elezebeth.

Foster, Nathiel and Hannah-Dinah Stryker.
25. Voorheese, Jaques and Dinah-Abraham.
1795.
Feb. 8. Van Clive, John and Sarah-Margereth.
19. Barkelow, Hendrick and Lenah-Frederick.
22. Gulick, Joakim and Caty-Isaac.
Meseloll, Abraham and Anne-John.
Apr. 19. Van Liewe, Cornelius and Mary-Frederick.
Hogeland, Derick and Matte-Derick.
Dehart, Cornelius and Else-Mary.
May 17. Sedam, Ryke and Rachel-Ryke.
25. Pipenger, Hendrick and Mary-Lucretia Coll.
Aug. 2. Van Hangelen, Cornelius and Elezebeth-John.
Williamson, Jorge and Idah-William.
Sedam, Laurance and Abigal-Peter.
Cortelyou, William and Mary-Abraham.
Oct. 4. Voorhees, Jaques and Sarah-Simon Wyckoff.
Nov. 8. Bastedo, William and Margereth-Margereth.
Hageman, Aaron and Frances-Wyckoff.
Veghte, Nicholas and Alche-Elezebeth.
Gerertson, John and Phebe-Abraham.
Voorheese, Isaac and Sophia-John.
Van Liewe, John and Magdelanah-Magdelanah.
Baker, John and Sarah-Mary.
Voorheese, Lucas and Anne-Charrithy.
1796.
Jan. 10. Stryker, John and Nelly-John.
Hageman, Hendrick and Lidia-Mary.
Johnson, Nicholas and Margereth-Elezebeth.
Dehart, Cornelius and Anne-Caterian.
10. Polhamus, Garret and Jenne-Daniel.
Veghte, John and Mary-Nicholas.
Feb. 21. Vanderbeek, Andrew and Alche-Ann.
Vannostrand, Jacob and Caty-John.
May 15. Furte, Henry and Anne-Sarah.
Skilman, Jacob and Nelle-Abraham.
Baker, More and Elezebeth-John.
Williamson, John and Mary-Charles Smith.
Dehart, Abraham and Sarah-Cornelius.
Williamson, Cornelius and Mary-James.

15. Slover, John and Nelle-Ritcherd.
July 3. Van Northwick, Hendrick and Nencey-Elezebeth.
Sept. 4. Williamson, William and Anne-Jane.
Pearse(?), Thomas and Elsey-Elsey.
Gulick, Benjamin and Elizabeth-John.
Nov. 20. Voorheese, Jaques and Dinah-Peter.
Nevius, David and Elezebeth-James Schureman.
Kortelyou, Hendrick and Elezebeth-Peter.
Stryker, Frederick and Suphiah-John.
Worthman, Abraham and Anne-John Duryea.
Sutphin, Peter and Martha-Margareth.
1797.
Feb. 5. Brown, Andrew and Anne-Mary Giffers.
Night, John and Jane-James.
Voorheese, Cornelius and Mary-Lucas.
Barcklo, Farrington and Hannah-Jacaminah; Elleanor.
June 25. Simonson, Cornelius and Mary-Sarah.
Sedam, Lawrence and Abigal-John.
Van Nothwick, Christian and Anne-Catherine.
Bennet, Peter and and Lideah-Jane.
Thonson or Johnson, Nicholas and-Margereth-Handrick Van Dike.
Williamson, George and Idah-John Pumyea.
Kortelyou, John and Nelle-Hendrick.
Perdun, John and Anna-David Pervast.
July 9. Bastedo, William and Margereth-John Stanle.
23. Vannostrand, Jacob and Caty-Isabel.
Meserol, Jonathan and Elizabeth-Barent.
Aug. 6. Provost, David and Mary-Mary.
20. Vanderveere, Lucas and Anne-Peter.
Kortelyou, William and Mary-Hendrick.
Sept. 3. Meseroll, Abraham and Anne-William Williamson.
Voorheese, Jaques and Sarah-Abraham.
Berian, John and Sarah-Cornele.
Gulick, Joachim and Caty-Mary.
17. Beekman, Abraham and Anne-Catherin Ann.
Oct. 29. Sedam, Ryke and Rachal-Sarah.
Pohamas, Garret and Jane-Johannah.
Nov. 27. Vanderbeek, Andrew and Alche-John Barricklow.
Van Liewe, James and Caty-Catherian Cornell.
Sedam, Joseph and Elezebeth-Mary.

27. Nevius, Garret and Mary-John.
Voorheese, Isaac and Sophiah-James.
Dec. 10. Gerretson, Peter and Mary-Gerret Terhune.
24. Hogeland, Lucas and Phebe-Christopher.
1798.
Jan. 7. Fine, David and Anne-John.
Voorheese, Abraham and Else-Catherian.
11. Blackwell, Hendrick and Margereth-Margereth.
Feb. 4. Veghte, Nicholas and Alche-Mary.
Vanpelt, Alche and Sarah.
18. Addes, Ritchard and Jemima-Simon.
Cock, John and Dorethe-Jane.
28. Farmer, Jesper and Elizebeth-Sarah.
Williamson, Cornelius and Mary-Martin Jonson.
Mar. 4. Voorheese, Jacob and Lemeche-Lenah.
Apr. 1. Hogeland, Jacob and Elezebeth-Garret.
Vanderveer, Garret and Deborah-Mary Voorheese.
15. Scot, William and Ame-Marten.
May 9. Wyckoff, Jacob and Mary-Alche.
Van Liewe, John and Magdalen-Catherine.
Kortelyou, Hendrick and Elezebeth-Anna.
Whitlock, John and Lideah-Elias.
Hager, David and Charity-Mary.
May 13. Williamson, John and Mary-Margereth.
Williamson, Cornelius and Martin Johnson.
27. Vantine, Ephaim and Anne-Sarah.
June 10. Hageman, Aaron and Frances-Aaron.
Hageman, Hendrick and Lida-Christina.
Gulick, Benjamin and Elezebeth-Rebecah.
24. Dehart, Cornelius and Anne-Johnson.
July 8. Slover, John and Nelle-Mariah.
22. Dehart, Cornelius and Elce-Hedrick.
Sept. 2. Cannon, R [Rev.] James Spencer and Caty Brevort-James Stoutenberg, b. Aug. 17.
Barkelow, Cornelius and Elesebeth-John Vanburen.
16. Nevius, John and Roeliphe-Catherian Stoothoff.
Nov. 12. Atcheson, Elesebeth-John Manlius.
Sedam, Peter and Leah-Abraham.
Dec. 23. Williamson, William and Anne-Sarah.
Voorheese, Isaac and Suphiah-Nellie Hogeland.

1799.
Feb. 17. Night, John and Jane-Sarah.
Mar. 31. Williamson, Joseph and Idah-Isaac.
Apr. 14. Simonson, Cornelius and Mary-Elezebeth.
Staats, Abraham and Dorothy-Hendrick Veghte.
Gerretson, John and Dinah-Garret.
Stryker, Lucas and Sarah-Lidiah.
Stryker, Fredrick and Suphiah-Caterian Ann.
Hager, David and Charity-Elezabeth.
May 10. Nevius, David and Elezebeth-Margereth.
June 10. Nevius, Peter P. and Gerritte-Hendrick Vrom.
23. Sutphin, Peter and Martha-Abraham.
Meserol, Jonathan and Elezebeth-Elezebeth.
July 7. Bastedo, William and Margereth-Thomas Vantilburg.
21. Sedam, Lawrence and Abigal-William Williamson.
Aug. 4. Cortelyoe, William and Mary-John.
Sparling, Isaac and Elezebeth-Jacob Gilliland.
18. Pumyea, John and Jane-Agness.
Sept. 1. Vanliewe, Peter and Scythe-James Cannon.
Barricklow, Cornelius and Elezebeth-Sarah Hogeland.
15. Pumyea, Peter and Sarah-Peter.
29. Voorheese, Abraham L. and Else-John.
Vannostrand, Jacob and Caty-Catherian.
Oct. 13. Geretson, John and Phebe-Johannah.
Dehart, Uriah and Margereth-Mariah.
Nov. 24. Voorheese, Jaques and Sarah-Peter.
Dec. 22. Spader, John and Abigal-Anne
1800.
Jan. 5. Blackwell, Henry and Margereth-Mary Ann. [Dated "Jan. 5, 1780/1800"].
Scot, William and Ame-Elezebeth.
19. Nevius, John P. and Charity-Peter.
Sedam, Joseph and Elezebeth-William. [Dated "Jan. 19,1780/1800"].
Feb. 2. Stryker, John and Nelle-Catherine Sarah Vandike.
Apr. 13. Voorheese, Jaques and Dinah-Cornelia.
Meserol, Abraham and Anne-Abraham.
Sedam, Ryke and Rachel-Cornelia Dehart.
Vanderveer, Lucas and Anne-Abigal.
Gulick, Cornelius and Elezebeth-Maryam.
Hogeland, John and Williampe-Hendrick.

May 11. Van Cleef, John and Sarah-Sarah.
Whitlock, Moses and Catherian-James Cannon.
25. Wyckoff, Jacob-Cornelius Waldrom.
June 8. Cortelyou, Hendrick and Elezebeth-Lucas.
22. Voorheese, Cornelius and Mary-Mary.
Johnson, Joseph and Rachle-Martin Johnson.
July 6. Dehart, Cornelius and Anne-John Gulick.
Veghte, Nicholas and Alche-James Lake.
Whitlock, John and Lidiah-Mary Ann.
Vanderveer, Gerret and Deborah-Jane.
July 20. Simonson, Thomas and Sarah-John Van Liewe; Magdalane Van Liewe.
Aug. 3. Perdun, John and Anne-Mary.
Skilman, Jacob and Mary-John.
Skillman, Joseph and Else-Else.
Johnson, Nicholas and Margereth-Mary Ann.
Aug. --. Gulick, Benjamin and Elezebeth-Catherian.
Williamson, Cornelius and Mary-Joseph.
Sept. 14 Farmar, Jasper and Elezebeth-Verdine Elsworth.
Jay, Joseph and Elenor-Nancy Northwyck.
Williamson, John and Mary-Maria.
Schank, Garret and Caty-Sarah.
Punyea, John and Jane-Peter.
Barricklow, Christopher and Mary-Elizabeth.
Oct. 1. Gulick, John and Hannah-Abraham.
Hageman, A. and Francys-Peter.
Sperling, ---m and ---eah-John Gillin.
12. Cortelyou, John and Nelley-Sarah.
Debart, Cornelius and Ame-Gorge.
Hageman, Aaron and Hannah-Abraham. [The whole of this entry crossed out in the original].
Quick, Abraham and Mary-Abraham.
Vliet, David and Anne-Lidia.
Hatfield, Joseph and Jane-John.
25. Rigtmire, J--s and Sarah-Jacob Vanpelt.
Garretson, Samuel and Lenah-Magdalenah.
Nov. 9. Fine, Isaac and Dezieh-John Voorhese.
Dec. 21. Cannon, Rev. James S. and Caty-Ma-Voorhees. ["Daughter, b. Nov. 24"].

BASKING RIDGE PRESBYTERIAN CHURCH - BAPTISMS, 1795-1800

Performed by Rev. Robert Finley. Abstracted by Miss Nettie Allen, Corresponding Secretary of the Basking Ridge Historical Society. From *The Genealogical Magazine of New Jersey*, Vol. VII, No. 2 (October, 1931)

Annin, Mary, daughter of Wm.- June 21, 1795.
Alward, Ann, daughter of Benjamin - Aug. 30, 1795.
Anderson, Gavin McCoy, son of James - Sept. 13, 1795.
Annin, Eliz., daughter of Alex'r - Dec. 31, 1795.
Annin, Wm., son of Alex'r - Dec. 31, 1795.
Ayers, Elias Jeffers, son of Richard - April 7, 1796.
Annin, Jacob Van Doren, son of John - July 10, 1796.
Ayres, Anne, daughter of Jno. arid Mary - May 13, 1797
Ayres, David, son of John and Mary - May 13, 1797.
Annin, Alexander, son of Alexander - June 18, - 1797.
Alward, Stephen, son of Benjamin - June 25, 1797.
Annin, Elizabeth, daughter of John - July 30, 1798.
Ayres, Julietta, daughter of John - July 30, 1798.
Ayres, Daniel Blackford, son of Rev'd - Dec. 26, 1798.
Anderson, Jane, daughter of James - March 31, 1799.
Annin, Margaret, daughter of Alex. - Dec. 12, 1799.
Boyd, Esther, daughter of Wm. - June 21. 1795.
Bayley, Phebe, daughter of Samuel - Sept. 12, 1795.
Bayley, Platt, son of Samuel - Sept. 12, 1795.
Bedell, Mary, daughter of Timothy - Jan. 13, 1796.
Burgie, Ann, daughter of Thomas - Jan. 31, 1796.
Breese, Nancy, daughter of Henry - Oct. 15, 1796.
Backman, James, son of Mrs. - Oct. 30, 1796.
Ball, Mary {widow) - May 7, 1797.
Baylis, Zephaniah, son of Samuel - Sept. 10, 1797.
Boylan, Jacob, son of Samuel and Hannah - June 8, 1798.
Beedle, Nathan, son of Timothy - June, 1799.
Baylis, Absalom, son of Samuel - July, 1799.
Bedell, _____of Timothy - July 12, 1800.
Coriell, Elias, son of Peter - Oct. 11, 1795.
Coriell, Philip, son of Peter - Oct. 11, 1795.
Cross, Robert, son of William, Jun'r - Nov. 1, 1795.
Cross, George Davidson, son of John, Jun'r - Jan. 31, 1796.

Cross, Joseph, son of John, Jun'r - May 8, 1796.
Coriell, Richard, son of Peter - July 3, 1796.
Canfield, Abraham, son of Jacob - Sept., 1796
Canfield, Charles, son of Jacob - Sept., 1796.
Canfield, Jacob, son of Jacob - Sept., 1796.
Canfield, Moses Munson, son of Jacob - Sept., 1796.
Canfield, George Oliver, son of Jacob - Sept., 1796.
Canfield, Archibald, son of Jacob - Sept., 1796.
Conkling, Sally, daughter of Wm. - Nov. 13, 1796.
Canfield, Harriot, daughter of Jacob - July 16, 1797.
Coriell, Israel Lindsley, son of Mr. - March 3, 1799.
Cross, Providence, daughter of John, Jun'r - Oct. 3, 1799.
Doty. Samuel, son of Daniel - June 28, 1795.
Dalglish. David, son of Samuel - .July 19, 1795.
Doty, Elizabeth, wife of Daniel - Dec. 25, 1796.
Doty, .Joseph, son of Daniel - May 7, 1797.
Day, Sophronia, daughter of Jared - June 11, 1797.
Dunham, Fanny, daughter of Sam'l - Feb. 24, 1799.
Dayton, Caty Anne, daughter of John - April 1, 1799.
Dayton, Sarah, daughter of John - April 1, 1799.
Doty, Daniel, son of Daniel - Dec. 22, 1799.
Farmar, Mary, daughter of George [New Brunswick] - May 16, 1796.
Fisher, Elizabeth (widow) - May 7, 1797.
Fisher, Sarah, daughter of Elizabeth - Sept. 30, 1797.
Finley, Mary Ogden, daughter of Rev'd Robert - June, 1799.
Finley, Anne, daughter of Alexander - Sept., 1799.
Finley, Hetty, daughter of Alexander - July 28, 1800.
Hand, Nancy, daughter of Jonathan - Oct. 11, 1795.
Hedgoss, Margaret, daughter of Sar. - Jan. 13, 1796.
Horton, Mr. Jason - May 21, 1796.
Horton, Sarah, daughter of Jason - June 28, 1796.
Horton, Uriah, son of Jason - June 28, 1796.
Horton, Elizabeth, daughter of Jason - June 28, 1796.
Horton, Mary, daughter of Jason - June 28, 1796.
Horton, Abigail, daughter of Jason - June 28, 1796.
Horton, Eunice, daughter of Jason - June 28, 1796.
Heth, Mr. John - Sept. 30, 1797.
Heth, Elizabeth, daughter of John - Sept. 30, 1797.
Hinds, Martha, wife of Isaac - Jan. 25, 1799.
Hand, Betsey, daughter of Jon'n - Aug. 25, 1799.

Hand, Wm., son of Aaron - Sept. 22, 1799.
Hall, Richard - Oct. 12, 1799.
Johnson, Eliz'th, daughter of Abner - Oct. 11, 1795.
Johnson, John Wright, son of Mr. [New Brunswick] - April 28, 1796.
Johnson, Joseph Gaston, son of Abner - Sept. 22, 1799.
Kirkpatrick, Mary, wife of David, Jun'r - Oct. 4, 1795.
Kirkpatrick, Walter, son of David, Jun'r - Oct. 4, 1795.
Kirkpatrick, Hugh, son of David, Jun'r - July 16, 1797.
Kirkpatrick, Jane, daughter of Alexander - July 30, 1798.
Kirkpatrick, Elizabeth, daughter of David - Feb. 9, 1800.
Lewis, Maria, daughter of Edward - June 28, 1795.
Lindsley, Julia, daughter of Isaac - Jan. 31, 1796.
Lockart, John, son of Andrew - May 22, 1796.
Layton, Sarah, daughter of John - Sept. 14. 1796.
Lewis, Henry Southard, son of Edw'd - May 7, 1797.
Layton, Phebe, daughter of John, Jun'r - Sept. 30, 1797.
Leach, Mary, daughter of Abner - Sept. 30, 1797.
Leach, John Hull, son of Abner - Sept. 30, 1797.
Leach, Nancy, daughter of Abner - Sept. 30, 1797.
Lewis, Sophia, wife of John (Blacksmith) - Jan. 20, 1799.
Lindsley, Silas, son of Isaac - Feb. 3, 1799.
Layton, Jesse Sexton, son of Charles - Feb 3, 1799
Layton, John, son of John, Jun. - June, 1799.
Lewis, _____, daughter of John (Blacksmith) - Oct. 20, 1799.
Mills, Matilda, daughter of Jed'k - June 28, 1795.
McCollum, Mary Pettit, daughter of Eleanor - Sept. 20, 1795.
McCane, Phebe, daughter of Wm. - Sept, 14, 1796.
McCane, James, son of Wm. - Sept. 14, 1796.
McCane, John, son of James - Sept. 14, 1796.
McMurtry, Samuel, son of Robert - Sept. 25, 1796
McCord, Jane, daughter of James - Sept. 25, 1796.
McCollum, William, son of Mr. John - May 29, 1798.
McCord, Nathaniel, son of James - June 16, 1798.
McMurtry, Daniel, son of Robert - July 30, 1798.
McMurtry, Eliza, daughter of Robert - July 30, 1798.
McCane, Abigail Ross, daughter of Jas. - April 21, 1799.
Nesbit, Nancy, daughter of James - Sept. 14, 1796.
Nesbit, _____, daughter of James - July 30, 1798.
Pruden, Henry, son of Benjamin - Nov. 29, 1795.
Pruden, Hannah, daughter of B'n - April 3, 1796.

Plumm, John Mersullis, son of John - July 17, 1796. [New Brunswick]
Peppard, Wm., son of Francis - Sept. 30, 1797.
Robinson, Collin, son of Isabell - June 28, 1795.
Sutton, Peter, son of Peter - June 21, 1795.
Sutton, Phebe, daughter of Peter - June 21, 1795.
Savage, Eliza, daughter of Wm. - July 19, 1795.
Stiles, Anny, daughter of _____ - June 25, 1797.
Southard, Finley, son of Henry, Esq. - Sept. 30, 1797.
Simpson, James, son of David - June 16, 1798.
Stout, Cornelius Augustus, son of Johnson - July 30, 1798.
Simpson, Phebe, daughter of John, Jr. - June, 1799.
Smith, _____, daughter of John Lewis B. - Oct. 20, 1799.
Simpson, _____, daughter of David - July 12, 1800.
Watkins, Isaac, son of Jonathan - July 12, 1795.
Whitkonack, John, son of Widow - Sept. 6, 1795.
Whitkonack, Providence, daughter of Widow - Sept. 6, 1795.
Whitkonack, Nathan, son of Widow - Sept. 6, 1795.
Whitaker, Annie, daughter of Stephen - May I 1796.
Watkins, Elizabeth, daughter of Jonathan - July 3, 1796.
Watkins, Joseph, son of Jonathan - July 3, 1796.
Wilkinson, _____ - July 6, 1796.
Whitaker, Hannah, daughter of Nath'l and Ruth - June 16, 1798.
Wright, Mary (Adult) - June, 1799.
Woods, Hannah, daughter of Abraham - Oct. 20, 1799.
Woods, Martha, daughter of Abraham - Oct. 20, 1799.
Woodward, William, son of John, AE, 17 - Jan. 13, 1800.

Heritage Books by F. Edward Wright:

18th Century Records of the German Lutheran Church at Philadelphia, Pennsylvania (St. Michael's and Zion): Volume 1, Baptisms, 1745–1769
Robert L. Hess and F. Edward Wright

18th Century Records of the German Lutheran Church at Philadelphia, Pennsylvania (St. Michael's and Zion): Volume 2, Baptisms, 1770–1786
Translated by Robert L. Hess, Ph.D. Edited by F. Edward Wright

18th Century Records of the German Lutheran Church of Philadelphia, Pennsylvania (St. Michael's and Zion): Volume 3, Baptisms, 1787–1800
Translated by Robert L. Hess, Ph.D. Edited by F. Edward Wright

18th Century Records of the German Lutheran Church at Philadelphia, Pennsylvania (St. Michael's and Zion): Volume 4, Marriages and Confirmations
Robert L. Hess and F. Edward Wright

18th Century Records of the German Lutheran Church at Philadelphia, Pennsylvania (St. Michael's and Zion): Volume 5, Burials
Robert L. Hess and F. Edward Wright

Abstracts of Bucks County, Pennsylvania, Wills, 1685–1785

Abstracts of Cumberland County, Pennsylvania, Wills, 1750–1785

Abstracts of Cumberland County, Pennsylvania, Wills, 1785–1825

Abstracts of Philadelphia County, Pennsylvania, Wills:
Volumes: 1682–1726; 1726–1747; 1748–1763; 1763–1784; 1777–1790; 1790–1802; 1802–1809; 1810–1815; 1815–1819; and 1820–1825

Abstracts of South Central Pennsylvania, Newspapers, Volume 1, 1785–1790

Abstracts of South Central Pennsylvania, Newspapers, Volume 3, 1796–1800

Abstracts of the Newspapers of Georgetown and the Federal City, 1789–99

Abstracts of York County, Pennsylvania, Wills, 1749–1819

Adams County [Pennsylvania] Church Records of the 18th Century

Baltimore Directory of 1807

Berks County, Pennsylvania, Church Records of the 18th Century, Volumes 1–4

Bible Records of Washington County, Maryland

Bucks County, Pennsylvania, Church Records of the 17th and 18th Centuries, Volume 1: German Church Records

Bucks County, Pennsylvania, Church Records of the 17th and 18th Centuries, Volume 2: Quaker Records: Falls and Middletown Monthly Meetings
Anna Miller Watring and F. Edward Wright

Bucks County, Pennsylvania, Church Records of the 17th and 18th Centuries, Volume 4

Caroline County, Maryland, Marriages, Births and Deaths, 1850–1880

Citizens of the Eastern Shore of Maryland, 1659–1750

Colonial Families of Cape May County, New Jersey, Revised 2nd Edition

Colonial Families of Delaware:
Volumes: Volume 1; Volume 2: Kent and Sussex Counties; Volume 3 (2nd Edition): Kent and Sussex Counties; Volume 4: Sussex County; Volume 5: New Castle; Volume 6: Kent County

Colonial Families of New Jersey, Volume 1: Middlesex and Somerset Counties

Colonial Families of Northern Neck, Virginia, Volume 1 and Volume 2
Holly G. Wright and F. Edward Wright

Colonial Families of the Eastern Shore of Maryland: Volumes 1 and 2
Robert W. Barnes and F. Edward Wright

Colonial Families of the Eastern Shore of Maryland: Volume 4
Christos Christou and F. Edward Wright

Colonial Families of the Eastern Shore of Maryland: Volumes 5, 6, 7, 8, 9, 11, 12, 13, 14, 16, and 19
Henry C. Peden, Jr. and F. Edward Wright

Colonial Families of the Eastern Shore of Maryland: Volumes 15 and 17
Ralph A. Riggin and F. Edward Wright

Colonial Families of the Eastern Shore of Maryland: Volumes 10, 18, 20, and 22
Vernon L. Skinner, Jr. and F. Edward Wright

Colonial Families of the United States of America, Volume II
Holly G. Wright and F. Edward Wright

Cumberland County, Pennsylvania, Church Records of the 18th Century

Delaware Newspaper Abstracts, Volume 1: 1786–1795

Early Charles County, Maryland, Settlers, 1658–1745
Marlene Strawser Bates, F. Edward Wright

Early Church Records of Alexandria City and Fairfax County, Virginia
F. Edward Wright and Wesley E. Pippenger

Early Church Records of Bergen County, New Jersey, 1740–1800

Early Church Records of Dauphin County, Pennsylvania

Early Church Records of Lebanon County, Pennsylvania

Early Church Records of New Castle County, Delaware, Volume 1: 1701–1800

Early Church Records of Rockingham County, Virginia

Early Church Records of Somerset County, New Jersey, Volume 1

Early Lists of Frederick County, Maryland, 1765–1775

Early Records of the First Reformed Church of Philadelphia, Volume 1, 1748–1780

Early Records of the First Reformed Church of Philadelphia, Volume 2, 1781–1800

Frederick County, Maryland, Militia in the War of 1812
Sallie A. Mallick and F. Edward Wright

Henrico County, Virginia, Marriage References and Family Relationships, 1654–1800

Inhabitants of Baltimore County, Maryland, 1692–1763

Judgment Records of Dorchester, Queen Anne's, and Talbot Counties [Maryland]

Kent County, Delaware, Marriage References and Family Relationships

King George County, Virginia, Marriage References and Family Relationships, 1721–1800
Anne M. Watring and F. Edward Wright

Lancaster County Church Records of the 18th Century, Volumes 1–4

Lancaster County, Pennsylvania, Church Records of the 18th Century, Volume 1
F. Edward Wright and Robert L. Hess

Lancaster County, Pennsylvania, Church Records of the 18th Century, Volume 3

Lancaster County, Pennsylvania, Church Records of the 18th Century, Volume 5

Lancaster County, Pennsylvania, Church Records of the 18th Century: Volume 6
Robert L. Hess and F. Edward Wright

Lancaster County, Virginia, Marriage References and Family Relationships, 1650–1800

Land Records of Sussex County, Delaware, 1769–1782

Land Records of Sussex County, Delaware, 1782–1789: Deed Book N No. 13
Elaine Hastings Mason and F. Edward Wright

Marriage Licenses of Washington, District of Columbia, 1811–1830

Marriage References and Family Relationships of Charles City, Prince George, and Dinwiddie Counties, Virginia, 1634–1800

Marriages and Deaths from Eastern Shore Newspapers, 1790–1835

Marriages and Deaths from the Newspapers of Allegany and Washington Counties, Maryland, 1820–1830

Marriages and Deaths from the York Recorder, *1821–1830*

Marriages and Deaths in the Newspapers of Frederick and Montgomery Counties, Maryland, 1820–1830

Marriages and Deaths in the Newspapers of Lancaster County, Pennsylvania, 1821–1830

Marriages and Deaths in the Newspapers of Lancaster County, Pennsylvania, 1831–1840

Marriages and Deaths of Cumberland County, [Pennsylvania], 1821–1830

Marriages, Births, Deaths and Removals of New Castle County, Delaware

Maryland Calendar of Wills:
Volume 9: 1744–1749; Volume 10: 1748–1753; Volume 11: 1753–1760; Volume 12: 1759–1764; Volume 13: 1764–1767; Volume 14: 1767–1772; Volume 15: 1772–1774; and Volume 16: 1774–1777

Maryland Eastern Shore Newspaper Abstracts
Volume 1: 1790–1805; Volume 2: 1806–1812; Volume 3: 1813–1818; Volume 4: 1819–1824; Volume 5: Northern Counties, 1825–1829
F. Edward Wright and Irma Harper;
Volume 6: Southern Counties, 1825–1829; Volume 7: Northern Counties, 1830–1834
Irma Harper and F. Edward Wright;
Volume 8: Southern Counties, 1830–1834

Maryland Eastern Shore Vital Records:
Book 1: 1648–1725, Second Edition; Book 2: 1726–1750; Book 3: 1751–1775; Book 4: 1776–1800; and Book 5: 1801–1825

Maryland Militia in the War of 1812:
Volume 1: Eastern Shore; Volume 2: Baltimore City and County; Volume 3: Cecil and Harford Counties; Volume 4: Anne Arundel and Calvert Counties; Volume 5: St. Mary's and Charles Counties; Volume 6: Prince George's County; and Volume 7: Montgomery County

Maryland Militia in the Revolutionary War
S. Eugene Clements and F. Edward Wright

Middlesex County Virginia, Marriage References and Family Relationships, 1673–1800

Middlesex County, New Jersey, Records of the 17th and 18th Centuries

New Castle County, Delaware, Marriage References and Family Relationships, 1680–1800

Newspaper Abstracts of Allegany and Washington Counties [Maryland], 1811–1815

Newspaper Abstracts of Cecil and Harford Counties [Maryland], 1822–1830

Newspaper Abstracts of Frederick County [Maryland], 1811–1815

Newspaper Abstracts of Frederick County [Maryland], 1816–1819

Northampton County, Virginia, Marriage References and Family Relationships, 1634–1800

Northumberland County, Virginia, Marriage References and Family Relationships, 1645–1800

Orphans' Court Proceedings of New Castle County, Delaware, 1742–1761

Quaker Minutes of the Eastern Shore of Maryland: 1676–1779

Quaker Records of Henrico Monthly Meeting and Other Church Records of Henrico, New Kent and Charles City Counties, Virginia

Quaker Records of South River Monthly Meeting, 1756–1800

Richmond County, Virginia, Marriage References and Family Relationships, 1692–1800

Sketches of Maryland Eastern Shoremen

St. Mary's County, Maryland, Marriage References and Family Relationships, 1634–1800

Stafford County, Virginia, Marriage References and Family Relationships, 1661–1800

Supplement to Maryland Eastern Shore Vital Records, Books 1–3

Sussex County, Delaware, Marriage References, 1648–1800

Sussex County, Delaware, Wills: 1800–1813

Tax List of Chester County, Pennsylvania, 1768

Tax List of York County, Pennsylvania, 1779

The Maryland Militia in the Revolutionary War
S. Eugene Clements and F. Edward Wright

Vital Records of Kent and Sussex Counties, Delaware, 1686–1800

Washington County [Maryland] Church Records of the 18th Century, 1768–1800

Western Maryland Newspaper Abstracts, Volume 1: 1786–1798

Western Maryland Newspaper Abstracts, Volume 2: 1799–1805

Western Maryland Newspaper Abstracts, Volume 3: 1806–1810

Wills of Chester County, Pennsylvania, 1766–1778

York County, Pennsylvania, Church Records of the 18th Century, Volume 1
Marlene S. Bates and F. Edward Wright

York County, Pennsylvania, Church Records of the 18th Century, Volume 2
Marlene Strawser Bates and F. Edward Wright

York County, Pennsylvania, Church Records of the 18th Century, Volume 3

York County, Virginia, Marriage References and Family Relationships, 1636–1800

York County, Virginia, Wills Inventories and Accounts, 1760–1783

www.ingramcontent.com/pod-product-compliance
Lightning Source LLC
Chambersburg PA
CBHW070543270326
41926CB00013B/2183

9781680349696